The Home Plans Book

The Home Plans Book

**David Snell and
Murray Armor**

EBURY PRESS

London

3   5   7   9   10   8   6   4   2

First published in the United Kingdom in 1999 by Ebury Press
Random House
20 Vauxhall Bridge Road
London SW1V 2SA

Random House Australia (Pty) Limited
20 Alfred Street, Milsons Point, Sydney
New South Wales 2061, Australia

Random House New Zealand Limited
18 Poland Road, Glenfield
Auckland 10, New Zealand

Random House South Africa (Pty) Limited
Endulini, 5a Jubilee Road, Parktown 2193, South Africa

Random House UK Limited Reg. No. 954009

A CIP catalogue record for this book is available from the British Library.

ISBN: 0 09 186953 6

This book contains only general advice, and neither the author nor the publishers will accept responsibility of any sort for
the consequence of the application of this advice to specific situations. In particular, planning and other legislation is
described in outline only, and professional help should always be obtained when dealing with these matters. No company
has paid for any of their material to be used in this book and the authors take no responsibility for the accuracy of any of
the plans reproduced.

Produced and designed by Colin Spooner and Myra Giles.
Printed in Hong Kong by Sheck Wah Tong.

Contents

This is not the first mainstream plan book to appear in recent years, nor is it even the first from the stable that includes *Building Your Own Home* as there are two other such books, *Plans For A Dream Home* and *Home Plans* that have already been published.

This book is, however, the first real attempt to create a plans book that gives a flavour of the plans and design ideas available across a wide cross section of the major players within the self build industry and it is certainly the first plans book where all of these companies and architects have co-operated from its inception to its creation. As such, I hope that you will be able to use this book, in conjunction with the other books, but in particular with *Building Your Own Home*, in order to make your minds up, not only about what sort of design you want to achieve, but, most importantly, who you want to achieve it with and through.

All of the plans within this book are the copyright of one or other of the companies or architects who have contributed to it and their names are clearly marked on the relevant pages with further details of just how you can get in touch with them or get hold of their brochures, at the rear of the book. At no stage are any of these plans published in order for you to simply take them away and build from them and, although there are companies who are prepared to sell you the detailed plans with a licence to build, the majority are only available as part of a wider package deal service or commission.

Maybe there's a plan in this book that suits what you're looking for down to the last detail, in which case you'll need to make a note of the address of the copyright holder immediately and get hold of them to see where you go from here. What's much more likely is that the ideal design for you and/or your site is an amalgam of several of the designs, and borrows bits from one and ideas from another. If that's the case, then I'm pleased that the book is leading you along the path of discovering and creating your own individual home and you may decide that the people or company who have contributed the most to your ideals are the ones that you feel you should contact in order to progress things further.

Without pre-empting the pages that follow, many of the plan layouts can be adapted to look completely different to the outside so as to fit in with the local vernacular or materials. Some of the plans have been formulated for a particular form of construction promoted by the contributory company whilst others can be built by any approved method. All of the companies are fully capable of providing you with an individual design worked up from scratch to your own specifications and requirements.

Some of the plans that are reproduced in this book may also appear in the company literature of the contributing companies but many more have evolved as bespoke designs. All of the plans have been chosen to provide an insight into the range of designs that are available within the industry. Perhaps, as a result of this book, there may be some cross pollination of ideas, but there is no doubt that the spark of individuality and ingenuity that has led up to the creation of many of these plans will continue to flourish, urged on by you, the self builders, who have done so much to demand the choices that are available and demonstrated within these pages.

Copyright

Copyright of any plans or drawings resides with the originator until or unless they agree otherwise. Even if you commission a drawing, or plan, to be prepared on your behalf by a company or practice, and even if you pay your bill in full, that does not mean that the copyright will pass to you, unless you have made specific arrangements for it to do so.

All of the plans and drawings within this book remain the copyright of the contributing companies and practices and they may not be used, copied or reproduced in any form or for any purpose, without the express permission of the copyright holders.

I should also stress that no contributor has been charged for the inclusion of their plan/s in this book.

What follows is a brief resume of the major points of consideration that can lead up to the choice of your selfbuild plan and your eventual new selfbuilt home. These points are considered in far greater detail in the companion book, *Building Your Own Home*, and, whilst this book is concerned with the choice of the plan of your new home, what leads up to that choice and how you make that choice, it is that book which then expands upon them and goes on to consider all of the other aspects of selfbuilding and just how one goes about translating your ideal plan into your new selfbuilt home.

The budget for your new home

Before any decision is made on the purchase of a site or the choosing of a plan, other than in the broadest sense, consideration has to be given to the budget.

For most people selfbuilding, the budget is made up of three elements:
* The equity that is realised from the sale of their existing house.
* The amount of mortgage they can command.
* Any savings or additional monies they have available.

Of course, there are quite a number of people who don't require a mortgage, as is evidenced by the differentials between the number of people selfbuilding, possibly as high as 18,000, and the number of selfbuild mortgages issued. Nevertheless the principle remains and it is only a very fortunate few who do not have to sit down and consider just how much money is available to put into their selfbuild, or how much it makes economic sense to put in. The rule must always be to start at the budget and work backwards and, having arrived at the total budget, you will then have to decide just how much you will dedicate to each of the two major elements in any selfbuild budget, the land cost and the building costs.

The land cost normally bears a direct relationship to the market value of any completed property and, as such, is likely to vary from area to area. If 1500 sq. ft. houses usually fetch £150,000 in your neighbourhood then land prices might well range between £40,000 and £60,000 depending on availability. On the other hand, if you live in the stockbroker belts of the major English cities and the same house would fetch £250,000 then a plot of land of exactly the same size could well fetch anywhere between £70,000 and £100,000 or even higher. And if you're in an area where land is particularly scarce, then the land prices, expressed as a percentage of the market value of the completed houses, may well rise even further. You need to establish just what you're likely to have to pay as the first point in the preparation of your budget and, perhaps, the easiest way of doing just that is to get hold of either of the two major magazines in the selfbuild world, *Homebuilding and Renovating* or *Build It,* both of which are available in most major newsagents or by subscription. These two magazines carry advertisements listing plots for sale and, as well as that, they feature either *Plotfinder* or *Landbank Services,* both of which can provide you with lists of plots in your chosen areas.

Having established what you are likely to have to pay for the land, you can then deduct this amount from your total budget to arrive at the amount that is available for the build and associated costs. What might surprise some people is the uniformity of build costs throughout the Kingdom. In the two examples of houses I have given above, although the land costs vary considerably, it's quite likely that, if built to the same specification, and by the same build route, the actual building costs would be practically identical. What does alter build costs is the specification, the complexity of the design, the choice of fittings and fixtures and the choice of external materials and I will briefly explore those points in the following pages. For the purpose of this section, however, when one is talking of the establishment of the initial budget, it is as well to confine our thinking to the various build routes that can affect the build costs.

Without doubt the most expensive way of achieving your individual home is to choose to build using a builder to carry out the whole of the works to an agreed specification. In many ways this is still selfbuilding as all of the choices, right from the design stage through to the selection of the fittings and fixtures remains in your hands. At the time of writing this way of going about things is likely to cost around £55 per sq. ft. and over. On the other hand, a selfbuilder electing to build by managing subcontract labour and purchasing all of the materials themselves, may well achieve the same house for as little as £40 per sq. ft. and under. Translate those figures into real money by reference to the hypothetical 1500 sq. ft. house in the other example and you have a difference in cost of £22,500.

It is important to realise that these two methods are not mutually exclusive and that there are half way houses and various permutations between building with a builder and building with subcontractors, the most popular of which is to get a builder to build to the point of a weathertight shell, and then to use subcontractors for the remainder of the build. It is important, also, to realise that these figures may alter between the time of me writing this book and you reading it but that that does nothing to invalidate the principles behind their demonstration. Again, probably by reference to the same magazines I have mentioned above, you will be able to glean the up to date figures and apply them to your circumstances.

Selfbuild mortgages
I am not going to list or even discuss any particular building society or bank within this section as the history of selfbuild mortgages is one where various banks and building societies have dipped in and out of the market like reluctant party goers, unable to ignore the noise yet unwilling to fully commit to the fun. The criteria for a selfbuild mortgage is just the same as for any mortgage, in that the amount that you can borrow is arrived at as a multiplier of your income or incomes. Some banks and building societies have schemes, at the time of writing, that are specifically tailored for the selfbuilder and provide mortgages in the form of stage payments, some of which include an advance on the land purchase. It's no longer feasible to think in terms of 100% finance and it's no longer feasible to think in terms of what used to be

known as 'roll up' mortgages where people used to live in one house paying their mortgage and then take out another loan for the new selfbuild project with the interest on the second loan being held over and added to the eventual mortgage when the first house was sold. Those days have gone, and quite rightly so, and, although, if you can demonstrate an ability to pay indefinitely for both mortgages, it's still possible for some building societies to entertain two mortgages running in tandem, in effect these are limited to those who are income rich in relation to their borrowings.

Once again the magazines run articles from time to time about the availability of selfbuild finance and the 'best buys' and it pays to make yourself aware of what's going on.

Building warranties
Even if you're not going to need finance yourself on any selfbuild, the chances are that if you want to sell your new selfbuilt house within ten years, any purchaser wanting a mortgage would find that their bank or building society would be reluctant to entertain any purchase where a recognised warranty scheme wasn't in place. Although it is possible, by means of comprehensive surveys and insurance policies, to achieve a retrospective guarantee, the chances are that any purchaser would have simply moved on to the next available and uncomplicated purchase by the time you had sorted things out. As well as all of this it surely is worthwhile considering one's own peace of mind and I do feel that serious selfbuilders should really consider putting a warranty scheme in place, whatever their circumstances.

The NHBC have their normal *Buildmark* scheme that gives the 10 year guarantee for those who use a builder to do either the whole job or the weathertight shell. For those who build using subcontract labour or their own labour they have another scheme called *Solo* which gives a 10 year warranty with some useful bolt on extras. Zurich Municipal have a scheme called *Custombuild* for those selfbuilding with either a builder or subcontractors and this gives a warranty of 10 years with the possibility of extending this to 15 years. They also have a scheme especially tailored for conversions and extensions that can give cover for 6 years extendable to 10. Another company, Project Builder have a scheme that gives cover for 10 years extendable to 12 and a further scheme, known as the Forest of Dean scheme offered by Trenwick Willis Corroon gives cover for 10 years, again extendable to 12. And, as if that's not enough to choose from, there is always the option of either Architects Progress Certificates or Architectural Supervision.

Finding a site

This is where many would think of starting but you'll forgive me for insisting on leaving it until second as my own view is that it's necessary to decide just how much one can afford to spend on the plot before one goes out looking for it. Nevertheless, this is where it comes to a grinding halt for many would be selfbuilders, when they can't find a suitable plot.

Perseverance and luck are the two main ingredients in finding a plot. Perseverance, in that you have to explore all avenues that could possibly lead to one and when they fail, you have to be prepared to go back and 'do the rounds again'. Luck, in that you have to be the one who's there when the plot of your dreams comes up.

Without, in any way, claiming to be comprehensive, some of the headings of ways of finding land could read as follows:-

Estate agents
Most land, even that for sale through other mediums, is for sale by or through estate agents and there's no doubt that they remain the single most important source of plots for selfbuilders. That said, you must not imagine for one moment, that simply putting your name on an estate agents register will be all that you need to do. Nearly all selfbuild stories tell of endless round after round of traipsing around estate agents, sometimes almost to the point of becoming a nuisance and that's where the perseverance and the luck often come together. If you can bring your name to the top of the agent's mind then, when that plot comes in and when you're there

on the scene, it'll probably be you who gets to hear of it first. Remember too, that sometimes the estate agents really don't want to sell that plot of land to you and would far rather sell it to a builder or developer. If an estate agent sells you a plot of land his commission will barely scrape above four figures. If, on the other hand, he sells that same plot to a builder then, not only will he get the same commission, but the chances are that he'll be retained to sell the house that the builder builds. And then he's not only into a far larger fee but on top of that he gets to keep his board, which after all is his street advertising hoarding, up for a great deal longer. That desire has to be balanced with a duty to the vendor and that's where your perseverance may pay off, especially if combined with other tacks as discussed below.

Auctions
These of course are conducted by estate agents but it's worth considering them separately. In a public auction, once the gavel goes down, if you're the highest bidder, you've effectively exchanged contracts. It's important, therefore, that you understand this and that your solicitor has a chance to do all of the necessary legal work and searches before you enter the auction room. In addition, it's vital that your finance is all arranged before you start bidding as, before you leave that auction room you will have had to hand over the 10% deposit and will have locked yourself into completion within a time frame of between 21 and 28 days. Many selfbuilders waste considerable amounts of time and money on trying to buy land at auction, compared to the relative few who are successful. Auctions are difficult things for lay people but, by rights, if you've done your homework properly, you should have an edge on the builder or developer insofar as you don't have to think in terms of an immediate profit.

Sometimes you'll come across a slightly different form of auction called a Tender, where sealed bids are called for to be opened at a specific time and day. In many ways it's like attending an auction without being able to hear the other bids but, unlike the auction, you might not necessarily be committed to purchase if your bid's the highest. The reverse side of that coin is that the vendors might not be obliged to accept your bid, even if it is the highest.

Newspapers

National, local, classified and some well known sales magazines are always a good source of land. And of course, the advertising can work two ways. You can advertise the fact that you're looking for a plot. You may get time wasters, you may get a string of no hope plots that would never attract planning permission, but you might, possibly, get the offer of a really good plot. It's always possible that you might also be offered a plot that has been for sale by an estate agent you're already in touch with, but who hasn't, for some mysterious reason, told you about it! And before you think that's unlikely, in the week before I am writing this, I've come across two such cases.

Selfbuild magazines

The selfbuild magazines are probably one of the best sources of plots at the moment, either directly through their advertising sections, or through the land finding agencies they support or control. Remember that what appears in the magazines may well have gone to print a couple of months before the magazine hits the shelves and that all that you see may not, therefore be up to date. Remember too though, that the services offering these plots, Landbank Services and Plotfinder, have to regularly update their subscription lists, and it is these lists, rather than what's shown in the magazine, that will give a true, up to date, reflection of what's on the market. Plotfinder staff, for instance, update their lists on a daily basis, maintaining nationwide coverage with both their advertisers and their subscribers through a comprehensive computer database that can be accessed on a faxback number.

The Internet

In the weeks preceding the writing of this section I have already met two couples who met via the Internet. In one case a couple who had found a double plot, had advertised on the net for another couple to share it with them. Presumably the same could have been achieved by advertising in other mediums but the use of the internet is something that I can see growing and with more and more selfbuild sites being set up on it, if you've got the facilities, then use them.

Local authorities

Some local authorities are well known for selling land and regularly set aside land and provide serviced plots for selfbuilders. Many more do absolutely nothing. Ring your local authority and ask them if they've got land for sale, or write to the Estates Department asking if there is any spare land that they can identify as being suitable. At any one time there may be a site in the offing or they may be able to identify land that they own but for which they have no other purpose.

The Commission for New Towns (CNT)

Most of the new towns have practically exhausted their supply of land although, as I write, some of them do have a small number of plots for sale. There is still a ready supply of serviced plots available in Milton Keynes and the CNT is still likely to be a smashing source of individual plots in this town, right up to and through the millennium.

The Public Utilities

In the old days a telephone relay exchange, a water pumping station or a gas pressure regulation station used to require a building the size of a small bungalow and, by the very nature of their requirement, they were often situated in street locations. Now all that used to go on in these buildings can be done in a fibreglass box the size of a small chest of drawers. Sometimes the land is advertised for sale but many more times the redundant building or land just lies fallow. Write to the Estates Department of your local utilities and ask if they have any such property, or else include it in:

Looking around

In all the dire warnings given about not buying

6

land without the benefit of planning permission, many of them given by me, there are circumstances where a piece of land that doesn't yet have planning can, nevertheless, be considered as a plot. Get out and about and look out for obvious gaps in the street scene and remember, infill plots don't just happen in the town, they can often occur in more rural surroundings. Sometimes there will be a gap in a village street with an unexplained tongue of land. Maybe it's the site of a main or a sewer and the land is sterile but, just maybe, it was the tongue of land the farmer retained as access to the fields at the back and maybe, with new and larger machinery, its whole raison d'être has disappeared and it awaits your interest.

Asking around

If you've chosen to concentrate your search in one particular area or village then asking around at local shops or at the pub could well produce results. Hairdressers and barbers usually know all that's going on in an area and so will the local busybody in the pub. Be prepared to have to explain that you're not completely mad and be prepared, also, to weed out the horror stories that usually happened to someone who knew someone who knew someone.

New for old

Nearly every selfbuild project I've come across in the South east corner of the Kingdom and quite a few in other areas, have come about as the result of replacing an existing dwelling with a new one. In many of those cases the estate agents selling the original dwelling had not twigged that the property was more suitable as a plot than in its original form. In some cases, young couple after young couple, attracted by the prospect of a cheap home had tried time and time again, without success, to get a mortgage. In all cases the selfbuilders had kept quite quiet about their intentions until such time as the purchase had gone through. Estate agents come in two varieties; the old established and professional agencies, dealing in all things from sales of land and houses through to livestock auctions, and the younger, more brash agents who concentrate

on the volume sales of houses. Whilst the former might well be trained to recognise the potential in any property they are called upon to evaluate, the latter often have no such background and, instead, are only interested in a high throughput. Consequently, whilst the established agents would seek planning and eventually put the plot on the market, maybe by auction, the other sort will often just seek to sell the property at face value and the discerning selfbuilder can often step in and realise the full potential.

There are distinct advantages in new for old in that, whilst the old property has to be demolished, in many of the cases this does not have to be done until after the new house is completed and in some cases that can solve a difficult temporary accommodation problem. In addition, things like the sewer connections, connections to services, driveways and gardens are often already done and when you add all that up it can often mean savings of several thousand pounds. Demolition is different for each property of course but again, there can often be hidden benefits and if the bricks and/or roof tiles or slates are recoverable, the salvage value can often outweigh the demolition costs. Beware where the bungalow or house to be demolished is made of, or contains, asbestos. Don't be tempted to cut corners and do take notice of the very strict regulations regarding the treatment and removal of the spoil. It will add considerably to the demolition costs but that's something you'll have to take on the chin.

HM Land Registry

Not all land is registered but quite a lot of it is and, if any of the headings above throw up a piece of land where you can't establish the owner, and if asking around and general enquiries draw a blank, then the Land Registry is the place to go. A registered title contains details of the address and location of the land and any owners, together with lists of any charges, covenants and easements affecting the land. If you find a piece of land and you need to establish the ownership then a simple application, with the appropriate fee, may well turn up all you need to know.

Planning registers

Not everyone realises it but the planning register is open for inspection by the public. It lists all applications, both current and recent, on land within that local authorities jurisdiction and, if you can fight your way past the company representatives paid to glean information from it, it can be a useful tool in finding land. Applications for detailed consents are less likely to be of interest, although not entirely so, as, in all probability, by going in for the detailed stages, the owners have established what they want to do with the land. Outline applications, on the other hand might well lead you to the vendor, even if an estate agent is listed as the applicant's agent, and a letter registering your interest could well produce results. At the very least it will let the vendor know you're out there and, if the agent drags his feet when selling the land, you could well hear from him.

Multiple sites

If you come across a site for more than one dwelling then there's always a possibility that you could join in with others to develop it, not as a formal selfbuild group but more in the capacity of a group of individuals. Quite often, if two or more individuals can join together, they can have an advantage in that sometimes, the land is too much for the small local builder but not big enough to interest the larger developer. Care needs to be taken over the division and responsibility for common parts and, in particular, the issue of drains, services and access or roads. In most cases where there are four plots or less, the driveway can remain as an unadopted roadway. Thought, however, needs to be given to the construction of any driveway and services, especially if their completion affects the occupation or enjoyment of any of the houses. If agreement cannot be reached to construct the driveway together, as part and parcel of the joint development, then it's perhaps best to construct the purchase around the premise that one party is responsible for the construction of the driveway and services within a certain time frame, with the other parties legally required to pay their portions of the costs. An alternative could

be to arrange for the work to be carried out by an independent contractor with all parties required to pay their due proportion. In a situation where the works are likely to spill over onto the public highway this is often the best idea as this work can only be carried out by approved and accredited contractors.

Often, once the land purchase and the ancillary works are sorted out, the individual selfbuilders go their own way but in some instances there may be advantages in sticking together a bit longer. Sometimes the plans and the designs can be jointly agreed and commissioned to a cost advantage and sometimes cooperation can stretch advantageously through to the build itself.

Evaluating a plot and its effects on the design and costs

Without a plot there is no selfbuild and with a plot, it is the plot and everything about it that will dictate the progress, and the nature of that selfbuild. Where it is, will dictate the style of your new home and the choice of external materials. Where it is will determine the optimum size of your proposed home and where it is may well influence the facilities you want or need to include. Some would-be selfbuilders feel that it's important to establish the design in intimate detail even before a plot is found and evaluated but this, in my opinion, is putting the cart before the horse and it is only once you've found and decided upon a plot that the final details of the design should be formulated to suit that plot. That doesn't mean that you can't or shouldn't be thinking about design right from the outset of your decision to selfbuild, but it does mean that the design should fit the plot and not vice versa.

In most cases the selfbuilder will be buying land that already has planning permission of one sort or another and this is discussed below. A golden rule would be to say that selfbuilders should only buy land that has some specific planning consent on it and that they should stay as selfbuilders and not venture into the realms of property speculation. To all rules there must be exceptions and, by the very entrepreneurial nature of the selfbuilders makeup, there are always going to be opportunities that it is right and proper to explore. Sometimes a person may own land already and, in such a case, it is only sensible to explore the possibilities of planning permission. In other cases it might, sometimes, be all right to buy land that does not have an express planning consent. I'm thinking here of where, for example, the planning department of the local authority agree that there is a pretty good chance of it or where, history has bypassed an obvious plot. In any such case, to guard against ending up with a useless parcel of land, or to prevent a vendor selling the land to someone else after a lot of hard work on your part, there are some precautions to be taken. Either the land should be purchased 'subject to receipt of satisfactory planning permission', which would mean that the contract is voided in the event of the planning failing or alternatively a legal option, possibly granted on some payment or other, might tie the vendor of the land to selling to you in the event that you are successful in gaining planning consent.

Planning permission

If a piece of land doesn't have planning permission then you should perhaps, subject to my comments above, move on to consideration of somewhere else. Even if a piece of land does have planning you need to check out whether the consent is valid and has not expired, and you need to check whether the conditions of the consent are suitable for that which you propose. Planning can come in various forms and it helps to understand them.

Outline Planning Permission lasts for five years and it means that, in principle, the land can be developed in accordance with the details and description on the consent. However, it usually does not give any consideration to the details of the design, its siting or its external appearance and these matters have to be determined by a further application known as:

Approval of Reserved Matters. This has to be made within a period of three years of the date of the granting of the outline consent and failure to make such an application can result in the technical expiry of the planning permission. This part of the planning process is sometimes referred to as detailed planning permission because it deals with the details of the design. In normal circumstances an *Outline* consent does not allow you to commence work, whilst an *Approval of Reserved Matters* cannot stand alone and must always relate back to a valid *Outline* consent.

Full Planning Consent rolls up the outline and detailed stages of the permission into one application and, as such, stands alone and is valid for the full five years.

Once work has started on a site, this has the effect of perpetuating the consent, although there are powers available to planning authorities, enabling them to serve a Notice to Complete.

Planning permission says that you *may* develop a piece of land in a certain way. It does not say that you *can* develop that land and there are pitfalls that the selfbuilder needs to watch out for, the first of which is:

Roads and access

Consideration needs to be given to the type of road that gives access to the plot and whether it is adopted or private and, if so, whether there is a legal right for the owner of the plot to use that access. Sometimes there may be a ransom strip where a strip of land in another party's ownership divides the land from the access and this will need to be looked out for, and sorted out, before the plot is purchased. The requirements of the local and highways authorities may impose conditions on the land which can radically affect its viability, or the size of any dwelling you construct on it, by means of stipulations about parking, turning, visibility splays and gates, all of which it's vital that you understand.

Footpaths

Do not imagine for one moment that if there is a footpath through or alongside your land, you can divert it or stop it off. Footpaths, however infrequently used, can only be ceased by an order from the council and such an order is by no means a foregone conclusion as there are powerful lobbies who make it their business to see that they remain open and unchanged.

Drains and sewage options

If mains drainage is available and connection is feasible then this is often the most favoured choice. There is a legal right for connection to a public sewer but in certain circumstances, such as with overloaded sewers, new connections are prohibited by means of the planning laws. In other instances the physical difficulties, and by implication the costs, make connection to the mains sewer impossible or unattractive. In these cases, as with plots where no mains drainage is available, there are alternatives, the first of which might be a *sewage treatment plant*. These work by means of electrically driven rotating blades or turbines slowly exposing the effluent to water and air borne bacteria that purify it to the extent whereby it can be released into a suitable water course or ditch. A cheaper alternative but one that is normally only acceptable to the local authority and the Environment Agency in rural rather than urban situations, is a *septic tank*. This works, without power, by baffles separating out the solids from the liquids in the effluent and exposing it to water borne bacteria that purify it to the point whereby it can be released into the sub strata of the soil by means of land drains. If neither of these systems are acceptable to the authorities then the final solution is the *cesspool*, which is effectively a huge holding tank in which the effluent is stored until it is pumped out and taken away. This latter alternative is the least popular and the most expensive of these options both in terms of its installation and its emptying costs. However, even the other two options do need de-sludging from time to time but the infrequency of this requirement means that the savings in sewerage rates will usually be more than adequate to cover this expense.

Surface water needs some consideration as, not only might it have to be connected to a mains drain in the normal way but, in other circumstances, provision might have to be made for the construction of quite elaborate soakaways if a ditch or water course is unavailable. Usually however it can be discharged into relatively cheap soakaways formed by filling holes with selected hardcore and then covering the top over with polythene prior to burying it in the topsoil.

Where drainage levels are wrong for any kind of gravity fall a pump might have to be employed to lift foul or surface water drainage to a higher level and, in some circumstances, particularly where there is an expensive road entry required to connect to a mains drain, it can even be cheaper to employ such a system to enable the drainage to be taken to another outlet. Which brings me neatly onto:

Easements and Covenants

Essentially they are very similar except that an easement usually gives rights to one party to pass over or do something on another party's land whilst a covenant more commonly, restricts the rights of an owner or occupier of land. As such, you can see that they can radically affect one's enjoyment of land and that they can act for or against you. An easement in your favour would be one that allowed you to take the drainage we've just been discussing over an adjoining owner's land. On the other hand an easement could exist giving that same neighbour the right to pass over your land for the purposes of access to his own or another parcel of land. Another kind of easement can exist in favour of the utilities giving them the right to pass over or under your land with their services and, in turn, you could benefit by that same easement bringing the services onto your land in the first place. Where the prospective selfbuilder has to be careful is where such easements are tied into a restriction or sterilisation of land such as with a high pressure main crossing a plot where there is a legal prohibition against development taking place over or near that service.

Covenants can be meaningless, such as one prohibiting the salting of pork on the land, or they can be more serious such as restricting or preventing the development of the land. Sometimes they can, to all intents and purposes, be deemed to have lapsed, in which case a simple Single Premium Indemnity policy can be arranged against the unlikely event of anyone endeavouring to enforce them. At other times it might be necessary to try to have them quashed by the Lands Tribunal, an expensive and lengthy process. Sometimes they are 'live' and they will either have to be bought off or adhered to. A covenant placed on a piece of land by a vendor who lives next door, requiring that no windows of habitable rooms shall face in his direction is such an example and, if that radically affects your ability to develop the land suitably then it will in turn affect either the viability of the plot or your willingness to purchase. On the other hand a covenant that the vendor reserves the right to approve the plans of your proposed new house, may be perfectly reasonable and, in any event, whether or not it specifically says so, the words 'such consent not to be unreasonably withheld' are implied. As such, if the planning authorities approve your proposals, it would be next to nigh impossible for the neighbour to object.

Adverse possession

Sometimes known as squatters' rights, these can affect land. If a person occupies land 'without let or hindrance' for a period of 12 years or more they can register a possessory title in the land and after a further 3 years they can register an absolute title. If there are signs that someone has occupied, or is using all or part of, the plot that you are preparing to buy, you need to establish, fairly quickly, whether or not they might be taking, or have taken that occupation further into an adverse possession. If the twelve years is not up, then any obstruction (hindrance) or agreement (let) will stop the clock. If the twelve years is up then the matter could go to court and, if they can establish proof of their continuous occupation, the squatters might well gain title. It works both ways of course, and plots do come onto the market where all or part of the land's title is established in this way. If you are buying land where the title is possessory rather than absolute, then you will need a Single Premium Indemnity policy to safeguard your interests.

Services

The provision and availability of services to a plot are of paramount importance to most people although there are a hardy few who relish the thought of alternatives. Most areas where development is going to be allowed have access to mains water and/or electricity. If the former is not available then an alternative can be a borehole but this is not always feasible and the quality of the water would need to be verified. Electricity can be self generated but again this is not always practicable and, I would suggest, is normally outside the scope of most selfbuilders. Gas is the one service that, whilst almost universally desirable, is not absolutely essential, in terms of our modern day life, which is why, perhaps, of all of the undertakers, I have always found them to be the most helpful. If the gas main is available and you can demonstrate that you intend to use gas for your central heating, then there is often no connection charge. Not so for water and electricity I'm afraid, although their charges have, especially in the case of the water boards, come down to more reasonable proportions in recent years. Most prudent selfbuilders will want to establish the costs of bringing the various services onto their land at an early stage although most will also not want to pay for these facilities before they have purchased the land. Remember, however, that there are specific timescales built in to all of these applications for supply and, particularly in the case of water, where a building supply is needed almost from the start of building, you do need to keep an eye on the lead in times.

Trees can be of paramount importance on a plot and they have quite an effect on several aspects of selfbuilding. Planners and neighbours can get very excited about trees, from the points of view of their possible removal, their maintenance and their replacement. In addition trees can have a profound effect on the design of a house and their foundations. The presence of trees on any plot needs to be investigated but this is particularly important in areas where the soil is heavy clay. Trees take considerable amounts of water from the subsoil and, if a tree is removed or killed off due to the building works, then the clay can retain the water and expand, causing what is known as 'heave'. The damage this can cause to unprotected buildings has to be seen to be believed, and in such a situation, it is very necessary to take precautions and employ special foundations.

Special foundations

Of course, trees and clay aren't the only combinations that can spell special foundations and any purchaser of a plot needs to establish the probable ground conditions right from the outset. Sometimes your advisors will take a look at a plot and know right away, from experience and, perhaps, from the type of vegetation it supports, that it needs a soil investigation and survey. Sometimes everything will seem all right and reference to other houses being built in the vicinity will indicate that no specific precautions need to be taken. If you're in any doubt on this then, in the first instance, try talking to the local Building Inspector. He'll have seen nearly everything that's been built in the locality and, even if he hasn't got any specific knowledge of your site, he'll know the general ground conditions and be able to give you some pointers. Modern advances mean that a requirement for special foundations is, in most cases, unlikely to preclude the development of your plot. Nevertheless, any proposed solutions could well mean that the design might have to be rationalised into a more simple shape and an increase in costs might also mean that the size and scope of your new home might have to be curtailed, if it is to stay within your budget.

If you do get a soil investigation and survey done and it recommends that special foundations are required then you'll need to understand the basic principles behind those recommendations and the effects that they will have on your costs.

A reinforced strip foundation is a simple solution to the problem of soft spots within the foundation or minor differences in the bearing capacity of the subsoil. All that's usually required is that mesh or bar reinforcement is placed within the foundation concrete which sometimes, but not always has to be thickened up a little or widened. Care has to be taken with the pouring of the ready mix, so as not to disturb the placing of the reinforcement which is often put 50mm from the top as well as from the bottom of the concrete. Where the ground is wet or where the time of year means that the trenches are likely to quickly fill with water, and in situations where

the sides of the trenches might become unstable, it can pay to consider changing to:

A trenchfill foundation. Here the concrete, instead of forming a layer at the bottom of the trench, is brought up to within 200mm of the surface. There are several advantages to this form of foundation, the first and most obvious of which is that one is out of the ground very quickly and, indeed, sometimes on the same day. In addition, so long as there are no other considerations and so long as the ground has a good bearing capacity, the trench can sometimes be narrowed to 450mm instead of the more usual 600mm, thus limiting the extra concrete required. This may mean that the savings in labour and materials, on the blockwork that would have been needed below ground, can offset, to a large degree, the costs of the extra concrete and, when the time factor is taken into consideration it can seem like the best option.

Clay and the presence of trees may, as I've presaged above, mean that precautions have to be taken against possible heave. In these cases, the answer is usually to employ a trenchfill foundation, only to take its depths down to subsoil levels where the effects of any drying out are limited. However, in certain situations, this is still not enough to prevent possible damage to the foundation and in these cases it might be necessary to line the sides of the trench with compressible material or slip membranes. Usually, it's only the inside edge of the trench that needs to be lined with this fairly expensive compressible material, but sometimes both faces have to be so treated and, with the extra widths and depths of foundation, the amounts of concrete and the amounts of spoil can rise to rather dramatic proportions. There comes a time when extra depth becomes impossible or ceases to be cost effective and one then slips into the next type of foundation that the selfbuilder is likely to come across.

Piled foundations used to strike terror into the heart of any selfbuilder but in recent years things have changed dramatically and, as a foundation genre, they have become much more user friendly. Essentially there are three types of piled foundation – driven, bored or dug. Driven foundations are perhaps the least friendly for most selfbuild situations as they do still involve a fairly large rig and they do involve a fair degree of noise and vibration, all of which can upset the neighbours. They use a shell of steel or concrete that is driven to the appropriate depth and then filled with concrete and reinforcement. Bored piles, on the other hand, can be put in place by a mini rig that can often be mounted on a Landrover or small lorry. Sometimes they drill a simple tube but other systems are designed to mushroom out below ground and, all are, of course, filled with concrete and reinforcement. Dug piles are pads of concrete that can sometimes be dug by the normal digger that one would find on a selfbuild site. The common factor in all of these methods is the fact that the piles are taken down to stable ground and they provide a bearing for a 'ground beam' or 'ringbeam' which then spans from pile cap to pile cap. The house walls are then built off this ringbeam which is reinforced by metal bars and a combination of mesh cages within the concrete. Sometimes the ringbeam itself has to be isolated from the ground in situations where there might be heave and this is done by using the same sort of compressible material that is sometimes used to line a trenchfill foundation. Sometimes the ringbeam is tied into the reinforcement of the piles and at other times a polythene slip membrane is employed to allow the ringbeam and the piles, usually dug piles, to move with a degree of independence. An innovation of recent years has been the introduction of pre-formed pile caps with pre-formed ringbeams that can be 'dropped' onto the caps, thus achieving in days what used to take weeks.

A reinforced raft foundation comes into use where the ground is inherently stable but there is likely to be movement below ground, caused by something like coal mining. There are various forms of this but essentially what is created is a solid slab foundation, often with a built in edge beam, that is able to withstand the ground movement and float, on the surface without cracking up. It involves quite a lot of concrete and reinforcement but taken altogether it does not involve much more work or material than

many other forms of foundation.

It's important to bear in mind that the various solutions will tend to become almost standard in certain areas and, for instance, in Nottinghamshire, a raft foundation might well be thought of as a normal foundation. Translate that same foundation to Essex and there would be much scratching of heads and an inflated price. Conversely, whilst the deep trenchfilled foundation is virtually universal in parts of Essex, Kent and Hertfordshire, in Nottinghamshire it would be looked upon as akin to civil engineering. Whatever foundation you have to employ, the likelihood is that, in your area, many others have had similar problems and a foundation type has been evolved as the best and most cost effective solution. In evaluating your potential plot you need to find out what that solution is and plan accordingly.

Radon gas has been in the news a lot recently and, if one was to believe the papers, everybody who lives in Devon should shine in the dark. Radon gas is a radioactive gas that seeps from the rock and is prevalent in certain areas, particularly the West Country. It is relatively easily, and cheaply, contained and ducted out from the substructure and necessity and the ways of dealing with it will be covered within any Building Regulations application.

Sloping sites are another factor that can affect the costs of developing a plot and the way people choose to build on sloping land can vary from county to county. In parts of Wales and the North of England, a flat site might well be a rarity, whereas, in parts of Cambridgeshire and Lincolnshire sites with a change of level of more than 300mm would be unusual. The first rule of any development of a site is that the design should reflect the levels of the land if it's to look at all right and if it's to be cost effective. A design that is formulated for a site that has a forty five degree slope on it will be expensive to construct on a flat site and will never really look right. A design that evolved around a flat site will require a great deal of underbuilding if it is transposed to a sloping site and that underbuilding might be extremely ugly and difficult to hide. Cut and fill might be the answer, where a median point is

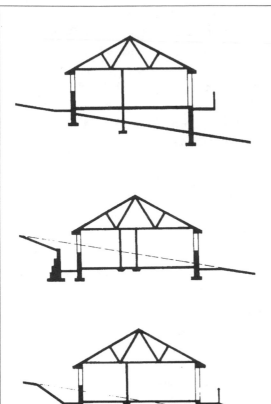

Option One. Build up above the slope. Involves suspended floors, some additional foundation costs, and the need for very careful landscaping to conceal the large area of brickwork below floor level. Will improve the view, especially from the balcony.

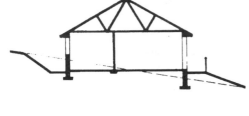

Option Two. Build into the slope. Permits a cost effective solid floor on natural ground, but may require a retaining wall or steep garden to the rear. Excavated material will have to be carted away unless it can be used for landscaping on stand.

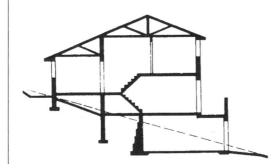

Option Three. 'Cut and Fill' ' This is the usual approach, combining the minimum foundation costs with the look of being built into the hillside. Care required with landscaping.

Option Four. Multi level Garage below with living accommodation above, following the slope. Gives interesting layouts with opportunities for balconies to take advantage of views, but construction costs will be high. Inevitable steps outside and changes of level inside may limit resale potential.

taken in the slope and a level plinth is cut back into the slope from that point, with the resultant material being deposited at the lower end of the ground to bring up the levels. Sometimes that isn't possible and the slope of the land is either too uneven or too much to employ this solution and, in those situations it might be as well to think in terms of a design that 'runs with the land'. Sometimes this can be a split or multi levelled design where all levels of the building 'ride out' of the land but at other times it might mean that certain storeys or parts of the building might find themselves wholly or partially below ground and that, of course, brings us onto consideration of basements.

Basements, in my opinion, are things that are best left to experts and builders who have previous experience of them. They are not a job that should be tackled lightly by the selfbuilder and I question whether, in many cases, unless they are dictated by the nature of the ground, they are something that most selfbuilders should entertain. Most of the 'experts' who advocate basements have never had first hand experience of building one. Most of the selfbuilders who are passionate about them have lived in Germany. In older houses the occupants love their basements and accept, without question that, just occasionally it can get a bit damp in them. In a new home, if only the slightest sign of damp becomes apparent then everybody stops sleeping at night and the entire structure is suspect. A full basement is a swimming pool in reverse. Instead of the water being within the pool, it is kept outside and the pressures for it to make its way through the structure are huge. Unlike a swimming pool, where it's relatively easy to empty the pool and attend to a leak, it's often next to impossible to go back on the waterproofing which is usually on the outside, buried beneath the rest of the structure.

Having said all that, I come back to the fact that the levels on the site may well dictate that one or more walls will find themselves below ground. In these cases the attention to the waterproofing, or tanking as it's called, is vital and care should be taken to follow the instructions and specification laid down by the designer. Remember also, that the basement wall is also a retaining wall and there may well be an element of reinforcement required.

Choosing the design and the influences on that choice

One of the largest single factors influencing the design of your proposed new home has to be the site, both in terms of its physical characteristics as I've discussed above and, also, just where it is. It's likely that you, and your architects or designers, will want to build in the established local style, or at least in a style that doesn't conflict with the local vernacular, and indeed the very characteristics of the local style are what probably attracted you to the area in the first place. That isn't to say that one necessarily sticks to rigid design guides or principles, but it is to say that, if a smooth passage is hoped for in your planning application, contention is best avoided.

Take a trip around the area you're going to be building in and make notes and take photographs of the architectural features and characteristics of the buildings. Take a close and particular look at any new or newish properties in the area for an indication of the way the local thinking goes and the sort of house or bungalow that gets consent. If you live in an area where most of the houses are red brick with distinctive detailing and features, then it's no good thinking that you're going to get an easy ride on a proposal to build a stone house. The planners would simply contend that the stone was non indigenous and reject your proposals out of hand. On the other hand, if most of the houses in your area and particularly the new ones employed a plain tile, but you could successfully argue that many of the traditional buildings had slate or pantiles, you might well have a valid case that the planners might listen to. Planning is law but it is law that is translated by opinion and opinions can vary, or be varied, by logical argument or persuasion.

Surprisingly, although style does of course have an effect on costs, it's not the greatest influence on them. External materials, particularly external walling and roofing materials, have the greatest impact on costs, although, to be fair, these choices are often part and parcel of the style in the first place. A roof which is made up of prefabricated trusses is always going to be cheaper and quicker to construct than a roof that involves fabrication on site with rafters, joists and purlins etc. But, either of those roof types are going to be cheaper to cover in flat profiled interlocking concrete tiles than they are in natural slate or plain clay handmade tiles. In turn, a simple rectangular roof of either sort is always going to be cheaper to construct than a complex shaped roof or one with dormer windows within or through the roof plane. Changing the walling material can have a huge knock on effect and, for example, if one was to change the external materials of a house from rendered blockwork to natural stone, one would be looking at an increase in the walling costs of something in the order of 400%! Now, before you go off having the vapours at the thought, that translates down to 10% on the overall costs of the project but, even then, that may still mean £6-8000 in cash terms.

Size isn't everything they say. Well as far as

building is concerned it is and that's why it's so easy to use £'s per sq. ft. as a ready reckoner for costs. Surprisingly, peculiar circumstances apart, they remain remarkably consistent, irrespective of whether it's a house or bungalow, although to be fair they do break down on the very large or the very small properties. Larger houses have an economy of scale that tends to reduce their costs per square foot but, having said that, the costs are quite often then raised by an increase in the specification for fittings and fixtures. Very small houses and bungalows lose all economies of scale, where, for instance, their sewage and service connections and even things like the cost of boilers may cost the same as for the larger house. A £2000 kitchen in a 900 sq. ft. bungalow amortises out at £2.22 per sq. ft., whereas, in a 2000 sq. ft. house it comes down to £1 a sq. ft. Carrying on with the same example, if you go on to think about the roof, then that little bungalow has a roof of practically the same size as the larger house and the costs, therefore, assuming the same specification, will be identical.

Well, that's the general bits covered but let's look at some of the more specific headings that you might need to think about in the preparation and formulation of your design ideals.

How long will you live there?
You may think it's going to be forever but statistics show that the chances are that you'll be moving on within 5-7 years and quite a few selfbuilders become serial selfbuilders, often building at least once if not twice more before they're done. If you're absolutely convinced that you're going out of the door feet first in a wooden box then by all means forget all about what other people might want and think only of yourselves. If you're likely to want to, or have to, sell then you've got to think in terms of the new homes attractiveness in general market terms, rather than any overtly peculiar or individual requirements.

House or bungalow?
As I've said the costs are pretty much the same but that doesn't translate to the value, where a

bungalow of, say, 1500 sq. ft. built next door to a house of the same size with the same specification, might well have a market value of 10% more. Why? Well, because bungalows are popular with older people and older people don't often need a mortgage and are able to pay that little bit more for what they want and need. In addition, bungalows take up more land than houses and therefore fewer of them get built, so supply and demand pushes their value up. Planning, and the street scene in general, are going to be the deciding factor in whether you can build a house or a bungalow. If you are buying a plot in a street of large houses then the chances are that the planners won't really entertain a bungalow and, conversely, in a street of small bungalows it's unlikely that you'd ever get consent for a house. Similarly in a sensitive area where the local vernacular was for low eaved properties, a bungalow, even if it had rooms in the roof space, might find more favour with planners who are concerned about ridge heights.

If you are going to build a bungalow and you're absolutely certain that you're never going to want to occupy the roof void, then by all means construct the roof cheaply with 'fink' trusses and enjoy living on one floor. If you do ever believe that you may need the extra space or if you ever contemplate selling and you feel that a prospective purchaser might welcome the opportunity of being able to employ the roof space, then do think about it at the design stage. Changing from 'fink' to attic trusses could add £1500 at the construction stages, assuming no immediate occupation, but it opens up a wealth of possibilities for the future.

Garages and carports
A garage can be 15% of the build cost of a property and, in many cases it's never even used for the purpose of its design. Try and market a new house or bungalow without a garage, however, and you'll pretty soon realise just how essential its provision is in the human psyche. Garages can be attached, detached or integral but whatever they are, it doesn't make sense in design terms to construct them in anything other

than similar materials to the dwelling.

In that circumstance, even a detached garage, whilst undoubtedly cheaper to construct in terms of pounds per square foot, becomes a small bungalow of between two and four hundred square feet and the costs cannot be discounted. In cases where the garage is an integral part of the design and is almost just another room, the costs, in per square foot terms, bear similarity with the costs of the house itself. After all, if the foundations, the walls and the roof are the same, if the windows and doors are the same and if almost one wall is taken up by an expensive garage door, then why should the costs be that different? Most selfbuilders will feel that the trades of plumber, electrician and, perhaps also plasterer, should have an input and, to be fair, the garage must also bear its fair share of the apportionment of any associated driveway and service costs. I have always, therefore recommended that, when considering the costs and the square footage of any proposed house, an integral or attached garage is counted in as part of the overall square footage. If that means that, somebody comes along one day and complains about having some money left over then I'd far rather live with that than entertain the many people who forget to cost the garage altogether and feel that, somehow, it comes either ludicrously cheap or for free.

Garages don't have to be boring rectangles. Cars come in various sizes and there's no earthly reason why garages have to have all bays the same size. Garages can also double up as workshops and, again, there's no reason why the provision of space has to be made by just lengthening the garage. Why not think of making the shape more complex? Why not, while you're at it, think in terms of the occupation or future occupation of the roof void for storage, hobbies or even office accommodation, by planning to use attic trusses?

Lastly on this subject, garage doors need careful attention and care needs to be taken not to make the open maw of the garage door the dominant architectural feature of your new home.

Children

Children arrive on the scene in neatly packaged sizes and with limited requirements and they grow up in all respects. If you're never going to have children, then that doesn't mean that you can necessarily forget all about the housing and requirements of the younger members of the species, especially if you're ever going to sell and move on. The chances are that anyone buying your house will want to know that their children can be properly accommodated and if you've arranged the accommodation, and in particular, the sleeping accommodation, in such a way that normal family life would be impossible, then you're cutting down the marketing opportunities for your house.

Even those who do have children often get it wrong. Children's requirements change. What suits the ten year old is not right for the seventeen year old and what suits a seventeen year old will be redundant when the twenty four year old has long since left home. Think about these changing requirements. Think of how the ten year old may well want to spend the early evening, before they go to bed, in the same lounge as mummy and daddy. Think of the same child at seventeen and by then they may well want to go to bed after you, will almost certainly want to watch different things on the telly, at a considerably higher volume than you might appreciate, and may well want to do so in company with eight of their friends. The answer is, of course, a family room or playroom where they can entertain their mates. But, what if that's just underneath your bedroom and you find it difficult to sleep to the sound of an extended base? What about its access and proximity to the other facilities? Late at night hordes of hungry teenagers may well need to find a fridge, larder or loo and do you really want them trooping all through your house?

Granny flats

There's an awful lot to think about here, not least whether the idea's a good one in the first place. The idea of the older generation being housed and looked after by the younger generation is a good, and a socially desirable one. For many the pooling of financial resources, and the possibility of a built-in friend, babysitter and house sitter is wonderful. For many others, the thought of someone coming to live in their home is as welcome as the onset of bubonic plague. Culturally many of us have lost the natural progressions of family and social life that lead up to the gentle inclusion of different generations within the same household. Personally we've lost the ability to exchange roles and inherit different hierarchies and it's as well to think these things through before any commitment is made, and especially before an older and more vulnerable member of the family is enthused or moved.

The financial implications of any joint selfbuild need to be carefully thought through and as much thought needs to be given to the possible future unravelling of any pooling of financial resources, as it does to their amalgamation. What if it all goes wrong? What if granny, or you, decides that it's no good and that you're going to have to split up again? What if granny gets ill and needs to go into an expensive nursing home? In any or all of these cases will granny be able to recover her monies and if she does, will that make your own occupation of the new home untenable?

Will granny simply pass over her share of the project in cash, in the knowledge that you will look after her for the rest of her days, or will she do so as part owner of the new home? In either of these cases, what security of tenure will granny have and how will she be able to recover her share if she needs to re-house herself somewhere else? All of these questions need an answer before a joint project is undertaken and not afterwards.

One way around things might be for granny to give you a private mortgage to the value of her input, negating or limiting your need to apply for outside finance. Granny now has an additional income and, in all probability, even if you pay her an amount that would be above the amount she could expect if she invested the money in a Building Society, you will be paying less than if you'd taken out a mortgage with that same society. If you project your thinking forward to the time when granny has to go into care, then, if

granny retains ownership of the property, she might well be required to sell it in order to fund her care accommodation. On the other hand, if her only interest in your new home is in the form of a mortgage and the income deriving from it, then the principle asset is safe and the income, added to her pension income, may well mean that she can be housed in more comfortable circumstances.

The important thing in all of this is forward planning and sound advice from solicitors and/ or accountants and, unsavoury as it seems, one has to look forward to the possibility of death. If granny dies first, then with any of the arrangements I've described above, it's important that any Will reflects your desire not to be turfed out of your home, and that the mortgage lapses or else granny's share of the home comes down to you. Siblings can complicate this and the need to accommodate their aspirations of inheritance may well, in their eyes, take precedence over the loving care you gave granny in her last years. And what if you predecease granny? Will she in turn be turfed out of house and home or will adequate provision be made for her re-homing and/or her extrication of her financial stake in the family home? I say again, as much care needs to go into the possible unravelling of the pooling of financial resources as it does with its amalgamation.

Given the social desirability of the elderly being housed within the bosom of a loving family, you might be surprised to learn that planners are often fairly hostile to the idea of separate or self contained accommodation within the home and, by their attitude in certain situations, you'd think you were asking for a block of flats rather than multi generational accommodation. Their fear is always, of course, that the separate accommodation will be hived off as a completely separate dwelling and in this respect there are things that you can do to alleviate their fears. Firstly consider whether or not it's absolutely essential for the granny annexe to have its own separate front entrance, at least in the first instance. Secondly, consider whether a full kitchen is required and, even if it is, then whether or not the annexe requires a separate utility room or whether it could share yours. If the objections are more deep rooted then think carefully about whether or not you designate the rooms involved as an annexe at all. The lounge for the annexe could just as easily be described as a family room and the bedroom could equally as easily be called a study. Now you may think that there's an element of pulling the wool over people's eyes here but there's nothing wrong with that. Your duty is to house your extended family and if you want to legitimately rearrange or re-designate the accommodation in your home to suit those requirements then you're doing nothing wrong.

Of course, it might not be the fact of the use of accommodation itself that brings about the planning officer's objections. That might well be the fact that the provision of the accommodation means that the house has got too big. In that case the arguments against what you're proposing gain a legitimacy that it's hard to refute, espe-cially as, by the very nature of its intended occupation, the granny annexe should normally be on the ground floor. Now, before you go running off thinking that all councils are against the provision of granny annexes, there are a great many who welcome them enthusiastically. Sometimes this has to do with a recognition of the benefits to society as a whole, of the care of the elderly within the family unit but, at other times, and in certain areas, it can also be generated by a recognition of the need for tourist accommodation.

But to stick to the point of this section, there are certain considerations that need to be carefully thought through, and planned for, if the accommodation is to properly fulfil its role. Firstly, as I've said, the annexe should normally be on the ground floor and unless you can demonstrate that there is, perhaps, a lift, the presumption will always be against the provision of accommodation on the top floors. Granny may well be concerned that the accommodation, especially when compared to her existing or previous home, is too small but, the planners, and perhaps your budget, might well require that it's not too large. Diplomacy is the key here. The furniture that you feel might easily be disposed

of, the pictures that would crowd out the walls in the annexe, the ornaments that you think of as a waste of space might well have connections and memories that far outweigh their face value. Try to interest granny in the practicalities of the design and stress the bits that are important.

Plugs and light switches can be set at hand height without any extra cost being involved. Taps can be provided that are easily turned on by those with arthritic hands. The sanitaryware can be designed for use by elderly people, with either a walk in bath, a shower with a seat or even one that can be accessed by a wheelchair. Doors should be 2'9" or even 3 feet wide to allow for wheelchair access, not only for granny but maybe for her friends, and while you're about it, think about ramps to all external doors or doors with cills.

And outside? Remember elderly people still like to walk and sit outside on a nice day and that they won't want to be cooped up in the house all the time. Think about pathways and patios with slopes instead of steps, and railings for them to hold on to. As well as that, think about the provision of suitable shady seating at strategic points throughout the garden so that an elderly person can gently progress from point to point rather than having to make a marathon route march to a comfortable seat.

And then you'll need to think about what use the accommodation can have when granny finally leaves it. Will it be suitable for a son or daughter to lead their lives in relative independence under your roof? Could there even be a reversal of roles with you eventually swopping over into the annexe and one of your children taking over the main house?

Home office accommodation
Working from home is a growing trend. The greater use of computers and the Internet obviates the need for a group of people working together to be in the same room, or even the same building, and that has allowed people and especially working mothers to opt to work from home. In addition companies have found that by the use of representatives working from home they can expand their sales operations into

different areas without having to go to the expense of setting up and renting new office accommodation.

But, before you go marking out a plush suite of offices in your new home, there are some considerations, the first of which is the attitude of the planners. Whilst it's unlikely to be as hostile as it can get towards granny flats, there may well be some suspicion. Your home is probably going to be built as the result of a planning consent for a dwelling house and any suspicion that its usage is going to be extended into an activity that might involve, staff, additional car parking requirements or noise will upset not only the planners but, in all probability, your neighbours. It's a question of degree. The representative or the aroma therapist working from a room in the home, that was probably designated as a study, will not attract too much attention and is, in most cases, perfectly acceptable. The busy marketing company with staff and vans coming and going at all hours will pretty soon attract the attention of the authorities.

Animals
Maybe, if you've got a daughter who's in to horses, it's that which has brought you to the selfbuild table. Fed up with having to escort her to out of the way fields at unearthly hours of the day, you've decided that the only course is to build a new home with stabling and a paddock. If so, thought needs to be given to ancillary accommodation such as tack rooms and feed rooms but in all probability these will be provided as separate accommodation. Thought also needs to be given to parking for the inevitable next step of a horsebox as well as to the dung heap and its proximity to the house.

Dogs come in varying sizes and degrees of dirtiness. The pampered pooch, who only ever walks on the footpath, needs no extra consideration but the Springer spaniel who delights in immersing himself in muddy water certainly does. Consider whether you want mud sprayed up the wall of your utility/laundry room and, if there's space, think about a dog room with a hose down floor and access to a run.

If you're fed up with coming home to find yet another pussy dead on the road, consider whether an aviary attached to the house could house Tiddles in comfort and safety. Consider also the resultant increase in the local bird population.

Extendibility
In other books this has been given a separate category in the plans section but it is my contention that all properties are capable of extension in some way, and that to try and design with extension in mind will lead to a building which is 'neither fish, flesh nor fowl'. There are things that can be done, however, to make future extension easier, or even possible, and I'm thinking here of the provision of attic trusses in the roof instead of 'fink' trusses and the possible inclusion of lintels built into walls where it is known, or it is likely, that a door or a window opening will be required.

Many extensions can be carried out under what is known as Permitted Development Rights. These give consent for certain classes of development of which, subject to certain conditions, an extension of usually no more that 15% of the volume of the original house is one. Other classes of permitted development are, alteration within the curtilage of a dwelling, which includes the roof space and the erection of a garage, where none exists. There are a whole host of different rules and regulations governing or modifying whether they are applicable and, in particular, in Conservation Areas, Areas of Outstanding Natural Beauty and in National Parks, the scope of any rights is severely curtailed or cancelled. Before you contemplate any extension it's as well to visit your local planning office to get a definitive ruling on whether or not what you're proposing can be built under Permitted Development Rights or whether it will need express planning consent.

Accommodation for disabled people
In many ways, many of the comments and suggestions I have made on design in the section on granny flats are equally applicable here. Careful thought needs to be given regarding

access to, and within, the home and think about just how friends and visitors who are disabled might be accommodated.

Larders & cold rooms

Even in an age of fitted kitchen units, the larder still holds sway in people's minds. In many modern kitchens, however, its inclusion is difficult, if the run of units is not to be disturbed. On the other hand, if there's space then it's interesting to note that a 6ft x 6ft larder with 18" shelves all around, will provide as much storage as a whole lorry load of units.

Agas, Rayburns & their generic cousins

To some a huge expense for what is often just a cooker, to others the very essence of the dream of a new home. Think about where it's going to go. Think about the flue that it might need, and the space that it will take up. Some of them are indeed only cookers but others can contribute to the hot water and even run the central heating as well.

Hobbies

If it's a swimming pool or an indoor badminton court you're after, and you've decided that their provision cannot be accommodated within a separate or purpose made building, then your house will need to have this area designed in as part and parcel of it and, in many respects, this aspect of the project may take on a dominant influence. More often it's a case of the provision of a room for things like sewing, model making, writing and things like that and that can be satisfied by simply setting aside a room or rooms for that purpose. Oh, and by the way, the roof void is the perfect place for hobbies like train sets.

Billiards and snooker tables need careful thought from two aspects. Firstly, it's no good providing a room that's big enough for the table if the space available doesn't allow you to stretch to the full extent of the cue and, secondly, if the table is going upstairs, then access has to be considered as well as the weight and whether the floor is capable of supporting it.

Energy conservation

The first thing to say about energy conservation is that it need not be expensive nor rely on advanced technology. Often the best results can be achieved with an expense of about 50p per square foot but it is important to consider these matters at the design stage. If energy conservation is high on your list of priorities, then it's important that you make your designers aware of this at the outset so that extra insulation can be built in and their savings reflected in, perhaps, a lesser boiler requirement.

Without going through the details of the SAP values and energy ratings in this book I suggest you read *Building Your Own Home* or obtain the leaflets from BRECSU, part of the Building Research Establishment. Suffice it to say here, that a SAP value of 100 is a better rating than one of 86 and in the examples set out below, I compare two identical houses, of 2500 sq. ft., to show just how you can increase the energy efficiency of your new home.

House 'A' – built to meet the Building Regulations requirements

* Basic wall insulation (U value of 0.45)
* 150mm loft insulation
* 30mm floor insulation
* Standard double glazing (6mm air gap)
* Gas wall mounted boiler serving radiators
* Room thermostat, programmer and thermostatic radiator valves
* 30mm sprayed on insulation to hot water cylinder

SAP rating = 86
Annual heating and hot water cost £476 (*1998/9)

House 'B' – built to provide low running costs

* South facing orientation
* Good wall insulation (U value of 0.3)
* 200mm loft insulation
* 50mm floor insulation
* Double glazing with 12mm air gap and low 'e' glass
* Gas condensing boiler serving radiators
* Room thermostat, programmer and thermostatic radiator valves
* 70mm sprayed on insulation to hot water cylinder

SAP rating = 100
Annual heating and hot water costs £306 (*1998/9)

Design Check List

House or bungalow? The planning permission or the plot may dictate this but it's obviously the first consideration. Even if it's to be two storeys, is there a restriction on the ridge height or eaves height and will you need to think in terms of dormer windows or roof lights? Remember, with a dormer house, the area of the upper part, that you can actually occupy, is often a lot smaller than the ground floor and may have sloping ceilings.

What is the local vernacular? Is it for simple or complex shapes? What are the local materials and what effect do they have on the design in terms of things like roof pitches and window types? Observe details in the local architecture that you feel would properly transfer to your new home.

Sloping site or flat site? Whichever it is, you need to make sure that the design you choose is one that is suitable for the lay of the land. A dwelling designed for a flat site will never really look right on a sloping site and vice versa.

Moving inside. Start with the hall. There is a refreshing modern trend to make this as large as possible after years of thinking of it as merely a waste of space. If guests enter into a room with a table in the centre with flowers on it, and doors off, it's much more impressive than having everybody crammed into a tiny space beside a staircase. On the continent the dining hall is very popular and as people spend more holidays over there the trend is coming this way. You either like it or you don't.

Staircases say an awful lot about your home and are probably one of the best ways to make an entrance area impressive. There are a myriad of styles and materials and even the most expensive won't cost as much as your kitchen units.

Moving through into the living area. Do you want one single open space or would you prefer the rooms to be separated, even if only by archways? Do you want a sitting room with a separate dining room or would you prefer a lounge/dining room or even a kitchen/dining room? A house over 1800 sq. ft. can probably give you a TV room or study and at over 2000 sq. ft., you can have both.

If you've got children, do you need a family room or a lounge that they can call their own? If so try to make sure that it's accessible from, or close by, the kitchen areas, that it's near to toilet facilities and that it's not directly below your bedroom.

Do you need a self contained annex to use either as a granny flat or office accommodation? Sometimes this is just a matter of setting rooms aside but at other times there are very important considerations to be taken into account. Think this one through very carefully and read up about it in this book and others before putting pen to paper.

If you want to provide accommodation for hobbies, then you have to decide whether this can be within the main body of the house, in a separate annex or purpose designed building or, possibly combined with garage or outhouse accommodation. The nature of your hobby or interests may well determine this.

What sort of atmosphere do you want from your principal rooms? Double doors and a higher than average ceiling height give a feeling of spaciousness. A large fireplace can look incongruous in a smaller room whilst a carefully proportioned one can make a room cosy. Fireplaces are important - they can't be changed very easily and some thought needs to be given to choosing a design that is appropriate to the style of home you're after.

If you want patio or french doors leading out onto a terrace give some thought as to how it will look from both inside and out and how you will arrange the furniture both in the room and outside on the terrace. Do you want this terrace to be an extension of the living area of the house or would you prefer to situate this outside sitting, or barbecue area, away from the house?

Give some thought to the dining room. Is it going to be just big enough to seat your immediate family or does it need to be big enough to entertain on a larger scale? Will it ever really get used or will it become the least used, most expensively furnished room in the house? Even if the plans of the house show the table in the room, is there going to be enough room for the chairs to be pulled back far enough for people to sit down?

The kitchen? Probably the most important room in the house as far as making a statement of your own ideals is concerned. Do you want a smallish kitchen with separate utility room? Does that utility room have to be very large? Do you even need it or would the space be better employed in creating a larger kitchen, especially now that washing machines and dishwashers don't sound like Concorde taking off. What sort of units do you want? Is there any need to spend a huge amount on these units or are there cheaper alternatives, which, with flair and imagination, can still be as impressive? Do you want to ever eat in the kitchen or do you always want to do so? What sort of flooring do you want?

Consider a projecting rear porch instead of a utility room. What do you use the utility room for? Is it connected in any way with the activities of the kitchen or is it really a laundry room? Is it even that or is it just somewhere to kick off the muddy boots, hang up the wet Barbour and park the dogs?

Do you want a downstairs or separate WC? If so think about whether it's going to be of more use to your lifestyle by being positioned nearer the front or the back door. Perhaps you need both or perhaps you don't want strangers going beyond a certain point when they call. Perhaps, too, you don't want to traipse through the house to go to the loo when you're busy gardening.

Are you going to be able to provide room to keep all those things that never seem to find a proper home like the vacuum cleaner and the brooms? Do you need to house a pram, pushchair or wheelchair?

Would you like a coats cupboard or are you happy with hooks in the hall or the downstairs loo?

Moving upstairs, do you want the master bedroom suite to be totally separate and private from all of the other bedrooms? Is sound transmission between these rooms, and the prevention of it, important to you?

Staying with the master suite, how large do you want it to be in comparison with the other rooms? On some houses the master suite will take up well over a third and, sometimes, approaching a half of the entire upper floor. Is this what you want?

How many bathrooms do you want? Does the main or communal bathroom have to be the biggest? Does it have to have things like a bidet or, will that only get used by the children for storing dirty socks. With children fighting to get ready for school each day would the provision of more than one wash basin be a good idea? Does the en-suite, assuming you want one, have to be big? Would you like to have a bath in it or do you prefer a shower?

If there are guest rooms, do they have to have en-suite facilities or could they or any of the other bedrooms do with a wash basin?

With the bedrooms - do they all have to be of

similar size or are there some that you would like bigger than others do? Children start off in different sizes but, long before they leave home, they all assume roughly the same proportions.

Going back to the master bedroom, or to any of the other bedrooms come to that, do they need dressing rooms?

Built in furniture for bedrooms and dressing rooms is cost effective but if you already own free standing wardrobes and are happy with them, then wouldn't it be better just to provide alcoves? Remember, when you move you can take your furniture but you can't take the fitted units.

These days with insulated tanks, which lose less than one degree a day in heat, the cylinder cupboard might not double up as an airing cupboard at all. Do you need or want a large linen cupboard? Do you need a separate storage cupboard upstairs for household implements?

Have you considered a built in vacuum?

With increasingly hot summers have you thought about whether you should considered air conditioning?

In similar vein and possibly in combination with the last point, have you considered whether you should install a heat recovery and ventilation system?

Will you want a conservatory now or in the future? If the answer is yes then you have to decide which rooms will it be entered from and plan for doors or french doors at that point.

What about a balcony? Planners have the vapours about them in built up areas, thinking that all sorts of perversions are likely to go on. In reality, how often can you use them in this country - in the winter it's probably too cold or wet and in the summer you could probably fry eggs on the tiles.

The garage. Is it to be attached, integral or detached? What are the requirements for parking and turning areas and what impact will they have on the area of the plot left available for the dwelling. Is the garage simply for parking cars in or can it double up or share its use with some other aspect of your lifestyle.

The orientation of the house is alluded to in Example 'B' and there's no doubt that if your house can be positioned to face south, plus or minus 45 degrees, there are advantages to be gained in energy terms. However, these are ideals and they might not be possible or practicable on your site. In addition in certain planning situations there is no doubt that considerations of energy conservation where they impact on external design or appearance, can come a very poor second in a planning officer's mind. A compact plan without extensions, and with the external wall surfaces minimised, reduces heat loss and reduces shading of parts of the structure. Whether that fits in with the local vernacular, or the trend in design terms, for more complex shapes is a different matter altogether.

If possible, position little used rooms or utility areas on the north of the building and get as many of the habitable rooms as possible to benefit from the passive solar gain of being on the southern side. Don't, however, ruin a design or the advantages of a site by a slavish compliance with these ideals.

Internal fittings, fixtures and the choices of heating and lighting systems are beyond the scope of this book but are considered in greater detail in the books and leaflets I have referred to.

Landscaping, planting and the garden
The surroundings for your new home are as much a consideration of its design as any other aspect of its layout. It is the external appearance and enjoyment of your home that will impart much of its value to it.

The driveway, paths and patios
In many new homes the driveway is the dominant feature of the front elevation and care needs to be given to its design and construction. Consider whether it needs to run straight up to the front of the garage or whether there's room for it to curve gently across the site. Consider whether by doing so you can gain privacy in the front garden or whether, if that's not possible, the pathway to the front door can run separately. Think about the surfacing of any driveway. Pea shingle might be fine in a rural situation but in

an urban one might look incongruous. Again it might be alright on a flat site but on a sloping driveway it will be forever migrating onto the highway. A tarmac or block paviour driveway may well look right in a suburban street but will look completely out of place and be equally as impracticable in some rural situations. Paths and patios don't have to be in straight lines and needn't all be of the same materials. Experiment with different shapes, surfaces and textures and consider whether the garden sitting areas should be allied to the house as an extension of the normal living space, or divorced to provide a separate environment.

Walls, fences and hedges
A walled garden can, as the Victorians discovered, create an Eco climate of its own and on top of that a wall will do far more to eliminate noise than any fence or hedge. If you are going to build a wall or walls as the boundary of your new home, then do it properly. Four inch brick walls with piers will always be unstable, unless they are dog legged at frequent intervals and I would suggest that you always think in terms of a nine inch or even a thirteen and half inch wall. Any wall needs to be properly founded and it's important not to forget the dpc and the capping if what is after all a fairly expensive construction is not to deteriorate quite quickly. Blockwork walls will need properly rendering and, as well as the dpc with a bellmouth drip, they will need a proper tiled or stone slate capping.

Dry stone walls may look easy to construct but do not imagine for one moment that all that it involves is simply plonking one stone on top of another. There are regional variations but all of them require a very careful choice and placing of each stone, usually with an inward batter to both faces and a rubble infill.

Retaining walls of any of these materials will need to be designed by an engineer, if they are called upon to retain more than 1.2M, and as much attention needs to be given to the drainage of the retained land behind the wall as it does with the actual strength of the wall itself.

If you're going to plant hedges, choose the species carefully and think about their eventual height and spread and just how high you want it to end up as. Please choose native species wherever possible and please don't plant *leylandii*.

There are many different types of fencing and they have all evolved to suit differing purposes. As a means of enclosure, to keep out stock or to denote an area where people are not expected to walk, the simple post with either a double or single rail fence is highly effective and relatively attractive. If privacy is required then the close boarded fence using proper straight or feather edged boarding securely nailed to arris rails is perfectly suitable and serviceable and, if not as much privacy is required, then the vertical sections can be nailed as hit and miss. Panels of woven fencing can only really be considered as temporary solutions to the immediate problems of privacy and enclosure.

Trees and landscaping
Trees and their effects on the foundations of your new home have already been considered but the planners might well want you to submit a tree planting scheme. When working one out, try, as far as is possible, to use native species and when positioning them on the plans think in terms of their eventual height and girth and the effect they will have on the structure of your home as well as the shade they will produce.

Whether or not you commission a formal landscaping scheme from a garden designer, you'll need to think about levels and the creation of your new garden at an early stage. Building a new home means that vast amounts of topsoil and subsoil have to be dug up and their removal to a tip can be very expensive and time consuming. How much more galling is it, therefore, if, at the end of your building you find yourself having to pay to import soil or fill to make up levels or to create a new landscape? Try to think forward and where possible, store topsoil and some subsoil for eventual use and, when you do, just in case you've got it wrong and you don't need it, store it in a place where access can be got to it by machinery. Incidentally, many a rockery in mature as well as new houses, owes its existence to the fact that it was once a spoil heap.

The contributory companies and practices

The actual building process is outside the scope of this book and you will need to turn to the pages of *Building Your Own Home* to read about how to go about getting all of the necessary consents and how to obtain and manage builders and labour. This book is concerned with the choice and the selection of your plans and, in this respect, it is, therefore, pertinent to briefly talk about the companies who have contributed plans to this book from a broad cross section of the major players within the selfbuild industry. Some of the plans within this book have been created or have evolved around a particular system of building and in some cases translation of those ideas to a differing system would be neither appropriate or possible. Other designs lend themselves to construction by any of the main methods of building and in many cases the companies or architects are able to take things forward on the basis of your preferred choice.

I have always maintained that there is no real argument about whether timber frame or brick and block construction are better or worse than one another. Both are equally valid methods of building and, in many cases, a lay person would be hard pushed to know whether one house or another was built in any particular way. What is important is that you are comfortable with the company or practice you are dealing with, with the design of your new home, and with the level and the cost of the service that you are being provided with. In many cases that satisfaction will far outweigh any interest about which building method they are promoting, whilst in others, what is being provided may be so unique to that company that that is what fuels your interest.

Associated Self Build Architects
This association, conceived and run to this day by Chartered Architects, Julian Owen and Adrian Spawforth, entered the selfbuild stage like a breath of fresh air in 1992. They set out to show just how much architects have to offer and to instil and promote, through a like minded membership, the principle of architects working

for and *with* their clients, in order to achieve what the selfbuilder wanted rather than that which the architect thought they should have. Their rules for membership mean that only the smaller practices can join and that they must be members of the RIBA or RIAS and carry the appropriate Professional Indemnity Insurance. ASBA architects must also agree to provide an initial consultation, free of charge, and, most importantly they require their members to have appropriate design skills and a general commitment to one off house designs as well as an approachable, unpretentious attitude to their work and their clients.
Telephone, Freephone: 0800 387310

Border Oak Design & Construction Ltd
Established in the mid eighties, Border Oak has principally built up a reputation based on its unique and traditional oak framed houses. This is sixteenth century construction methods brought into the modern age with a massive skeleton of heavy oak timbers forming the frame. This frame is fabricated in their workshops from the finest coppiced trees of English Oak and is test assembled in the 'framying' ground before being marked and disassembled ready for erection on site. It is single skin building and the infill panels are fitted with a sophisticated system of trims, water bars, weather seals and drainage channels to ensure that the building can withstand the worst that the British climate can provide. This is not a twee modern copy of a style – this is the real thing.

Border Oak can do anything from the design and feasibility through to a full 'turnkey' package but they find that most of their clients prefer to commission them to prepare the base, manufacture and erect the oak frame, fit the infill panels, the external joinery and roof coverings to provide a waterproof structure that can be completed at leisure. They also have a 'Victorian' range of timber framed houses that replicate the architectural values and styles of that period, together with an 'Arthouse' range. These are provided on either a supply only or a supply and erect basis.
Telephone: 01568 708752
Fax: 01568 708295

Custom Homes Ltd
Custom Homes started off life over 30 years ago as ASPP and have a long experience in dealing with one off selfbuilders. Their service can revolve around one of the many designs in their comprehensive and informative brochure but it is much more likely that it will be based on an individual design formulated and reached after a series of on site meetings and a feasibility study.

Their service is based on an energy efficient timber frame package, covering everything, including the planning and Building Regulations applications though to the supply and erection of the timber frame. Some of their clients prefer to self manage their projects, whilst others take advantage of their Project Management service where, from the outset, they will provide a trade by trade guide to budget costing moving on to the engagement of suitable local tradesmen and the day to day running of the project.

As a result of bulk purchasing direct from the manufacturers they are also able to offer a wide variety of optional extras and ancillary materials, details of which are available on request.
Telephone: 01293 822898
Fax: 01293 782229

Designer Homes
This company, with its breathtaking designs, can supply plans only for a fixed fee or else can arrange to supply you with a timber frame/brick and block package.
Telephone/fax: 01835 823806

Design & Materials Ltd
This is undoubtedly one of the most respected and longest established companies to specialise in the selfbuild market. Formed in 1971, their reputation has been principally gained though their championing of the brick and block forms of construction, although they can, and will, provide their service on the basis of the supply and erection of a timber frame.

Essentially they are a package deal company providing a complete architectural service, to include all the necessary applications for planning and Building Regulations, together with the supply of a comprehensive package of materials, each one specifically tailored to the clients' requirements and quoted at a fixed price.

Although they have many 'standard' designs in their brochure, most of their clients choose to have an individual design especially formulated for them and their drawing office is recognised as a prime mover in the cause of innovative and progressive design. Quality, choice and high level of service are the hallmarks of this company.

Whichever build route you choose, they are able to help with the recruitment of labour, by introducing builders who have worked successfully for past clients or by providing the self-builder with everything they need to recruit subcontractors. Regional Managers, their fully qualified architect and all head office staff are on hand to assist in any, and every, aspect of their clients selfbuild project.

Telephone: 01909 730333
Fax: 01909 731201

Kingpost Design Company Ltd.
Keith Bishop & Andrew Smith, both chartered architects, provide the driving force behind the company. They have over 30 years of individual home design and a number of civic awards behind them and their designs, and the detail they express, are breathtakingly exciting.

They provide a comprehensive and professional service from initial site analysis, through planning, working drawings, materials and site supervision, based on either their standard designs or one tailored to a client's individual requirements.

Although basically a design company, they are able to arrange for the supply and erection of a top quality timber frame, for a home to one of their designs.

Telephone/Fax: 01684 566494

Potton Ltd/The Bungalow Company
'People get Potton like they get religion'. Perceived by many as being the market leader, their success in the selfbuild market is largely founded on their 'Heritage' range of houses, backed up by their 'Rectory' and 'Shire' ranges and now by their specialist branch, The Bunga-

low Company. However, what many seem to lose sight of in all of this success is that they are fully able to offer a bespoke design service, where they will start from scratch and create a plan that is totally individual.

The Heritage range of houses involve a unique form of construction, called the aisle frame system, where the major loadings, instead of being borne, solely, by the walling panels, are taken by massive timber uprights supporting a skeleton frame. Other designs use standard open panel timber frames, or a combination of these methods, and all their packages include a full erection service.

As you'd expect, with a company with their unrivalled track record, they maintain a register of customer recommended builders and subcontractors, the performance of whom is constantly monitored. There are also a whole host of inclusions and bolt on extras such as insurances, structural guarantees, supplier discounts and financial advice and packages.

They hold regular and free seminars at their Wyboston Lakes Business and Leisure Park and there are a number of fully furnished show houses at their show village in Cambridgeshire.

Telephone: 01767 263300
Fax: 01767 263311

Scandia-Hus Ltd
During over a quarter of a century of unparalleled success, this company has done more than any other to marry the ideas and ideals of Scandinavian design and technology with the traditions of British architecture. For many, this company is the epitome of package deal and timber frame kit companies and a visit to their show homes and offices at East Grinstead, Sussex, will confirm the luxurious quality of their product, reflected in the designs, the feel and warmth of the exposed timber and the level of the comprehensive specification.

From a manufacturing base in Wales, where they use selected timber imported from Sweden, they continually strive to increase the specification and have designed their new 'Fabric 25' timber frame system to be 'air tight' as the next step forward in improving upon the energy efficiency offered by insulation alone.

Their service ranges from the manufacture and supply and erection of the kit though to a full 'turnkey' package where they take on the role of the main contractor by taking on full responsibility for the whole project. Alternatively they will assist their clients to find and contract with local builders to undertake the work or they are able to put them in contact with Project Managers who will oversee the construction and completion of the new home on a fixed fee basis.

Telephone: 01342 327977
Fax: 01342 315139

The Swedish House Company Ltd
Formerly known as Hedlunds Swedish Houses Ltd., this company actually imports its closed panel timber framed kits from its own factory in Sweden where they are manufactured under highly supervised and controlled conditions from timber grown in their own forests and cut and processed in their own sawmills. Thus there is quality control right from the planting through to the completion of the new home.

This is much more than just a timber frame and, instead, as so much more is included, it can, more properly be described as a kit. This kit is delivered to site, prefabricated in storey high sections up to nine metres long, all fully insulated and with the vapour barrier pre-fitted. Triple glazed windows and a whole host of fixtures and fittings are standard and, as you would expect, the completed houses have an ultra low heating and maintenance requirement.

All fees for Planning and Building Regulations applications are included in their prices and either their own designs can be utilised or else they will work with their clients in the creation of a bespoke design. The service ranges from the supply and erection of the weathertight kit, right through to the provision of a full 'turnkey' service. Help can also be provided in sourcing builders and subcontractors where necessary.

Telephone: 01892 665007
Fax: 01892 665125

The plans that are shown in this book are reproduced at their face value. Their inclusion does not impart or imply any warranty, recommendation or approval of, or for, the contributory companies, their plans or the services or products they provide.

It should also be stressed that no company has paid for their material to be included in this book.

Bungalows under 1500 sq. ft.

When one thinks of small bungalows in this country, one usually thinks of a simple rectangular shape with gable ends, the like of which exists in row upon row in parts of the West Country. There is still an affection for these uncomplicated shapes and indeed, in areas where your new home is going to be an addition to an existing street scene of such dwellings, it would not make sense to make to many radical departures from the norm in architectural terms.

However, there is no need for all small bungalows to look like railway carriages, with few if any notable external features, and a brief look through the following pages will confirm that the flair of some of the current designers is able to take this group into new and exciting realms.

One word of warning about the smaller bungalows, in that, whilst the smaller size is often dictated by budget, buildings of this nature often lose all economies of scale. That means that although the cost of building may well be low, in pounds per square foot terms it is often appreciably higher than larger dwellings. This comes about by virtue of the fact that many of the features, fittings, and requirements, such as driveways, sanitaryware, kitchen units and boilers, do not cost any less than they would for, say, a house almost twice the size.

Contributors in this section:

ASBA Reed Architects
Border Oak
Custom Homes
Design & Materials Ltd.
Designer Homes
Kingpost Design Co
Potton Ltd.
Scandia-Hus

81.4 sq.m./875 sq.ft.

Apperley

The copyright belongs to Kingpost Design Co

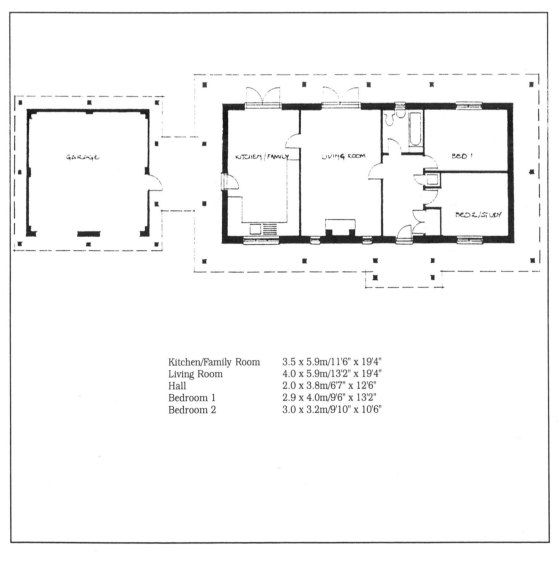

Kitchen/Family Room	3.5 x 5.9m/11'6" x 19'4"
Living Room	4.0 x 5.9m/13'2" x 19'4"
Hall	2.0 x 3.8m/6'7" x 12'6"
Bedroom 1	2.9 x 4.0m/9'6" x 13'2"
Bedroom 2	3.0 x 3.2m/9'10" x 10'6"

An attractive barley twist chimney and traditional thatched roof makes this the ideal home for the small country plot. Two spacious bedrooms, a large kitchen/diner and a full house width lounge with French doors opening to the garden make this a most comfortable dwelling. Thatch is surprisingly low maintenance. Overhanging eaves give welcome respite from the midday sun while allowing the morning and evening sun to light the house. The timber support posts are just asking for roses to be trained over them. There is also a functional and spacious double garage.

110 sq. m.

The copyright belongs to Border Oak

Bailey Lodge

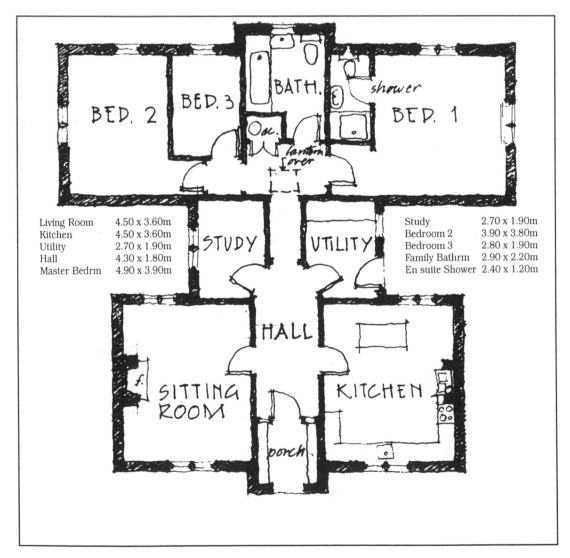

Living Room	4.50 x 3.60m
Kitchen	4.50 x 3.60m
Utility	2.70 x 1.90m
Hall	4.30 x 1.80m
Master Bedrm	4.90 x 3.90m

Study	2.70 x 1.90m
Bedroom 2	3.90 x 3.80m
Bedroom 3	2.80 x 1.90m
Family Bathrm	2.90 x 2.20m
En suite Shower	2.40 x 1.20m

A reworking of the traditional gatehouse which graces many of our country estates. Appropriate reference is made to the Arts and Crafts movement, the use of diminishing course stone tiles or slates, reconstituted stone parapets and window labels/moulds underline the good taste and restraint of a deceptively spacious single storey building. The progression of the entrance hall and circulation spaces give clear sight lines and long perspectives which are often absent in small modern buildings. A 'lantern' provides an interesting interplay of light and shade contributing to the delight of a building which would make an acceptable domicile for the Lord of the Manor.

1100 sq. ft.

The copyright belongs to Scandia-Hus

Athena

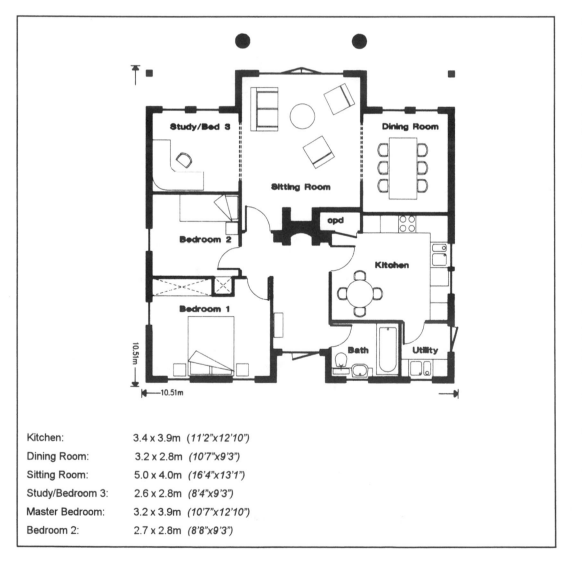

Kitchen:	3.4 x 3.9m *(11'2"x12'10")*
Dining Room:	3.2 x 2.8m *(10'7"x9'3")*
Sitting Room:	5.0 x 4.0m *(16'4"x13'1")*
Study/Bedroom 3:	2.6 x 2.8m *(8'4"x9'3")*
Master Bedroom:	3.2 x 3.9m *(10'7"x12'10")*
Bedroom 2:	2.7 x 2.8m *(8'8"x9'3")*

The Athena is a Greek inspired bungalow which dispels the notion of bungalows being uninteresting, buildings under low, straight roof lines. This is a small bungalow with a square footprint and will fit onto the narrowest of plots. The attractive front elevation will make it blend into most landscapes or street scenes, while the rear elevation is spectacular. The interior layout is very different from the norm, with a real fire greeting you as you enter the hallway. It has two bedrooms, with a third bedroom or study off the central sitting room. The open plan living areas give this bungalow an incredible feeling of space, and the covered patio area extends the space available throughout the summer months.

1367 sq. ft.

The copyright belongs to Scandia-Hus

Bjorkham

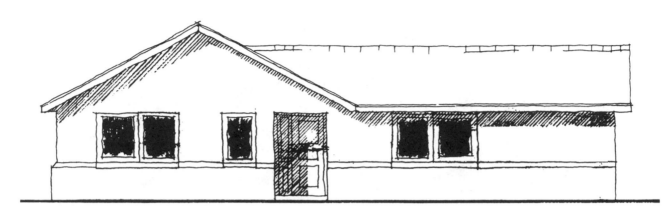

Kitchen:	3.0 x 3.1m *(9'10"x10'2")*
Dining Area:	4.1 x 3.7m *(13'5"x12'2")*
Sitting Room:	7.1 x 4.8m *(23'2"x15'9")*
Master Bedroom:	3.9 x 3.8m *(12'11"x12'5")*
Bedroom 2:	3.0 x 3.8m *(9'10"x12'6")*
Bedroom 3:	3.0 x 2.5m *(9'10"x8'4")*
Bedroom 4:	3.0 x 2.5m *(9'10"x8'4")*

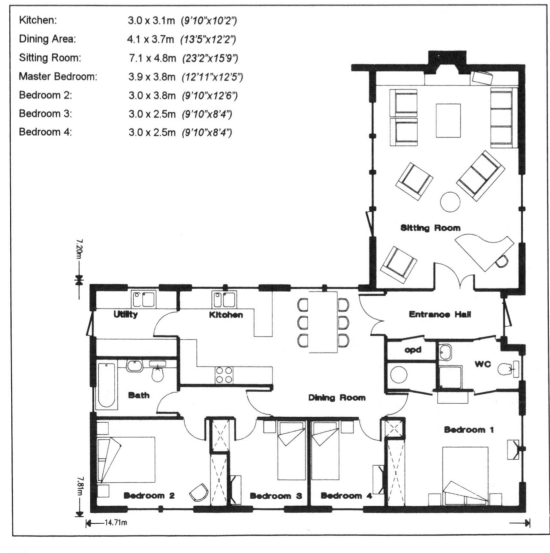

This classic L-shaped bungalow offers a family home with comfort, privacy and plenty of style. The open-plan kitchen/family room is the centre of activity, with the sitting room housed in a separate wing. Deep picture windows and French doors open on to the part-covered patio area, and an open fireplace is just one of the features that can be incorporated into all our designs. Any type of central heating can be installed and, thanks to the energy-efficiency of all Scandia-Hus homes, a cost-effective electric system is a perfectly viable option.

1184 sq. ft.

The copyright belongs to Scandia-Hus

Onsala

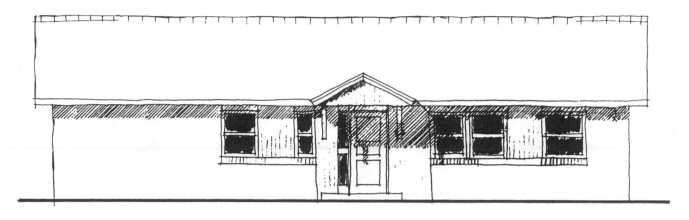

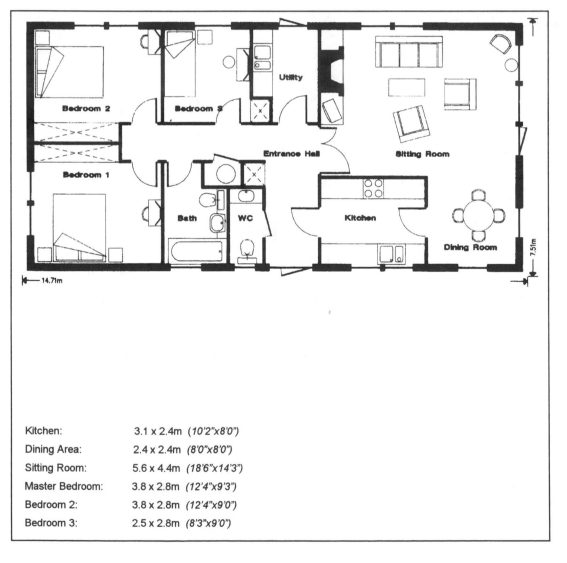

Kitchen:	3.1 x 2.4m	*(10'2"x8'0")*
Dining Area:	2.4 x 2.4m	*(8'0"x8'0")*
Sitting Room:	5.6 x 4.4m	*(18'6"x14'3")*
Master Bedroom:	3.8 x 2.8m	*(12'4"x9'3")*
Bedroom 2:	3.8 x 2.8m	*(12'4"x9'0")*
Bedroom 3:	2.5 x 2.8m	*(8'3"x9'0")*

The Onsala bungalow is a Scandia-Hus 'classic'. The choice of a two, or a three bedroom version of this bungalow is not the only option open to those interested in this compact, yet deceptively spacious design. By using brick, stone, block and render or timber - or indeed a combination of any of these - the Onsala can be made to blend into the local vernacular in any part of the country. The large L-shaped sitting room and dining area features deep picture windows and French doors which cast a well-lit look of luxury over an impressive interior. The Onsala offers economy of scale without any reduction in quality or style.

1346 sq. ft.

The copyright belongs to Scandia-Hus

Ekudden

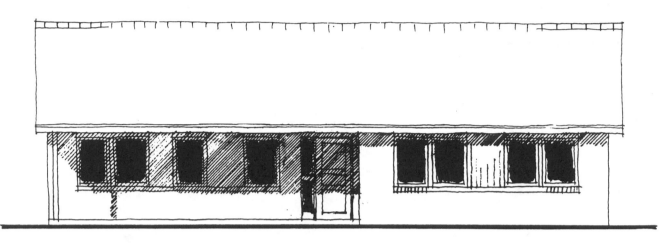

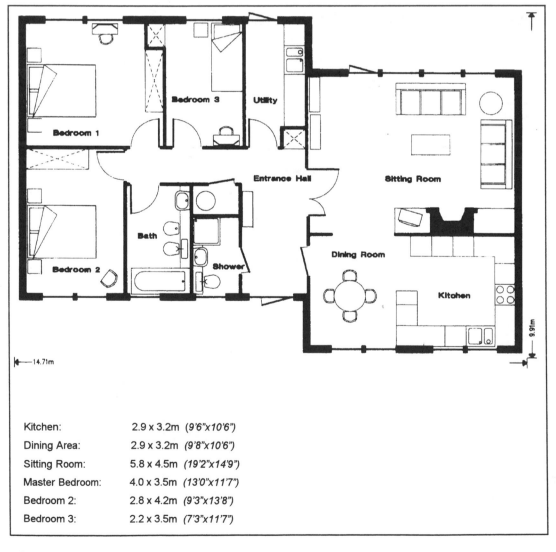

Kitchen:	2.9 x 3.2m	*(9'6"x10'6")*
Dining Area:	2.9 x 3.2m	*(9'8"x10'6")*
Sitting Room:	5.8 x 4.5m	*(19'2"x14'9")*
Master Bedroom:	4.0 x 3.5m	*(13'0"x11'7")*
Bedroom 2:	2.8 x 4.2m	*(9'3"x13'8")*
Bedroom 3:	2.2 x 3.5m	*(7'3"x11'7")*

Providing Scandinavian open-plan lifestyle, coupled with the privacy of self-contained bedroom accommodation, the Ekudden is a fine example of the inspired simplicity of Scandia-Hus design. Warm and welcoming in winter, the optional fireplace adds a traditional feel to the generously proportioned sitting room. In summer, the picture windows and French doors lead straight out to the covered patio area which is ideal for barbecues, or just for relaxing in the shade. The recess forming the front verandah provides an attractive and practical covered entrance and a sunny spot for afternoon tea or pre-dinner drinks.

1367 sq. ft.

The copyright belongs to Scandia-Hus

Boscobel

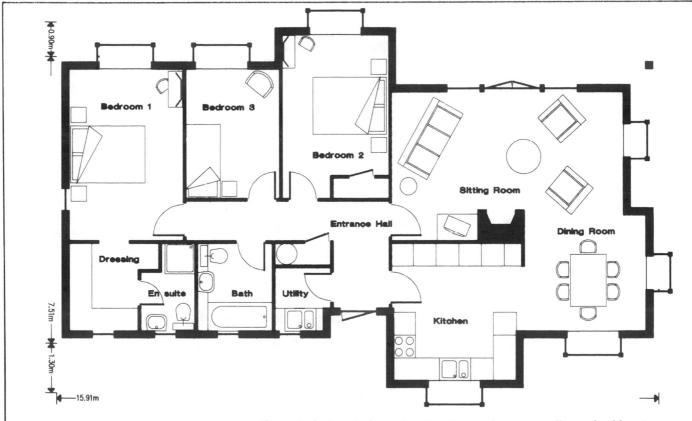

Kitchen:	3.4 x 3.6m *(11'0"x11'9")*
Dining Area:	3.2 x 3.0m *(10'7"x9'10")*
Sitting Room:	6.1 x 3.9m *(20'0"x12'8")*
Master Bedroom:	3.0 x 4.4m *(9'8"x14'3")*
Bedroom 2:	2.9 x 4.2m *(9'4"x13'9")*
Bedroom 3:	2.4 x 3.4m *(8'0"x11'0")*

The main footprint of this bungalow is a basic rectangle, but its regular shape is broken up by the two projections to the front and rear elevations, as well as by the attractive window bays. The open-plan kitchen, dining and sitting room layout makes the Boscobel feel very spacious and light. As none of the internal walls are load-bearing, you are free to move or remove any of them - at any time – to suit your own needs and preferences.

1480 sq. ft.

47 ft. x 43 ft.

Bedlington

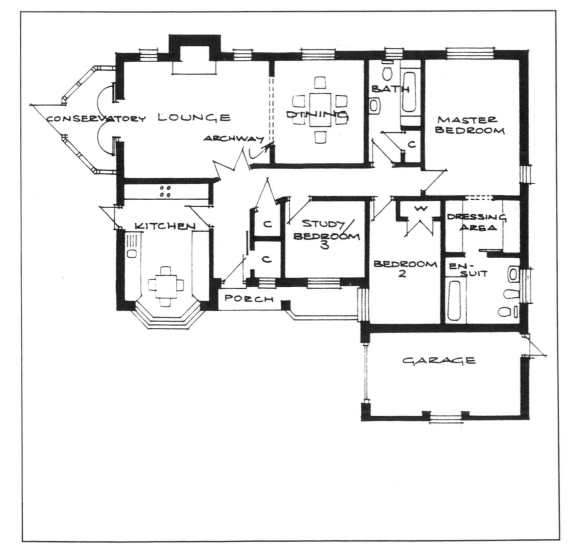

This pretty bungalow will appeal to couples who are retired or about to retire and the build costs won't crack your nest egg! The garage creates a natural courtyard area and could easily be increased to a double if required. There is a comfortable master bedroom suite, a spare guest bedroom and a third bedroom which can double as a study.

1375 sq. ft.

44 ft. x 42 ft.

The copyright belongs to Design & Materials Ltd.

Clevedon

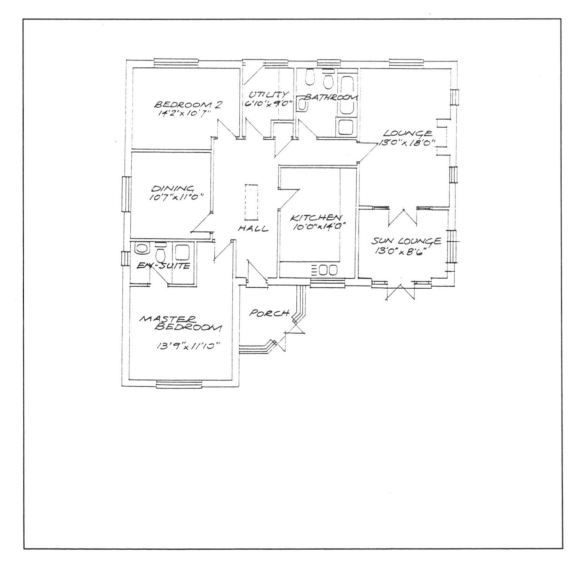

This bungalow would make an ideal retirement home for a plot with a southerly aspect to the front. Illustrated here in render with brick features, plain roof tiles and casement windows the design incorporates a glazed porch and sun room to catch the afternoon or early evening sunshine. There is a comfortable master bedroom with en suite plus a good sized spare bedroom for visiting relatives or friends.

1475 sq. ft.

59 ft. x 40 ft.

The copyright belongs to Design & Materials Ltd.

Ruddington

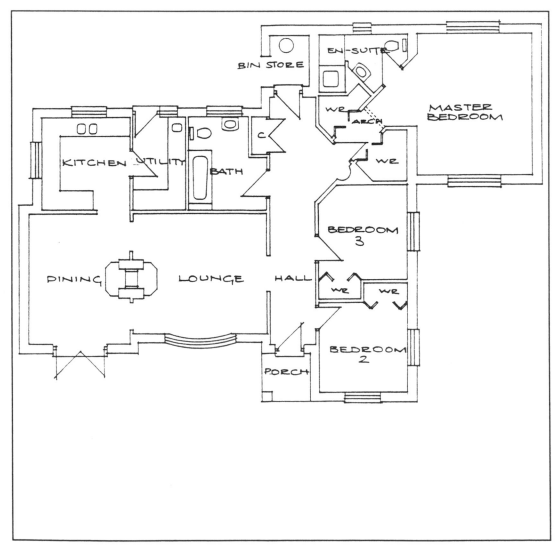

The skilled designer should be able to adapt the external appearance of an existing houseplan to suit most situations. To illustrate this we have shown this attractive bungalow with an alternative elevational treatment.

1251 sq. ft.
Copyright refer to Designer Homes
Alder

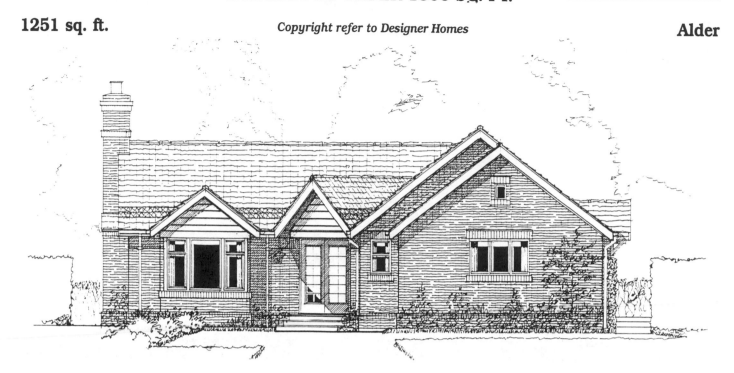

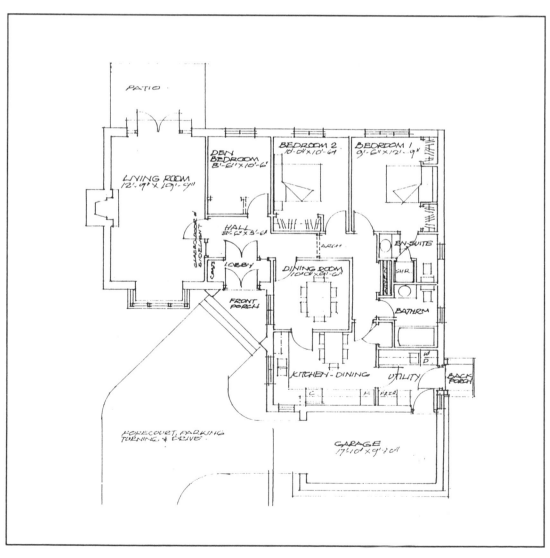

What a wonderful design this is. By taking the simple bungalow and, by clever use of the angled entrance in concert with the varied rooflines of the forward projection, interest and excitement are brought to relatively modest accommodation.

251.52 sq. m.

12.57m x 20.01m

The copyright belongs to Potton Ltd.

97-148

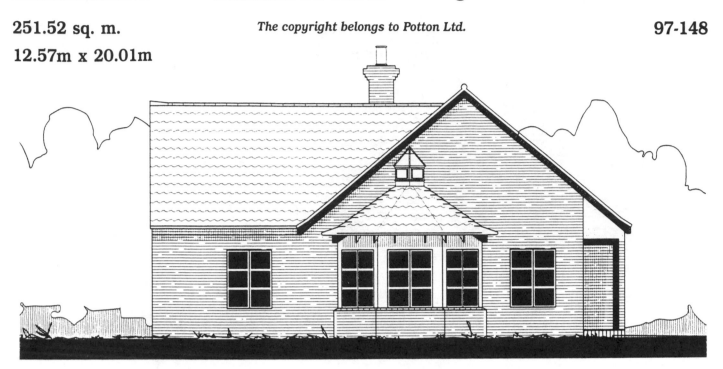

Family Room	3.50 x 4.16m/11'6" x 13'8"	Lounge	6.91 x 5.11m/22'8" x 16' 9"
Workshop	1.84 x 4.81m/6'0" x 15'9"	Dining	5.86 x 4.61m/19'3" x 15'2"
Garage	6.00 x 5.48m/19'8" x 18'0"	Sunroom	3.51 x 3.40m/11'6" x 11'2"
Bedroom 1	4.76 x 2.81m/15'8" x 9'3"	Kitchen	6.66 x 3.75m/21'10" x 12'4"
Bathroom	3.30 x 1.90m/10'10" x 6'3"	Utility	3.10 x 1.84m/10'2" x 6'0"
Bedroom 2	4.80 x 4.25m/15'9" x 13'11"	Larder	1.49 x/4.11m/4'11" x 6'0"
En suite	2.11 x 2.42m/6'11" x 7'11"	W/C	9.00 x 2.70m/2'11" x 8'10"

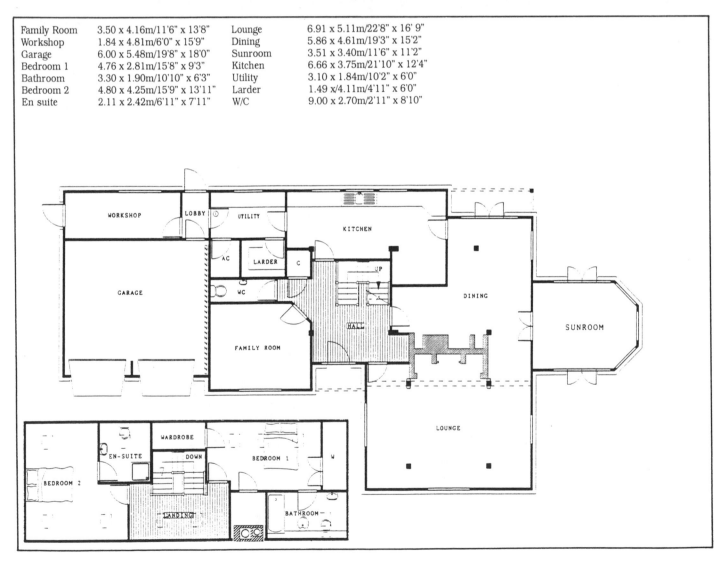

1000 sq. ft.

The copyright belongs to ASBA
Reed Architects

Boultibrook

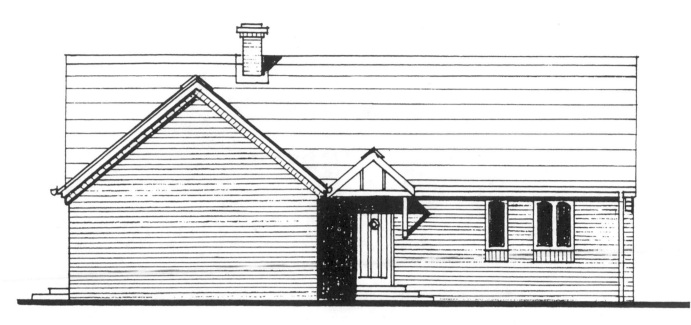

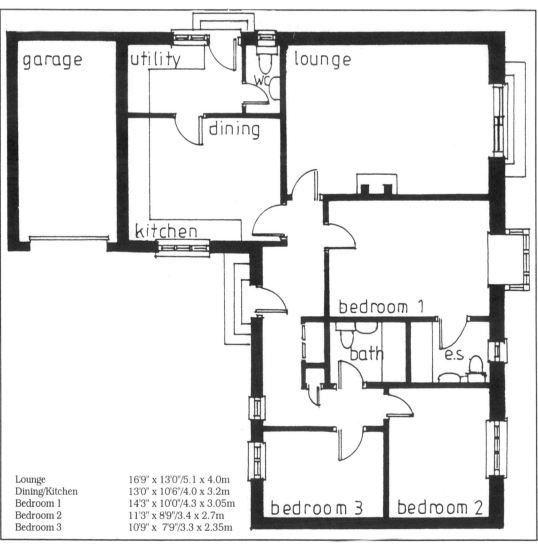

A family bungalow with en suite bathroom to the master bedroom and children's wing with separate bathroom. This corridor could have a further door to provide sound insulation from the living areas.

Lounge	16'9" x 13'0"/5.1 x 4.0m
Dining/Kitchen	13'0" x 10'6"/4.0 x 3.2m
Bedroom 1	14'3" x 10'0"/4.3 x 3.05m
Bedroom 2	11'3" x 8'9"/3.4 x 2.7m
Bedroom 3	10'9" x 7'9"/3.3 x 2.35m

1210 sq. ft./112 sq. m.

The copyright belongs to Custom Homes

Dartmoor

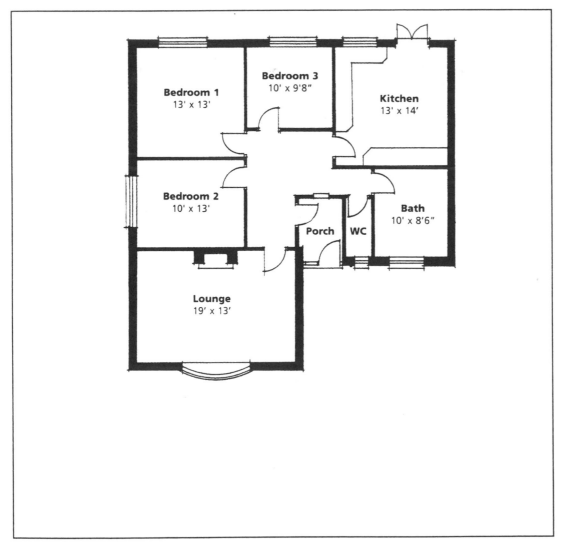

A bungalow that would fit into many a street scene. Whether or not the bedroom could be redisignated as a dining room or study would be up to the self builder.

112 sq. m.

The copyright belongs to Custom Homes

Clovelly

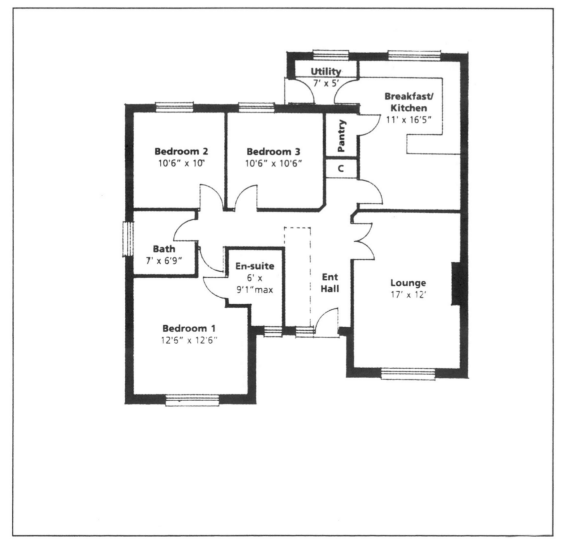

Utility
7' x 5'

Breakfast/
Kitchen
11' x 16'5"

Pantry

C

Bedroom 2
10'6" x 10'

Bedroom 3
10'6" x 10'6"

Bath
7' x 6'9"

En-suite
6' x
9'1"max

Ent
Hall

Lounge
17' x 12'

Bedroom 1
12'6" x 12'6"

There is quite a wealth of accommodation in this little bungalow and its arrangement manages to successfully divide living from sleeping accommodation. In addition there is obviously scope for occupation of the main roof void.

118 sq. m.

The copyright belongs to Custom Homes

Brixham

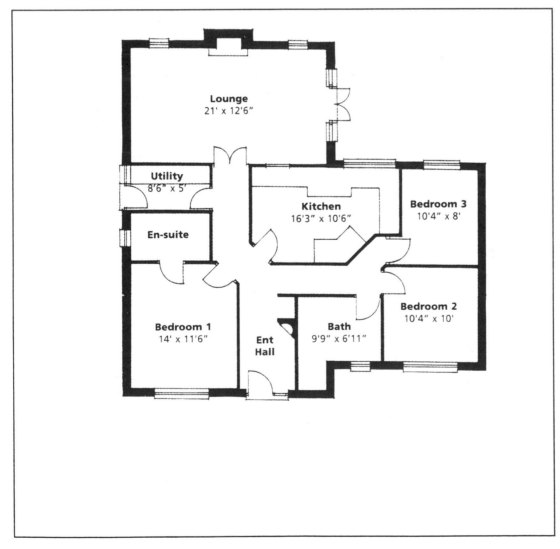

Lounge
21' x 12'6"

Utility
8'6" x 5'

En-suite

Kitchen
16'3" x 10'6"

Bedroom 3
10'4" x 8'

Bedroom 1
14' x 11'6"

Ent
Hall

Bath
9'9" x 6'11"

Bedroom 2
10'4" x 10'

The positioning of the lounge in the rear projection would obviously be of best advantage where there was a private garden direction. Clever angling of the main corridor allows for a great deal of accommodation to be provided in a relatively small space.

957 sq. ft./89 sq. m.

The copyright belongs to Custom Homes

Hampton

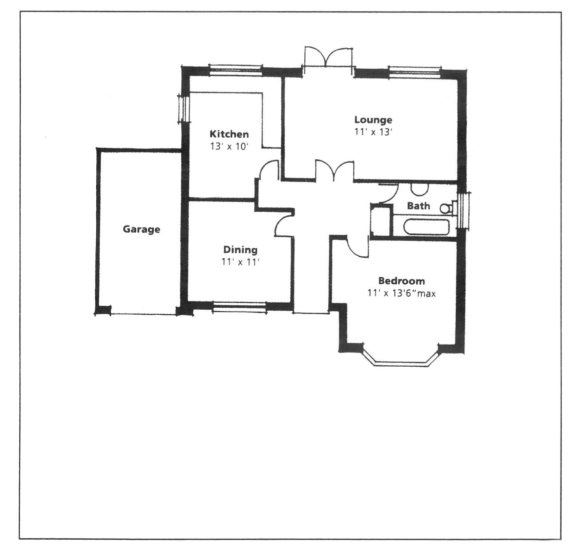

It's not often one comes across a really small bungalow but this one manages to project a presence far beyond its limited size. Restricted as the accommodation is, the dining room could always double up as a spare bedroom.

Kitchen
13' x 10'

Lounge
11' x 13'

Garage

Bath

Dining
11' x 11'

Bedroom
11' x 13'6"max

Bungalows over 1500 sq. ft.

The larger bungalows can really spread their wings in design terms and some very interesting and innovative designs can result. Although still classed as bungalows, many of these larger buildings lend themselves to occupation of the roof void and, even if it's decided that this isn't required in the first instance, it often makes sense to consider constructing the roof in such a way as to make its occupation physically possible in the future.

Care needs to be taken with bungalow designing so as not to muddle up the living and sleeping accommodation, as there is not the natural division between these two aspects of living that one gets in a house. In some of the medium and larger sized bungalows, it is possible to arrange for doors to divide the sleeping and living accommodation.

Bungalows often need a larger plot than a house of a similar square footage and additional care needs to be taken regarding proximity of windows to boundaries. Complex shapes can often create room for windows to look in all four directions and the clever use of design, so splendidly illustrated in the following pages can often mean that a bungalow can occupy a plot that would otherwise be unsuitable.

Contributors in this section:

ASBA David H. Anderson
ASBA Keith Bishop
ASBA Julian Owen Associates
Custom Homes
Design & Materials Ltd.
Designer Homes
Kingpost Design Co
Potton Ltd.
Scandia-Hus
Swedish Homes

170 sq. m./1830 sq. ft.　　*The copyright belongs to Scandia-Hus*　　**Harvard**

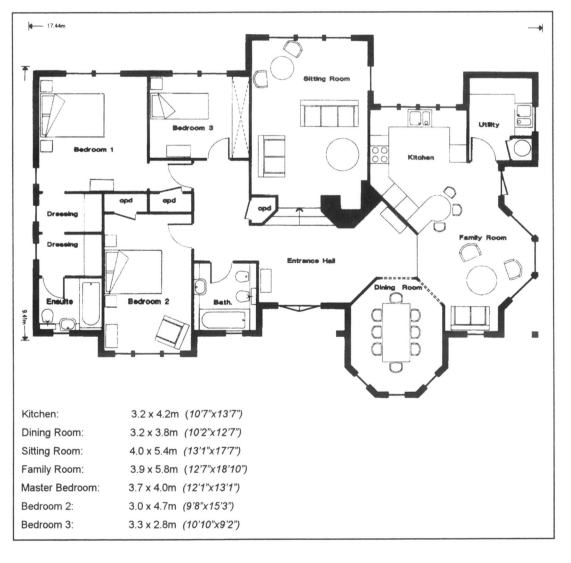

Kitchen:	3.2 x 4.2m *(10'7"x13'7")*
Dining Room:	3.2 x 3.8m *(10'2"x12'7")*
Sitting Room:	4.0 x 5.4m *(13'1"x17'7")*
Family Room:	3.9 x 5.8m *(12'7"x18'10")*
Master Bedroom:	3.7 x 4.0m *(12'1"x13'1")*
Bedroom 2:	3.0 x 4.7m *(9'8"x15'3")*
Bedroom 3:	3.3 x 2.8m *(10'10"x9'2")*

This American-inspired, modern bungalow has a striking front elevation with irregular projections. The imposing entrance 'tower' seems made for a circular clock above the double doors, and the hexagonal dining room projection lends added interest. The separate bedroom section has been segregated from the open-plan living/ entertaining section. The dining room is located on the same level as the entrance hall with steps leading down to the family room and kitchen. The different levels and angles allow you a free hand to create an ambience to suit your taste and lifestyle.

154 sq. m./1658 sq. ft.   *The copyright belongs to Scandia-Hus*   **Acacia**

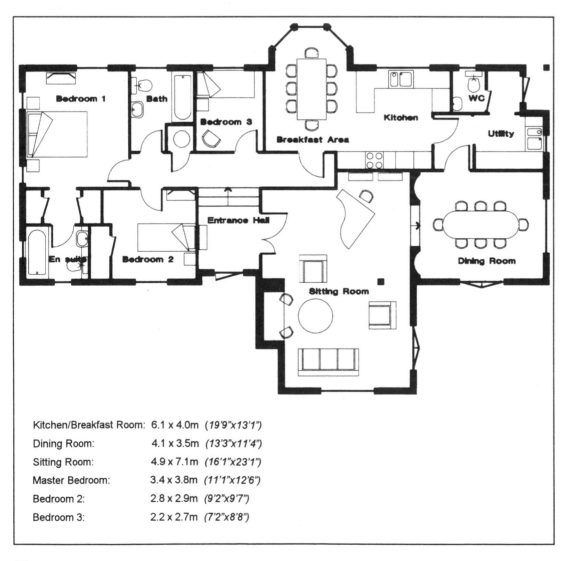

Kitchen/Breakfast Room: 6.1 x 4.0m *(19'9"x13'1")*

Dining Room: 4.1 x 3.5m *(13'3"x11'4")*

Sitting Room: 4.9 x 7.1m *(16'1"x23'1")*

Master Bedroom: 3.4 x 3.8m *(11'1"x12'6")*

Bedroom 2:   2.8 x 2.9m *(9'2"x9'7")*

Bedroom 3:   2.2 x 2.7m *(7'2"x8'8")*

The period features of a rural school or chapel conversion are captured in the external features of this unique addition to the Scandia-Hus range of homes. Inside, however, the layout could not be more suited to the practical aspects of modern living. The split level accommodation provides a distinctive lower level entrance hall and sitting room with steps leading up to the spacious dining room. The layout neatly divides the residence, separating the comfortable living area from the seclusion of the bedrooms. Norfolk knapped flints complete the old English quality of the Acacia, complementing perfectly the unusual window and authentic chimney features.

171 sq. m./1841 sq. ft.

The copyright belongs to Scandia-Hus

Stocksund

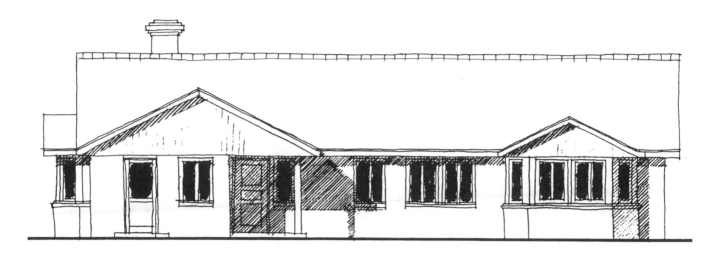

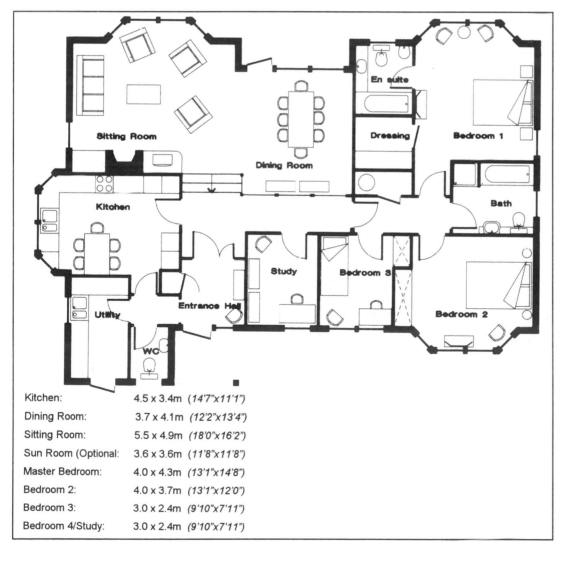

Kitchen:	4.5 x 3.4m	*(14'7"x11'1")*
Dining Room:	3.7 x 4.1m	*(12'2"x13'4")*
Sitting Room:	5.5 x 4.9m	*(18'0"x16'2")*
Sun Room (Optional:	3.6 x 3.6m	*(11'8"x11'8")*
Master Bedroom:	4.0 x 4.3m	*(13'1"x14'8")*
Bedroom 2:	4.0 x 3.7m	*(13'1"x12'0")*
Bedroom 3:	3.0 x 2.4m	*(9'10"x7'11")*
Bedroom 4/Study:	3.0 x 2.4m	*(9'10"x7'11")*

With its attractive bay windows and split-level reception rooms, the Stocksund has a unique character, offering an abundance of interesting nooks and crannies an interior designer dream. The lower level dining and sitting rooms offer airy, open aspects of the patio and garden which can be further enhanced by incorporating the optional sun room into the plan. The floor plan and elevation drawing provide a feel of the quality of life that comes with the Stocksund but, as with all Scandia-Hus designs, it is the finer details that make all the difference. A dressing room, a vestibule, arches and a covered entrance porch – all come as part of the standard specification.

207 sq. m./2228 sq. ft.

The copyright belongs to Scandia-Hus

Gotland

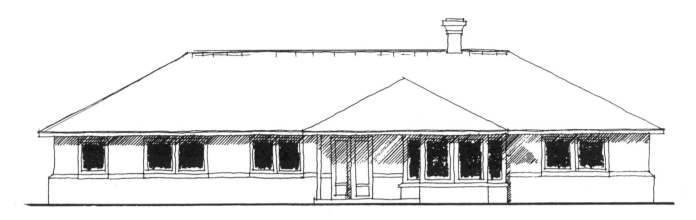

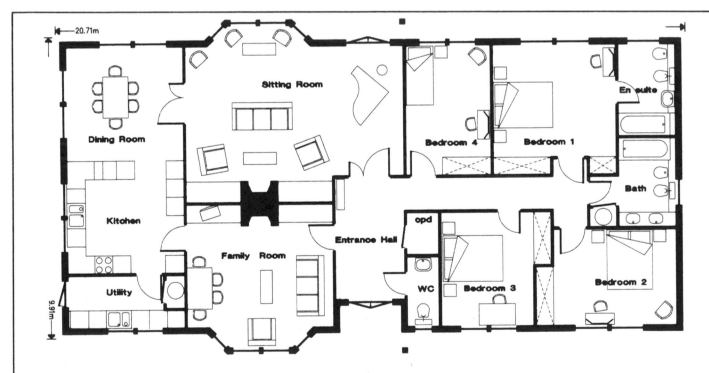

Kitchen:	3.7 x 3.9m (12'2"x12'11")
Dining Area:	3.8 x 3.9m (12'6x12'11")
Sitting Room:	5.7 x 7.1m (18'7"x23'4")
Family Room:	4.9 x 4.8m (16'0"x15'9")
Master Bedroom:	3.6 x 4.0m (11'10"x13'1")
Bedroom 2:	3.2 x 4.1m (10'6"x13'6")
Bedroom 3:	3.8 x 2.9m (12'5"x9'5")
Bedroom 4:	4.2 x 2.8m (13'9"x9'1")

This spacious bungalow would blend with the vernacular architecture in any part of the country. The sheltered entrance porch lends it a traditional appearance accentuating its classic lines, and its impressive double doors take you straight through glazed doors into the large sitting room. A double-backed chimney can be incorporated to provide open fires in both the family and sitting rooms and, as with so many of the Scandia-Hus designs, the bedrooms have been separated from the living and entertaining parts of this home providing a typically Scandinavian life-style.

230 sq. m./2476 sq. ft. *The copyright belongs to Scandia-Hus* **Uppland**

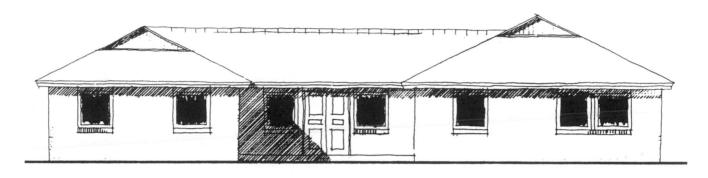

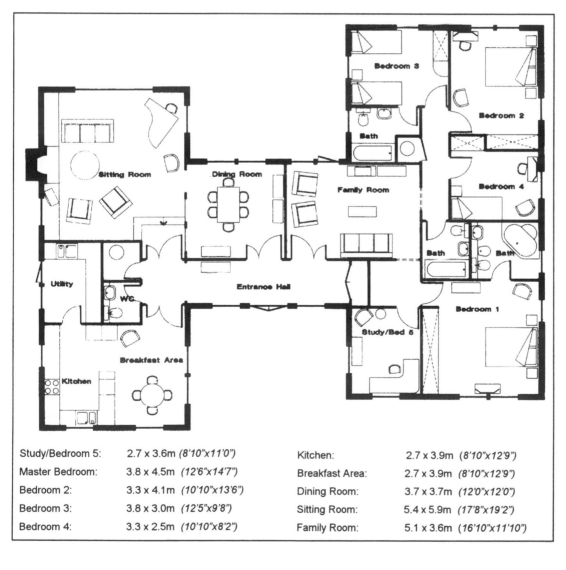

One of the largest single storey designs in the Scandia-Hus range, the Uppland is a family home, offering four spacious bedrooms, three bathrooms and a separate study/fifth bedroom. The bedroom wing, with its own family room, is conveniently separated from the main reception rooms. The variation in levels of the opposite wing gives the sitting room an interesting stepped feature, and the added ceiling height and large patio doors lend the room a light and airy feel. Two steps higher, through three graceful arches, the dining room is perfectly sited for stylish entertaining and overlooks the sheltered rear courtyard, which can be converted into a conservatory or sun room.

Study/Bedroom 5:	2.7 x 3.6m (8'10"x11'0")		Kitchen:	2.7 x 3.9m (8'10"x12'9")
Master Bedroom:	3.8 x 4.5m (12'6"x14'7")		Breakfast Area:	2.7 x 3.9m (8'10"x12'9")
Bedroom 2:	3.3 x 4.1m (10'10"x13'6")		Dining Room:	3.7 x 3.7m (12'0"x12'0")
Bedroom 3:	3.8 x 3.0m (12'5"x9'8")		Sitting Room:	5.4 x 5.9m (17'8"x19'2")
Bedroom 4:	3.3 x 2.5m (10'10"x8'2")		Family Room:	5.1 x 3.6m (16'10"x11'10")

150 sq. m./1614 sq. ft.   *The copyright belongs to ASBA David H. Anderson*   **Mourne Retreat**

Conceived as a design to front a busy road where there was little or no view to open countryside, this design manages to present mainly utility and non habitable rooms to the road elevation. A more contemporary elevation is possible at the rear with the inclusion of the sun deck.

Upper Living Area	2.95 x 3.60m
Lower Living Area	5.10 x 3.60m
Kitchen/Dining	5.10 x 3.50m
Utility	2.95 x 3.50m
Bedroom 1	5.10 x 2.90m
Bedroom 2	5.10 x 3.10m

2233 sq. ft.

The copyright belongs to ASBA
David H. Anderson

The New Old House

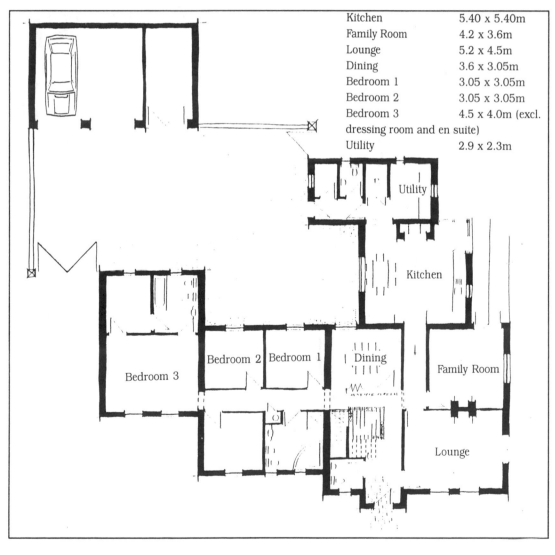

Kitchen	5.40 x 5.40m
Family Room	4.2 x 3.6m
Lounge	5.2 x 4.5m
Dining	3.6 x 3.05m
Bedroom 1	3.05 x 3.05m
Bedroom 2	3.05 x 3.05m
Bedroom 3	4.5 x 4.0m (excl.
dressing room and en suite)	
Utility	2.9 x 2.3m

The architectural expression resembles a vernacular style and the designer has included some modern detailing, subtly inserted such as the kitchen with its cut away glazed corner and natural top lighting.

The copyright belongs to Kingpost Design Co

213 sq. m./2287 sq. ft.

Beaufort

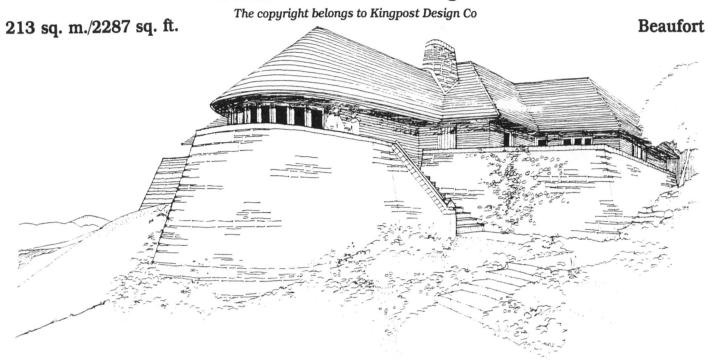

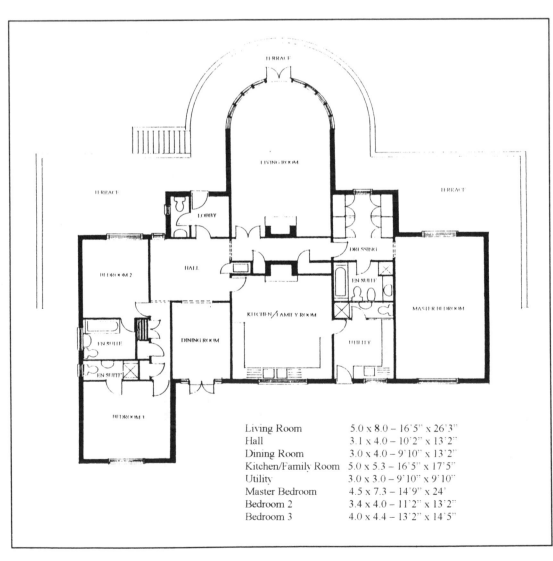

A stylish modern bungalow designed for a hilltop, panoramic views. Deep eaves provide shade at noon but the rooms are still well lit by the morning and evening sun. The large bayed living room enjoys panoramic views and French doors to the terrace. Three good sized bedrooms, all en suite, a kitchen/diner and a utility room combined with a spacious entrance hall give a spacious home.

Living Room	5.0 x 8.0 – 16'5" x 26'3"
Hall	3.1 x 4.0 – 10'2" x 13'2"
Dining Room	3.0 x 4.0 – 9'10" x 13'2"
Kitchen/Family Room	5.0 x 5.3 – 16'5" x 17'5"
Utility	3.0 x 3.0 – 9'10" x 9'10"
Master Bedroom	4.5 x 7.3 – 14'9" x 24'
Bedroom 2	3.4 x 4.0 – 11'2" x 13'2"
Bedroom 3	4.0 x 4.4 – 13'2" x 14'5"

146.8 sq. m./1577 sq. ft.   *The copyright belongs to Kingpost Design Co*   **Arlington**

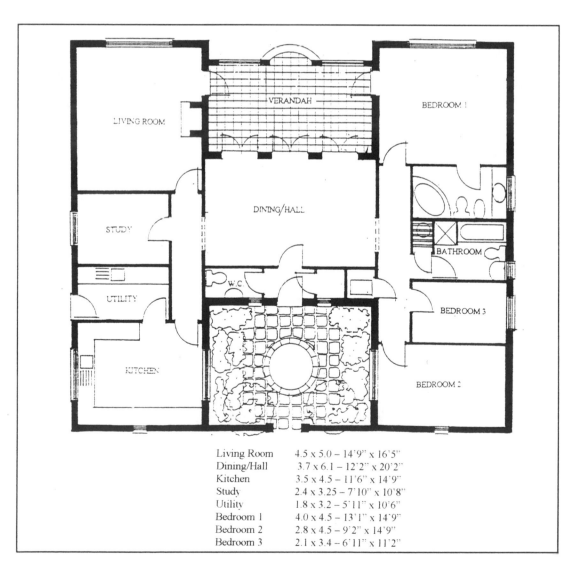

Living Room	4.5 x 5.0 – 14'9" x 16'5"
Dining/Hall	3.7 x 6.1 – 12'2" x 20'2"
Kitchen	3.5 x 4.5 – 11'6" x 14'9"
Study	2.4 x 3.25 – 7'10" x 10'8"
Utility	1.8 x 3.2 – 5'11" x 10'6"
Bedroom 1	4.0 x 4.5 – 13'1" x 14'9"
Bedroom 2	2.8 x 4.5 – 9'2" x 14'9"
Bedroom 3	2.1 x 3.4 – 6'11" x 11'2"

If hot summer days are here to stay, how nice to be able to sit on a shady veranda with a cool drink. This well planned bungalow allows you to do just this while also offering a walled court-yard garden with a small pool at the front. The design allows this bungalow to be built quite close to the road with the windows to the kitchen and bedroom looking into the couryard. The large dining hall has a high cathedral ceiling with a dormer window at high level to allow light to fill the room.

1936 sq. ft./180 sq. m.

The copyright belongs to Custom Homes

Peacehaven

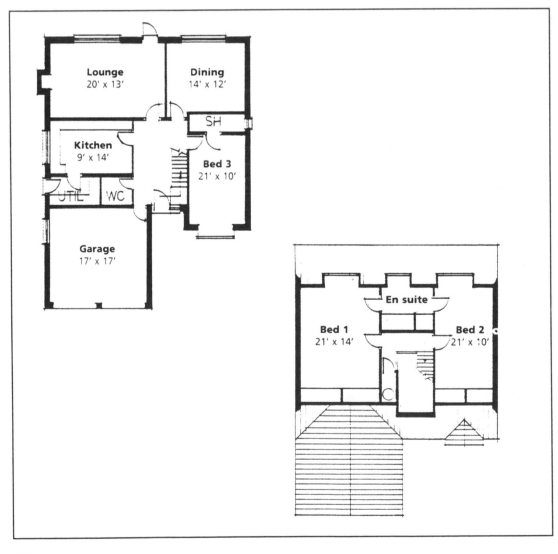

The appearance from the street scene for this compact dwelling is of a standard bungalow and it is only when one views it from the back that it is apparent that there's a lot more to it than meets the eye.

2178 sq. ft./202 sq. m.

The copyright belongs to Custom Homes

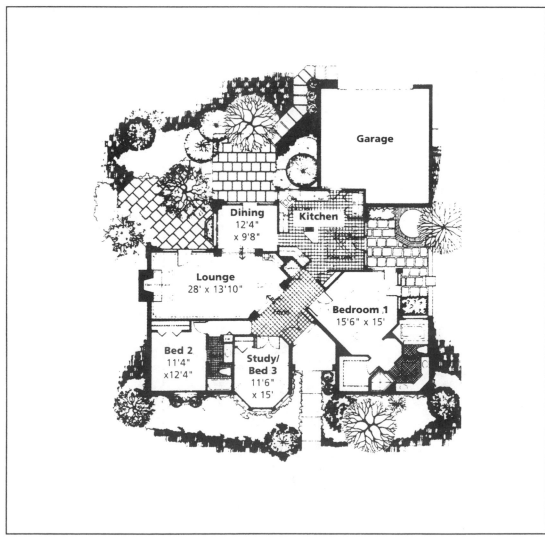

Complex roof shapes, and varying eaves levels succeed in taking this bungalow into another league. The same ethos is reflected in the internal layout of the accommodation to create what is a totally attractive property.

2266 sq. ft./210 sq. m.

The copyright belongs to Custom Homes

Detroit

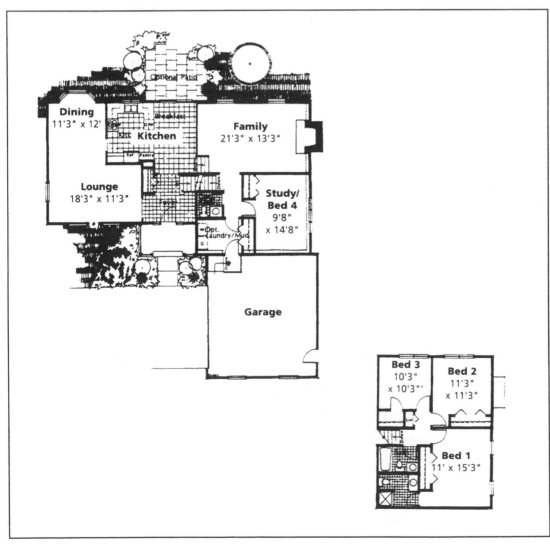

Dining
11'3" x 12'

Kitchen

Breakfast

Family
21'3" x 13'3"

Lounge
18'3" x 11'3"

Study/ Bed 4
9'8" x 14'8"

Opt. Laundry/Mud

Garage

Bed 3
10'3" x 10'3"

Bed 2
11'3" x 11'3"

Bed 1
11' x 15'3"

This split level house provides accommodation in three levels with the ground floor having two levels. A slight slope across the plot tends to favour the design so as to prevent too much underbuilding on the lounge section.

1727 sq. ft./160 sq. m.

The copyright belongs to Custom Homes

Dallas

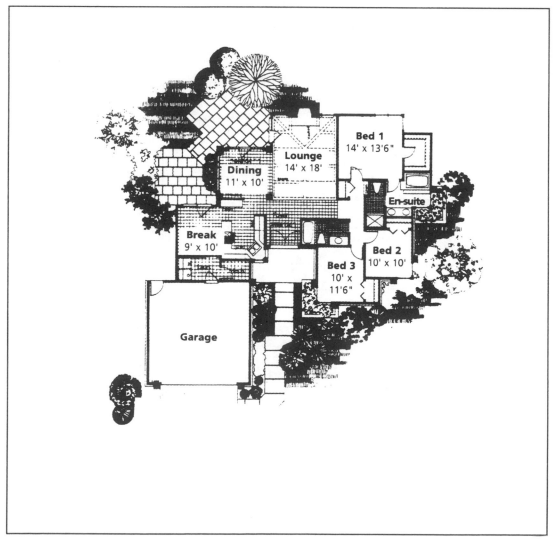

Dining
11' x 10'

Lounge
14' x 18'

Bed 1
14' x 13'6"

En-suite

Break
9' x 10'

Bed 3
10' x 11'6"

Bed 2
10' x 10'

Garage

Visually from the front the roof plans of this bungalow seem to layer back on each other giving depth and character to the design. This is reflected in the stepped progression of accommodation that maintains the proper division of living and sleeping areas.

1560 sq. ft.

60 ft. x 35 ft.

Greenwood

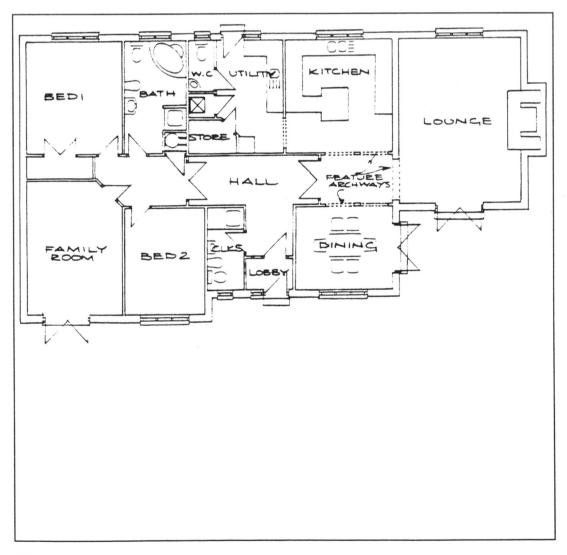

The Greenwood is a charming family bungalow with well proportioned rooms throughout and a really traditional appearance.

The forward projecting gable and lounge annexe both help avoid the ranch style often associated with wide bungalows.

1650 sq. ft.
40 ft. x 59 ft.

The copyright belongs to Design & Materials Ltd.

Holywell

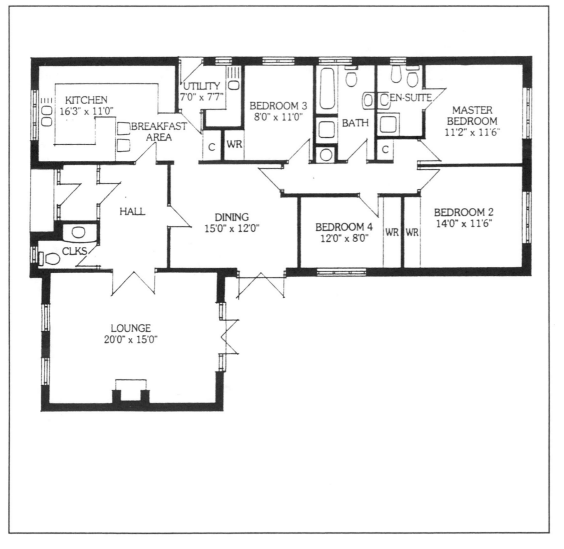

KITCHEN
16'3" x 11'0"

UTILITY
7'0" x 7'7"

BREAKFAST
AREA

BEDROOM 3
8'0" x 11'0"

BATH

EN-SUITE

MASTER
BEDROOM
11'2" x 11'6"

C   WR

C

HALL

DINING
15'0" x 12'0"

BEDROOM 4
12'0" x 8'0"

WR   WR

BEDROOM 2
14'0" x 11'6"

CLKS

LOUNGE
20'0" x 15'0"

This design is something of a 'wolf in sheep's clothing' in that the front elevation conveys the impression of a relatively modest dwelling. However, in reality, it is a spacious family home with four bedrooms, two bathrooms, kitchen/ breakfast, dining room and well proportioned lounge. The plot has a reasonable frontage but narrows to the rear and the brief was to create a large bungalow to maximise the potential of the site.

1800 sq. ft.

55 ft. x 52 ft.

The copyright belongs to Design & Materials Ltd.

Strathblane

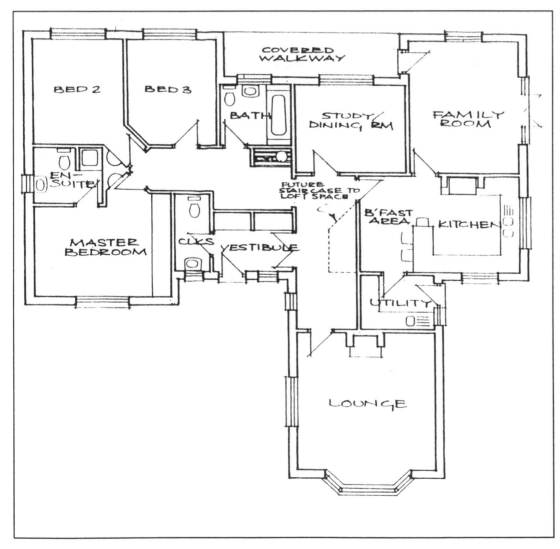

This bungalow is ideal for a busy family and features generous, plentiful rooms including a family room and large lounge. There is potential to convert the loft space if necessary.

1750 sq. ft.

58 ft. x 59 ft.

Wimborne

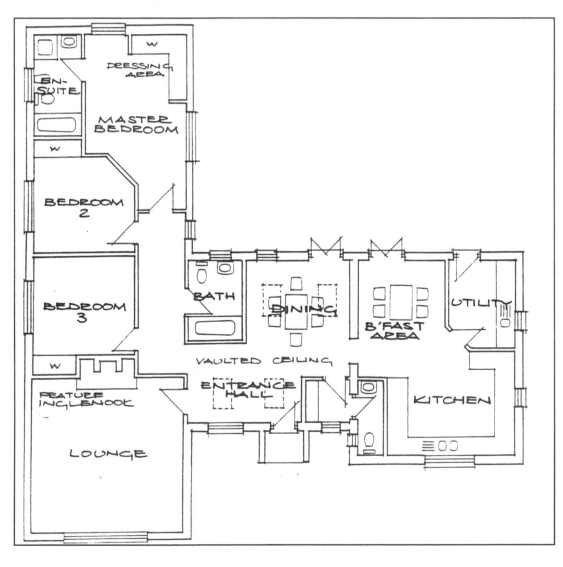

An interesting bungalow with an open-plan hall and dining area, incorporating a full height cathedral ceiling and roof lights. The master bedroom suite includes a dressing area and there are two further good sized bedrooms. A blend of traditional and contemporary.

2050 sq. ft.

62 ft. x 58 ft.

Broadheath

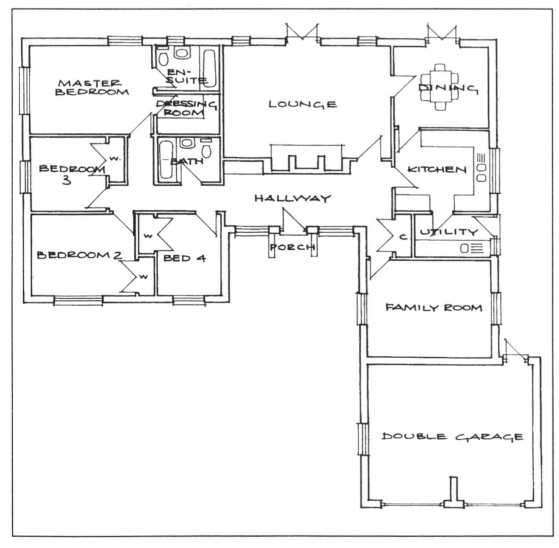

This large family bungalow includes four bedrooms in a separate wing, well away from the main living areas. The lounge has a large inglenook fireplace.

2350 sq. ft.

79 ft. x 50 ft.

Ballyntyre

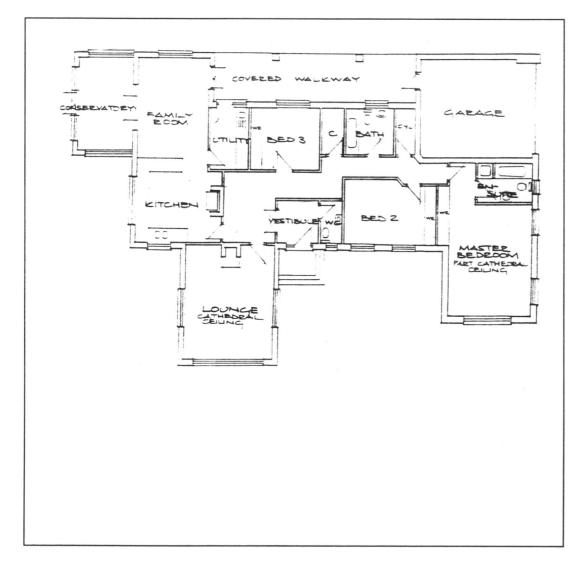

An interesting bungalow with lots of space and designed to allow for future conversion of the big loft area. The lounge and conservatory both have cathedral ceilings, and there is an open plan kitchen and family room with Aga range.

2900 sq. ft.
48 ft. x 54 ft.

The copyright belongs to Design & Materials Ltd.

Aldborough

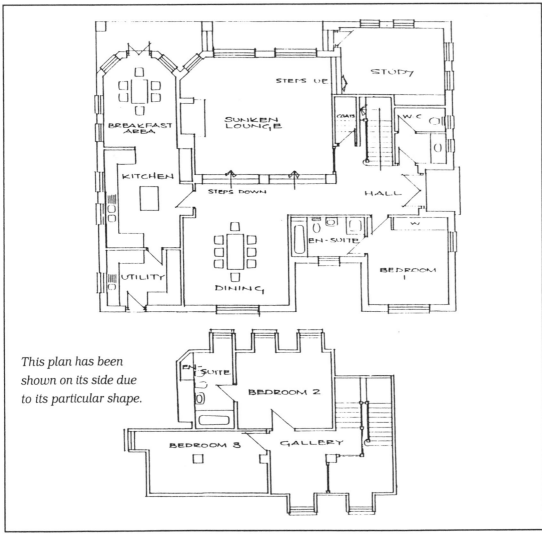

BREAKFAST AREA

SUNKEN LOUNGE

STEPS UP

STUDY

COATS

W.C.

KITCHEN

STEPS DOWN

HALL

EN-SUITE

W

UTILITY

DINING

BEDROOM 1

This plan has been shown on its side due to its particular shape.

EN-SUITE

BEDROOM 2

BEDROOM 3

GALLERY

This impressive bungalow has many interesting design features. The main living area is open-plan and includes a dining room leading down to a sunken lounge, which in turn steps up to a large study.

2180 sq. ft.
47 ft. x 55 ft.

The copyright belongs to Design & Materials Ltd.

Galloway

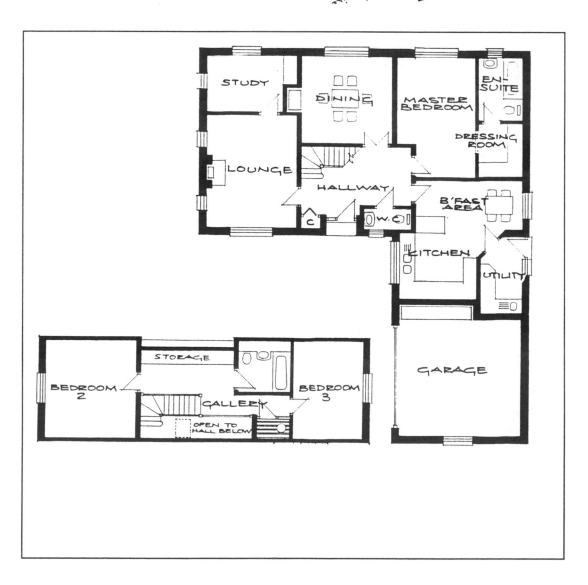

This attractive dormer bungalow packs a lot of accommodation into a relatively small footprint and the simplicity of the design makes the bungalow particularly suitable for infill or corner plots and the absence of dormer windows should ensure the design is also popular with planning officers. This design would make an ideal retirement home and can be built in two phases.

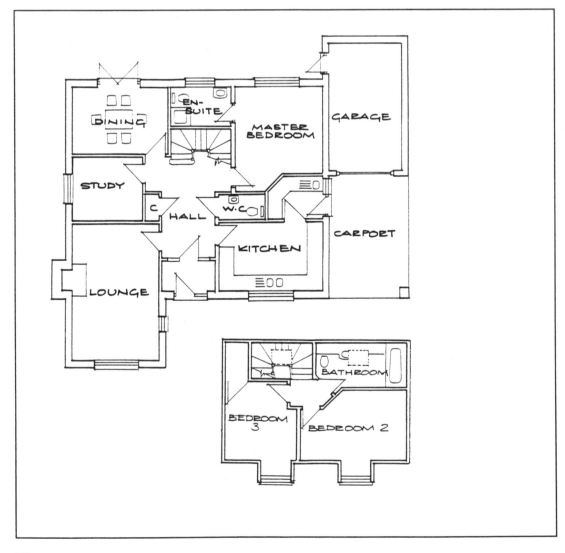

This pretty dormer bungalow provides well planned and surprisingly spacious accommodation. For the retired couple in particular, the design gives you everything you need on one floor, whilst the dormer bedrooms are ideal for weekend guests.

2680 sq. ft.

62 ft. x 57 ft.

Kelburn

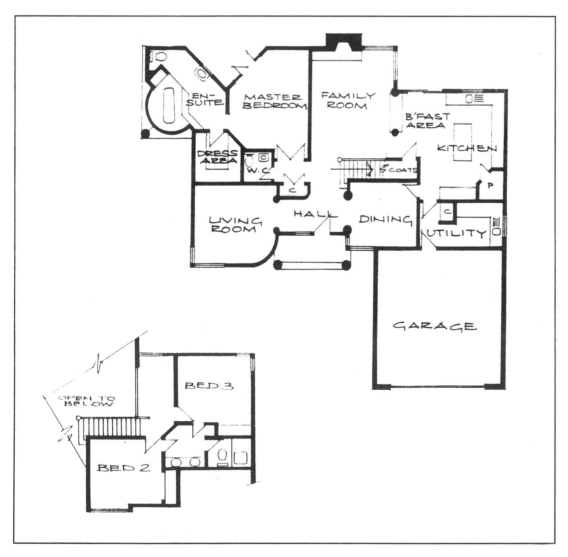

Large bungalows are too often boring - not this one! The exciting layout is mainly open-plan, with the big family room incorporating a vaulted ceiling. Two further bedrooms are housed in the roof space.

120.72 sq. m.

10.17m x 11.87m

97-340

At first sight this is a plain bungalow but there are areas of the country where that very simplicity would be seen as an asset. Nevertheless, the lounge projection at the rear would serve to make the garden elevation much more exciting and the accommodation has a feeling of spaciousness.

Kitchen/ Dining Room	7.31 x 3.70m/22'0" x 12'2"
Lounge	5.78 x 4.20m/19'0" x 13'9"
Bedroom 1	3.30 x 2.38m/10'10" x 7'10"
Bedroom 2	4.69 x 2.95m/15'5" x 9'8"
Bathroom	2.30 x 1.80m/7'7" x 5'11"

126 sq. m.

8.69m x 14.5 m

The copyright belongs to Potton Ltd.

97-065

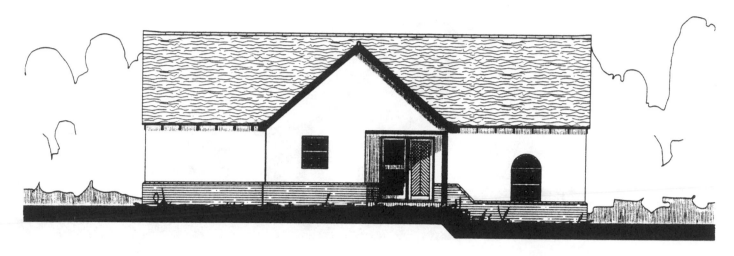

Dining/Lounge	6.50 x 3.50m
Kitchen	4.30 x 3.00m
Utility	3.00 x 2.80m
Bathroom	3.36 x 2.30m
Study	4.15 x 2.91m
Bedroom 1	3.91 x 3.50m
Bedroom 2	7.31 x 3.55m
En suite	3.55 x 3.46m
Wardrobe	3.30 x 3.17m
Gallery	6.50 x 3.50m

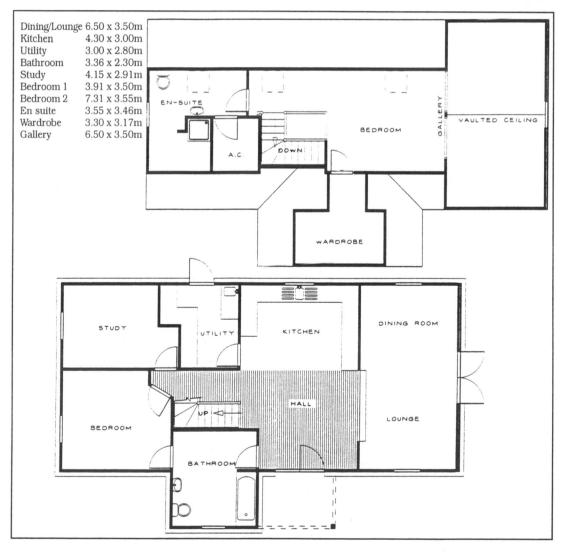

A deceptively spacious design which once again, would prove very useful in a sensitive planning situation. The sunken lounge, whilst an important feature, is not essential to the design and the flexible scope of the accommodation provided makes the bungalow suitable for many different situations.

132.38 sq. m.

12.28m x 10.78m

The copyright belongs to Potton Ltd.

97-066

Dining Room	3.91 x 5.41m/12'10" x 17'9"	
Utility	3.31 x 2.21m/10'10" x 7'3"	
Lounge	4.77 x 5.73m/15'8" x 18'10"	
Bathroom	2.35 x 2.90m/7'9" x 9'6"	
Study	2.35 x 2.90m/7'9" x 9'6"	

Flexibility is the key to this design and the dwelling could be used as one single large accommodation, or alternatively the upper part could be used to provide a separate and virtually self contained master suite.

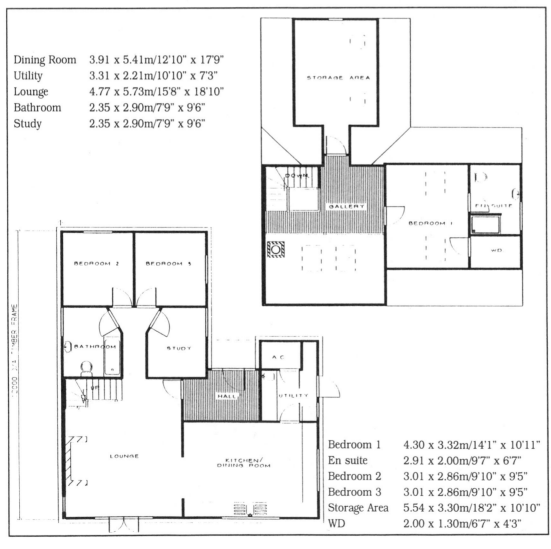

Bedroom 1	4.30 x 3.32m/14'1" x 10'11"	
En suite	2.91 x 2.00m/9'7" x 6'7"	
Bedroom 2	3.01 x 2.86m/9'10" x 9'5"	
Bedroom 3	3.01 x 2.86m/9'10" x 9'5"	
Storage Area	5.54 x 3.30m/18'2" x 10'10"	
WD	2.00 x 1.30m/6'7" x 4'3"	

338.18 sq. m.
20.44m x 16.55

The copyright belongs to Potton Ltd.

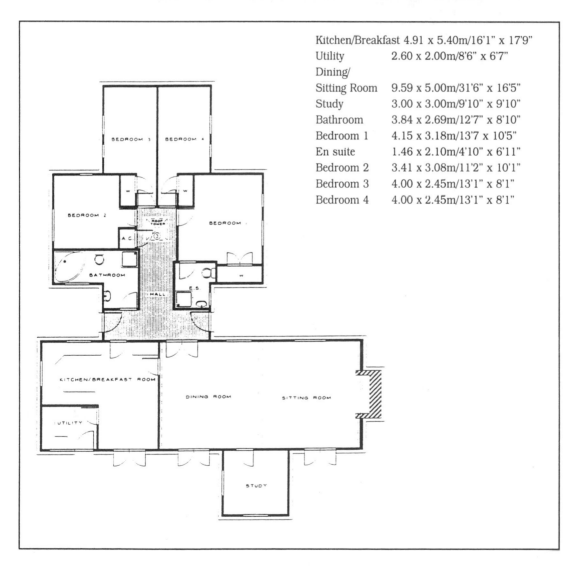

Kitchen/Breakfast	4.91 x 5.40m/16'1" x 17'9"
Utility	2.60 x 2.00m/8'6" x 6'7"
Dining/ Sitting Room	9.59 x 5.00m/31'6" x 16'5"
Study	3.00 x 3.00m/9'10" x 9'10"
Bathroom	3.84 x 2.69m/12'7" x 8'10"
Bedroom 1	4.15 x 3.18m/13'7 x 10'5"
En suite	1.46 x 2.10m/4'10" x 6'11"
Bedroom 2	3.41 x 3.08m/11'2" x 10'1"
Bedroom 3	4.00 x 2.45m/13'1" x 8'1"
Bedroom 4	4.00 x 2.45m/13'1" x 8'1"

Interesting and varied shapes combine to make this bungalow reflect the stable blocks or out-houses that are obviously its inspiration. It could either stand alone as an architectural unit in its own right or it could be positioned to blend in and compliment a larger house.

The copyright belongs to Potton Ltd.

297.30 sq. m.

17.55m x 16.94m

97-164

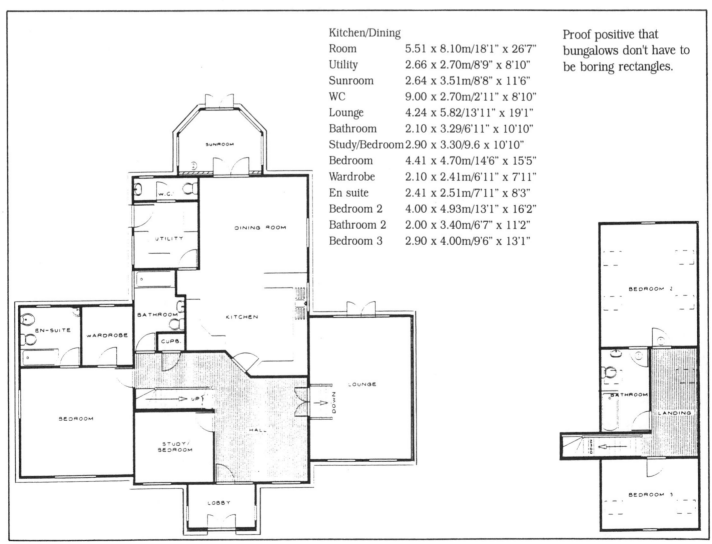

Kitchen/Dining Room	5.51 x 8.10m/18'1" x 26'7"
Utility	2.66 x 2.70m/8'9" x 8'10"
Sunroom	2.64 x 3.51m/8'8" x 11'6"
WC	9.00 x 2.70m/2'11" x 8'10"
Lounge	4.24 x 5.82/13'11" x 19'1"
Bathroom	2.10 x 3.29/6'11" x 10'10"
Study/Bedroom	2.90 x 3.30/9.6 x 10'10"
Bedroom	4.41 x 4.70m/14'6" x 15'5"
Wardrobe	2.10 x 2.41m/6'11" x 7'11"
En suite	2.41 x 2.51m/7'11" x 8'3"
Bedroom 2	4.00 x 4.93m/13'1" x 16'2"
Bathroom 2	2.00 x 3.40m/6'7" x 11'2"
Bedroom 3	2.90 x 4.00m/9'6" x 13'1"

Proof positive that bungalows don't have to be boring rectangles.

259.81 sq. m.
14.67m x 17.71m

97-208

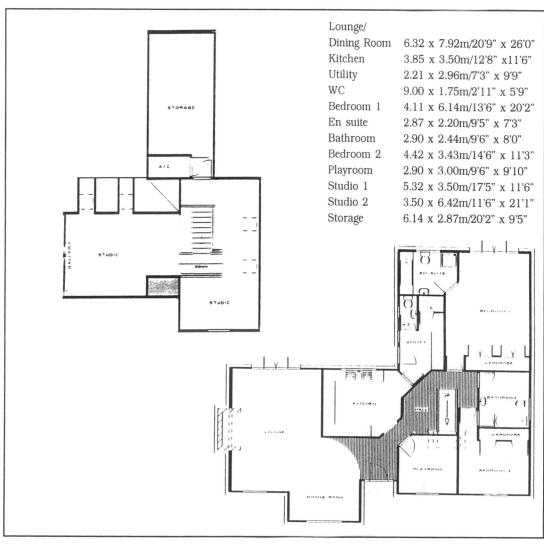

Lounge/		
Dining Room	6.32 x 7.92m/20'9" x 26'0"	
Kitchen	3.85 x 3.50m/12'8" x11'6"	
Utility	2.21 x 2.96m/7'3" x 9'9"	
WC	9.00 x 1.75m/2'11" x 5'9"	
Bedroom 1	4.11 x 6.14m/13'6" x 20'2"	
En suite	2.87 x 2.20m/9'5" x 7'3"	
Bathroom	2.90 x 2.44m/9'6" x 8'0"	
Bedroom 2	4.42 x 3.43m/14'6" x 11'3"	
Playroom	2.90 x 3.00m/9'6" x 9'10"	
Studio 1	5.32 x 3.50m/17'5" x 11'6"	
Studio 2	3.50 x 6.42m/11'6" x 21'1"	
Storage	6.14 x 2.87m/20'2" x 9'5"	

This bungalow design has a truly rural feel to it and could take its place on many a country plot. The true beauty of the design is available when one studies the varied and interesting layout of all of the rooms.

243.13 sq. m.
12.81m x 18.98m

96-341

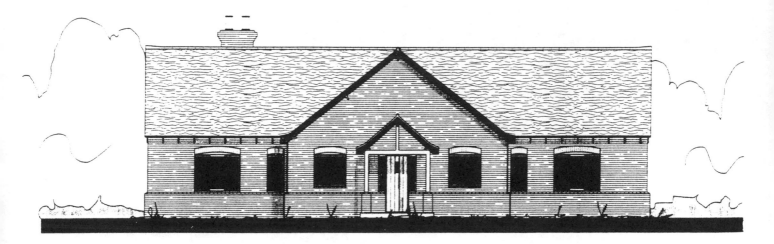

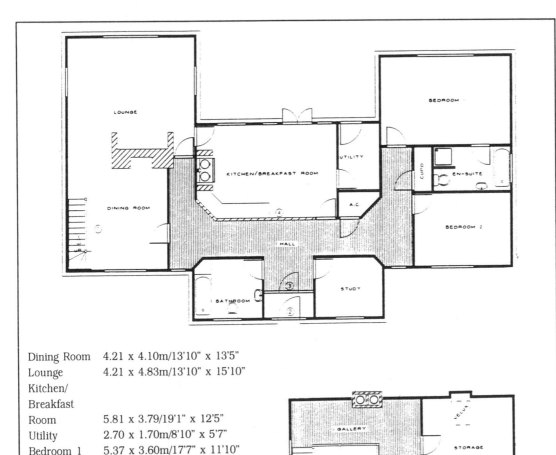

The houseshoe shape of this bungalow seems to enclose the rear patio area and by positioning the principal accommodation at this point, the effect is to bring the outside space within the composition of the accommodation.

Dining Room	4.21 x 4.10m/13'10" x 13'5"
Lounge	4.21 x 4.83m/13'10" x 15'10"
Kitchen/ Breakfast Room	5.81 x 3.79/19'1" x 12'5"
Utility	2.70 x 1.70m/8'10" x 5'7"
Bedroom 1	5.37 x 3.60m/17'7" x 11'10"
En suite	1.80 x 3.20m/5'11" x 10'6"
Bedroom 2	4.00 x 2.94m/13'1" x 9'8"
Study	2.80 x 2.40m/9'2" x 7'10"
Bathroom	2.80 x 2.40m/9'2" x 7'10"
Storage	3.75 x 3.85m/12'4" x 12'8"

The copyright belongs to Potton Ltd.

446.81 sq. m.

20.84m x 21.44m

97-226

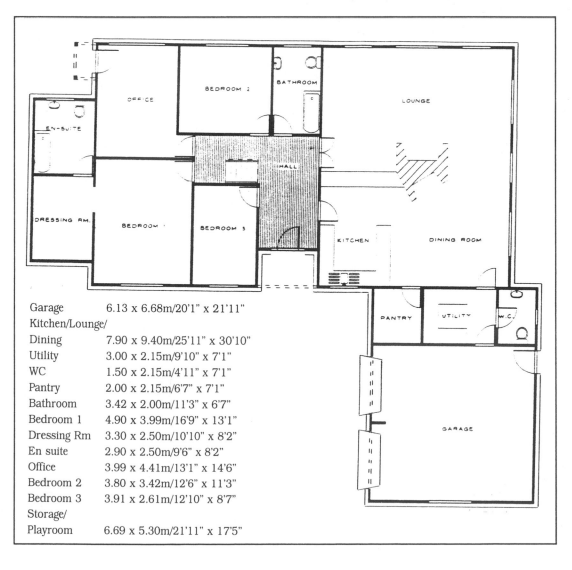

The open plan living area of this house seems to reinforce the impression of space that this large bungalow projects. With the occupation of the upper part this could be increased to provide a very substantial home.

Garage	6.13 x 6.68m/20'1" x 21'11"
Kitchen/Lounge/	
Dining	7.90 x 9.40m/25'11" x 30'10"
Utility	3.00 x 2.15m/9'10" x 7'1"
WC	1.50 x 2.15m/4'11" x 7'1"
Pantry	2.00 x 2.15m/6'7" x 7'1"
Bathroom	3.42 x 2.00m/11'3" x 6'7"
Bedroom 1	4.90 x 3.99m/16'9" x 13'1"
Dressing Rm	3.30 x 2.50m/10'10" x 8'2"
En suite	2.90 x 2.50m/9'6" x 8'2"
Office	3.99 x 4.41m/13'1" x 14'6"
Bedroom 2	3.80 x 3.42m/12'6" x 11'3"
Bedroom 3	3.91 x 2.61m/12'10" x 8'7"
Storage/	
Playroom	6.69 x 5.30m/21'11" x 17'5"

The copyright belongs to Potton Ltd.

178.39 sq. m.

14.61m x 12.21m

97-279

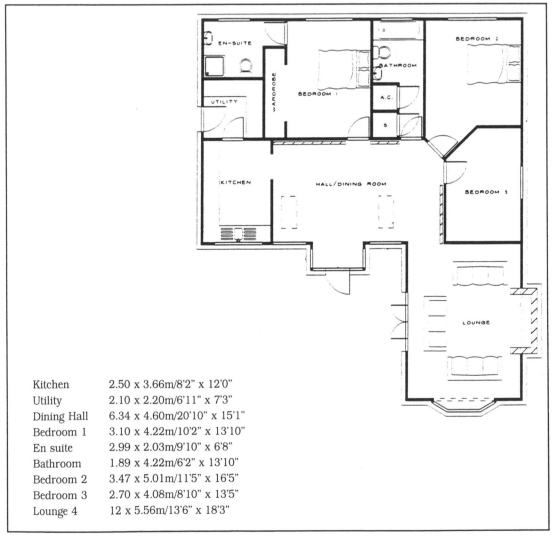

This is a deceptively spacious design where the living accommodation is deliberately concentrated on the front elevation whilst the bedroom accommodation is set to the rear. It would suit a plot where the dwelling was set back on the land.

Kitchen	2.50 x 3.66m/8'2" x 12'0"
Utility	2.10 x 2.20m/6'11" x 7'3"
Dining Hall	6.34 x 4.60m/20'10" x 15'1"
Bedroom 1	3.10 x 4.22m/10'2" x 13'10"
En suite	2.99 x 2.03m/9'10" x 6'8"
Bathroom	1.89 x 4.22m/6'2" x 13'10"
Bedroom 2	3.47 x 5.01m/11'5" x 16'5"
Bedroom 3	2.70 x 4.08m/8'10" x 13'5"
Lounge 4	12 x 5.56m/13'6" x 18'3"

The copyright belongs to Potton Ltd.

410.67 sq. m.
19.03m x 21.58m

97-263

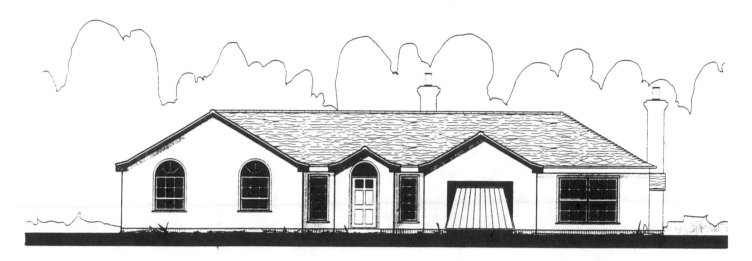

Dining Room	6.88 x 7.65m		Bedroom 2	4.30 x 2.93m
Living Room	6.00 x 6.91m		Bedroom 3	3.41 x 3.60m
Utility	1.90 x 2.41m		Bedroom 4	3.40 x 2.93m
Study	3.40 x 3.48m		Bathroom	2.22 x 4.90m
Bedroom 1	4.26 x 2.51m		Garage	4.07 x 6.01m
En suite	2.55 x 3.41m			

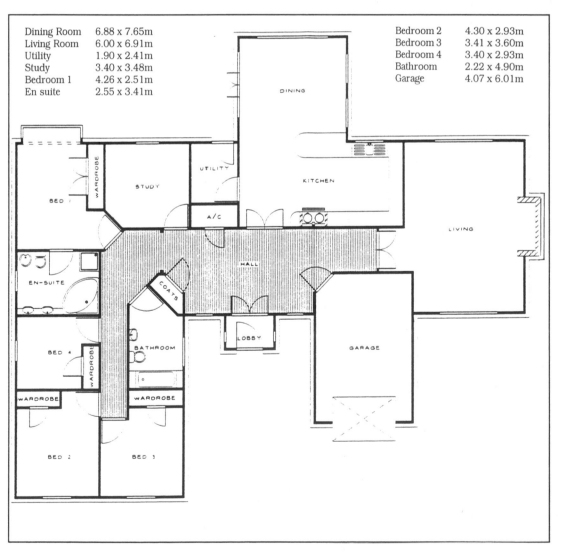

So often the integral garage is tacked on to the end of the dwelling site as some sort of afterthought, whereas here the architect is making a bold statement that this is an integral and important part of the accommodation and deserves its space at the centre of it.

178.76 sq. m.

13.33m x 13.41m

97-045

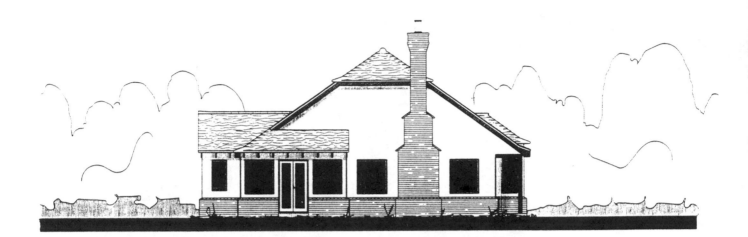

Kitchen	4.50 x 5.00m	Bedroom 1	3.30 x 5.60m
Lounge/Dining	4.96 x 7.18m	En suite	2.71 x 2.40m
Utility	2.00 x 3.10m	Shower Room	2.71 x 2.00m
Sunroom	2.90 x 4.00m	Bedroom 2	4.15 x 4.41m

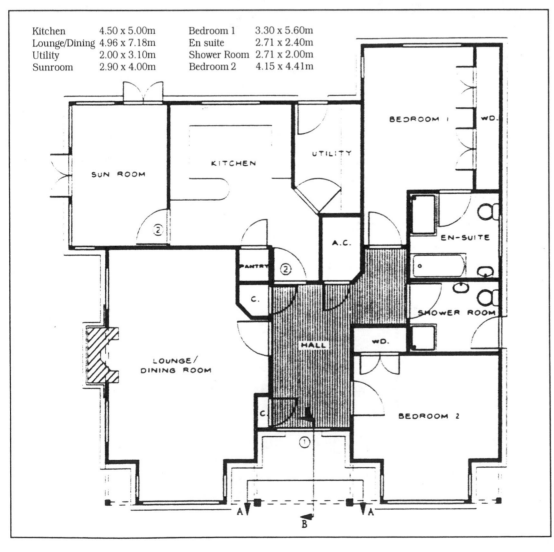

A basically square design where clever features combine to deceive the eye into revealing the complex and interesting shapes that are available. Then again the living and sleeping accommodations are properly divided by a roomy hallway that doesn't take up too much valuable space.

246 sq. m.

The copyright belongs to ASBA Keith Bishop

Vernon

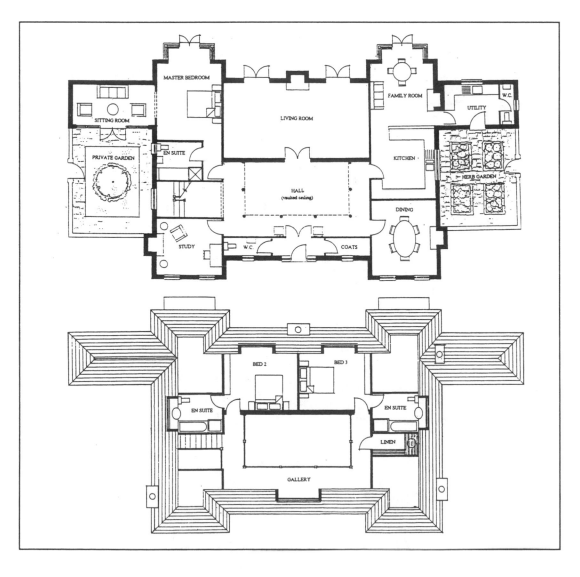

A spacious house for the larger site. The master bedroom suite is on the ground floor and benefits from its own private sitting room which looks out onto a private garden. The elegant hall and living room combine to make an imposing entertaining area. Upstairs, in the American style, the emphasis is not on the number of bedrooms but rather on providing relaxed and comfortable accommodation, so here both of the double bedrooms have their own bathrooms.

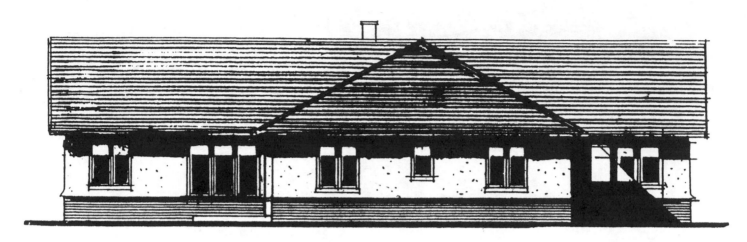

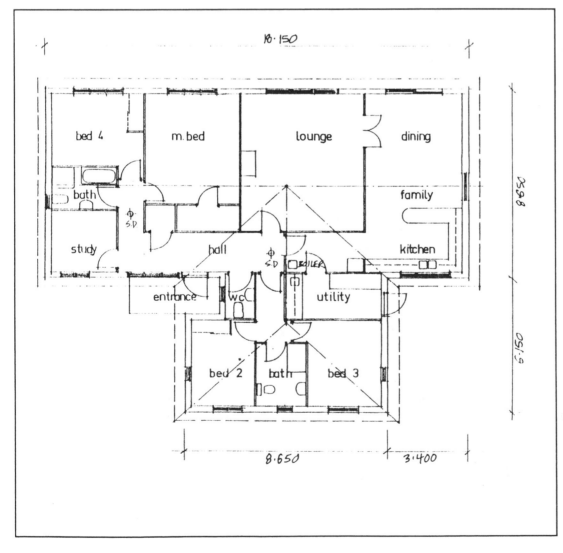

Scandinavian ideals of space and the importance of light are obviously the guiding factors in the creation of his design. The hallway becomes an important feature whilst giving access to all the rooms, without taking up too much of the floor space.

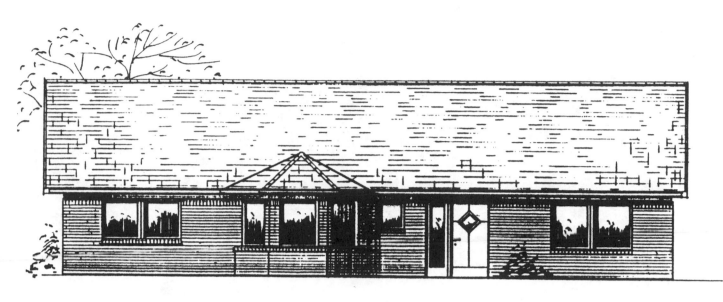

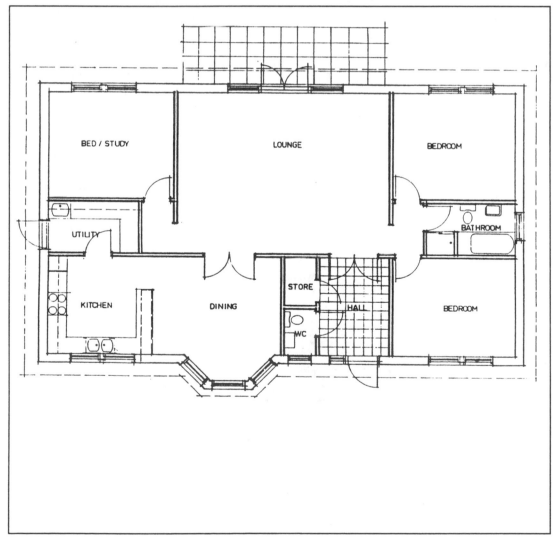

BED / STUDY

LOUNGE

BEDROOM

UTILITY

BATHROOM

KITCHEN

DINING

STORE

HALL

WC

BEDROOM

A wonderfully compact and beautifully laid out bungalow that seems to make the large lounge the dominant feature of the design. Simplicity of shape will mean that the design is also to be cost effective in constructional and energy efficiency terms.

1573 sq. ft. *Copyright refer to Designer Homes* **The Wren**

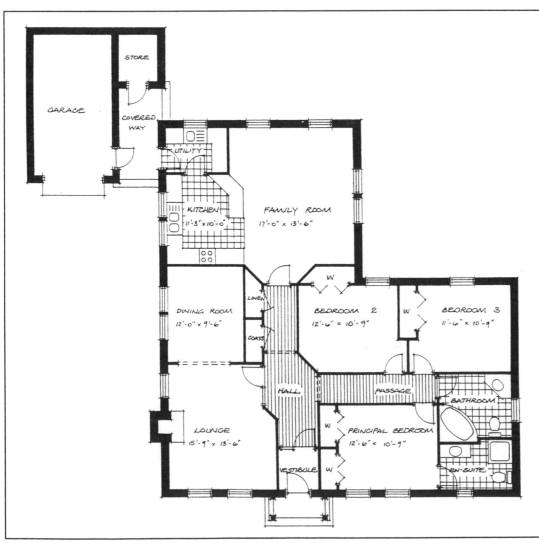

STORE

GARAGE

COVERED WAY

UTILITY

KITCHEN
11'-3" x 10'-0"

FAMILY ROOM
17'-0" x 13'-6"

DINING ROOM
12'-0" x 9'-6"

LINEN

COATS

BEDROOM 2
12'-6" x 10'-9"

BEDROOM 3
11'-6" x 10'-9"

W

HALL

PASSAGE

BATHROOM

LOUNGE
15'-9" x 13'-6"

W

PRINCIPAL BEDROOM
12'-6" x 10'-9"

VESTIBULE

W

EN-SUITE

Considerable care has gone into the preparation of this bungalow design with the proper division of living and sleeping accommodation and the concentration of the main reception rooms to one side of the property. This is carried forward in the semi detached nature of the garage and ancillary accommodation off the utility room. Note the especially large family room off the kitchen area.

140.56 sq. m./1513 sq. ft.   *Copyright refer to Designer Homes*   **The Snowfinch**

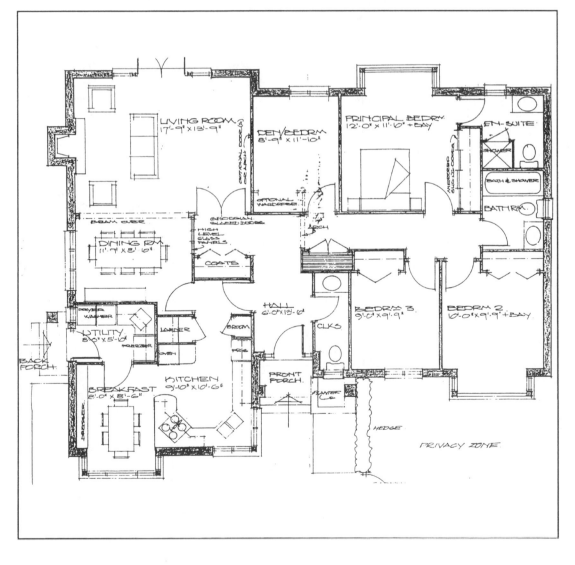

Whether you wish to think of this bungalow in terms of it having four good sized bedrooms or whether you prefer to think in terms of the fourth bedroom becoming a study, there's no doubting the fact that this is a classical bungalow design. Be that as it may it does not fall into the trap of being at all boring and clever use of architectural features adds interest to the appearance.

1783 sq. ft.

Copyright refer to Designer Homes

The Chaffinch

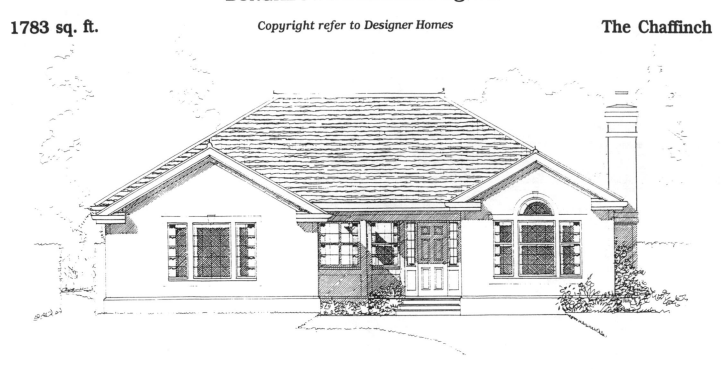

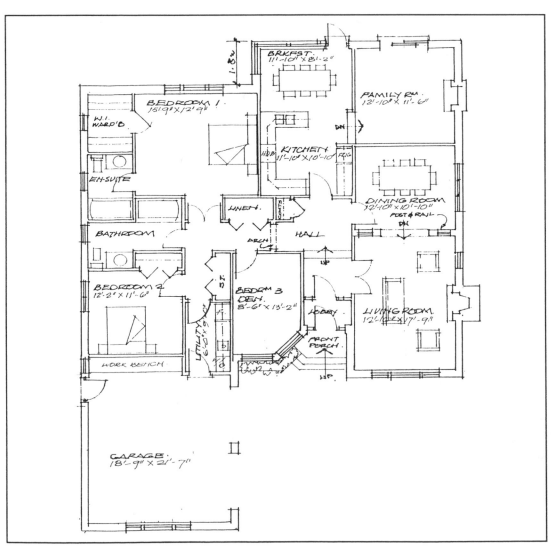

BEDROOM 1
15'9" X 12'9"

W.I. WARD'D

EN-SUITE

BATHROOM

BEDROOM 2
12'2" X 11'-6"

WORK BENCH

UTILITY 6'-0" X 9'-9"

BEDRM 3 DEN.
8'-6" X 13'-2"

LINEN

ARCH

HALL

UP

LOBBY

FRONT PORCH

BRKFST.
11'-10" X 8'-2"

KITCHEN
11'-10" X 10'-10"

HOB

DN

COATS

DN

FAMILY RM.
12'-10" X 11'-6"

DINING ROOM
12'-10" X 10'-10"

POST & RAIL

DN

LIVING ROOM
12'-6" X 17'-9"

GARAGE.
18'-9" X 21'-7"

Even though there's a large double garage to the front of this bungalow, by arranging the garage doors to look across the plot it avoids making them the dominant architectural feature of the front elevation. By balancing out the gable end of the garage with an introduced gable over the front of the living room, extra interest is given to the whole facade.

143.88 sq. m./1549 sq. ft.   *Copyright refer to Designer Homes*   ## The Hawk

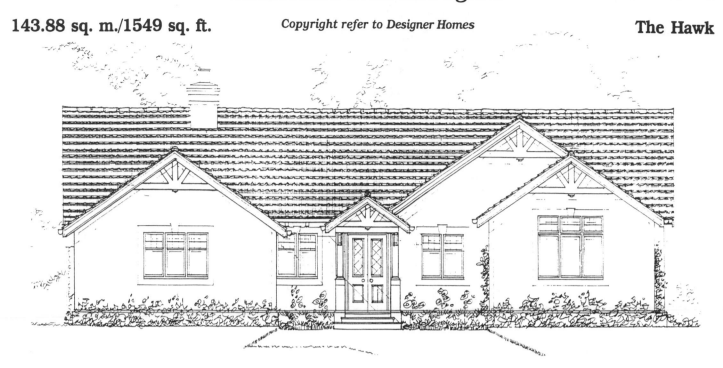

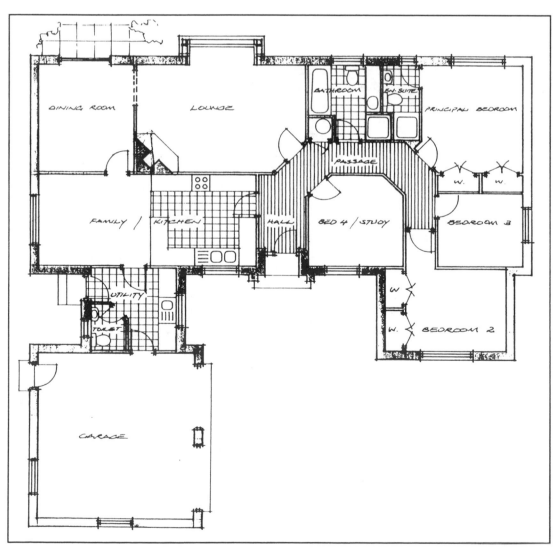

In this bungalow the garage is brought to the front and almost detached from the main body of the house by a linking section containing the utility room. Further interest is then given to the elevation by the pitched roof over the porch and the double gable over the bedroom sections.

1513 sq. ft.

Copyright refer to Designer Homes

The Skylark

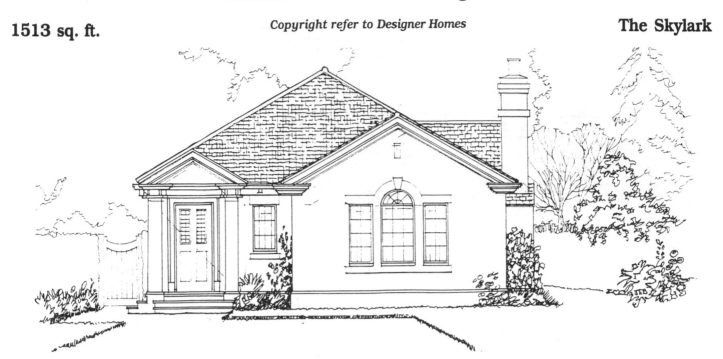

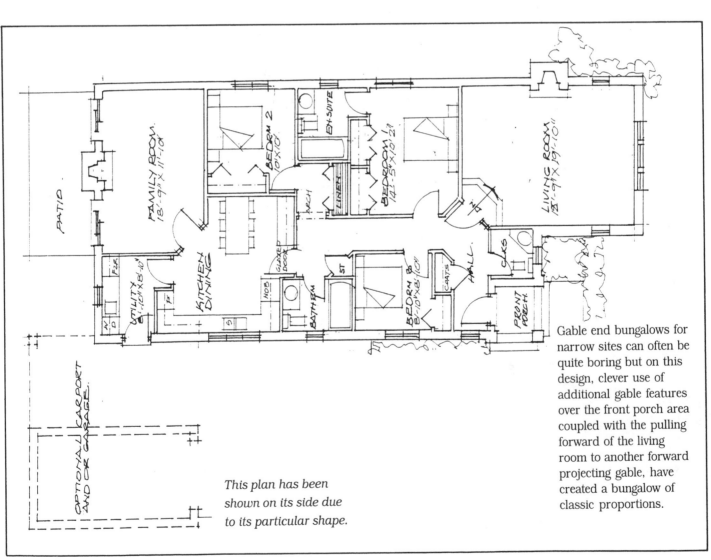

PATIO

FAMILY ROOM 18'-9" X 11'-10"

BEDROOM 2 10' X 10'

EN-SUITE

BEDROOM 1 14'-5" X 10'-2"

LIVING ROOM 13'-9" X 19'-10"

UTILITY 9'-10" X 8'-0"

KITCHEN DINING

GLAZED DOOR

HOB

BATHRM

ST

BEDRM 3 8'-10" X 8'-10"

COATS

HALL

CLKS

FRONT PORCH

LINEN

OPTIONAL CARPORT AND CR GARAGE.

Gable end bungalows for narrow sites can often be quite boring but on this design, clever use of additional gable features over the front porch area coupled with the pulling forward of the living room to another forward projecting gable, have created a bungalow of classic proportions.

This plan has been shown on its side due to its particular shape.

90

141.78 sq. m.

Copyright refer to Designer Homes

The Redstart

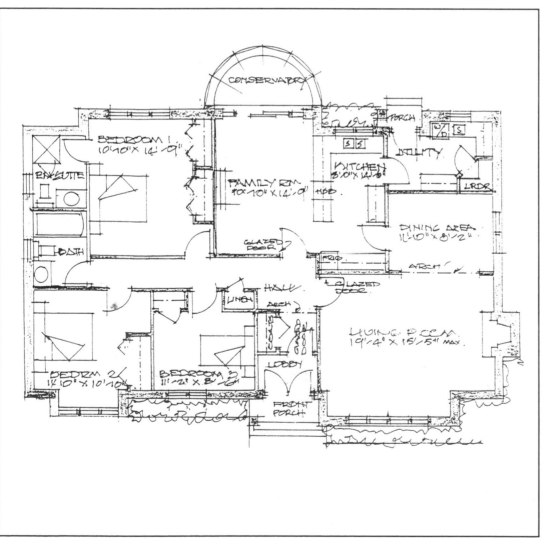

Not a lot of space is wasted by hallways and passage ways in this bungalow and the interlinking of the main living areas provides a degree of open plan living whilst retaining the separate identity of each area. A glazed door to the rear of the hall would give a splendid view through the house from the front door to the conservatory.

1604 sq. ft.

The Heron

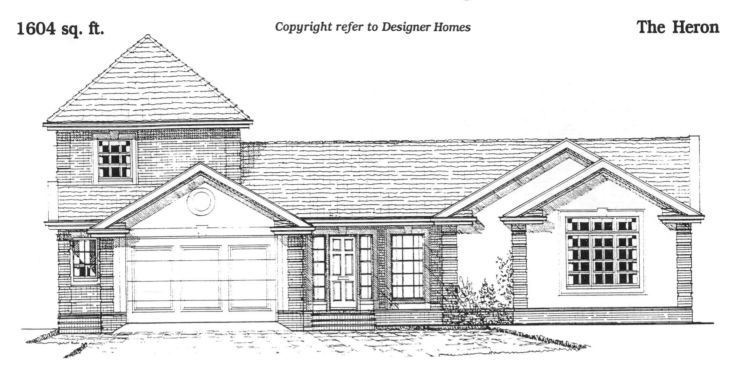

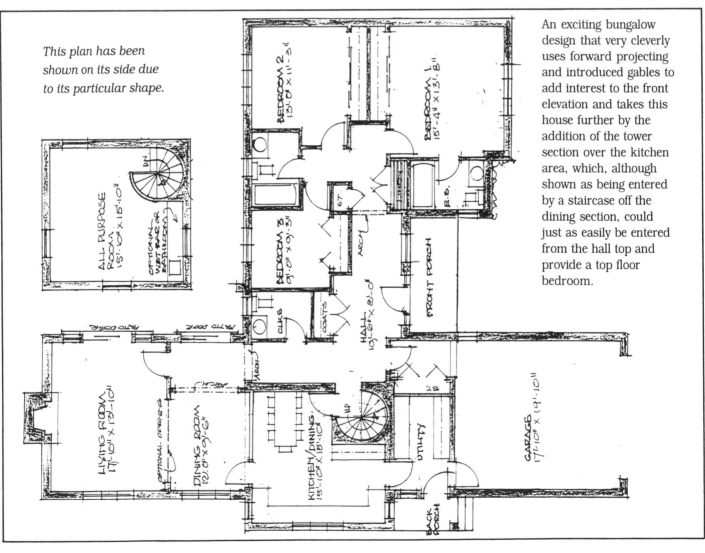

This plan has been shown on its side due to its particular shape.

An exciting bungalow design that very cleverly uses forward projecting and introduced gables to add interest to the front elevation and takes this house further by the addition of the tower section over the kitchen area, which, although shown as being entered by a staircase off the dining section, could just as easily be entered from the hall top and provide a top floor bedroom.

181.2 sq. m./1950 sq. ft.   *Copyright refer to Designer Homes*   **The Goldeneye**

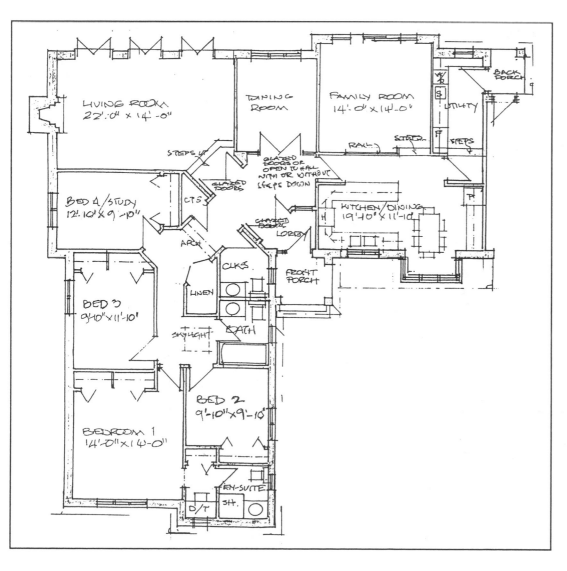

At first sight the front elevational drawing of this bungalow gives the impression of a fairly modest size but reference to the plans shows that this is a large bungalow with much of the accommodation one would expect in a big family house. Once more the designers have used clever architectural features to add interest to the elevations and you might particularly note the combination of the gable ends and the hipped roof that the most forward one lays back upon.

154 sq.m. - 1660 sq.ft. *The copyright belongs to Kingpost Design Co* **Cheriton**

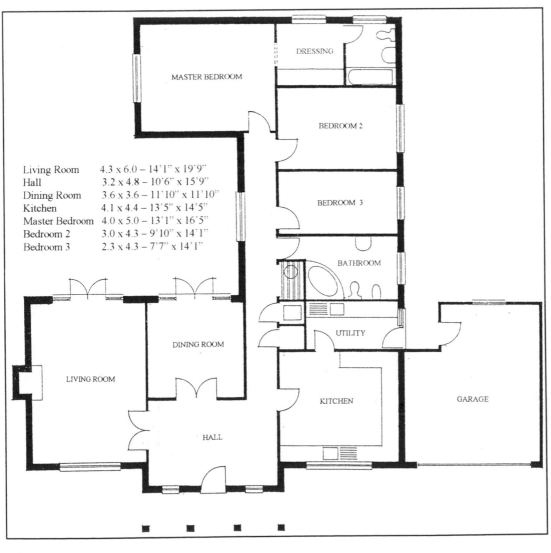

Living Room	4.3 x 6.0 – 14'1" x 19'9"
Hall	3.2 x 4.8 – 10'6" x 15'9"
Dining Room	3.6 x 3.6 – 11'10" x 11'10"
Kitchen	4.1 x 4.4 – 13'5" x 14'5"
Master Bedroom	4.0 x 5.0 – 13'1" x 16'5"
Bedroom 2	3.0 x 4.3 – 9'10" x 14'1"
Bedroom 3	2.3 x 4.3 – 7'7" x 14'1"

A contemporary styled bungalow offering generously sized accommodation with a rear patio area that would easily accommodate a large conservatory. The three good sized bedrooms, two bathrooms, and impressive hall make this a comfortable home for a family or the active retired.

94

2250 sq. ft.

21m x 17m/69ft x 56ft

Orchard

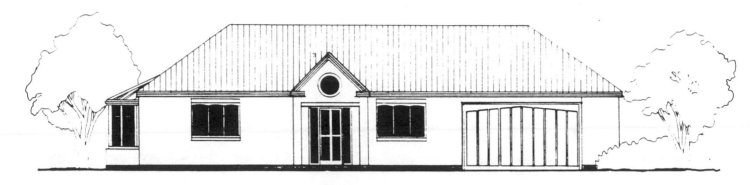

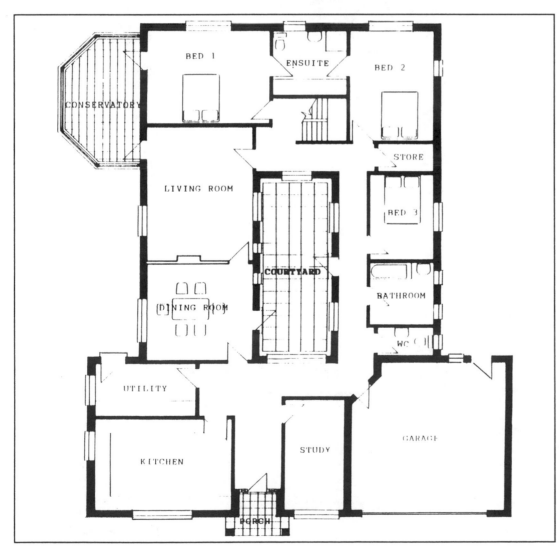

This bungalow has been designed to avoid the two main problems of bungalows - too much roofscape and long corridors without natural light. Both are solved by the introduction of a central courtyard, which reduced the roof pitches and bring daylight and sun into the heart of the building. It also provides a pleasant, private outdoor space.

The copyright belongs to Potton Ltd.

105.15 sq. m.
14.01m x 7.5m

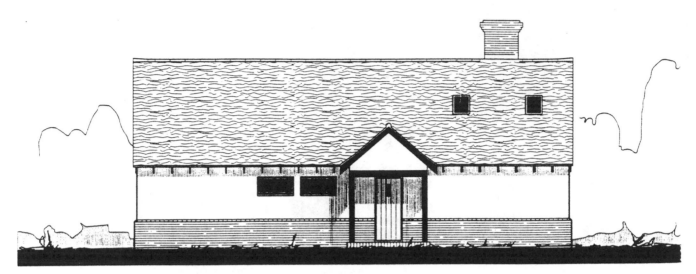

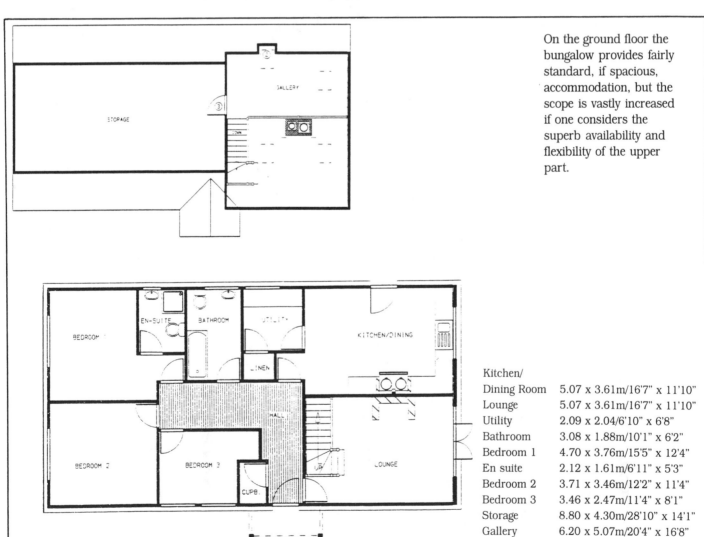

On the ground floor the bungalow provides fairly standard, if spacious, accommodation, but the scope is vastly increased if one considers the superb availability and flexibility of the upper part.

Kitchen/Dining Room	5.07 x 3.61m/16'7" x 11'10"
Lounge	5.07 x 3.61m/16'7" x 11'10"
Utility	2.09 x 2.04/6'10" x 6'8"
Bathroom	3.08 x 1.88m/10'1" x 6'2"
Bedroom 1	4.70 x 3.76m/15'5" x 12'4"
En suite	2.12 x 1.61m/6'11" x 5'3"
Bedroom 2	3.71 x 3.46m/12'2" x 11'4"
Bedroom 3	3.46 x 2.47m/11'4" x 8'1"
Storage	8.80 x 4.30m/28'10" x 14'1"
Gallery	6.20 x 5.07m/20'4" x 16'8"

2400 sq. ft.
56 ft. x 44 ft.

The copyright belongs to Design & Materials Ltd.

Lambert

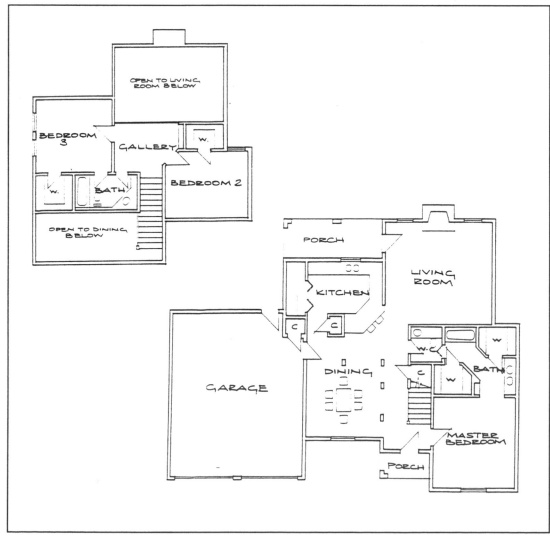

This bungalow has an unusual free flowing arrangement of the main rooms, with the lounge and dining room open to the gallery above. The roof space provides two further bedrooms and a bathroom.

2420 sq. ft./225 sq. m.

The copyright belongs to Custom Homes

Sovereign

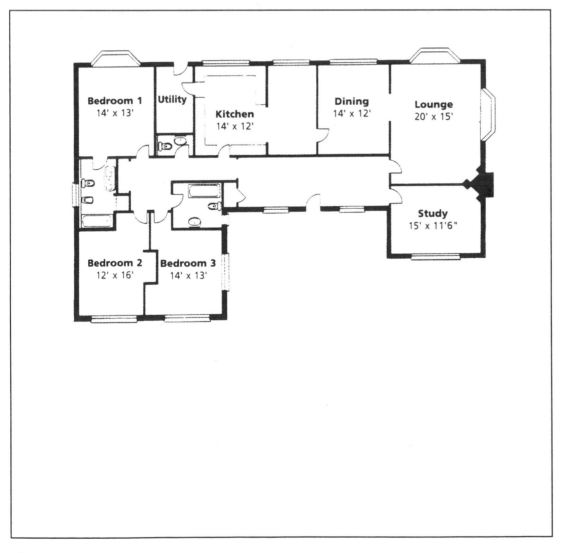

A design that is obviously conceived to take advantage of a plot where it is required that as many of the principal rooms as possible take advantage of a view to the rear. All the rooms to the front are secondary bedrooms and the study, and this design would suit a busy road environment.

Cottage Style Homes

This is a category that is really in the eye of the beholder but it is usually confined to the smaller to medium sized dwelling on one or two floors, that has a distinctly rural, village street feel to it. That said, they don't all have to look as if they belong on the front of a chocolate box and they certainly don't have to necessarily be thatched. A cottage in Lakeland is always going to be significantly different to one in Sussex and perhaps the real definition is that they should closely follow the local vernacular and contain many of the intimate design details and features expressed in the local architecture.

Garages are the things that often ruin the modern day cottage, and indeed many other types of home. When village streets first evolved the motor car didn't exist and, for most peasants living in the country, it was not preceded by a pony and trap or by any other form of transport other than Shanks' pony. So it's no use trying to pretend that your garage is replacing the old stable building, which, more properly, belonged to the squire's house. Nevertheless if you are going to build a garage, that's the closest you can get in historical terms, and if the design, therefore, can emulate the design of a small coach house or stable, then it's less likely to stick out like a sore thumb.

Contributors in this section:

ASBA Reed Architects
Border Oak
Custom Homes
Design & Materials Ltd.
Designer Homes
Kingpost Design Co
Scandia-Hus

1236 sq. ft.

The copyright belongs to Kingpost Design Co

Foxglove Cottage

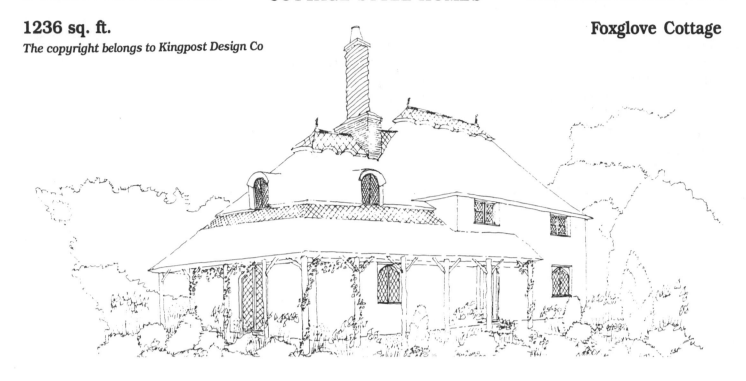

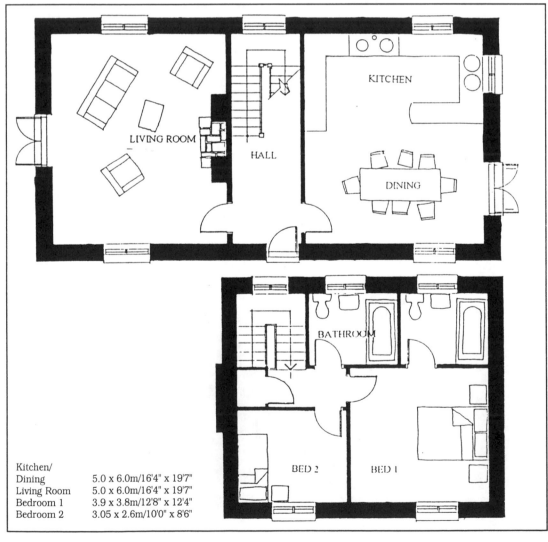

A classic country cottage in the picturesque style. The simple accommodation is highlighted by the double height living room which has three high level dormers which fill the room with light. The kitchen/dining room and the two bedrooms complete the accommodation which is attractively accentuated by the traditional thatched roof and surrounding verandah.

Kitchen/Dining	5.0 x 6.0m/16'4" x 19'7"
Living Room	5.0 x 6.0m/16'4" x 19'7"
Bedroom 1	3.9 x 3.8m/12'8" x 12'4"
Bedroom 2	3.05 x 2.6m/10'0" x 8'6"

98 sq. m.

The copyright belongs to Border Oak

Shaws Cottage

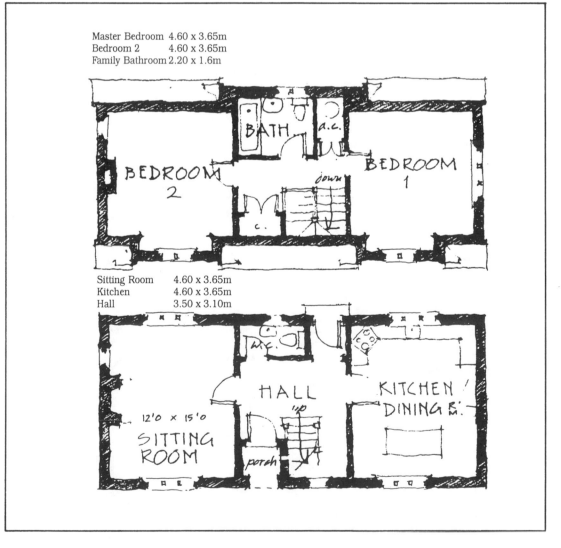

Master Bedroom 4.60 x 3.65m
Bedroom 2   4.60 x 3.65m
Family Bathroom 2.20 x 1.6m

BATH   a.c.

BEDROOM 2

down

c.

BEDROOM 1

Sitting Room   4.60 x 3.65m
Kitchen   4.60 x 3.65m
Hall   3.50 x 3.10m

w.c.

HALL

up

KITCHEN DINING R.

12'0 x 15'0
SITTING ROOM

porch

A pleasing fusion of rendered elevations, stone quoins, oak doors and window surrounds. A building which would be equally acceptable in Yorkshire or Devon. A cottage to catch the smell of woodsmoke and to recapture the toll of the angelus from a lost church across the valley. English oak beam ceiling or heavy and ornate plaster covings enhance the interiors, ledged and boarded cottage doors with blacksmith made fittings, flagstone floors and vaulted ceilings complete the picture.

123 sq. m./1324 sq. ft.   *The copyright belongs to Scandia-Hus*   **The Croft**

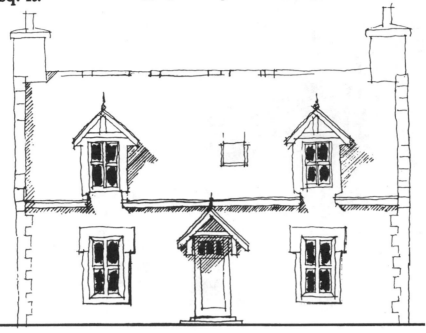

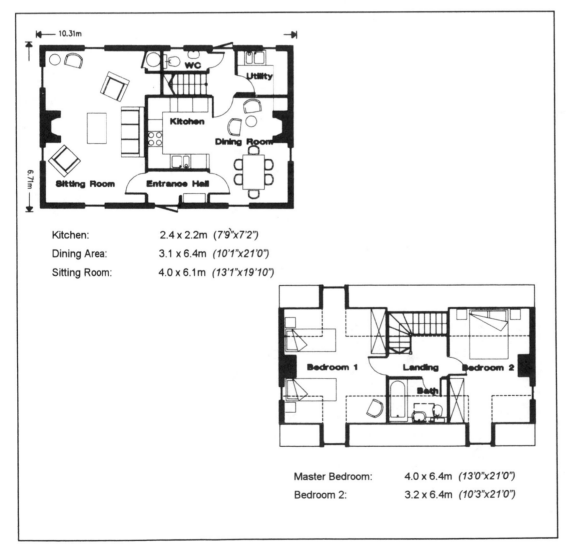

Kitchen:	2.4 x 2.2m	(7'9"x7'2")
Dining Area:	3.1 x 6.4m	(10'1"x21'0")
Sitting Room:	4.0 x 6.1m	(13'1"x19'10")

| Master Bedroom: | 4.0 x 6.4m | (13'0"x21'0") |
| Bedroom 2: | 3.2 x 6.4m | (10'3"x21'0") |

Although this traditional design is reminiscent of a Scottish Highland crofter's cottage, it would be at home anywhere in the British Isles. It has a large sitting room and farmhouse kitchen and, as no cottage would be complete without an open fire, provision has been made for a fireplace in both rooms. The first-floor bedrooms have small dormer windows, which give the elevations a very cottagey, yet symmetrical look. The windows feature glazing bars as standard, and the entrance porches further enhance the exterior of this attractive cottage.

96 sq. m.

The copyright belongs to Border Oak

Bicton Cottage

BEDROOM 4.9 × 3.5

c. down wc bath

BEDROOM 3.0 × 2.5

BEDROOM 3.1 × 2.5

SITTING ROOM 4.9 × 3.5

W.C. c.

up

KITCHEN 4.9 × 3.1

HALL 3.4 × 3.0

A three bay one-and-a-half storey cottage which can be constructed in conventional cavity masonry or utilising a modern softwood frame. A simple cost effective design which works well. Dormer windows and semi-vaulted ceilings at first floor level reinforce the cottage theme. Inglenook fireplaces and aga recesses provide interest to the sitting room and farmhouse kitchen. A spacious entrance hall can be opened up to the sitting room. A well mannered and affordable home.

80 sq. m.

The copyright belongs to Border Oak

Mere Lodge

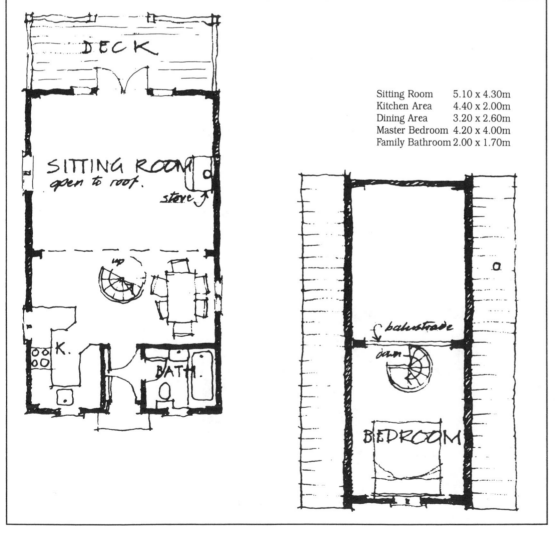

Sitting Room   5.10 x 4.30m
Kitchen Area   4.40 x 2.00m
Dining Area   3.20 x 2.60m
Master Bedroom   4.20 x 4.00m
Family Bathroom   2.00 x 1.70m

An unusual proposal for a holiday home. The use of a steeply pitched two bay oak frame with massive crucks combined with stressed skin panel external skin clad with horizontal weatherboarding. The sleeping loft with spiral staircase looks out onto the vaulted sitting room with French doors to the sun deck. Roof coverings can either be dark coloured profiled industrial sheeting or even oak or cedar shingles. The low eaves and steeply pitched roof are intriguing elements and would suit a woodland or lakeside setting.

115 sq. m.

Pensax Cottage

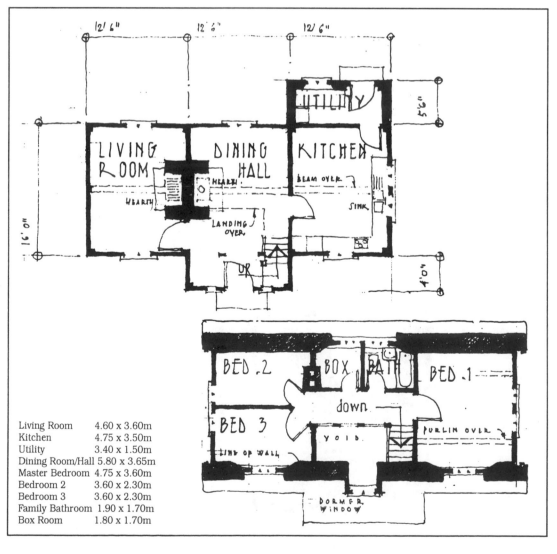

Living Room 4.60 x 3.60m
Kitchen 4.75 x 3.50m
Utility 3.40 x 1.50m
Dining Room/Hall 5.80 x 3.65m
Master Bedroom 4.75 x 3.60m
Bedroom 2 3.60 x 2.30m
Bedroom 3 3.60 x 2.30m
Family Bathroom 1.90 x 1.70m
Box Room 1.80 x 1.70m

A classic three bay oak framed cottage. A 55 degree roof pitch enables the use of traditional thatch. The 'catslide' to the central bay on the front elevation sweeps the eaves down to meet the ground. 'Eyebrow' dormers emphasise the 'tea cosy' look of the thatch. Back to back inglenooks share a handmade brickwork chimney stack. A galleried staircase leads to a bathroom and box room which can be converted into a family bathroom and en suite facilities for bedroom 1 which has a vaulted or cathedral ceiling. A home which draws inspiration from the honest logic of the oak frame.

1782 sq. ft./166 sq. m.

The copyright belongs to Custom Homes

Halsham

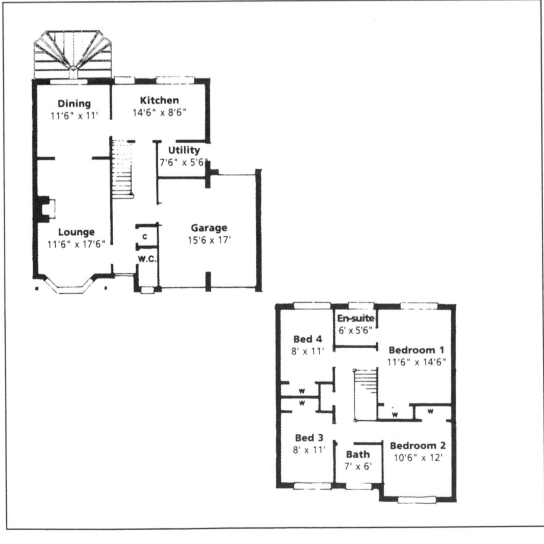

One of the garages to this family home is in a bungalow section that adds interest to the elevations and creates a more complex shape whilst still retaining a cost effective structure. The kitchen and dining room at the rear together with the conservatory would take full advantage of a nice back garden.

86 sq. m./924 sq. ft.

The copyright belongs to Kingpost Design Co

Bredon

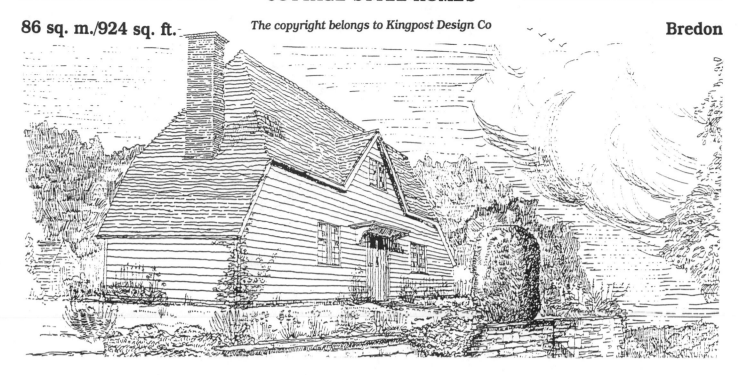

A traditional two bedroom cottage providing flexible accommodation with plenty of storage space and a useful study. The living room has French windows opening to the garden while the upstairs rooms have dormer windows to maximise the use of the high pitched roof.

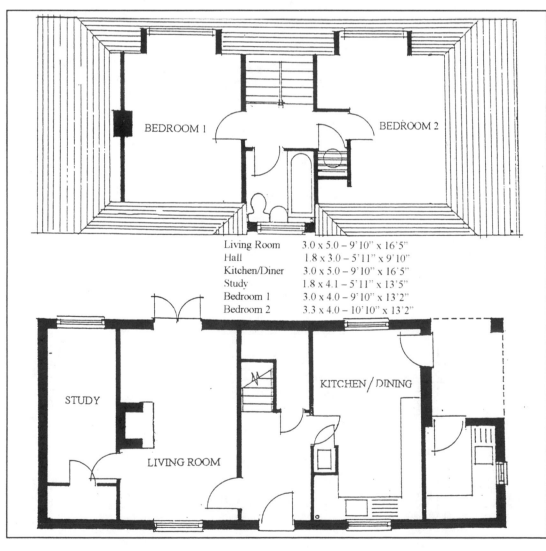

Living Room	3.0 x 5.0 – 9'10" x 16'5"
Hall	1.8 x 3.0 – 5'11" x 9'10"
Kitchen/Diner	3.0 x 5.0 – 9'10" x 16'5"
Study	1.8 x 4.1 – 5'11" x 13'5"
Bedroom 1	3.0 x 4.0 – 9'10" x 13'2"
Bedroom 2	3.3 x 4.0 – 10'10" x 13'2"

980 sq. ft.

D&M-1

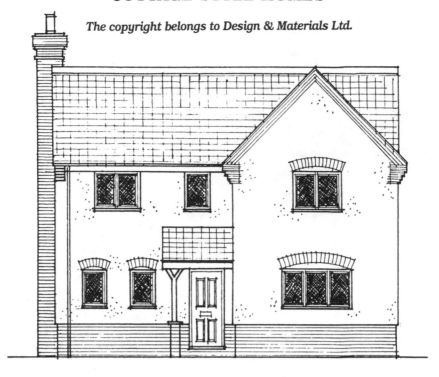

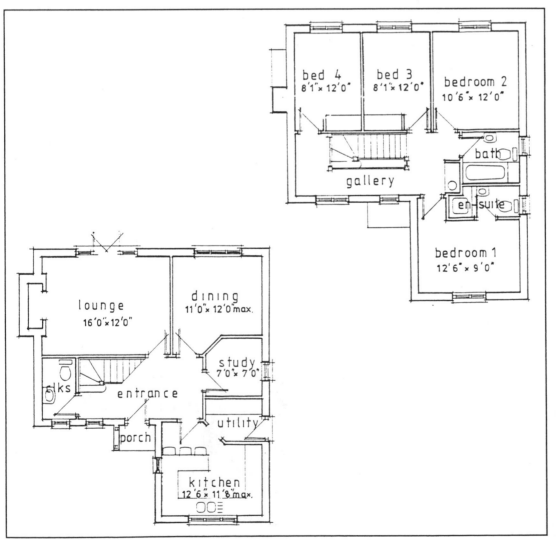

A compact home that was conceived for an infill plot in a suburban street o sit alongside Victorial villas. A feeling of space is guaranteed by the extensive hallway and galleried landing above.

88 sq. m.

The copyright belongs to Border Oak

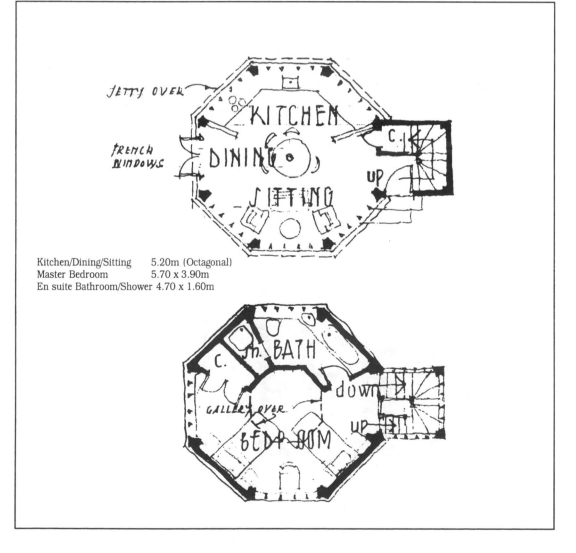

JETTY OVER

FRENCH WINDOWS

KITCHEN

DINING

SITTING

C.

UP

Kitchen/Dining/Sitting   5.20m (Octagonal)
Master Bedroom   5.70 x 3.90m
En suite Bathroom/Shower 4.70 x 1.60m

C. sh. BATH

down

up

GALLERY OVER

BEDROOM

The epitome of the English folly, albeit designed for a Japanese businessman! Nevertheless, a building with many virtues. Basically an octagon with an attached stairtower for convenient access. The third floor gallery makes use of the dramatic soaring roof. An exuberant design but with economical use of space. A building with a dreamlike quality with its feet firmly on the ground.

133 sq. m.

The copyright belongs to Border Oak

Singleton Court

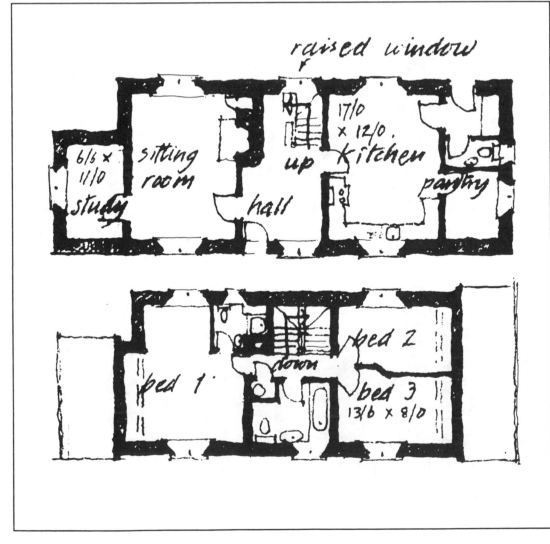

A Sussex home of brick and flint with a teracotta eiderdown of the handmade clay tile. Oak chamber and secondary joists provide attractive beamed ceilings in the sitting room, kitchen and entrance hall. A simple straightforward plan but with all the elements required for modern living. The study, pantry and en suite bathroom are welcome additions to a 17th Century design. Other elevational treatments are possible including handmade brick and tile hanging at first floor level. Painted or stained weatherboarding is another option for consideration.

132 sq. m.

The copyright belongs to Border Oak

Cobblers Cottage

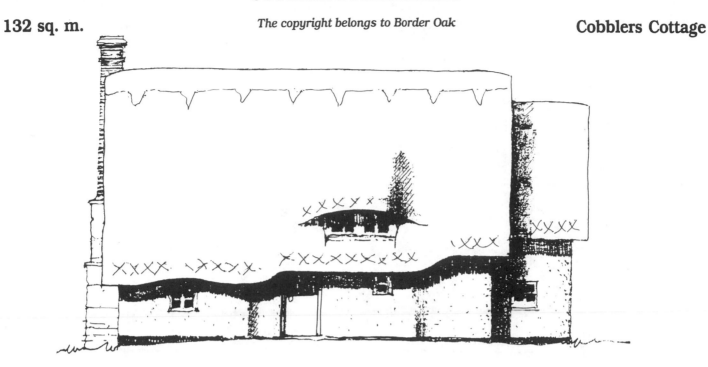

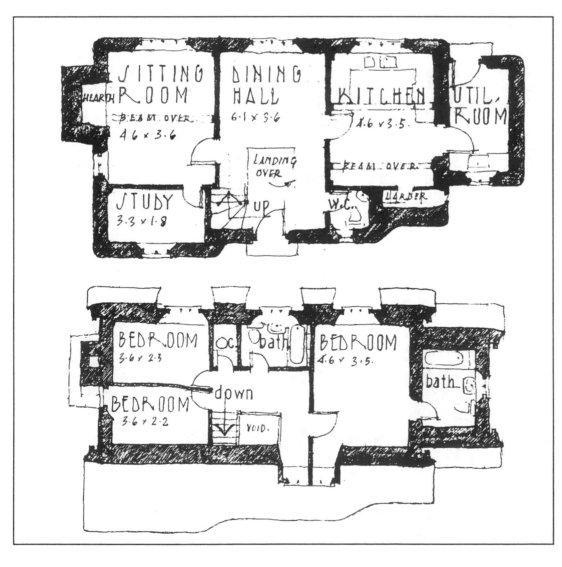

A design which draws inspiration from the traditional cob cottages of Devon and Dorset. Cob walls were traditionally constructed with rammed earth and were typically 18ins - 2ft wide. The 20th century enables the use of lightweight insulation blocks to achieve the same outline, the wide walls and exceptional insulation standards. Internal walls are executed in oak framing with rendered panels, massive oak chamber joists, and secondary (ceiling) joists provide visual interest. The master bedroom has a vaulted ceiling with exposed oak purlins and ornamental oak windbraces.

111

132 sq. m.

The copyright belongs to Border Oak

310.2

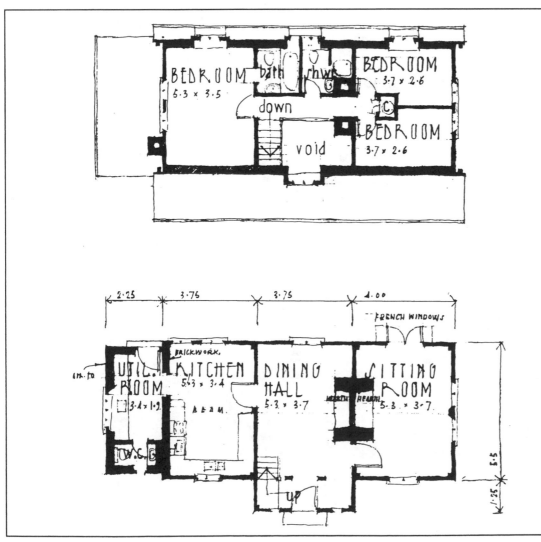

This is the true essence of a cottage property where simple shapes are extended to provide interest. Additive development is a distinctive part of many rural properties but its emulation has to be very carefully considered. In this design it all really works.

140 sq. m.

363.1A

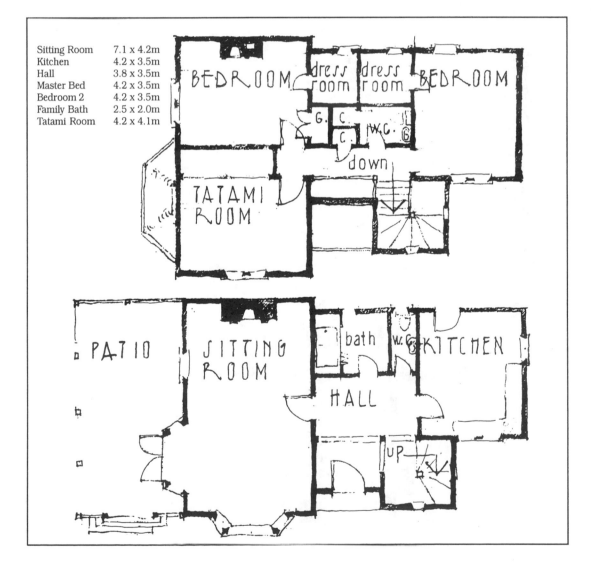

Sitting Room	7.1 x 4.2m
Kitchen	4.2 x 3.5m
Hall	3.8 x 3.5m
Master Bed	4.2 x 3.5m
Bedroom 2	4.2 x 3.5m
Family Bath	2.5 x 2.0m
Tatami Room	4.2 x 4.1m

So much that is good in our traditional architecture comes home to roost in this lovely design. The acommodation may not be vast but its interesting and careful arrangement reflects the beauty of all external appearance.

110 sq. m.

Paxton Cottage

Sitting Room	3.80 x 3.40m
Kitchen	4.50 x 3.80m
Utility	2.10 x 1.40m
Hall	3.50 x 2.80m
Master Bedroom	3.80 x 3.00m
Bedroom 2	3.80 x 3.40m
Bedroom 3	3.80 x 3.00m
Family Bathroom	2.70 x 1.50m
En suite Shower	2.70 x 1.50m
Study	3.80 x 3.00m

A logical layout with the hall and circulation space at the centre of the building provides generous and well proportioned living areas. The entrance hall with its unusual half-hexagonal staircase leads to the landing and provides access to the family bathroom and 3 bedrooms with gable windows and sloping ceilings. Outside, the building is complemented by decorative vertical tile hanging and masonry or rendered ground floor elevations.

84 sq. m.

The copyright belongs to Border Oak

The Gatehouse

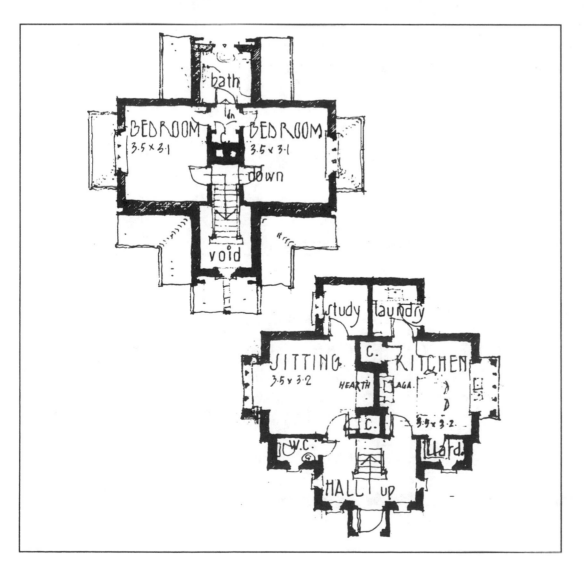

A deceptively spacious two-bedroomed mid-Victorian cottage with central back to back inglenook, impressive entrance hall with central staircase and geometric patterned traditional floor tiles. A small but useful sitting room with a bay window to increase the feeling of space and capable of accepting a window seat. A generous kitchen with bay window which accommodates a range of units, a useful larder and well-proportioned bedrooms with a shared lobby to a small but pretty bathroom. Decorative finials, 'cocks comb' ridge tiles, moulded ornate bargeboards and small paned windows complete the picture.

School House Cottage

90 sq. m.

The copyright belongs to Border Oak

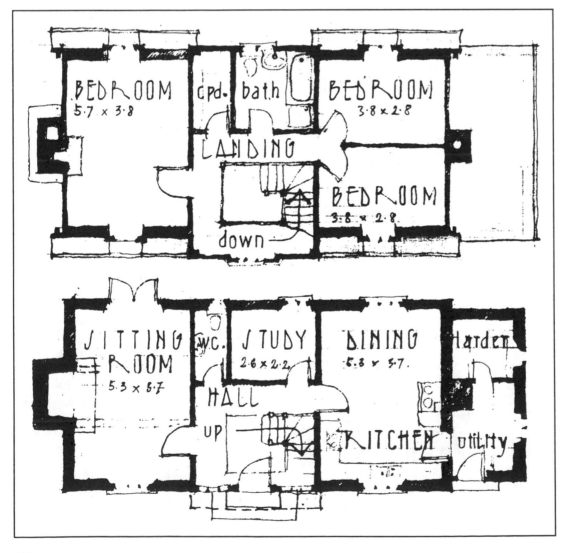

An harmonious mix of soft orange facing bricks combining with the silvery-grey and saffron hue of the oak frame and infill panels. An English oak planked front door with blacksmith made fittings opens onto an entrance hall with a minstrels gallery and a sense of drama. The cloakroom and study for the computer acknowledge the 20th Century. The inglenook in the sitting room, the farm-house kitchen and adjacent larder hark back to the 17th Century. A simple but effective first floor layout provides generous rooms and scope for revision to provide four bedrooms and perhaps two bathrooms. A no-nonsense building which learns from its past but accepts the 20th Century.

990 sq. ft.

Ditton Priors

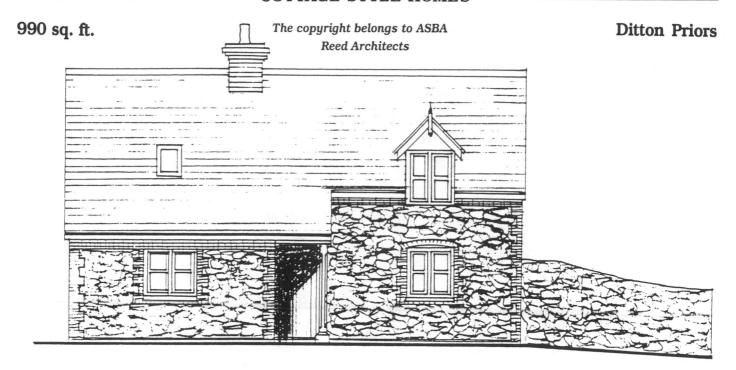

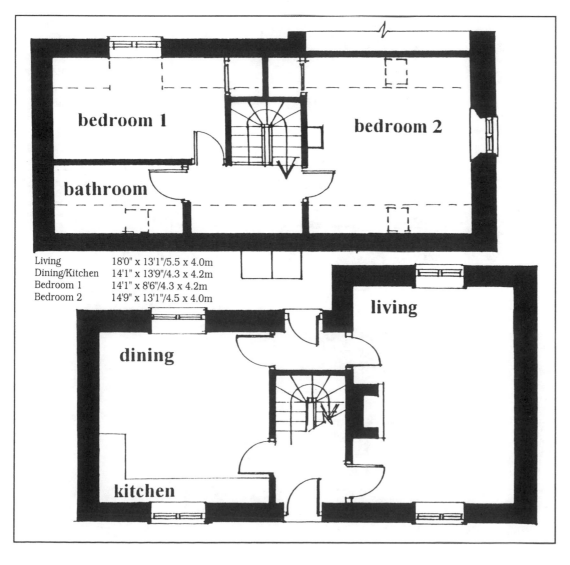

A simple country cottage suitable as a second home. The porch on the garden elevation is an ideal place to leave the walking boots after a hike in the country.

Living	18'0" x 13'1"/5.5 x 4.0m
Dining/Kitchen	14'1" x 13'9"/4.3 x 4.2m
Bedroom 1	14'1" x 8'6"/4.3 x 4.2m
Bedroom 2	14'9" x 13'1"/4.5 x 4.0m

The copyright belongs to Design & Materials Ltd.

1310 sq. ft.
45 ft. x 21 ft.

Tavistock

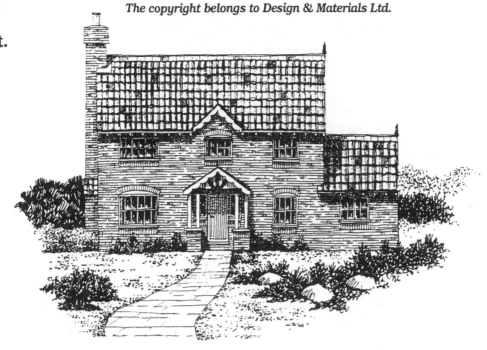

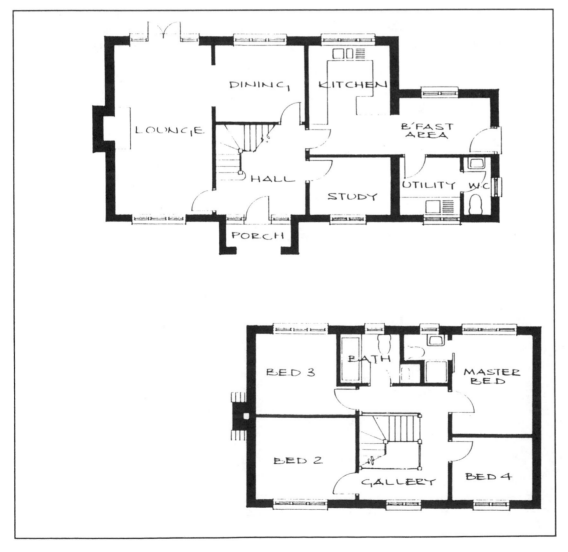

The size, shape, proportions and detailing make this a classic cottage in every sense. The central staircase has an open gallery with natural light and overall the design wastes not an inch of space. Almost any combination of external materials will look just as good.

1450 sq. ft.

32 ft. x 40 ft.

Chirbury

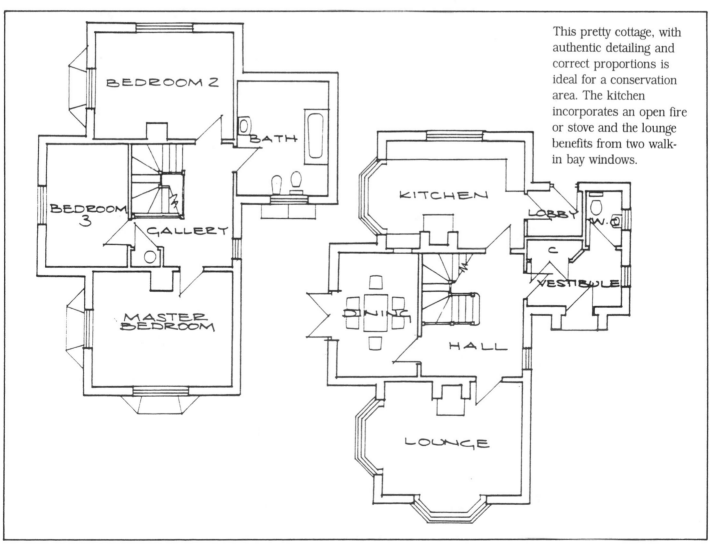

This pretty cottage, with authentic detailing and correct proportions is ideal for a conservation area. The kitchen incorporates an open fire or stove and the lounge benefits from two walk-in bay windows.

BEDROOM 2

BATH

BEDROOM 3

GALLERY

MASTER BEDROOM

KITCHEN

LOBBY

W.C

C

VESTIBULE

DINING

HALL

LOUNGE

The copyright belongs to Design & Materials Ltd.

1200 sq. ft.
40 ft. x 26 ft.

Lynstead

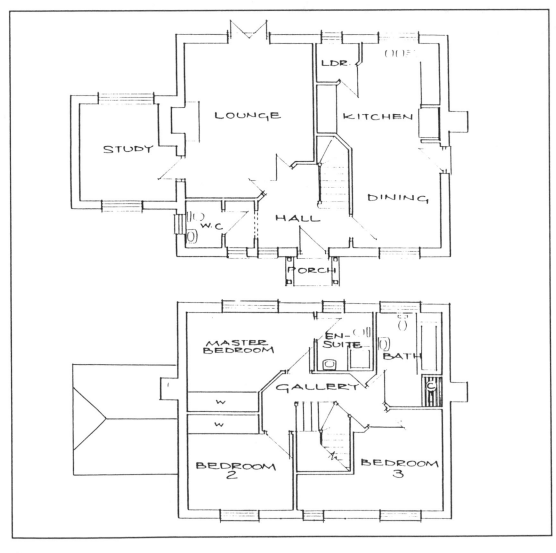

This pretty cottage is illustrated in Kentish clapboard, but could be built anywhere with appropriate materials. Its straightforward shape makes for cost-effective building and will appeal to those on a limited budget.

148 sq. m./1588 sq. ft.

The copyright belongs to Scandia-Hus

The Thatch

Scandia-Hus' range includes all styles and periods – from olde-worlde to hi-tech – all built to the same standards of Swedish technology. The Thatch derives its inspiration from a traditional, thatched, British cottage. The small windows and cottage door lend it a completely authentic look. The interior layout continues the cottagey theme, with an inglenook fireplace in the sitting room. However, it has a difference. A large dining area leads off the entrance hall, which is open right up to the first floor gallery, affording an impressive an unusually spacious feel to an otherwise traditional cottage design.

1050 sq. ft.

Castle Cottage

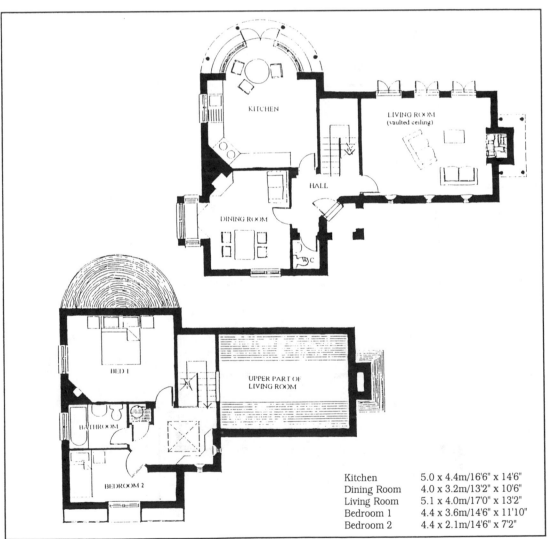

Kitchen	5.0 x 4.4m/16'6" x 14'6"
Dining Room	4.0 x 3.2m/13'2" x 10'6"
Living Room	5.1 x 4.0m/17'0" x 13'2"
Bedroom 1	4.4 x 3.6m/14'6" x 11'10"
Bedroom 2	4.4 x 2.1m/14'6" x 7'2"

A picturesque country cottage which is based on the self-consciously pretty 'cottage ornee' of the early nineteenth century. The gothic style arched windows and porch contrast interestingly with the painted weather boarding and decorative barge boards to the gable. The gothic style is evident in the timbered vaulted ceiling to the living room and the castellated tower and decorative chimney stack add an imposing touch to what is quite a simple two bedroomed cottage. Definitely a design for a rural site, and one which should find favour with the planners and the most 'nimbyish' neighbours.

725 sq. ft.

Copyright refer to Designer Homes

Tweed

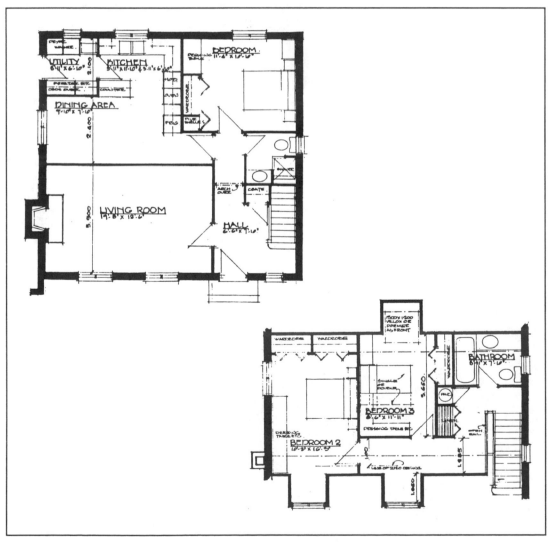

This very attractive modern cottage design breaks the rule that the garage plays no part in a cottage style. the proportions of it are exactly right and the clever offset which is reflected on the roof line over the front door, make it all look right.

90.7 sq. m.

Copyright refer to Designer Homes

1556/1285

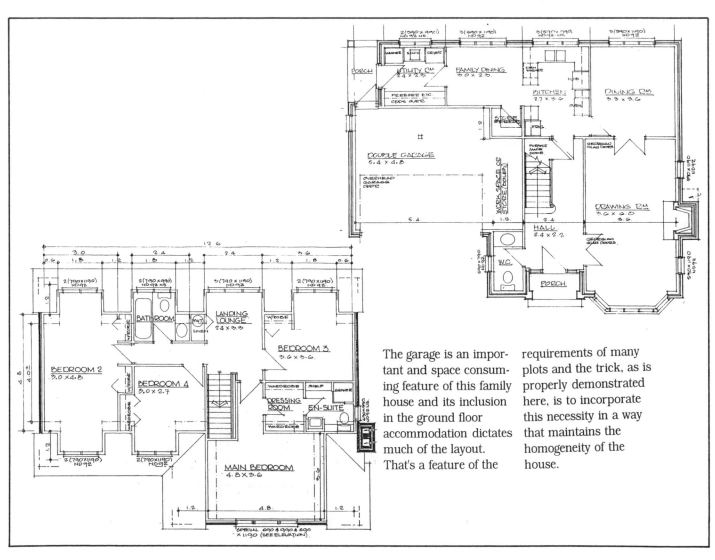

The garage is an important and space consuming feature of this family house and its inclusion in the ground floor accommodation dictates much of the layout. That's a feature of the requirements of many plots and the trick, as is properly demonstrated here, is to incorporate this necessity in a way that maintains the homogeneity of the house.

Copyright refer to Designer Homes

Who says a small family house has to be boring. A large living room and plenty of ancillary accommodation to the ground floor repeats to the top floor where a few simple changes could turn the dressing room into an en-suite.

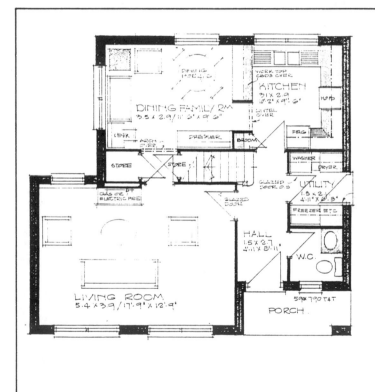

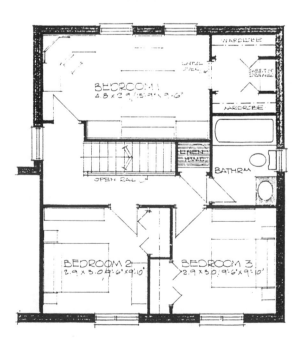

144.36 sq. m.

Copyright refer to Designer Homes

Bedrule

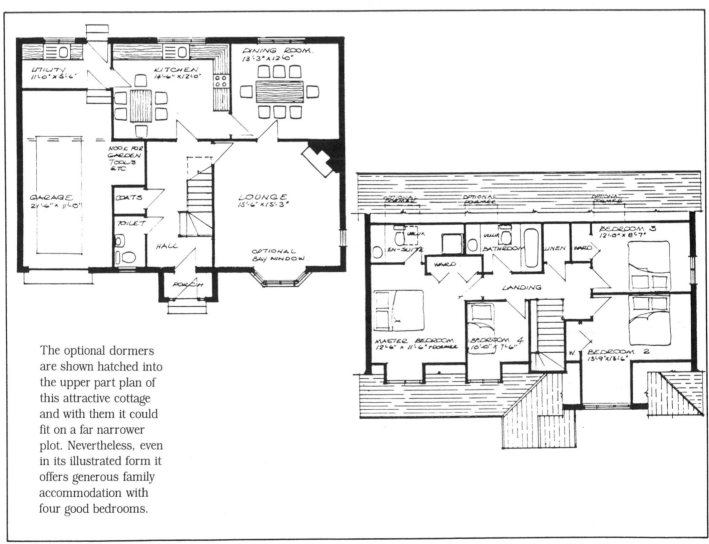

The optional dormers are shown hatched into the upper part plan of this attractive cottage and with them it could fit on a far narrower plot. Nevertheless, even in its illustrated form it offers generous family accommodation with four good bedrooms.

212.5 sq. m. /2287 sq. ft.   *Copyright refer to Designer Homes*   **Ledbury**

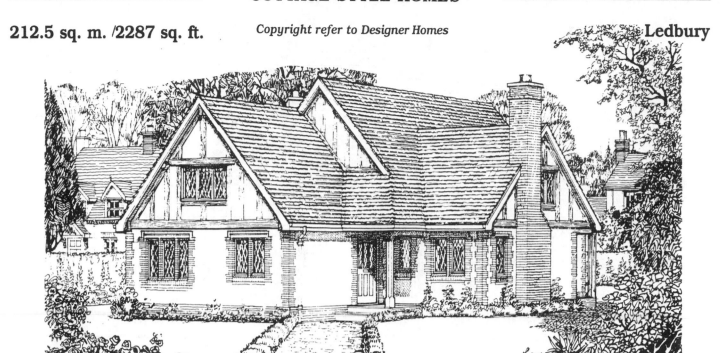

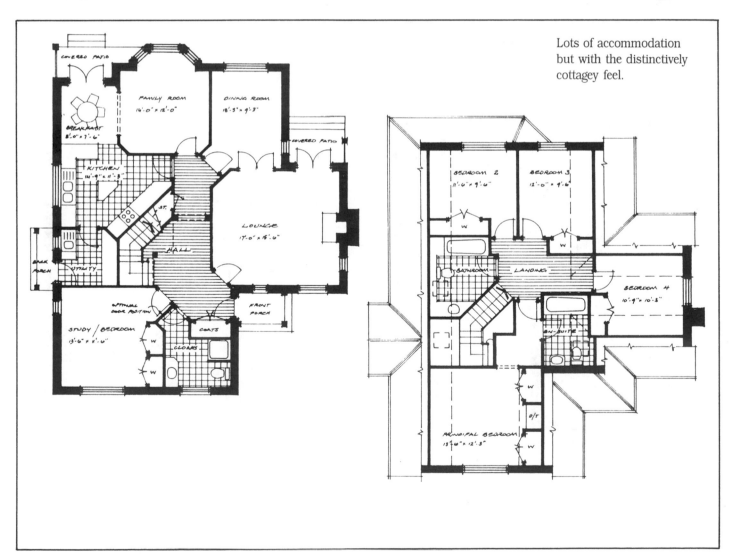

Lots of accommodation but with the distinctively cottagey feel.

163.05 sq. m./1755sq. ft.

Copyright refer to Designer Homes

Herongate

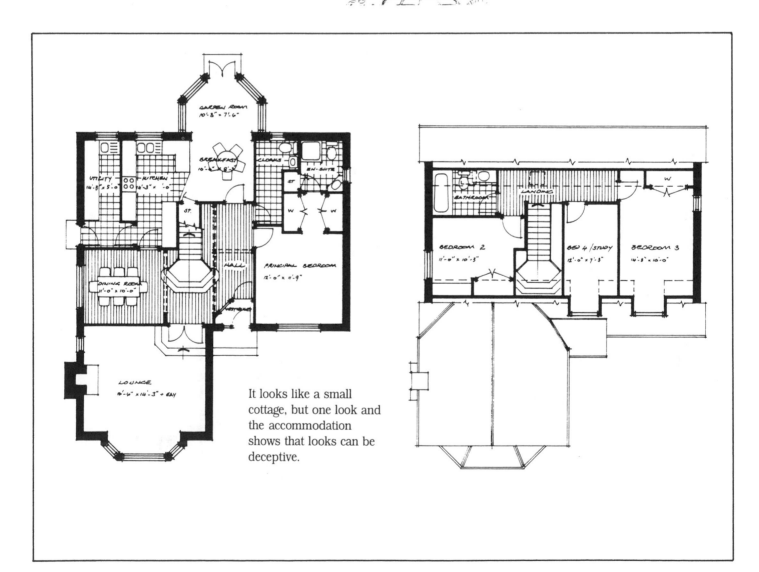

GARDEN ROOM
10'-8" x 7'-6"

BREAKFAST
10'-0" x 8'-0"

CLOAKS

EN-SUITE

UTILITY
14'-3" x 5'-0"

KITCHEN
16'-3" x 9'-0"

ST.

W   W

ST.

HALL

PRINCIPAL BEDROOM
12'-0" x 11'-9"

DINING ROOM
11'-0" x 10'-0"

VESTIBULE

LOUNGE
18'-6" x 14'-3" + BAY

BATHROOM

LANDING

W

BEDROOM 2
11'-0" x 10'-3"

BED 4/STUDY
12'-0" x 7'-3"

BEDROOM 3
14'-3" x 10'-0"

It looks like a small cottage, but one look and the accommodation shows that looks can be deceptive.

165.2 sq. m./1778 sq. ft.

Copyright refer to Designer Homes

Patterdale

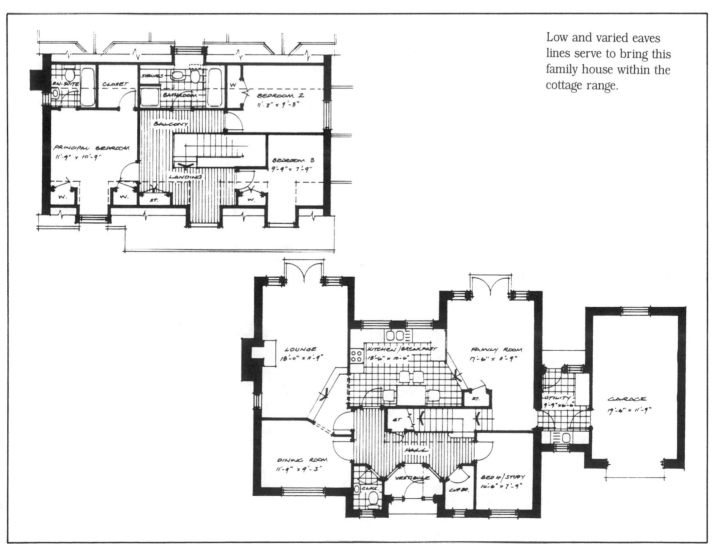

EN-SUITE
CLOSET
SHELVES
BATHROOM
W
BEDROOM 2
11' 3" x 9' 3"

PRINCIPAL BEDROOM
11' 9" x 10' 9"

BALCONY

BEDROOM 3
9' 9" x 7' 9"

LANDING

W.
W.
ST.
W.

Low and varied eaves
lines serve to bring this
family house within the
cottage range.

LOUNGE
18' 0" x 11' 9"

KITCHEN/BREAKFAST
13' 6" x 10' 6"

FAMILY ROOM
17' 6" x 8' 9"

ST.

UTILITY
9' 9" x 6' 6"

GARAGE
19' 6" x 11' 9"

DINING ROOM
11' 9" x 9' 3"

HALL

VESTIBULE

CUPBD.

BED 4/STUDY
10' 6" x 7' 9"

164.8 sq. m./1775 sq. ft.

Copyright refer to Designer Homes

Yarrow

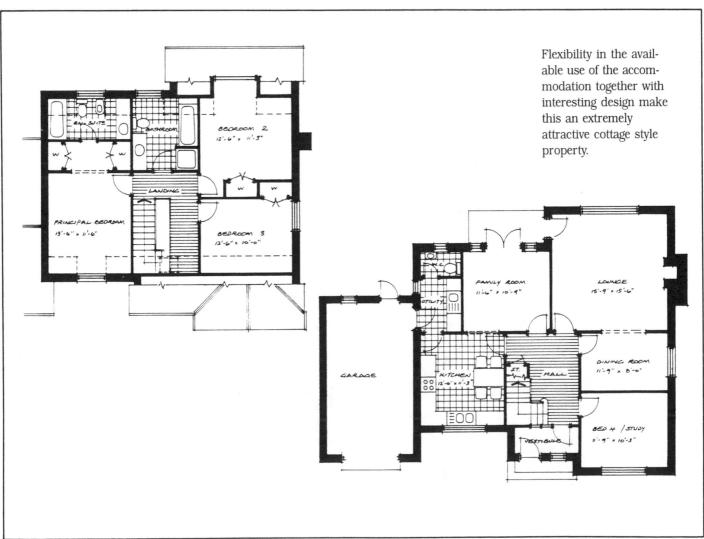

Flexibility in the available use of the accommodation together with interesting design make this an extremely attractive cottage style property.

150.80 sq. m./1139 sq. ft. *Copyright refer to Designer Homes*

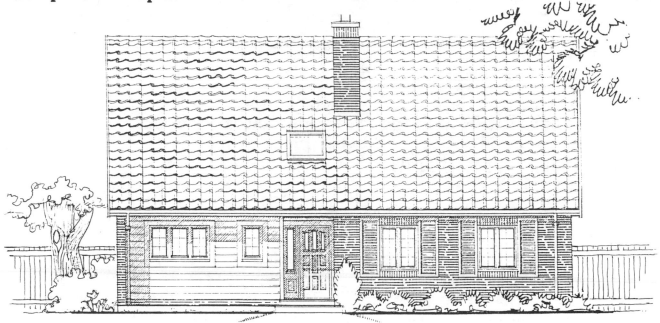

This cottage style bungalow with its high roofline would impress the planners in areas where bungalows were the norm. Do note however, the considerable amount of accommodation hidden within the roof where windows have been placed on the gable end and are therefore not visible from the front.

170.6 sq. m./1836 sq. ft.

Copyright refer to Designer Homes

Humbie

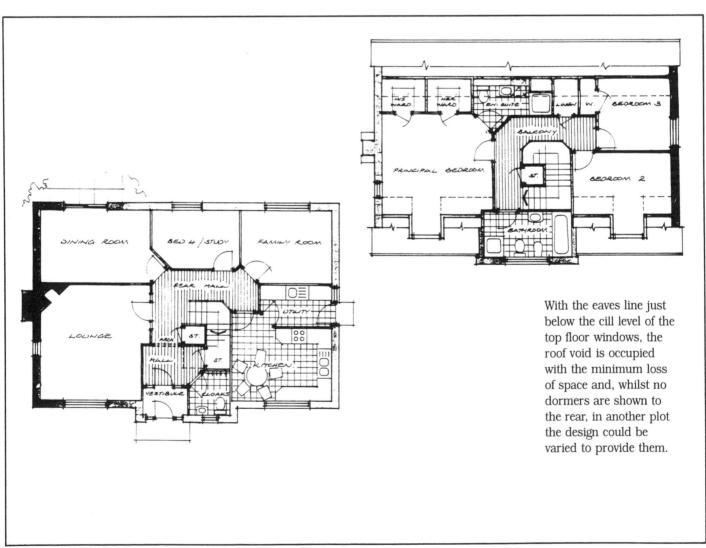

With the eaves line just below the cill level of the top floor windows, the roof void is occupied with the minimum loss of space and, whilst no dormers are shown to the rear, in another plot the design could be varied to provide them.

173.28 sq. m./1865 sq. ft.

Copyright refer to Designer Homes

Troon

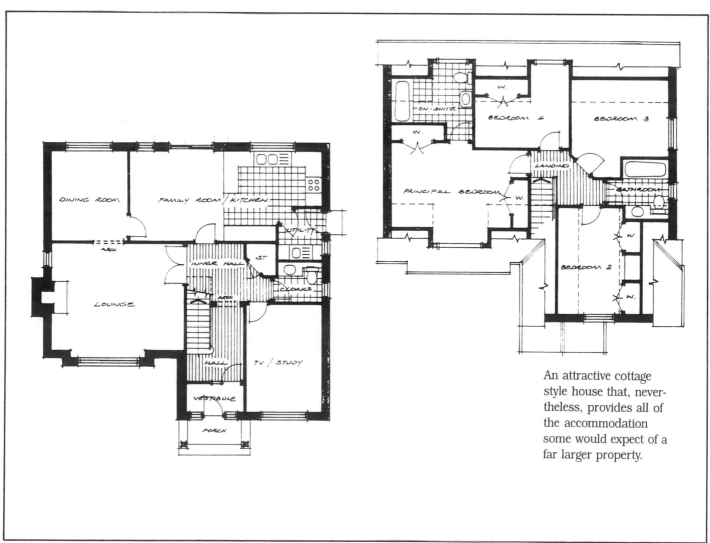

An attractive cottage style house that, nevertheless, provides all of the accommodation some would expect of a far larger property.

Houses under 1500 sq. ft.

The average four bedroomed house on a mass developer's estate is 1200 sq. ft., compared to the average size of a three bedroomed semi-detached house, which is usually no more than about 900 sq. ft.

You can see, therefore, that in this category there is scope to increase the level of the accommodation quite considerably and, with careful design, the impression can be given of quite a large house. The layout is important but with the standard groupings of the main reception rooms, it is often possible for houses of this size to include rooms like utility rooms and en suite shower rooms, especially if the major rooms and, in particular, the hallways and landings, don't take up too much space.

You have to decide at an early stage whether you want fewer larger rooms or more smaller rooms. For example do you want a larger combined lounge/dining room or does the pattern of your lifestyle mean that the separate but smaller lounge and dining room would be of more use. With the kitchen, if you've got two mud loving Springer spaniels, and you're not that fond of cooking, you might decide that a small kitchen with a utility lobby, is going to be of much more use to you than the larger kitchen.

Once again the motor car can complicate matters because, in the main, these smaller houses tend to occupy smaller plots and the requirements for space on the plot for driveways, parking and turning areas can eat into the plot quite considerably. Try not to make the garage door the dominant architectural feature of the new house. If at all possible try to have the garage at right angles to the main house with its garage door looking across the frontage rather than towards the road. If that's not possible and the garage has to either be integral or at the side of the dwelling, then try to offset or inset the garage door from the frontage of the building and think carefully about the style of that door.

Contributors in this section:

ASBA Reed Architects
Border Oak
Custom Homes
Design & Materials Ltd.
Kingpost Design Co
Scandia-Hus

138 sq. m./1485 sq. ft.   *The copyright belongs to Scandia-Hus*   **The Gables**

GROUND FLOOR

Kitchen:	2.9 x 3.0m	*(9'4"x9'9")*
Breakfast Area:	2.9 x 2.1m	*(9'4"x6'10")*
Dining Room:	3.9 x 2.9m	*(12'8"x9'6")*
Sitting Room:	3.8 x 2.9m	*(12'6"x9'4")*

FIRST FLOOR

Master Bedroom:	3.2 x 5.4m	*(10'6"x17'8")*
Bedroom 2:	3.9 x 2.9m	*(12'7"x9'6")*
Bedroom 3:	3.5 x 2.9m	*(11'3"x9'4")*

This Victorian home combines the best of both worlds – British architecture and tradition with Swedish quality and engineering techniques. The attractive wooden entrance veranda and window glazing bars help give this house that real Victorian feel, and the internal layout is also remarkably true to the period. A fitted kitchen, separate utility room and en-suite facilities may be slightly ahead of the time, but the pine staircase, panelled white doors and spruce kitchen ceiling are contemporary Victorian features. This compact three-bedroom design is remarkably versatile, providing comfortable, stylish family accommodation.

139 sq. m./1496 sq. ft.

The copyright belongs to Scandia-Hus

Highgrove

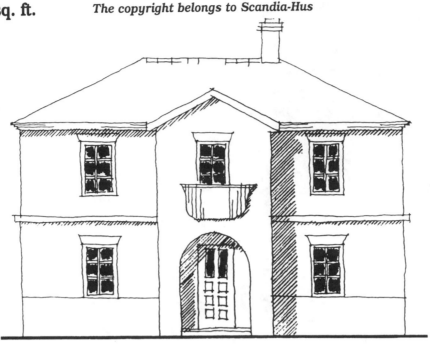

Master Bedroom: 3.4 x 4.0m *(11'0"x13'2")*

Bedroom 2:   3.5 x 3.2m *(11'3"x10'7")*

Bedroom 3:   3.5 x 2.5m *(11'3"x8'3")*

Kitchen/Breakfast Area   2.6 x 4.2m *(8'6"x13'9")*

Dining Room: 3.3 x 3.0m *(10'8"x9'10")*

Sitting Room: 3.4 x 5.9m *(11'0"x19'2")*

The Highgrove is a Georgian-style Scandia-Hus home, which would blend naturally into the street scene of most market towns. Its narrow frontage and relatively small foot print means that it can be squeezed into confined infill sites. Despite this, the Highgrove provides spacious family accommodation on two floors, with three double bedrooms, two reception rooms and a spacious family kitchen and breakfast area. The authentic Georgian look of this design is combined with the Swedish technology and energy-efficiency that are the hall marks of all Scandia-Hus homes.

1336 sq. ft.

The copyright belongs to ASBA
Reed Architects

Yatton

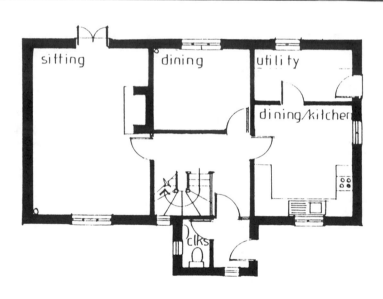

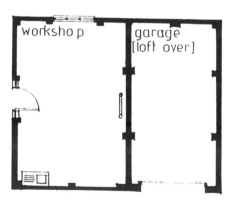

This one and a half
storey cottage provides
cosy family accommoda-
tion and the workshop to
the rear is reached via a
timber-framed covered
way for all-weather use.

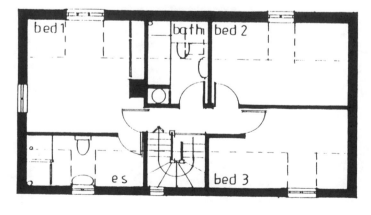

Sitting	19'0" x 13'0"/5.8 x 3.95m
Kitchen/Dining	12'8" x 10'10"/3.85 x 3.3m
Utility	10'10" x 5'11"/3.3 x 1.8m
Dining	10'8" x 9'2"/3.25 x 2.8m
Bedroom 1	12'10" x 11'2"/3.9 x 3.4m
Bedroom 2	15'1" x 9'6"/4.6 x 2.9m
Bedroom 3	15'5" x 9'0"/4.7 x 2.75m
Workshop	18'4" x 11'10"/5.6 x 3.6m

1320 sq. ft./123 sq. m.

The copyright belongs to Custom Homes

Salisbury

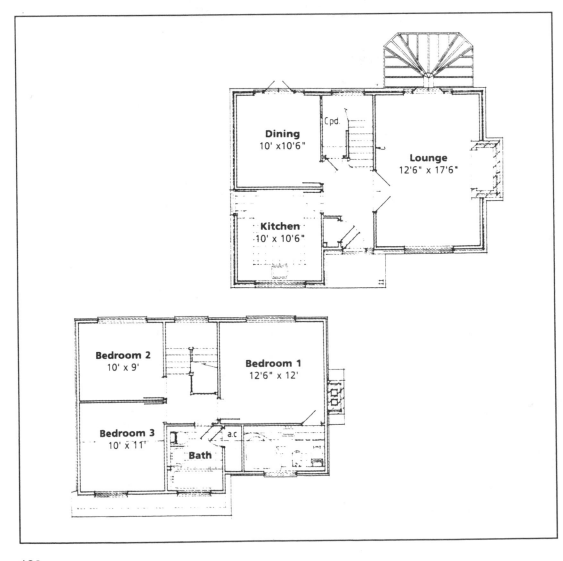

This is the same size as many of the four bedroomed houses on estates and, indeed if the extra large ensuite bathroom hadn't been required, then the upper part accommodation could quite easily be rearranged to provide the fourth bedroom.

1320 sq. ft./123 sq. m.

The copyright belongs to Custom Homes

Talbot

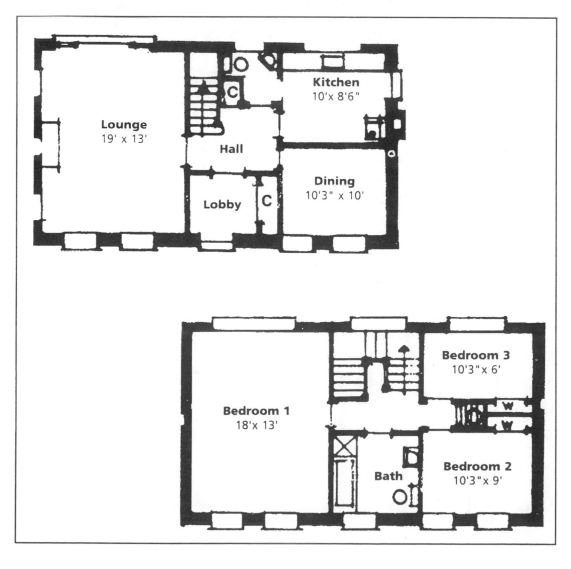

This design gives the impression of being a lot bigger than it actually is. The symmetry of the design and the window layout is broken slightly by the fact of the house only having one chimney in the illustration but, as you can see from the plans, there is scope for there to be one at each end.

1300 sq. ft.

Mill House

Sitting Room/	
Study	22'11" x 12'10"/7.0 x 3.9m
Dining	11'6" x 10'2"/3.5 x 3.1m
Kitchen	11'0" x 10'2"/3.35 x 3.1m
Utility	11'6" x 9'4"/3.5 x 2.9m
Bedroom 1	15'1" x 12'6"/4.6 x 3.8m
Bedroom 2	11'6" x 8'7"/3.5 x 2.6m
Bedroom 3	12'8" x 8'3"/3.85 x 2.5m
Bedroom 4	10'0" x 7'3"/3.0 x 2.2m

This house is for a stream-side site. The workshop is linked by a covered way for access to the family business in all weathers.

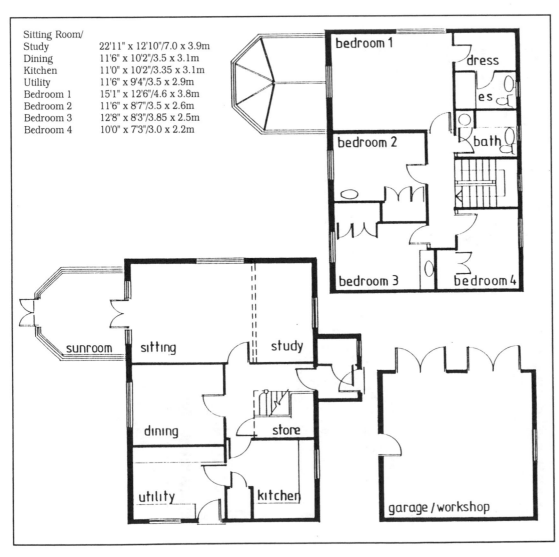

113 sq. m.

The copyright belongs to Border Oak

The Rectory

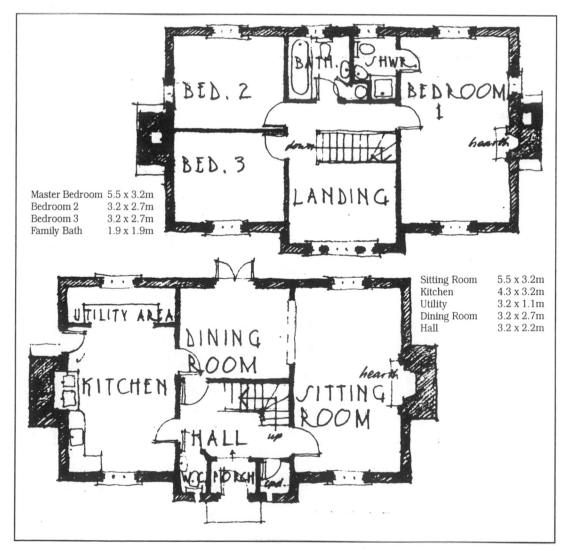

Master Bedroom 5.5 x 3.2m
Bedroom 2   3.2 x 2.7m
Bedroom 3   3.2 x 2.7m
Family Bath   1.9 x 1.9m

Sitting Room 5.5 x 3.2m
Kitchen   4.3 x 3.2m
Utility   3.2 x 1.1m
Dining Room   3.2 x 2.7m
Hall   3.2 x 2.2m

A home with echoes of the tradition and detailing of late Georgian/early Victorian period. Small paned sash windows, central venetian window and a proud front door with correctly detailed case, surround, architraves and portico greet the visitor. Internal accommodation is uniform without slavish regard to symmetry. The French doors from the dining room are ready to receive a future conservatory. The first floor landing will lend itself to quiet contemplation, perhaps the space to sulk! The third floor awaits its noisy teenage occupants. Brickwork, render or stone elevations will work equally well.

120 sq. m.

The copyright belongs to Border Oak

The Dower House

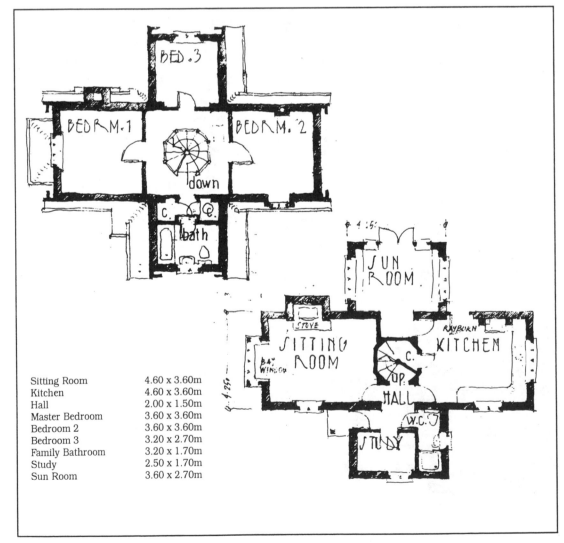

Sitting Room	4.60 x 3.60m
Kitchen	4.60 x 3.60m
Hall	2.00 x 1.50m
Master Bedroom	3.60 x 3.60m
Bedroom 2	3.60 x 3.60m
Bedroom 3	3.20 x 2.70m
Family Bathroom	3.20 x 1.70m
Study	2.50 x 1.70m
Sun Room	3.60 x 2.70m

Inspired by 'picturesque' cottages commissioned by the gentry. A home with echoes of the Arts and Crafts tradition, tile hanging and carved bargeboards add visual interest. The cruciform plan is unusual and works well. The central staircase provides easy circulation - a house that will absorb the day to day activities of a busy family yet provide a sense of privacy for all its occupants.

1495 sq. ft.
34 ft. x 33 ft.

Limegrove

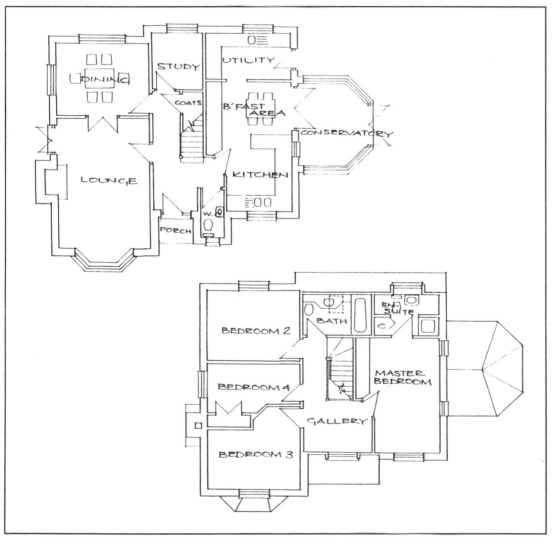

This very pretty house caters for all the needs of family life today. There is a breakfast kitchen, study, utility, four bedrooms and two bathrooms. The conservatory can be added later if the budget is tight.

143

1430 sq. ft.

The copyright belongs to Kingpost Design Co

Horncastle

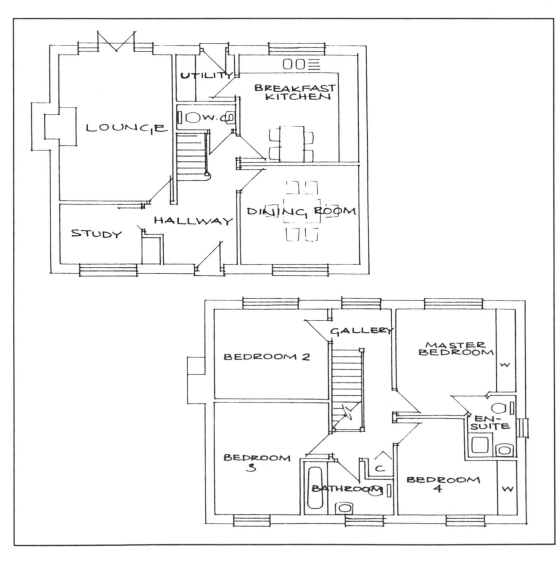

This design provides comfortable and well balanced accommodation for the established family. The central hallway leads directly to all main reception rooms which alight on to a well-lit gallery.

129 sq.m./1390 sq.ft.

The copyright belongs to Kingpost Design Co

Belvedere

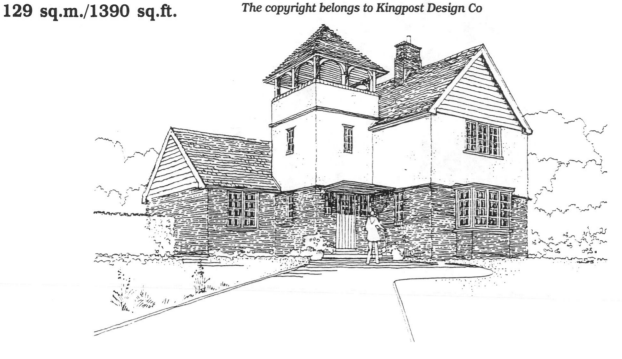

Living Room	3.7 x 4.6 – 12'2 x 15'1"
Hall	3.0 x 3.0 – 9'10 x 9'10"
Kitchen	2.6 x 3.7 – 8'6" x 12'2"
Family Room	3.3 x 3.7 – 10'10" x 12'2"
Belvedere	3.2 x 3.2 – 10'6" x 10'6"
Utility	1.8 x 3.5 – 5'11" x 11'6"
Bedroom 1	3.5 x 3.9 – 11'6" x 12'9"
Bedroom 2	3.7 x 4.7 – 12'2" x 15'5"
Bedroom 3	2.9 x 3.7 – 9'6" x 12'2"

To survey your rolling acres what could be better than this compact design with its raised observation deck, or belvedere. The tower provides a focal point and leads you to the entrance. The stairs eventually lead up to a private patio at roof level. A good sized kitchen/diner and a living room with a walk in bay window comprise the reception rooms while upstairs there are two good sized bedrooms. The master bedroom on the ground floor, with its en suite bathroom, makes life easier either for the older householder or for those who want to get away from noisy children.

1385 sq. ft.

Alderney

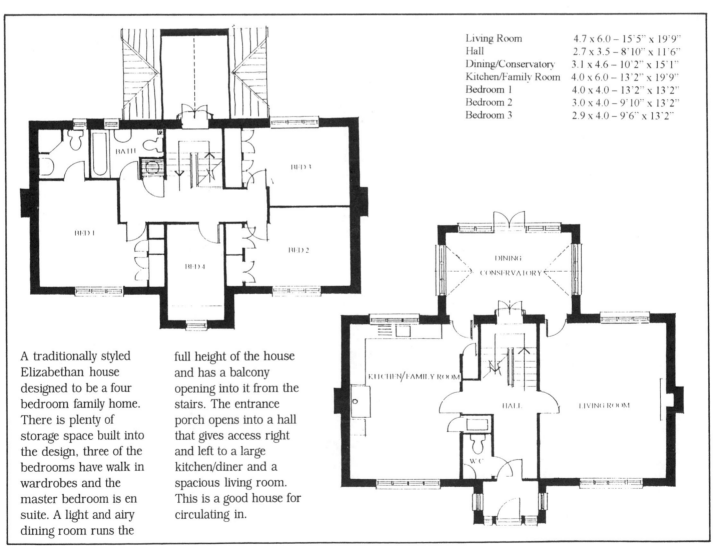

Living Room	4.7 x 6.0 – 15'5" x 19'9"
Hall	2.7 x 3.5 – 8'10" x 11'6"
Dining/Conservatory	3.1 x 4.6 – 10'2" x 15'1"
Kitchen/Family Room	4.0 x 6.0 – 13'2" x 19'9"
Bedroom 1	4.0 x 4.0 – 13'2" x 13'2"
Bedroom 2	3.0 x 4.0 – 9'10" x 13'2"
Bedroom 3	2.9 x 4.0 – 9'6" x 13'2"

A traditionally styled Elizabethan house designed to be a four bedroom family home. There is plenty of storage space built into the design, three of the bedrooms have walk in wardrobes and the master bedroom is en suite. A light and airy dining room runs the full height of the house and has a balcony opening into it from the stairs. The entrance porch opens into a hall that gives access right and left to a large kitchen/diner and a spacious living room. This is a good house for circulating in.

The copyright belongs to Kingpost Design Co

Allsop

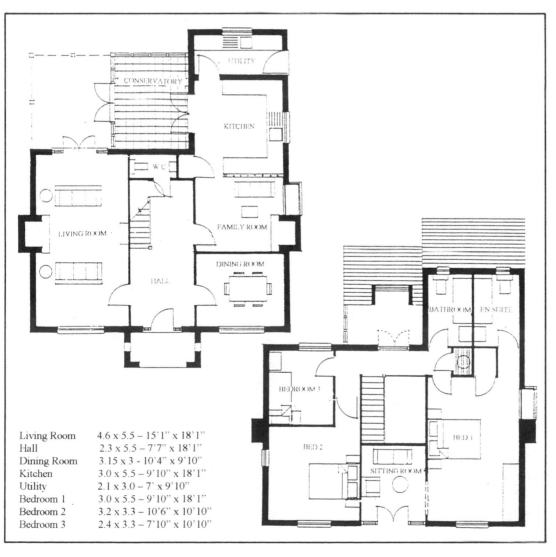

Living Room	4.6 x 5.5 – 15'1" x 18'1"
Hall	2.3 x 5.5 – 7'7" x 18'1"
Dining Room	3.15 x 3 – 10'4" x 9'10"
Kitchen	3.0 x 5.5 – 9'10" x 18'1"
Utility	2.1 x 3.0 – 7' x 9'10"
Bedroom 1	3.0 x 5.5 – 9'10" x 18'1"
Bedroom 2	3.2 x 3.3 – 10'6" x 10'10"
Bedroom 3	2.4 x 3.3 – 7'10" x 10'10"

A comfortable three bedroomed house with a design based on the Chedworth, but with interesting changes. Opening off the master bedroom is a comfortable private sitting room which has a Victorian style balcony over the front porch. To the rear is a double height conservatory viewed from a window on the galleried landing. The large kitchen/family room is the perfect focus for family gatherings, with a large fireplace ensuring a cosy atmosphere on cold winter evenings.

1400 sq. ft.

The copyright belongs to Kingpost Design Co

Avening

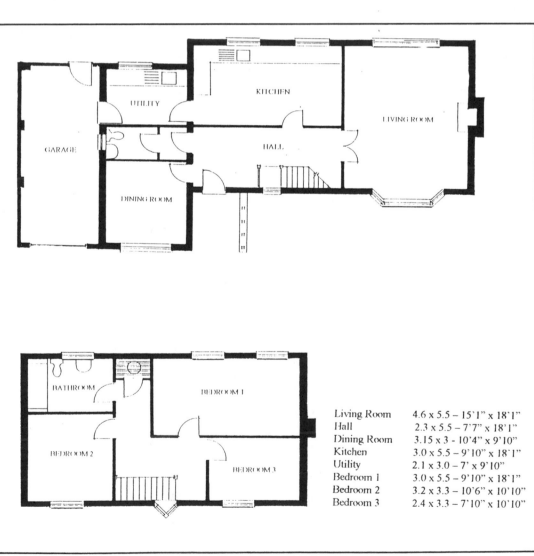

A straightforward design for a fairly wide plot. Three generously sized bedrooms share one bathroom but an en suite could easily be provided for the master bedroom. Downstairs the large hall gives easy access to the dining room, kitchen, and living room. A house with a lot of space in a compact 1400 sq. ft.

Living Room	4.6 x 5.5 – 15`1" x 18`1"
Hall	2.3 x 5.5 – 7`7" x 18`1"
Dining Room	3.15 x 3 - 10`4" x 9`10"
Kitchen	3.0 x 5.5 – 9`10" x 18`1"
Utility	2.1 x 3.0 – 7' x 9`10"
Bedroom 1	3.0 x 5.5 – 9`10" x 18`1"
Bedroom 2	3.2 x 3.3 – 10`6" x 10`10"
Bedroom 3	2.4 x 3.3 – 7`10" x 10`10"

Houses 1501 – 1750 sq. ft.

When you start to get to these sizes you're talking about houses that are almost twice the size of the average semi-detached house and, although not yet classed as big houses, many of the features and accommodation provided by the larger houses start to come into play. The need to decide between a reasonable sized lounge and a separate dining room has largely fallen away by this size, as has the necessary choice between a larger kitchen versus a utility room. In addition it's often possible for the en suite to become more than just an enclosure for a shower and to become more of a proper bathroom.

The one thing that the extra space does allow for is an increase in the size of the hallway and the upper landing or gallery, and the effect and interest this can add to the home takes it into a different league.

Once again the motor car can have a deleterious effect on the design unless it is very carefully thought through but a house of this size will often come about as a result of a slightly larger plot. There may, therefore, be room to consider detaching the garage and positioning it in an interesting relationship to the main house and, perhaps, linking it to the house by means of a wall so as to properly divide the private garden area from the driveway and parking areas.

Contributors in this section:

ASBA Reed Architects
Border Oak
Custom Homes
Design & Materials Ltd.
Kingpost Design Co
Potton Ltd.
Scandia-Hus
Swedish Homes

147 sq. m./1582 sq. ft.   *The copyright belongs to Scandia-Hus*   **Corlione**

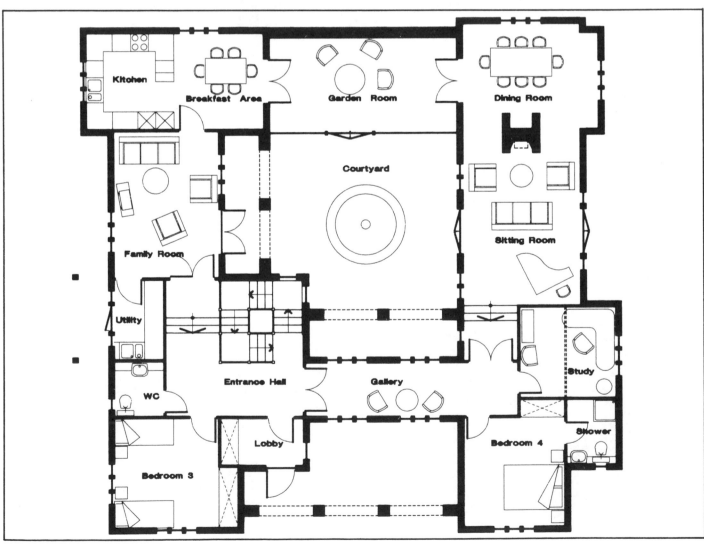

GROUND FLOOR

Kitchen/Breakfast Area:	3.6 x 5.9m *(11'8"x19'4")*
Dining Room:	3.5 x 4.7m *(11'5"x15'4")*
Sitting Room:	3.9 x 5.6m *(12'8"x18'4")*
Family Room:	3.9 x 3.5m *(12'8"x11'5")*
Tower Room:	4.5 x 4.5m *(14'8 x14'8")*
Study:	3.2 x 3.0m *(10'5"x9'8")*

FIRST FLOOR

Master Bedroom:	3.3 x 4.8m *(10'8"x15'7")*
Bedroom 2:	4.1 x 3.6m *(13'5"x11'8")*
Bedroom 3:	3.4 x 3.6m *(11'2"x11'8")*
Bedroom 4:	3.3 x 4.2m *(10'8"x13'8")*

The Corlione, which is reminiscent of an Italian palazzio, must surely be one of Scandia-Hus' most stunning designs. It is built on three floors and is brimming with interesting features such as Italian columns and arches, a courtyard and a tower room and a beautiful open-tread, ash staircase. It also features a vast, lower-level reception room, featuring a high, vaulted ceiling, and split in two by a central fire place, creating a generous sitting room at one end and a spacious dining room at the other. This is a magnificent home that incorporates everything a discerning family could possibly want, combined with true style and a genuine, Mediterranean atmosphere.

152 sq. m.

The copyright belongs to Border Oak

Carey Cottage

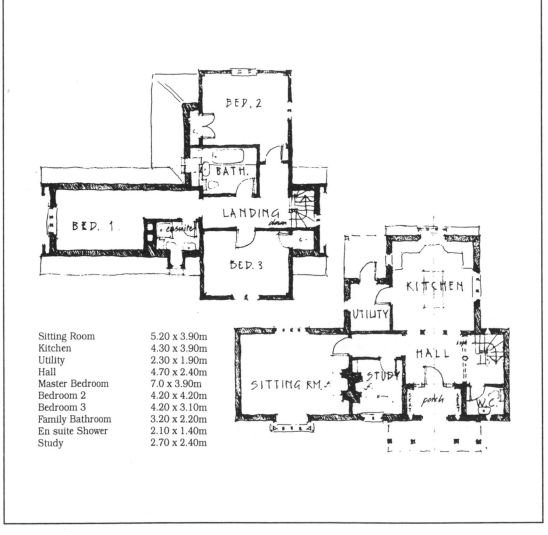

Sitting Room	5.20 x 3.90m
Kitchen	4.30 x 3.90m
Utility	2.30 x 1.90m
Hall	4.70 x 2.40m
Master Bedroom	7.0 x 3.90m
Bedroom 2	4.20 x 4.20m
Bedroom 3	4.20 x 3.10m
Family Bathroom	3.20 x 2.20m
En suite Shower	2.10 x 1.40m
Study	2.70 x 2.40m

An harmonious blend of local stone and oak framing, a jettied gable supported on massive oak pillars provide shelter to the entrance porch with seating leading to an inner hall and arched openings to a well-proportioned spacious kitchen. A landing to the side leads to the study and the sitting room both with fireplaces. A staircase with winders gains access to the landing with a master bedroom with en suite facilities, two further bedrooms and a family bathroom. A well mannered and well proportioned building.

162 sq. m.

The copyright belongs to Border Oak

Pembridge House

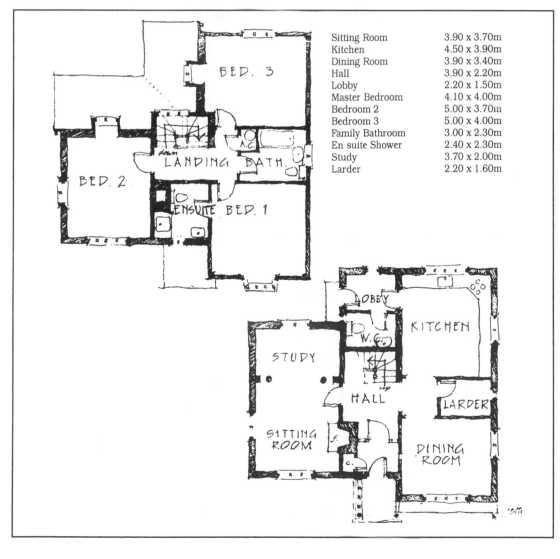

Sitting Room	3.90 x 3.70m
Kitchen	4.50 x 3.90m
Dining Room	3.90 x 3.40m
Hall	3.90 x 2.20m
Lobby	2.20 x 1.50m
Master Bedroom	4.10 x 4.00m
Bedroom 2	5.00 x 3.70m
Bedroom 3	5.00 x 4.00m
Family Bathroom	3.00 x 2.30m
En suite Shower	2.40 x 2.30m
Study	3.70 x 2.00m
Larder	2.20 x 1.60m

A charming house with an intricate open porch leading through an inner lobby to the entrance hall adorned with teracotta tiles. This in turn leads to the formal sitting room with study alcove, a kitchen wing with integral dining area separated by an unusual larder area. A dogleg staircase leads to a galleried landing with access to three sizable bedrooms, with en suite and family bathroom. The external elevations have purpose made windows with arched heads, diamond leaded lights, jetties, oriel windows, properly detailed tile hanging with fishtail tile decoration and small clay tiles to the roof crowned with cocks comb ridge tiles, finials and an imposing chimney stack.

164 sq. m./1765 sq. ft.

The copyright belongs to Scandia-Hus

The Rectory

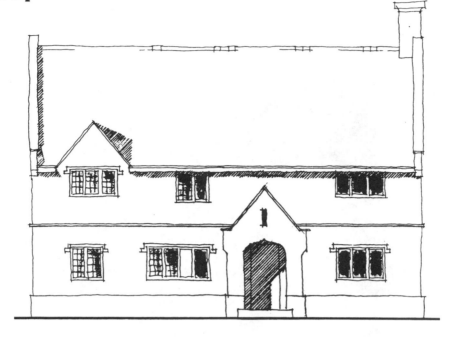

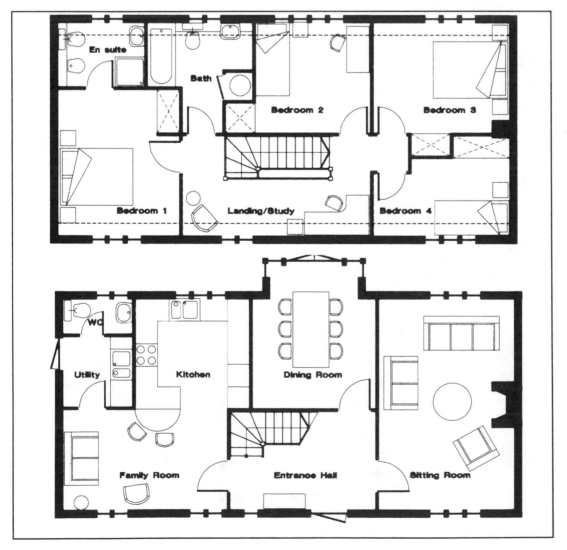

Inspiration for this traditional two-storey family home comes from the Cotswolds. And, although the exterior can be finished in any material, the design lends itself to stone cladding with attractive stone-mullioned windows, optionally fitted with leaded lights. The stone entrance porch leads into a spacious entrance hall featuring a beautiful pine staircase. The accommodation includes a large kitchen and breakfast room with a separate dining room which, depending on your needs, can be turned into a family room, and the first-floor gallery is large enough to accommodate a home office, keep-fit area or hobby room.

157 sq. m./1690 sq. ft.

The copyright belongs to Scandia-Hus

Tronning

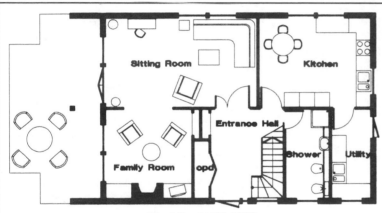

Kitchen:	4.5 x 3.7m *(14'9"x12'3")*
Sitting Room:	5.9 x 3.7m *(19'5"x12'3")*
TV Lounge:	3.4 x 3.4m *(11'2"x11'2")*

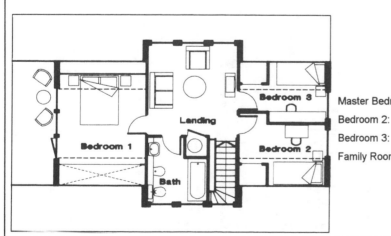

Master Bedroom:	3.4 x 4.0m *(11'2"x13'2")*
Bedroom 2:	3.4 x 2.4m *(11'2"x7'11")*
Bedroom 3:	3.4 x 2.4m *(11'2"x7'11")*
Family Room:	3.5 x 3.6m *(11'5"x11'8")*

Ideal for the young family, the Tronning, like many of the Scandia-Hus designs, can initially be completed as a single storey dwelling, leaving the second floor to be finished as a later option. The spacious sitting room leads into an intimate 'snug' with its own open fire, and upstairs the sloping ceilings add distinctive lines to the bedrooms and the family room. French doors from the master bedroom lead onto a sheltered balcony and the timber cladding, which is standard for the balcony gable head on this design, may be extended to front and rear elevations to create an attractive continental look.

181 sq.m.

Avon

The copyright belongs to Kingpost Design Co

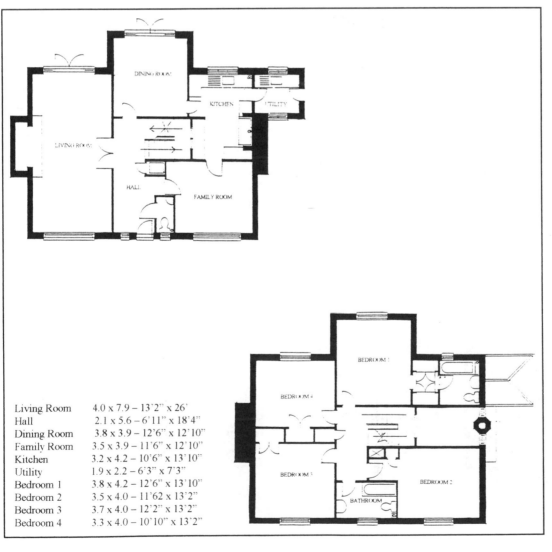

The two distinctive chimneys and exposed wooden beams give this house an authentic feel of Elizabethan elegance. Upstairs, four spacious bedrooms compliment the three large reception rooms on the ground floor. Two of these reception rooms have French windows opening out to the garden.

Living Room	4.0 x 7.9 – 13'2" x 26'
Hall	2.1 x 5.6 – 6'11" x 18'4"
Dining Room	3.8 x 3.9 – 12'6" x 12'10"
Family Room	3.5 x 3.9 – 11'6" x 12'10"
Kitchen	3.2 x 4.2 – 10'6" x 13'10"
Utility	1.9 x 2.2 – 6'3" x 7'3"
Bedroom 1	3.8 x 4.2 – 12'6" x 13'10"
Bedroom 2	3.5 x 4.0 – 11'62" x 13'2"
Bedroom 3	3.7 x 4.0 – 12'2" x 13'2"
Bedroom 4	3.3 x 4.0 – 10'10" x 13'2"

134 sq.m./1440 sq.ft. — *The copyright belongs to Kingpost Design Co* — **Chedworth**

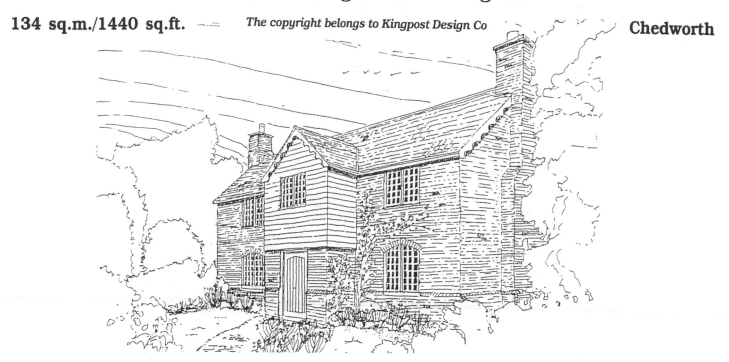

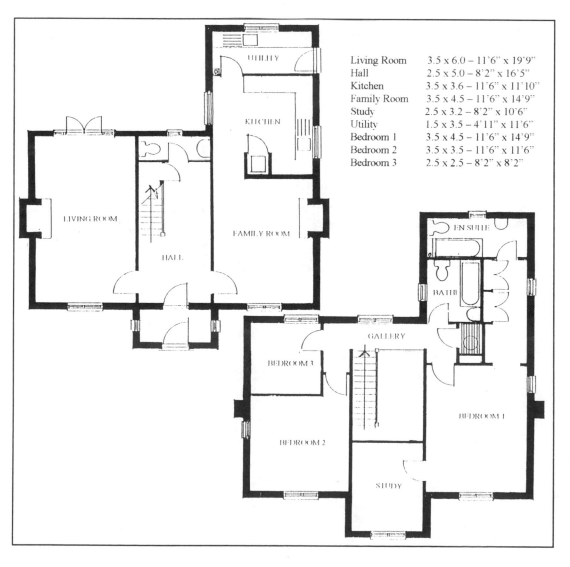

Living Room	3.5 x 6.0 – 11'6" x 19'9"
Hall	2.5 x 5.0 – 8'2" x 16'5"
Kitchen	3.5 x 3.6 – 11'6" x 11'10"
Family Room	3.5 x 4.5 – 11'6" x 14'9"
Study	2.5 x 3.2 – 8'2" x 10'6"
Utility	1.5 x 3.5 – 4'11" x 11'6"
Bedroom 1	3.5 x 4.5 – 11'6" x 14'9"
Bedroom 2	3.5 x 3.5 – 11'6" x 11'6"
Bedroom 3	2.5 x 2.5 – 8'2" x 8'2"

A compact three bedroom house with attractive arched windows and a timber finish over the entrance. The master bedroom has an en suite bathroom, dressing area with wardrobes and an adjoining study, which could also be used as a nursery or sewing room. Downstairs the large family room with inglenook fireplace provides the perfect surroundings for cosy family life.

160 sq.m./1718 sq.ft.   *The copyright belongs to Kingpost Design Co*   **Cheltenham**

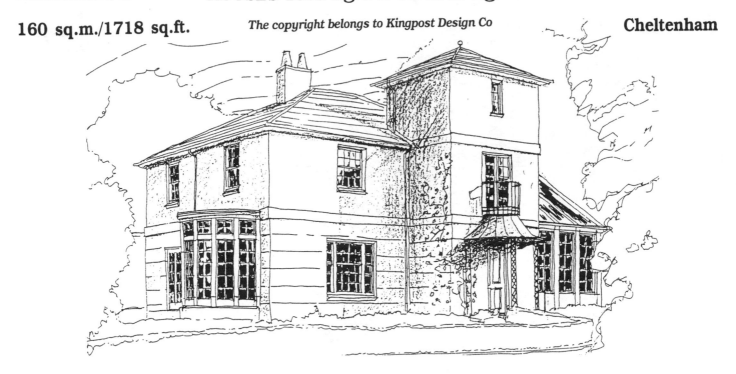

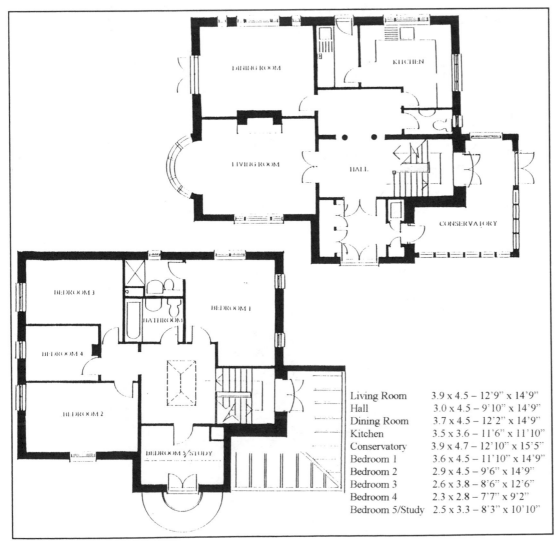

This is a spacious and comfortable family home with five bedrooms and a conservatory. The conservatory wraps round the house and allows light through the staircase via French doors. The tower is an attractive feature that not only acts as a focal point but also provides storage on the upper level. There are generous reception rooms with either French windows leading to the garden or walk in bay windows.

Living Room	3.9 x 4.5	12'9" x 14'9"
Hall	3.0 x 4.5	9'10" x 14'9"
Dining Room	3.7 x 4.5	12'2" x 14'9"
Kitchen	3.5 x 3.6	11'6" x 11'10"
Conservatory	3.9 x 4.7	12'10" x 15'5"
Bedroom 1	3.6 x 4.5	11'10" x 14'9"
Bedroom 2	2.9 x 4.5	9'6" x 14'9"
Bedroom 3	2.6 x 3.8	8'6" x 12'6"
Bedroom 4	2.3 x 2.8	7'7" x 9'2"
Bedroom 5/Study	2.5 x 3.3	8'3" x 10'10"

1700 sq. ft.

The copyright belongs to Kingpost Design Co

Whithington

Living Room	3.9 x 6.5	12'10" x 21'4"
Hall	2.4 x 5.2	7'10" x 17'1"
Dining Room	4.0 x 5.2	13'2" x 17'1"
Kitchen	4.0 x 3.9	13'2" x 12'10"
Study	3.1 x 4.0	10'2" x 13'2"
Master Bedroom	4.1 x 5.6	13'6" x 18'5"
Bedroom 2	3.7 x 6.6	12'2" x 21'8"
Bedroom 3	3.2 x 4.0	10'6" x 13'2"
Bedroom 4	3.3 x 4.0	10'10" x 13'2"

The traditional Georgian style lends character to this elegant four bedroom house with plenty of storage space. The large living room has French doors opening to the garden. The dining room has curved walls in the 18th century manner, with niches to display ornaments and an alcove for the sideboard.

1720 sq. ft.

The copyright belongs to Kingpost Design Co

Burford

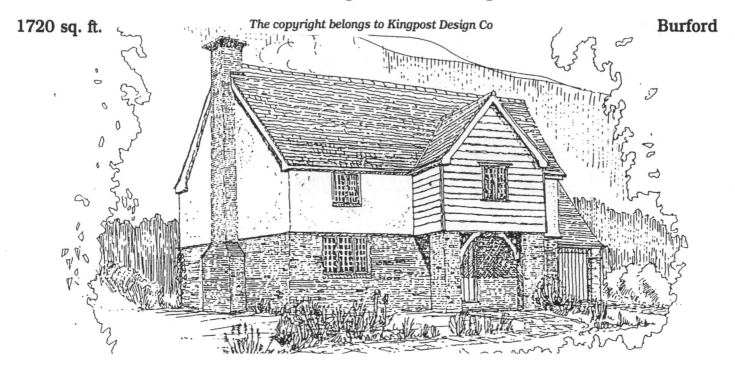

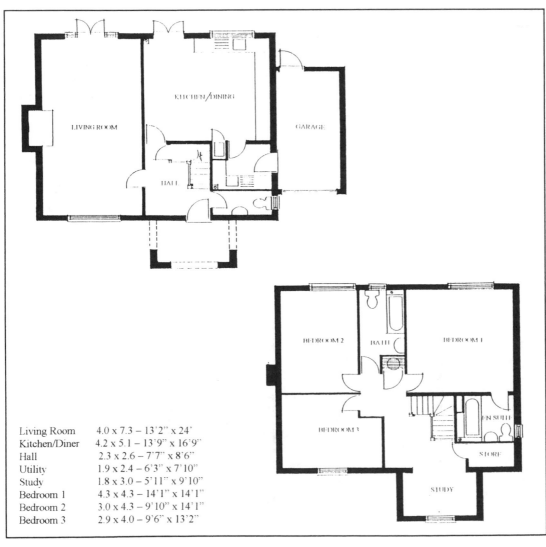

An ideal plan for a small house on a small site which still provides for three good sized bedrooms, a large kitchen/diner and a good sized living room. In order to further save space on the site the garage is attached to the house. The area over the porch provides a study which could be used as a comfortable sitting area.

Living Room	4.0 x 7.3 – 13'2" x 24'
Kitchen/Diner	4.2 x 5.1 – 13'9" x 16'9"
Hall	2.3 x 2.6 – 7'7" x 8'6"
Utility	1.9 x 2.4 – 6'3" x 7'10"
Study	1.8 x 3.0 – 5'11" x 9'10"
Bedroom 1	4.3 x 4.3 – 14'1" x 14'1"
Bedroom 2	3.0 x 4.3 – 9'10" x 14'1"
Bedroom 3	2.9 x 4.0 – 9'6" x 13'2"

158 sq. m.

The copyright belongs to Border Oak

Magnolia Cottage

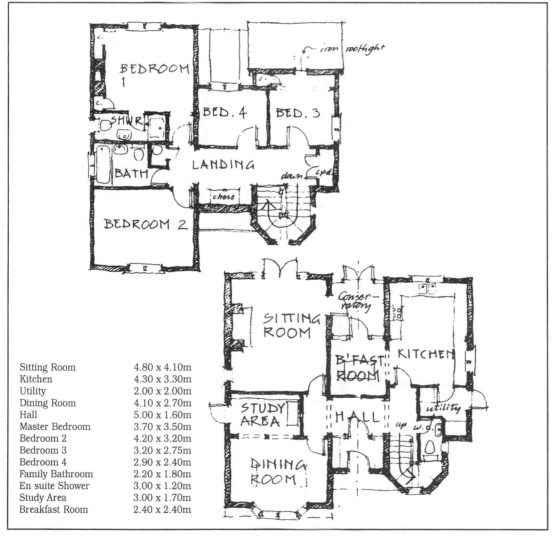

BEDROOM 1

SHWR

BED. 4

BED. 3

iron rooflight

BATH

LANDING

down

cpd

chest

BEDROOM 2

Conservatory

SITTING ROOM

KITCHEN

B'FAST ROOM

STUDY AREA

HALL

utility

up

w.c.

DINING ROOM

Sitting Room	4.80 x 4.10m
Kitchen	4.30 x 3.30m
Utility	2.00 x 2.00m
Dining Room	4.10 x 2.70m
Hall	5.00 x 1.60m
Master Bedroom	3.70 x 3.50m
Bedroom 2	4.20 x 3.20m
Bedroom 3	3.20 x 2.75m
Bedroom 4	2.90 x 2.40m
Family Bathroom	2.20 x 1.80m
En suite Shower	3.00 x 1.20m
Study Area	3.00 x 1.70m
Breakfast Room	2.40 x 2.40m

A cottage with intriguing detailing. First floor tile hanging permits a jetty which shelters a bay window, a faceted stairtower produces an unusual staircase. A galleried landing looks down on an entrance lobby with stained glass screens. A spacious kitchen leads via an exuberant plaster archway to a small breakfast room with access to a conservatory with French doors to the garden. The ground floor includes sitting room, study area and dining room as well as cloak-room and utility areas. The first floor includes master bedroom with shower room, three other bedrooms and a family bathroom. An unusual building equally at home in an urban or rural setting.

160 sq. m.

The copyright belongs to Border Oak

Whitton Court

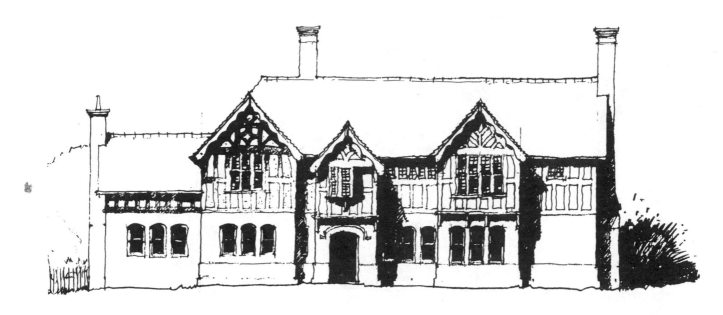

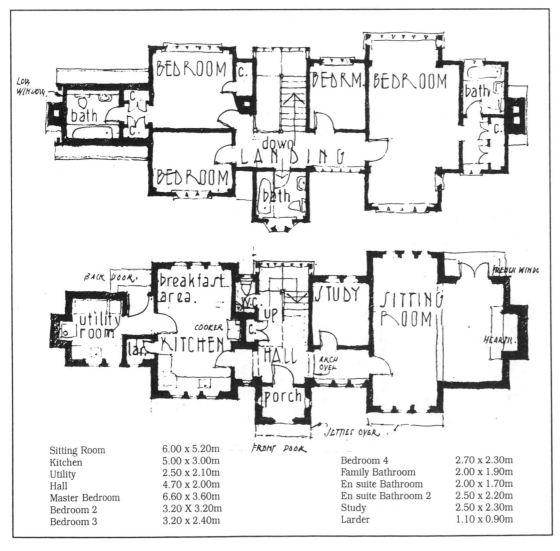

Sitting Room	6.00 x 5.20m		Bedroom 4	2.70 x 2.30m
Kitchen	5.00 x 3.00m		Family Bathroom	2.00 x 1.90m
Utility	2.50 x 2.10m		En suite Bathroom	2.00 x 1.70m
Hall	4.70 x 2.00m		En suite Bathroom 2	2.50 x 2.20m
Master Bedroom	6.60 x 3.60m		Study	2.50 x 2.30m
Bedroom 2	3.20 X 3.20m		Larder	1.10 x 0.90m
Bedroom 3	3.20 x 2.40m			

An Edwardian manor house in the Tudor style. A porch with an arched entrance gives access to the hall with staircase and long gallery. A feature of the ground floor are the triple banks of sash windows with arched heads. The large sitting room features a full inglenook with French windows to the side. The study could double as a working office, the kitchen and breakfast area would be recognised by Mrs. Beaton. The master bedroom has 'sitting alcoves' housed in attractive gables with dressing room and en suite bathroom. Bedroom 2 has its own en suite facilities and bedrooms 3 and 4 share a family bathroom.

1710 sq. ft./159 sq. m.

The copyright belongs to Border Oak

Bathcott House

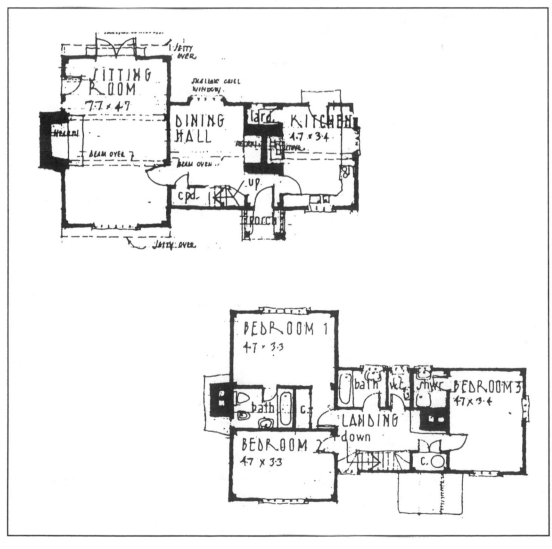

You can almost imagine that if buildings could ask for comfort they would plead to be covered in thatch. Hunkered down under its pale golden comforter, bonneted and shawled, this house, with its massive inglenooks, the warm, woodbroken walls, the reassuring sculptures of its beams, is the epitome of cosiness.

61.98 sq. m.

9.87m x 6.28m

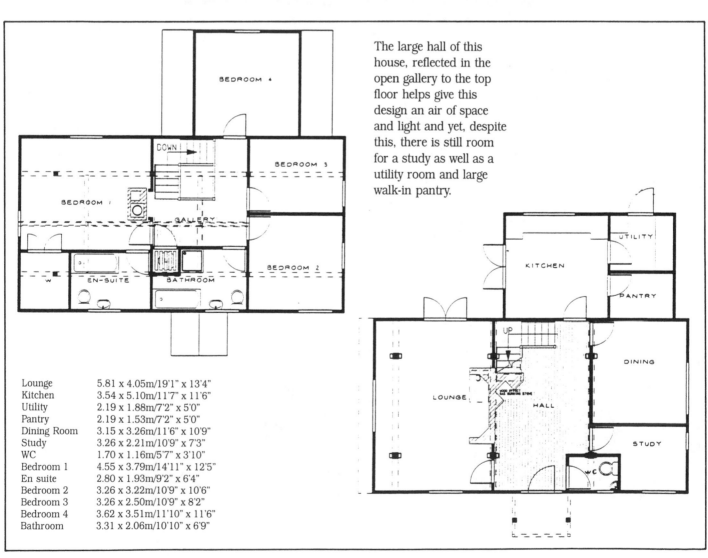

The large hall of this house, reflected in the open gallery to the top floor helps give this design an air of space and light and yet, despite this, there is still room for a study as well as a utility room and large walk-in pantry.

Lounge	5.81 x 4.05m/19'1" x 13'4"
Kitchen	3.54 x 5.10m/11'7" x 11'6"
Utility	2.19 x 1.88m/7'2" x 5'0"
Pantry	2.19 x 1.53m/7'2" x 5'0"
Dining Room	3.15 x 3.26m/11'6" x 10'9"
Study	3.26 x 2.21m/10'9" x 7'3"
WC	1.70 x 1.16m/5'7" x 3'10"
Bedroom 1	4.55 x 3.79m/14'11" x 12'5"
En suite	2.80 x 1.93m/9'2" x 6'4"
Bedroom 2	3.26 x 3.22m/10'9" x 10'6"
Bedroom 3	3.26 x 2.50m/10'9" x 8'2"
Bedroom 4	3.62 x 3.51m/11'10" x 11'6"
Bathroom	3.31 x 2.06m/10'10" x 6'9"

113.81 sq. m.
10.87m x 10.47m

The copyright belongs to Potton Ltd.

97-002

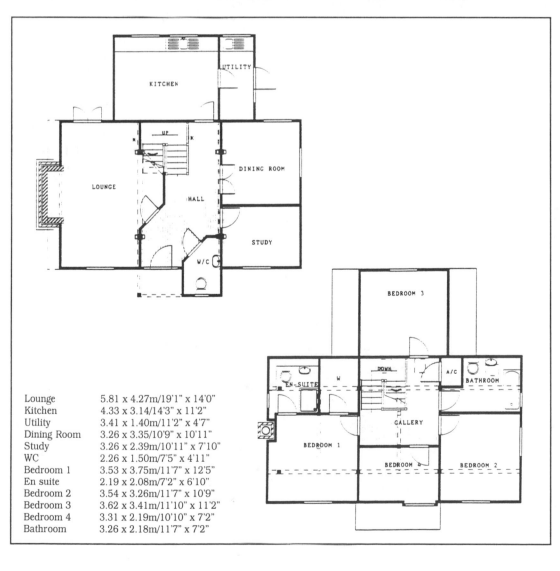

The half landing stair-
case arrangement gives
interest to the hallway,
creates a central upstairs
gallery and allows extra
space to be devoted to
the lounge in this
interesting family house.
The double aspect of the
dining room means that
the house could be set
on quite a narrow plot or
that a garage could quite
easily be attached to that
side.

Lounge	5.81 x 4.27m/19'1" x 14'0"
Kitchen	4.33 x 3.14/14'3" x 11'2"
Utility	3.41 x 1.40m/11'2" x 4'7"
Dining Room	3.26 x 3.35/10'9" x 10'11"
Study	3.26 x 2.39m/10'11" x 7'10"
WC	2.26 x 1.50m/7'5" x 4'11"
Bedroom 1	3.53 x 3.75m/11'7" x 12'5"
En suite	2.19 x 2.08m/7'2" x 6'10"
Bedroom 2	3.54 x 3.26m/11'7" x 10'9"
Bedroom 3	3.62 x 3.41m/11'10" x 11'2"
Bedroom 4	3.31 x 2.19m/10'10" x 7'2"
Bathroom	3.26 x 2.18m/11'7" x 7'2"

103.20 sq. m.

8.48m x 12.17m

97-063

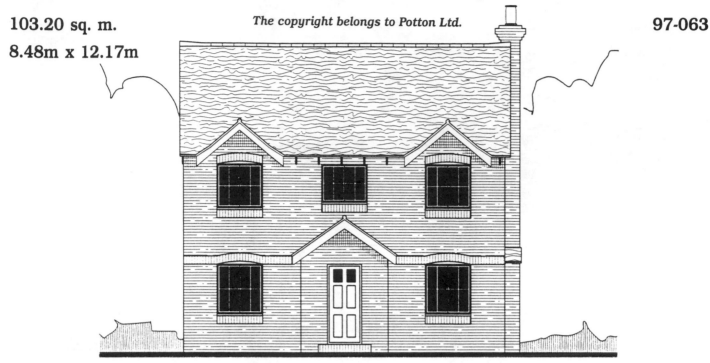

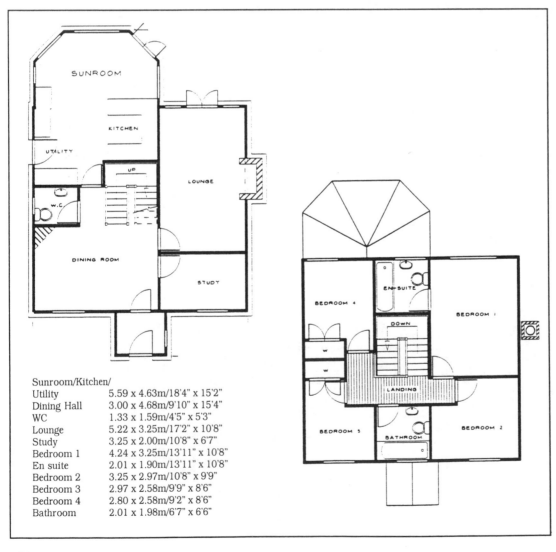

Sunroom/Kitchen/	
Utility	5.59 x 4.63m/18'4" x 15'2"
Dining Hall	3.00 x 4.68m/9'10" x 15'4"
WC	1.33 x 1.59m/4'5" x 5'3"
Lounge	5.22 x 3.25m/17'2" x 10'8"
Study	3.25 x 2.00m/10'8" x 6'7"
Bedroom 1	4.24 x 3.25m/13'11" x 10'8"
En suite	2.01 x 1.90m/13'11" x 10'8"
Bedroom 2	3.25 x 2.97m/10'8" x 9'9"
Bedroom 3	2.97 x 2.58m/9'9" x 8'6"
Bedroom 4	2.80 x 2.58m/9'2" x 8'6"
Bathroom	2.01 x 1.98m/6'7" x 6'6"

The whole ethos of this house revolves around the magnificent sunroom extension to the kitchen living area. The dining/hall might not appeal to everybody but, combined with the separate storm porch, provides an economical use of space. An ideal family house where the main activities of day to day living can be kept apart from the quieter reception rooms of the lounge and study.

74.36 sq. m.

7.37m x 10.09m

The copyright belongs to Potton Ltd.

97-190

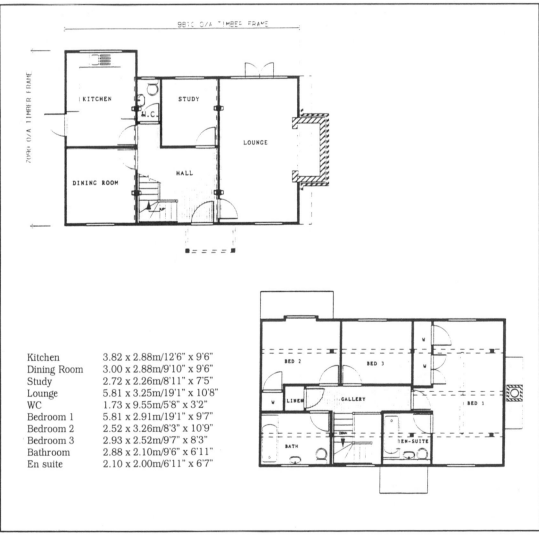

Although designated as a study, the size of the room means that it could well double up as a proper family room or second lounge for the children. The master bedroom suite is quite large in comparison with the rest of the upper part.

Kitchen	3.82 x 2.88m/12'6" x 9'6"
Dining Room	3.00 x 2.88m/9'10" x 9'6"
Study	2.72 x 2.26m/8'11" x 7'5"
Lounge	5.81 x 3.25m/19'1" x 10'8"
WC	1.73 x 9.55m/5'8" x 3'2"
Bedroom 1	5.81 x 2.91m/19'1" x 9'7"
Bedroom 2	2.52 x 3.26m/8'3" x 10'9"
Bedroom 3	2.93 x 2.52m/9'7" x 8'3"
Bathroom	2.88 x 2.10m/9'6" x 6'11"
En suite	2.10 x 2.00m/6'11" x 6'7"

133.81 sq. m.
10.47m x 12.78m

The copyright belongs to Potton Ltd.

98-002

Kitchen/	
Breakfast	5.75 x 6.31m/18'10" x 20'9"
Utility	1.83 x 3.01m/6'0" x 9'10"
Study	2.50 x 4.56m/8'2" x 15'0"
WC	2.06 x 2.26m/6'9" x 7'5"
Dining/	
Lounge	5.56 x 8.01m/ 18'3" x 26'3"
Master Bed	3.76 x 4.46m/12'4" x 14'8"
Wardrobe	1.85 x 1.96m/5'11" x 6'5"
En suite	1.96 x 2.56m/6'5" x 8'5"
Bathroom	2.13 x 2.32m/7'0" x 7'7"
Bedroom 2	3.12 x 3.26m/10'3" x 10'9"
Bedroom 3	2.60 x 3.26m/8'6" x 10'9"
Bedroom 4	3.01 x 4.00m/9'10" x 13'1"

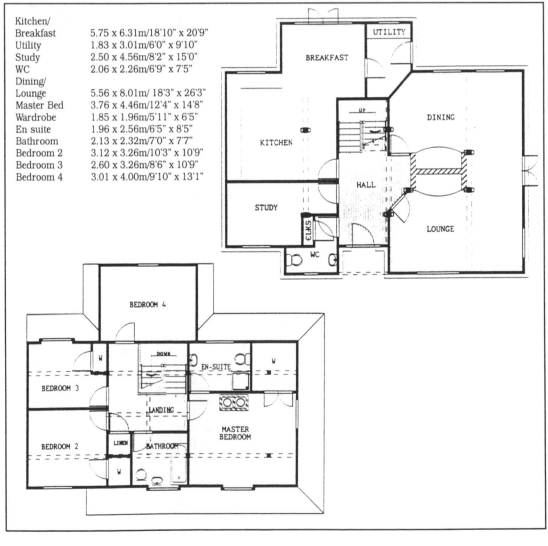

What an interesting layout this has to the ground floor, with its double fireplace linking the dining and lounge areas and the offset layout of the kitchen breakfast areas. Upstairs the accommodation provides a generous master suite in combination with three other double bedrooms.

246.93 sq. m. 15.89m x 15.54m

97-201

The copyright belongs to Potton Ltd.

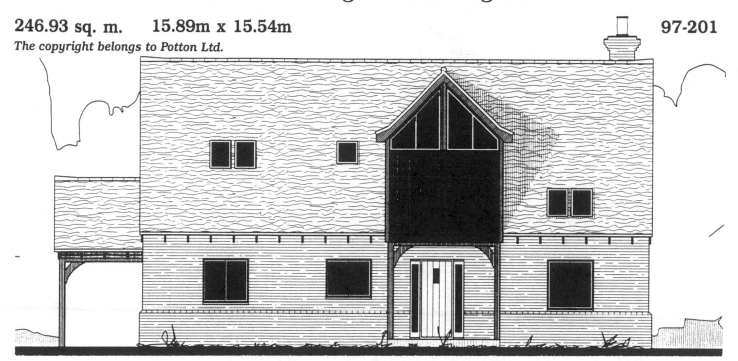

Kitchen/Breakfast

Room	5.56 x 6.17m/18'3" x 20'3"
Dining	3.87 x 6.53m/12'8" x 21'5"
Utility	2.40 x 2.83m/7'10" x 9'4"
Lounge	3.61 x 6.05m/11'10" x 19'10"
Study	2.44 x 3.61m/8'0" x 11'10"
Shower Room	1.83 x 2.64m/6'0" x 8'7"
Bedroom 1	2.74 x 3.81m/9'0" x 12'6"
Bedroom 2	2.82 x 3.81m/ 9'3" x 12'6"
Bedroom 4/	
Dressing Rm	8.01 x 4.10m/26'3" x 13'5"
En suite	2.67 x 3.04m/8'9" x 10'0"
Bedroom 3	2.79 x 4.58m/9'2" x 15'0"
Bathroom	1.80 x 2.75m/5'11" x 9'0"

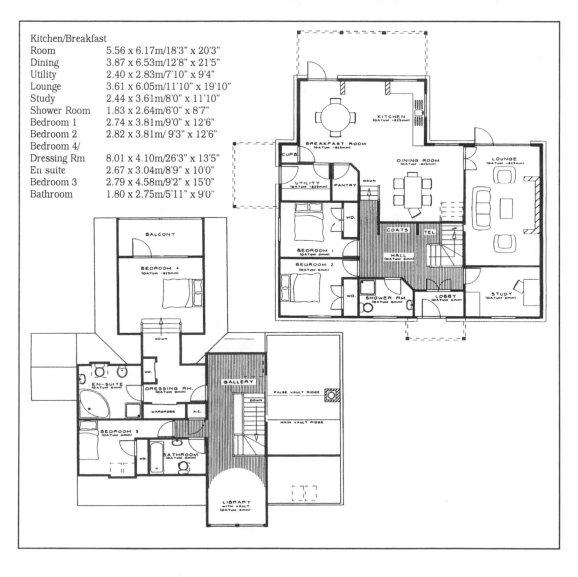

The gallery/library is the dominant architectural feature to the front elevation of this family house and inside it continues to provide a focal point to the design. A closer, look, however, will reveal the versatile nature of the accommodation and the fact that so many of the bedrooms have en suite facilities.

97.87 sq. m.

7.37m x 13.28m

The copyright belongs to Potton Ltd.

91-136

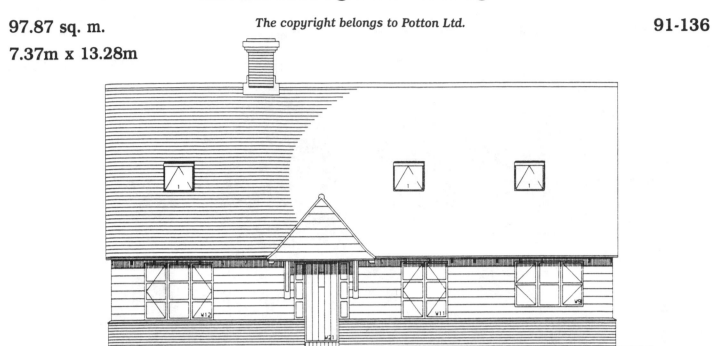

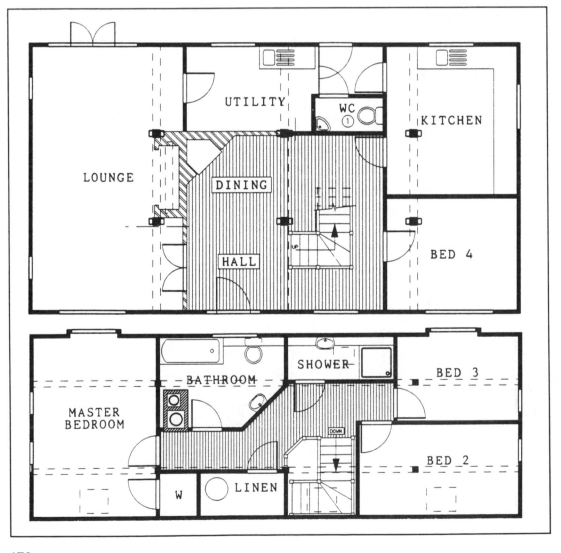

Clever use of the idea of a dining hall means that most of the major rooms to the ground floor can be grouped around and off it. The external appearance of the house also means that it could find favour in a planning situation where a bungalow would have been preferred.

Kitchen	3.42 x 3.91m
Utility	2.26 x 5.20m
WC	9.00 x 1.80m
Lounge	4.02 x 6.91m
Master Bed	3.26 x 4.71m
Bedroom 2	2.40 x 4.18m
Bedroom 3	2.22 x 3.19m
Bedroom 4	2.90 x 3.42m
Bathroom	2.37 x 3.31m
Shower Rm	1.13 x 2.78m

1575 sq. ft.
45 ft. x 28 ft.

The copyright belongs to Design & Materials Ltd.

Elsworth

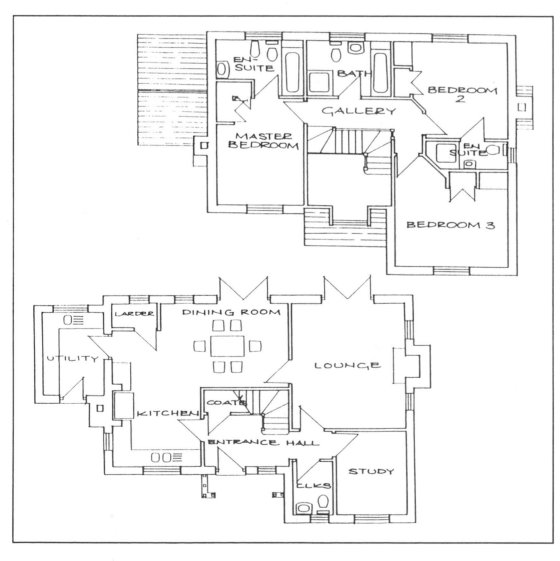

This delightful cottage style design will appeal to individuals who prefer three larger bedrooms although the layout is flexible enough to include a fourth bedroom if required. The main features are the open plan kitchen/family/dining room with Aga range and upper gallery which is open to the hall below. The main bedroom includes a full en suite bathroom.

1598 sq. ft.

39 ft. x 25 ft.

Marbury

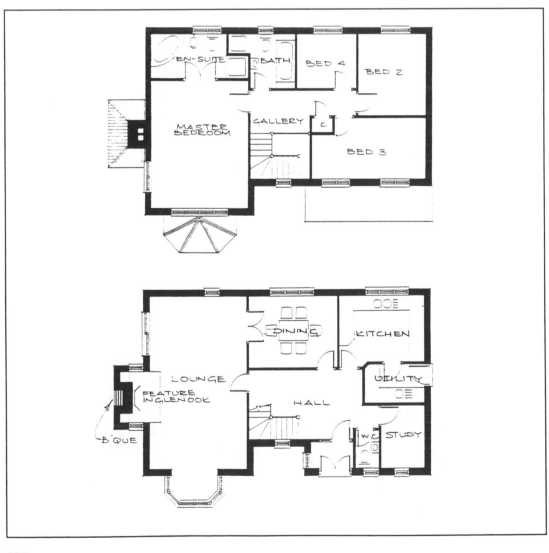

This design was drawn up to suit a plot of limited depth and the resultant short roof span means a relatively low ridge height.

The overall height of a dwelling can often be of concern to planning officers, particularly in infill situations.

1650 sq. ft.

42 ft. x 50 ft.

The copyright belongs to Design & Materials Ltd.

Harborough

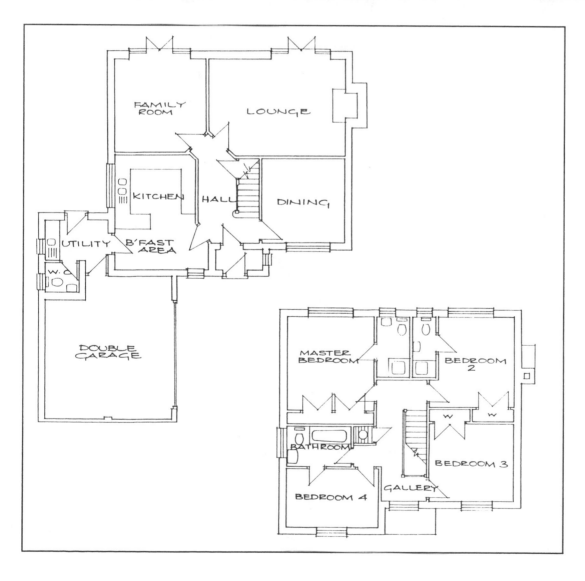

This traditional family home will fit comfortably on a plot well under 50' wide. The garage is sited to the front, of and at right angles to, the house, creating a natural courtyard and turning area.

173

1750 sq. ft./163 sq. m.

Stratton

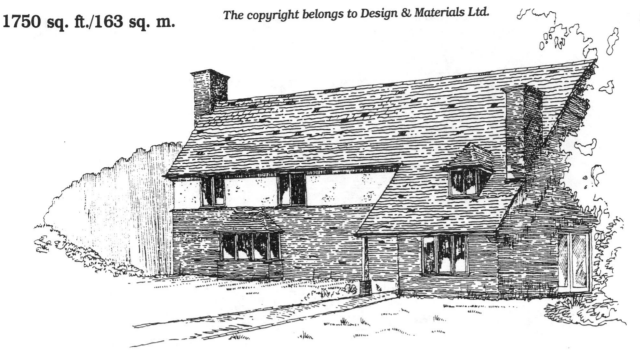

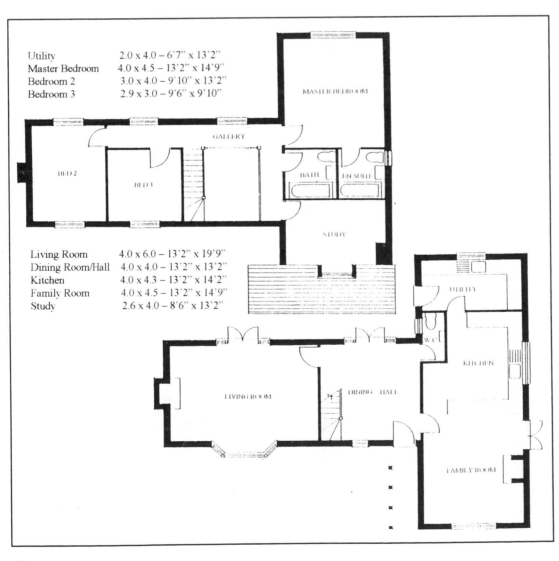

Utility	2.0 x 4.0 – 6'7" x 13'2"	
Master Bedroom	4.0 x 4.5 – 13'2" x 14'9"	
Bedroom 2	3.0 x 4.0 – 9'10" x 13'2"	
Bedroom 3	2.9 x 3.0 – 9'6" x 9'10"	

Living Room	4.0 x 6.0 – 13'2" x 19'9"	
Dining Room/Hall	4.0 x 4.0 – 13'2" x 13'2"	
Kitchen	4.0 x 4.3 – 13'2" x 14'2"	
Family Room	4.0 x 4.5 – 13'2" x 14'9"	
Study	2.6 x 4.0 – 8'6" x 13'2"	

A design based on old cottage architecture, with a long 'cat slide' roof on the front sheltering the front door. The design shown here is in brick and render, but other materials would look equally well, perhaps stone and half timbering or brick and dark stained boarding. The large dining/hall opens on to the rear terrace and the kitchen is combined with a good sized family room with its own fireplace which would be perfect for a woodburning stove. The study on the first floor could well serve as a fourth bedroom.

1752 sq. ft./163 sq. m.   *The copyright belongs to Kingpost Design Co*   **Batsford**

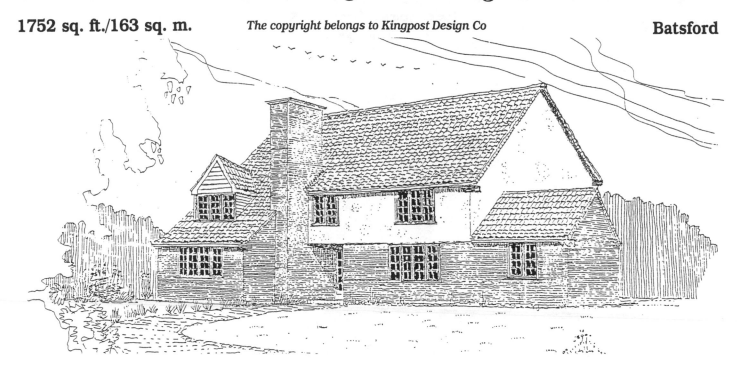

Living Room	4.0 x 6.0 – 13'2" x 19'9"
Hall	3.0 x 3.1 – 9'10" x 10'2"
Dining Room	3.0 x 4.0 – 9'10" x 13'2"
Kitchen/Family Room	4.0 x 6.5 – 13'2" x 21'4"
Utility	2.5 x 3.0 – 8'3" x 9'10"
Bedroom 1	3.4 x 5.1 – 11'2" x 16'9"
Bedroom 2	3.9 x 4.0 – 12'10" x 13'2"
Bedroom 3	3.0 x 4.0 – 9'10" x 13'2"

A clean, contemporary design given emphasis by the massive chimney stack next to the front door. Here the main idea has been to provide generous, uncramped space without attempting to maximise the number of rooms. The three bedrooms are all well sized and can each easily accommodate a double bed. The large landing gets light from both back and front and the large kitchen/family room is the perfect 'heart of the home' for the family.

1740 sq. ft.

The copyright belongs to ASBA
Reed Architects

Clunton

This handsome house suits a village location. The generous lounge is better with a higher than average ceiling height and the deep-cilled windows take advantage of country views.

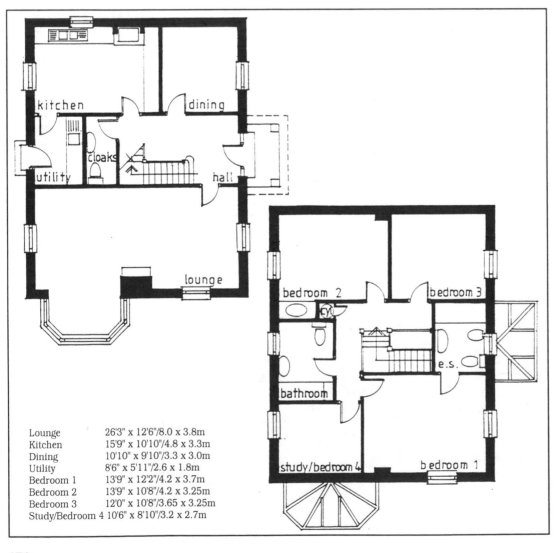

Lounge	26'3" x 12'6"/8.0 x 3.8m
Kitchen	15'9" x 10'10"/4.8 x 3.3m
Dining	10'10" x 9'10"/3.3 x 3.0m
Utility	8'6" x 5'11"/2.6 x 1.8m
Bedroom 1	13'9" x 12'2"/4.2 x 3.7m
Bedroom 2	13'9" x 10'8"/4.2 x 3.25m
Bedroom 3	12'0" x 10'8"/3.65 x 3.25m
Study/Bedroom 4	10'6" x 8'10"/3.2 x 2.7m

176

1615 sq. ft./150 sq. m.   *The copyright belongs to Border Oak*   ## Longmeadow Farm

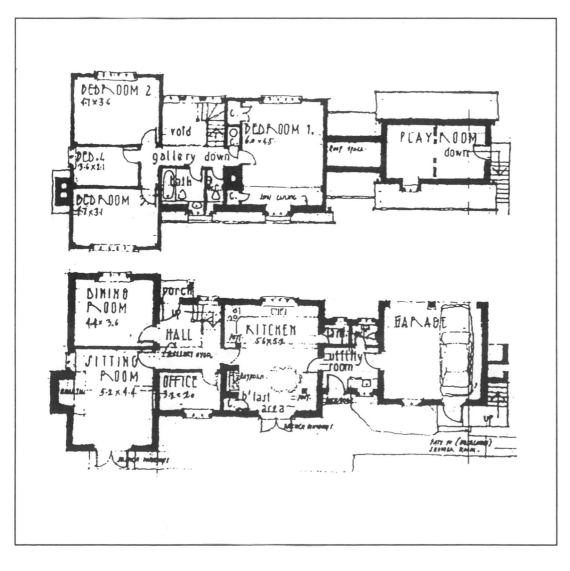

A spacious, fluid, linear design, reminiscent of an improved Border longhouse. The stepping of the ridge heights, and the graduation of materials, oak framing, warm red brick, and weatherboarding, impart an architectural harmony to the whole. The only additions required are the slow growth of moss, and the embracing spread of wisteria.

1738 sq. ft./161 sq. m.

The copyright belongs to Custom Homes

Newbury

The spacious hall of this family home would give it a grandeur that it well deserved.

1738 sq. ft./161 sq. m.

The copyright belongs to Custom Homes

Cambridge

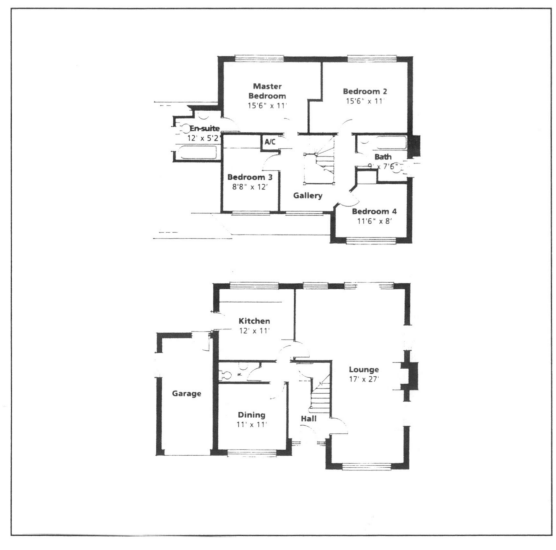

A house design that could fit in a suburban street scene as well as a more rural situation. The large lounge area could just as easily be subdivided to provide a study and an exciting feature of the design is the open and well lit gallery.

1516 sq. ft./141 sq. m.

The copyright belongs to Custom Homes

Bleaklow

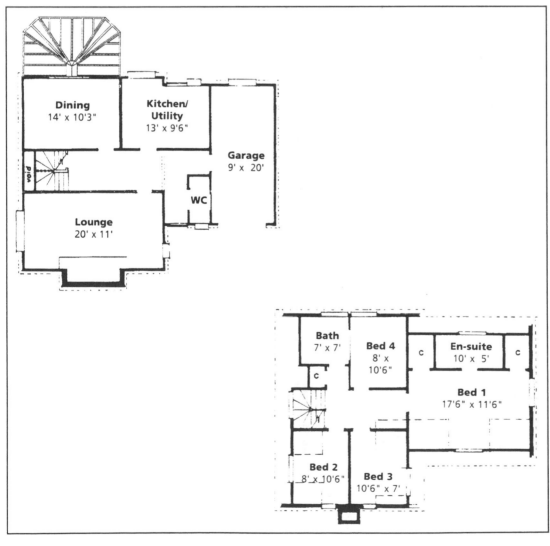

Compact and attractive accommodation is provided in this neat house where the large master suite is self contained as a large proportion of the upper part. The illustration of the lounge with its windows to the two sides, means that there would have to be a reasonable distance to the side boundaries but, having said that, there's room for one or more windows to the front elevation if required.

The copyright belongs to Custom Homes

1540 sq. ft./143 sq. m.

Petworth

The attachment of the garage on the side of this house allows for the provision of the generous en-suite accommodation to the main bedroom and also serves to take off some of the symmetry from the external appearance. The cat slide roof would also help if the site was one where the property to that side was, say, a bungalow, serving to create a visual bridge between the two different dwelling types.

1641 sq. ft./152 sq. m.

The copyright belongs to Custom Homes

Harringworth

A very nicely proportioned family house with a lovely and generously sized kitchen area. If a study wasn't needed then this could very easily become a breakfast room or else a utility room. With no windows to any of the side elevations, this house could fit on quite a small plot.

1540 sq. ft./143 sq. m.

The copyright belongs to Custom Homes

Diplomat

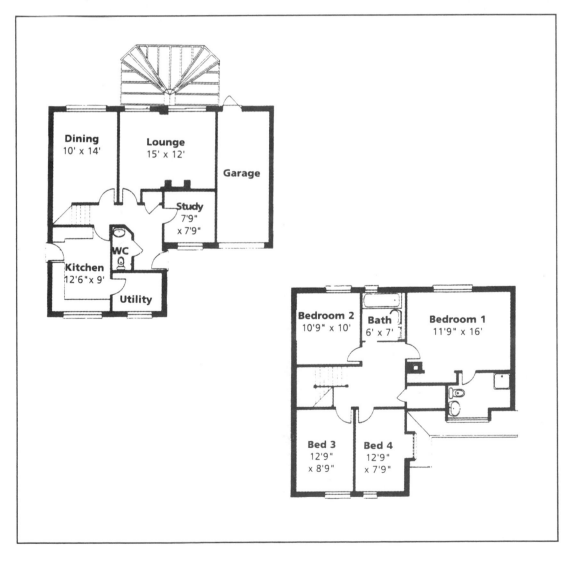

There's a lot of accommodation in this compact, yet impressive, design and with the inclusion of the garage within the main body of the house it's eminently suitable for a reasonably sized plot. The kitchen and utility areas are brought to the front of the house leaving the major reception rooms and the principal bedrooms free to enjoy the garden views.

Dining
10' x 14'

Lounge
15' x 12'

Garage

Study
7'9"
x 7'9"

WC

Kitchen
12'6" x 9'

Utility

Bedroom 2
10'9" x 10'

Bath
6' x 7'

Bedroom 1
11'9" x 16'

Bed 3
12'9"
x 8'9"

Bed 4
12'9"
x 7'9"

1650 sq. ft./153 sq. m.

The copyright belongs to Custom Homes

Wilmington

A modern house that has overtones of immediate post war design, as far as the external appearance is concerned. Indoors this is reflected in the layout of the ground floor. The upper part, on the other hand is essentially modern in concept with the provision of three almost equally sized bedrooms and a generous master suite.

The copyright belongs to Swedish Homes

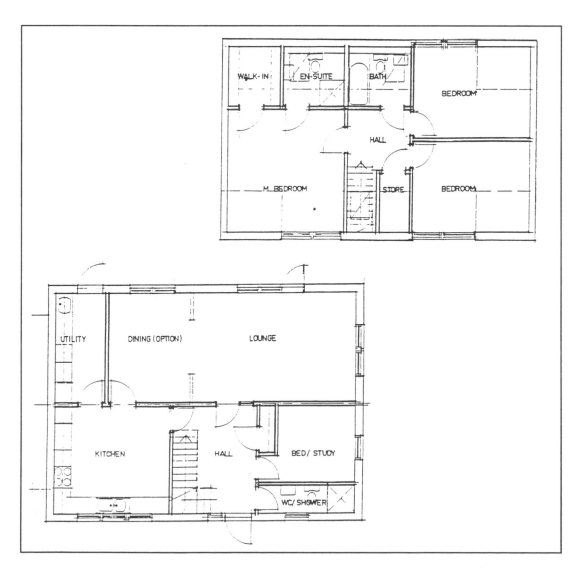

An energy efficient and cost effective design that, nevertheless, manages to provide interesting and spacious living accommodation. The ground floor bedroom could just as easily have the wc/ shower room incorporated as an ensuite, making it suitable for an older or infirm person's occupation.

Houses 1751 – 2000 sq. ft.

Houses of this size are, perhaps, part of the group that forms the largest contingent of self built homes and, for many, this is the size of home that personifies the ideal size for a family house. As such, the provision of a study as part of the ground floor layout and the extension of the kitchen area to include a breakfast room or, at the very least a dining area within the kitchen, is almost standard.

The bedrooms, if they are to stay as four in number, start to all be double rooms and there is often space for fitted wardrobes to each of them with the master suite, sometimes having space for a dressing room.

With the house getting bigger, the garage, as a proportion of its size, becomes less intrusive and can therefore take its place as part and parcel of the overall design. This can either be as an attached bungalow section or, on the larger plots, it can form a proper outhouse as a detached entity bearing a distinct architectural relationship to the main structure.

Contributors in this section:

ASBA Timothy Mostyn
ASBA Reed Architects
ASBA Andrew Smith Associates
Border Oak
Custom Homes
Design & Materials Ltd.
Designer Homes
Kingpost Design Co
Scandia-Hus

1800 sq. ft.

The copyright belongs to ASBA
Timothy Mostyn

North Shropshire

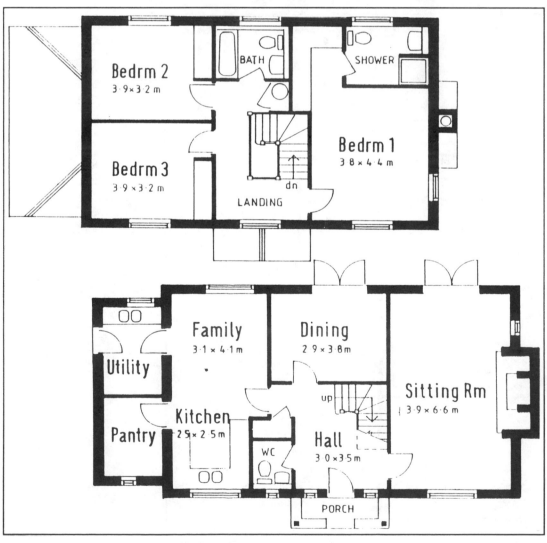

Bedrm 2
3·9 × 3·2 m

BATH

SHOWER

Bedrm 3
3·9 × 3·2 m

Bedrm 1
3·8 × 4·4 m

dn

LANDING

Utility

Family
3·1 × 4·1 m

Dining
2·9 × 3·8 m

Sitting Rm
3·9 × 6·6 m

up

Pantry

Kitchen
2·5 × 2·5 m

WC

Hall
3·0 × 3·5 m

PORCH

This cottage style home has traditional brick detailing and small clay tiles on the roof and is complimented internally with oak floor boards, ledge and brace oak doors and black iron latches and hinges. The sitting room features a huge inglenook fireplace. High standards of insulation give this cottage an excellent SAP energy rating.

1800 sq. ft.

Constable Cottage

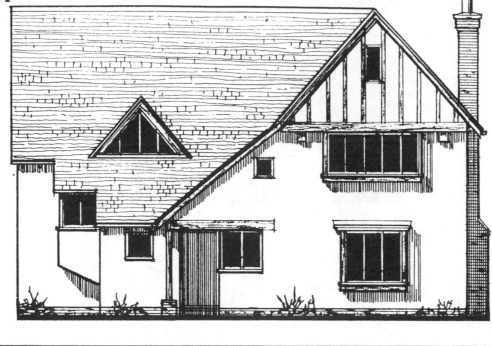

Set in the Constable Country of the Essex/ Suffolk border this replacement village house fits in comfortably with its surroundings. It is of timber frame construction which is honestly expressed externally in places with exposed structural oak beams. The staircase cantilevers out at the side to form an unusual feature. Because of the steeply pitched roof, there is space in the loft to provided ancillary accommodation such as a playroom which could be accessed in the future via a permanent stair- case installed on the generous landing.

1935 sq. ft.

The copyright belongs to ASBA Andrew Smith Associates

Diamond House

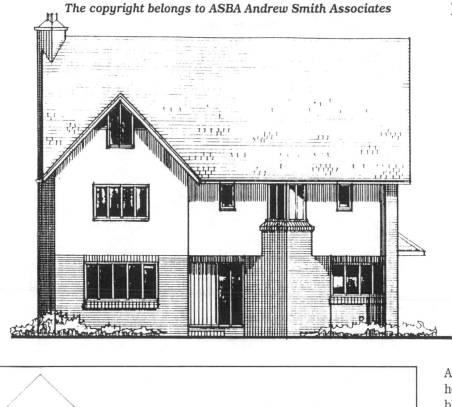

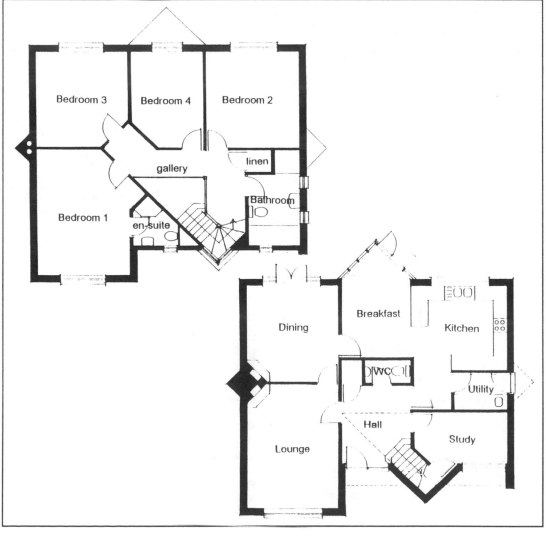

A compact modern house is of brick and block construction and incorporating traditional forms to harmonise with its village setting. Interesting spaces are created by the dramatic diagonal positioning of the staircase which is echoed at the rear by a triangular conservatory projecting from the breakfast room and at the sides by a diamond shaped chimney and small triangular canopy over the utility room door. The huge loft would form an excellent games room and could be fully converted to living accommodation in the future with the addition of a staircase.

189

1841 sq. ft.

The copyright belongs to ASBA
Reed Architects

Cricketwood

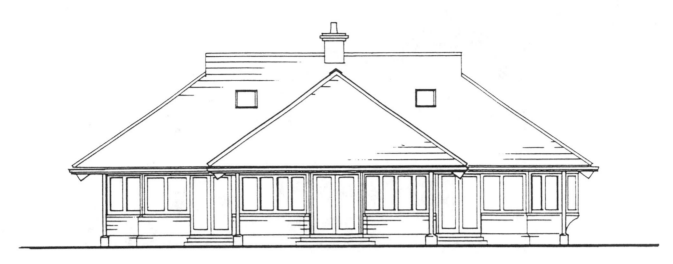

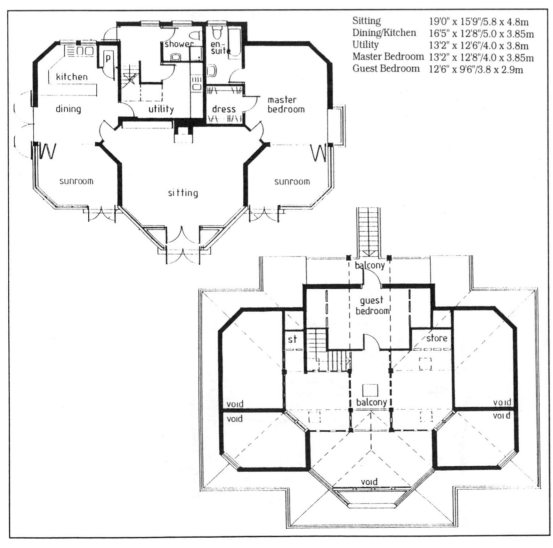

Sitting	19'0" x 15'9"/5.8 x 4.8m
Dining/Kitchen	16'5" x 12'8"/5.0 x 3.85m
Utility	13'2" x 12'6"/4.0 x 3.8m
Master Bedroom	13'2" x 12'8"/4.0 x 3.85m
Guest Bedroom	12'6" x 9'6"/3.8 x 2.9m

An unusual post and beam structure creates the freedom to use the floor either as a gallery or to provide two further bedrooms. The pavilion style incorporates sunrooms that open into the living accommodation to give a climatic buffer zone and provide ideal sitting spaces. This is a house for garden lovers in all seasons.

1894 sq. ft.

The copyright belongs to ASBA
Reed Architects

Bury Park

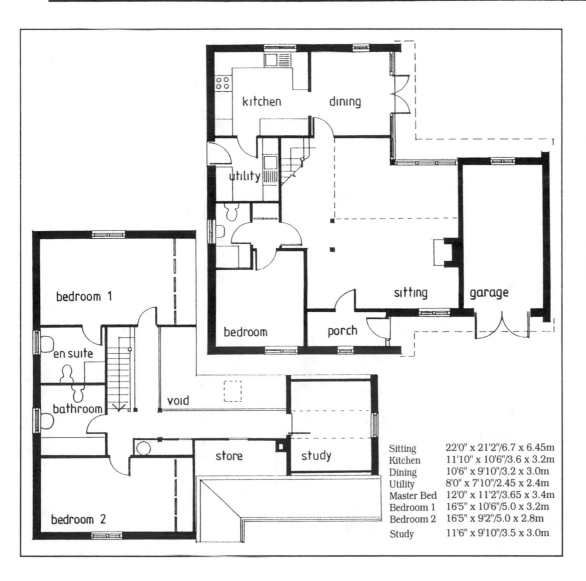

kitchen

dining

utility

bedroom 1

en suite

sitting

garage

bathroom

void

bedroom

porch

store

study

bedroom 2

Many people building a house for retirement require an en suite ground floor bedroom to continue to be able to use the house into old age. This house combines that facility with a galleried living area with first floor accommodation which includes a study over the garage, space often wasted in schemes with detached garages. The south and west facing windows form a sheltered sun trap for outdoor dining.

Sitting	22'0" x 21'2"/6.7 x 6.45m
Kitchen	11'10" x 10'6"/3.6 x 3.2m
Dining	10'6" x 9'10"/3.2 x 3.0m
Utility	8'0" x 7'10"/2.45 x 2.4m
Master Bed	12'0" x 11'2"/3.65 x 3.4m
Bedroom 1	16'5" x 10'6"/5.0 x 3.2m
Bedroom 2	16'5" x 9'2"/5.0 x 2.8m
Study	11'6" x 9'10"/3.5 x 3.0m

185 sq. m.

The copyright belongs to Border Oak

Whitcliffe House

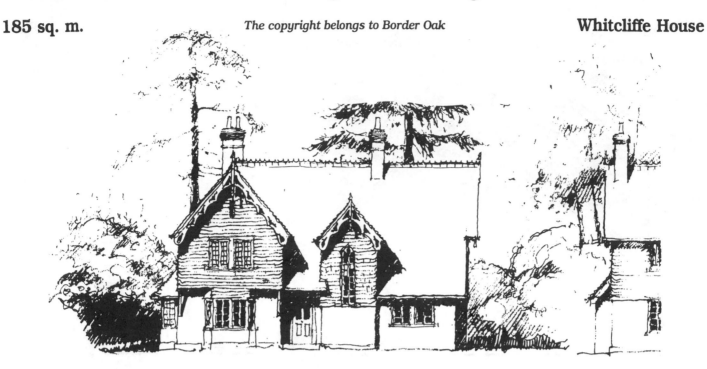

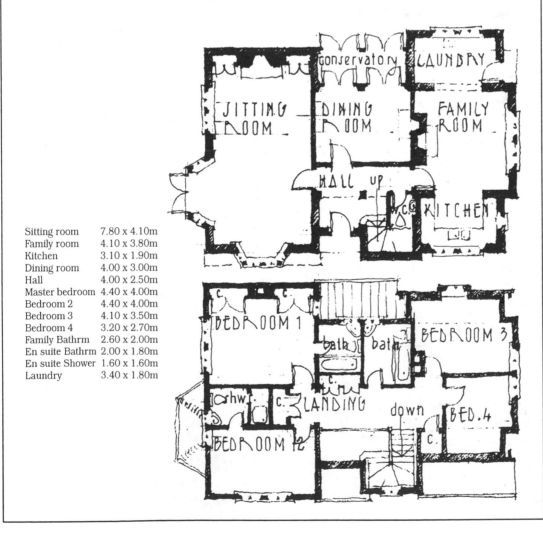

Sitting room	7.80 x 4.10m
Family room	4.10 x 3.80m
Kitchen	3.10 x 1.90m
Dining room	4.00 x 3.00m
Hall	4.00 x 2.50m
Master bedroom	4.40 x 4.00m
Bedroom 2	4.40 x 4.00m
Bedroom 3	4.10 x 3.50m
Bedroom 4	3.20 x 2.70m
Family Bathrm	2.60 x 2.00m
En suite Bathrm	2.00 x 1.80m
En suite Shower	1.60 x 1.60m
Laundry	3.40 x 1.80m

The basic plan is a simple T-shape but is changed with the introduction of a stairtower, front and rear lean-to's and a conservatory in the alcove between the sitting room and the laundry. The external elevations are intriguing. A tile hung gable enables an overhanging jetty which shelters and emphasises the ground floor bay window. A matching bay to the side elevation provides French doors. The kitchen, family room and laundry work well as interconnecting spaces and reinforce the theme of a home for a family. A galleried landing provides efficient circulation to the four bedrooms and three bathrooms. A wealth of cupboards show the thoughtful and practical interior design. A home that works.

170 sq. m.

The copyright belongs to Border Oak

The Smithy

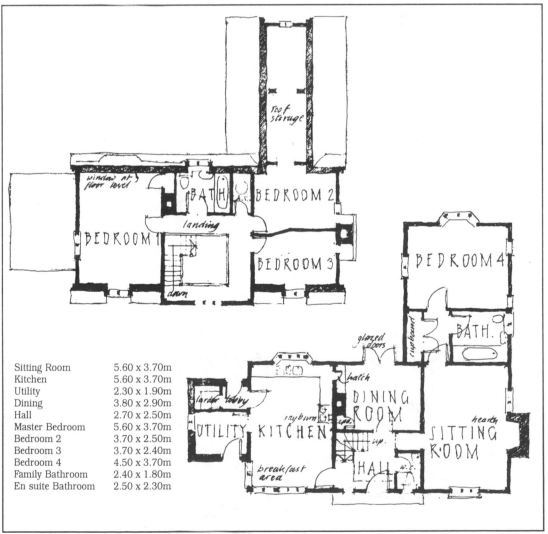

Sitting Room	5.60 x 3.70m
Kitchen	5.60 x 3.70m
Utility	2.30 x 1.90m
Dining	3.80 x 2.90m
Hall	2.70 x 2.50m
Master Bedroom	5.60 x 3.70m
Bedroom 2	3.70 x 2.50m
Bedroom 3	3.70 x 2.40m
Bedroom 4	4.50 x 3.70m
Family Bathroom	2.40 x 1.80m
En suite Bathroom	2.50 x 2.30m

A classic three bay oak framed cottage with coloured panels and oak framing. The subtle textures and colours of the clay tiled roof merge the building with its surroundings. Overhanging gables, dormer windows and random chimney stacks add to the whole. The farmhouse kitchen with breakfast area works on a practical level. The utility room, lobby and larder are typical of the no-nonsense approach. The sitting room is generously proportioned and enhanced by the classic inglenook. A single storey structure design to resemble an outbuilding provides self-contained and private accommodation perhaps for an elderly relative or an independent youngster.

180 sq.m./1934 sq.ft.

The copyright belongs to Kingpost Design Co

Tower House

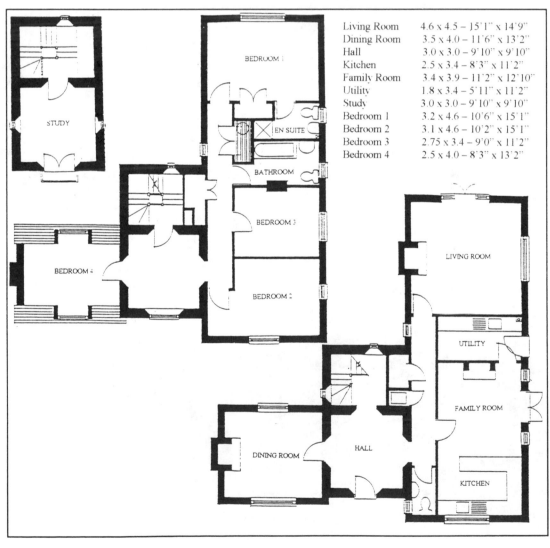

Living Room	4.6 x 4.5	15'1" x 14'9"
Dining Room	3.5 x 4.0	11'6" x 13'2"
Hall	3.0 x 3.0	9'10" x 9'10"
Kitchen	2.5 x 3.4	8'3" x 11'2"
Family Room	3.4 x 3.9	11'2" x 12'10"
Utility	1.8 x 3.4	5'11" x 11'2"
Study	3.0 x 3.0	9'10" x 9'10"
Bedroom 1	3.2 x 4.6	10'6" x 15'1"
Bedroom 2	3.1 x 4.6	10'2" x 15'1"
Bedroom 3	2.75 x 3.4	9'0" x 11'2"
Bedroom 4	2.5 x 4.0	8'3" x 13'2"

The central tower acts as a focal point for this four bedroom house. The top floor of the tower with French windows to a balcony can be used as a study or library. Downstairs a large kitchen/diner, living room and family room gives plenty of space for the family. There is also plenty of storage space in the house.

1960 sq. ft.

The copyright belongs to Kingpost Design Co

Kelmscott

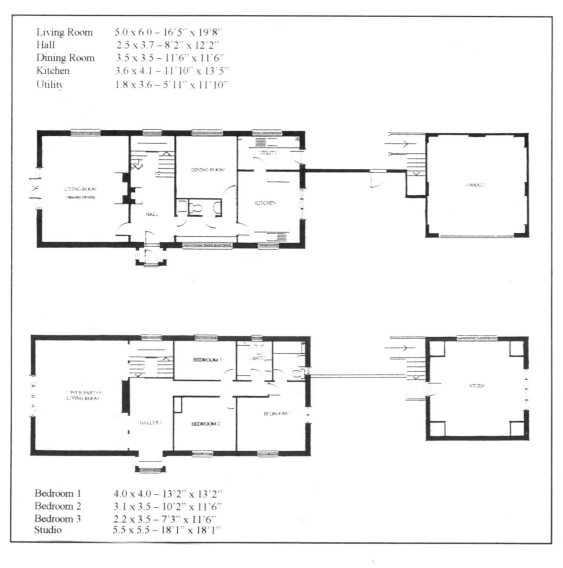

Living Room	5.0 x 6.0 – 16'5" x 19'8"
Hall	2.5 x 3.7 – 8'2" x 12'2"
Dining Room	3.5 x 3.5 – 11'6" x 11'6"
Kitchen	3.6 x 4.1 – 11'10" x 13'5"
Utility	1.8 x 3.6 – 5'11" x 11'10"

Bedroom 1	4.0 x 4.0 – 13'2" x 13'2"
Bedroom 2	3.1 x 3.5 – 10'2" x 11'6"
Bedroom 3	2.2 x 3.5 – 7'3" x 11'6"
Studio	5.5 x 5.5 – 18'1" x 18'1"

An executive residence with detached office or games room over a double garage. The ground floor boasts a large kitchen, a utility room with direct access to the garden and a dining room. The spacious, full height living room with access to the garden through French doors is an attractive focal point of the living accommodation. Upstairs there are three good sized bedrooms, the master bedroom having its own en suite bathroom. All in all, a good family house with generous bedrooms and reception rooms.

1760 sq. ft.

The copyright belongs to Kingpost Design Co

Kemble

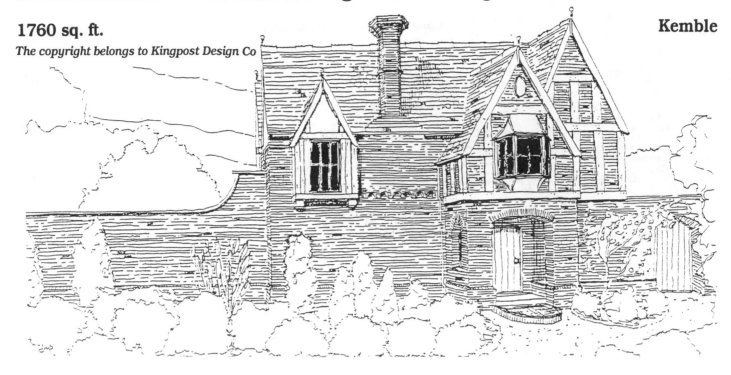

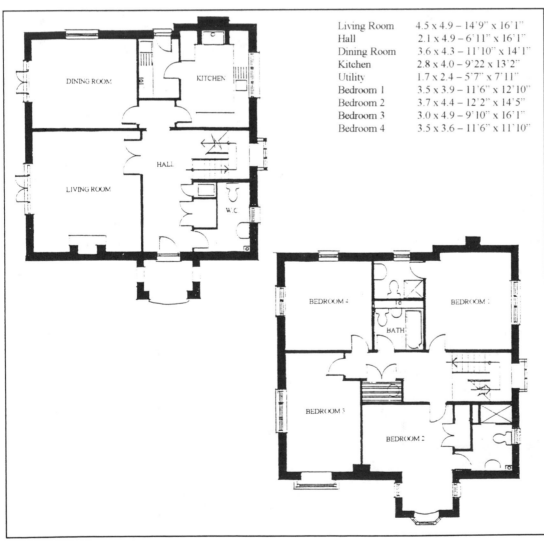

Living Room	4.5 x 4.9 – 14'9" x 16'1"
Hall	2.1 x 4.9 – 6'11" x 16'1"
Dining Room	3.6 x 4.3 – 11'10" x 14'1"
Kitchen	2.8 x 4.0 – 9'22" x 13'2"
Utility	1.7 x 2.4 – 5'7" x 7'11"
Bedroom 1	3.5 x 3.9 – 11'6" x 12'10"
Bedroom 2	3.7 x 4.4 – 12'2" x 14'5"
Bedroom 3	3.0 x 4.9 – 9'10" x 16'1"
Bedroom 4	3.5 x 3.6 – 11'6" x 11'10"

A compact Victorian style home with four generous bedrooms, two of which are en suite. One of the bedrooms cleverly uses the space over the front entrance hall. Both the living room and the dining room have French doors opening to a walled garden.

1910 sq. ft.

The copyright belongs to Kingpost Design Co

Mickleton

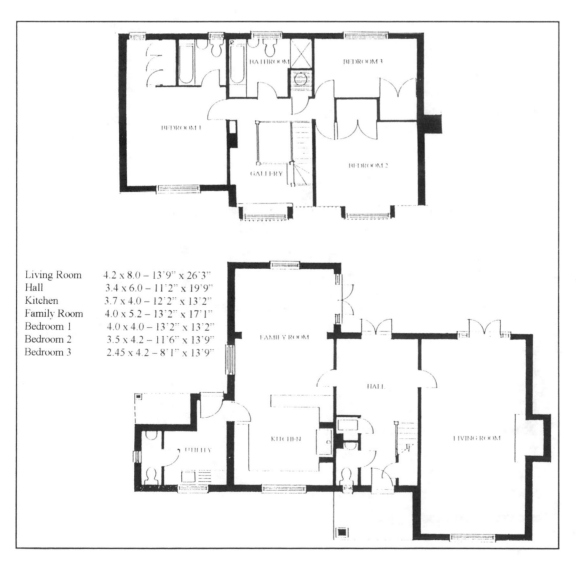

Living Room	4.2 x 8.0 – 13'9" x 26'3"
Hall	3.4 x 6.0 – 11'2" x 19'9"
Kitchen	3.7 x 4.0 – 12'2" x 13'2"
Family Room	4.0 x 5.2 – 13'2" x 17'1"
Bedroom 1	4.0 x 4.0 – 13'2" x 13'2"
Bedroom 2	3.5 x 4.2 – 11'6" x 13'9"
Bedroom 3	2.45 x 4.2 – 8'1" x 13'9"

A good sized family home. Three well proportioned bedrooms with plenty of storage space, each having walk-in wardrobes. There is a kitchen/diner and spacious lounge both of which are accessed through the galleried hall. Both rooms also have access to the garden through French windows as does the hall. The utility room can also be directly accessed from the garden. An ideal home for a family who love being in and out all day.

165 sq. m.

The copyright belongs to Border Oak

Back Lane House

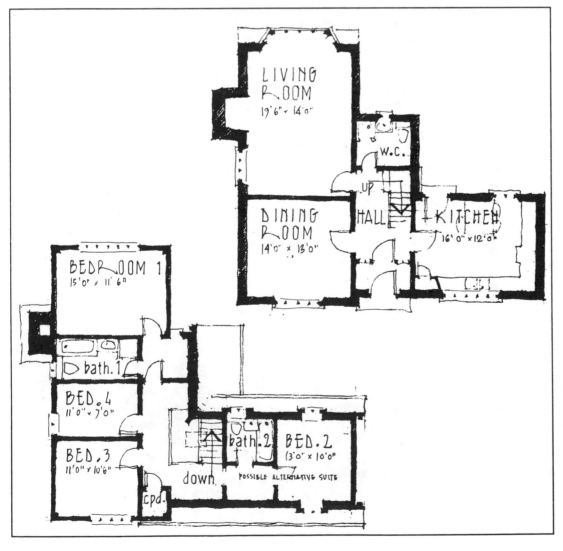

An unusual building with a quirky design, that has adapted to meet the changing needs of its successive owners. The rectangular entrance hall could serve two living areas. To the left a dining room/kitchen and living room, three bedrooms and a bathroom and to the right perhaps a kitchen/living room with first floor bedroom and bathroom. A building that could be shared by two generations, both keeping their independence or, indeed, as drawn, a large family house with a very individual layout.

1800 sq. ft.

34 ft. x 37 ft.

The copyright belongs to Design & Materials Ltd.

Monmouth

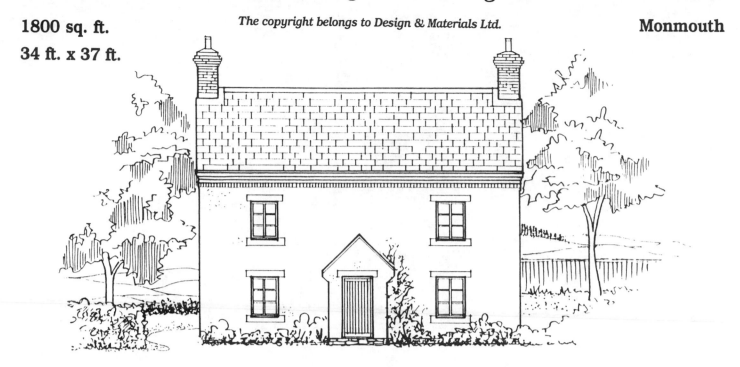

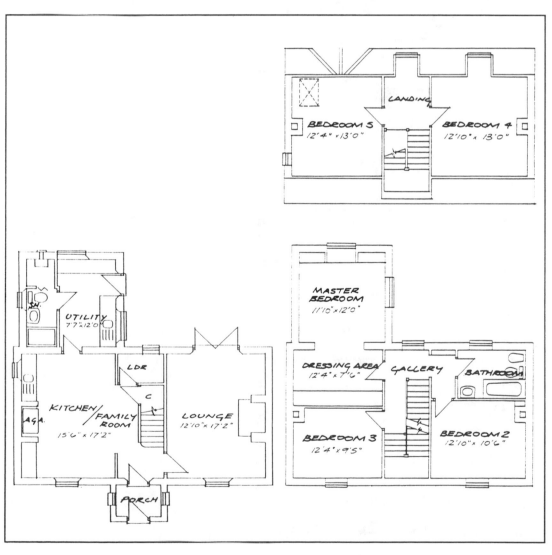

BEDROOM 5
12'4" x 13'0"

LANDING

BEDROOM 4
12'10" x 13'0"

MASTER BEDROOM
11'0" x 12'0"

DRESSING AREA
12'4" x 7'6"

GALLERY

BATHROOM

BEDROOM 3
12'4" x 9'5"

BEDROOM 2
12'10" x 10'6"

UTILITY
7'7" x 12'0"

LDR

C

KITCHEN/ FAMILY ROOM
15'6" x 17'2"

AGA

LOUNGE
12'10" x 17'2"

PORCH

This traditional cottage style design, illustrated here in render with a slate roof provides spacious family accommodation with five bedrooms over three floors, whilst maintaining the appearance from the front elevation of being a much smaller dwelling - a common planning requirement. Light to the top floor comes from rear dormers and roof lights. The floorplan maximises available space with a large living kitchen, utility, larder, small lobby and no hall.

The copyright belongs to Design & Materials Ltd.

Barminster

2000 sq. ft.
41 ft. x 22 ft.

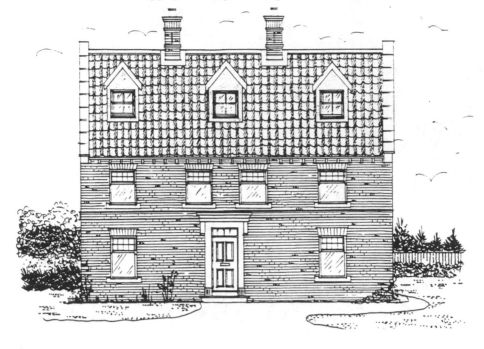

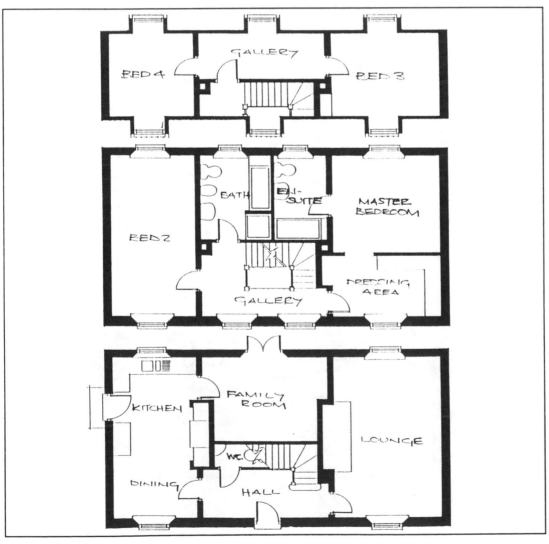

Here we have a prestigious country house on three storeys and with more than a flavour of the Queen Anne period. The Barminster has such classic proportions that it can be built in almost any combination of external materials. This makes it suitable for most regions of the country and because it is not a complex design, the build costs can be surprisingly economical depending on your choice of specification.

1975 sq. ft.
48 ft. x 33 ft.

The copyright belongs to Design & Materials Ltd.

Sevenoaks

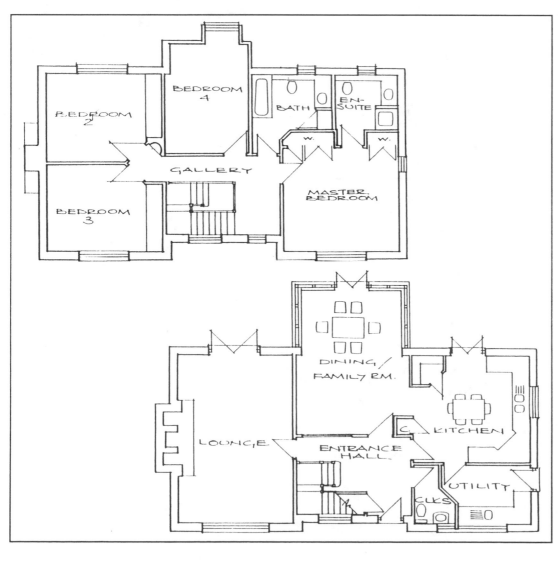

This very attractive Tudor house provides excellent family accommodation with good sized rooms throughout. Main features are the family/dining room with glazed projection which flows freely into the kitchen, and the jetted first floor which is typical of houses from this period.

1850 sq. ft.

45 ft. x 35 ft.

Oakhampton

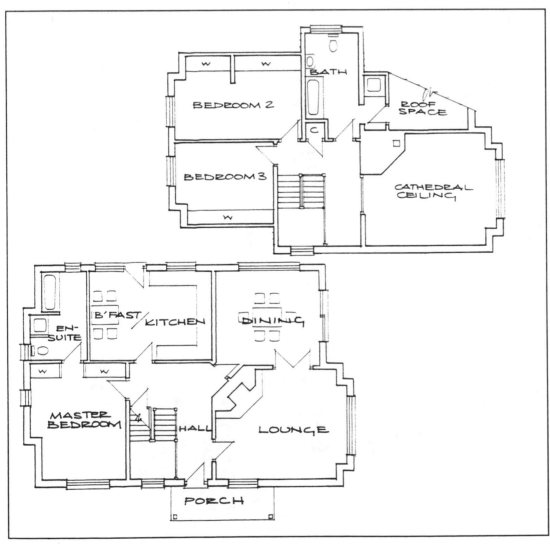

A design which will interest those looking for something a bit different. The lounge has a full height cathedral ceiling with feature window and is overlooked from the upper gallery.

1700 sq. ft.

37 ft. x 34 ft.

The copyright belongs to Design & Materials Ltd.

Roxburgh

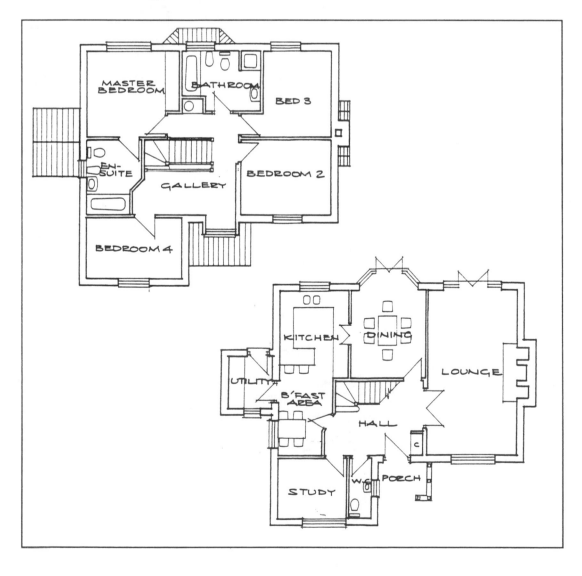

Although shown here in render under pantiles, this pretty cottage-style home can be built with a variety of external materials. The well planned interior satisfies all the demands of contemporary style.

1995 sq. ft.

41 ft. x 40 ft.

Stambourne

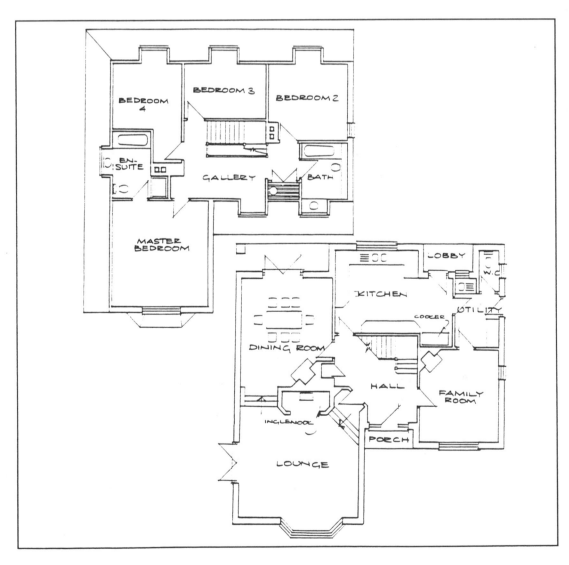

The external appearance of this delightful cottage belies its spacious interior. The sunken lounge features a large inglenook and there is an Aga range in the kitchen.

1775 sq. ft.

35 ft. x 44 ft.

Thameside

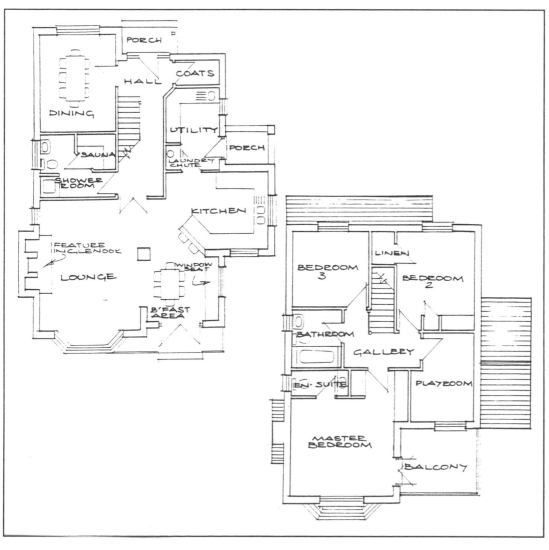

This attractive family home is designed to take advantage of any outstanding views in the area. The main features include an open-plan kitchen/breakfast/lounge with inglenook fireplace and a good sized balcony off the main bedroom.

1800 sq. ft.

72 ft. x 37 ft.

The copyright belongs to Design & Materials Ltd.

Glamorgan

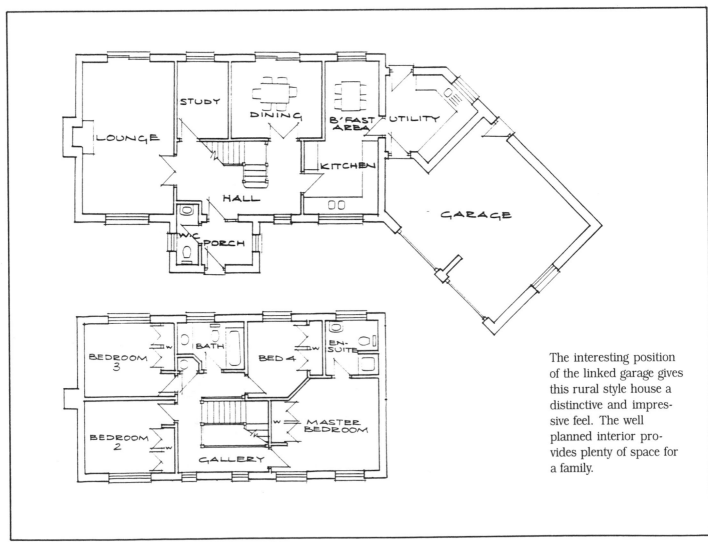

The interesting position of the linked garage gives this rural style house a distinctive and impressive feel. The well planned interior provides plenty of space for a family.

1948 sq. ft./181 sq. m.   *The copyright belongs to Scandia-Hus*   ## Lovesta

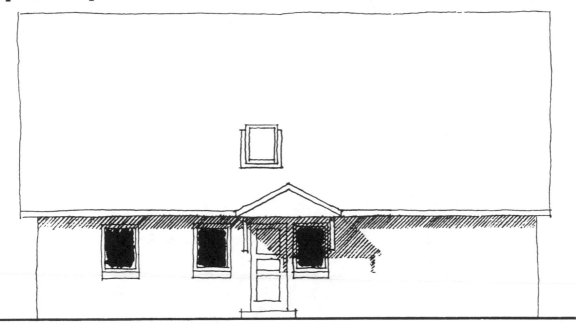

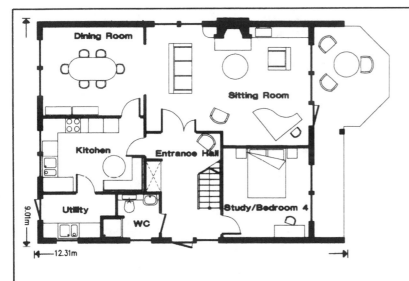

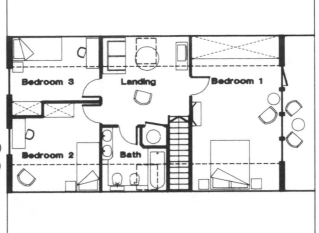

Master Bedroom:	3.4 x 5.1m *(11'2"x16'10")*
Bedroom 2:	3.4 x 3.4m *(11'2"x11'2")*
Bedroom 3:	3.4 x 2.7m *(11'2"x8'4")*
Landing Lounge:	3.5 x 3.5m *(11'5"x11'5")*
Kitchen:	4.0 x 3.1m *(13'2"x10'2")*
Dining Room:	4.0 x 3.6m *(13'2" x 11'8")*
Sitting Room:	6.4 x 4.7m *(20'11"x15'6")*
Study/Bedroom 4:	3.4 x 3.6m *(11'2"x11'8")*

This distinctive design is ideally proportioned for narrow building plots, and breakfast on a Swiss style balcony will add glamour wherever this chalet is sited. All the first floor bedrooms feature sloping ceilings, giving them a charming and individual character, and the large picture windows in the sitting room and separate dining room offer an attractive outlook over the patio which is sheltered under the overhanging first floor balcony. A practical entrance porch, timbered veranda or deck and dormer windows are but a few of the optional features which can easily be incorporated into any Scandia-Hus design, ensuring that your new home will be as individual as you are.

207

1819 sq. ft./169 sq. m.   *The copyright belongs to Scandia-Hus*   ## Dovecote

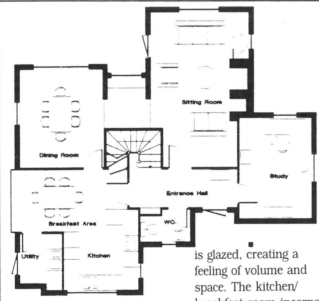

Kitchen:	3.0 x 2.1m	*(9'7"x7'1")*
Breakfast Area:	3.6 x 2.4m	*(11'8"x7'9")*
Dining Room:	3.3 x 3.8m	*(10'8"x12'3")*
Sitting Room:	3.9 x 6.0m	*(12'8"x19'6")*
Study:	2.8 x 3.9m	*(9'2x12'8")*
Master Bedroom:	3.9 x 3.2m	*(12'8"x10'5")*
Bedroom 2:	3.0 x 3.9m	*(9'9"x12'8")*
Bedroom 3:	3.7 x 2.6m	*(12'0"x8'6")*
Landing Lounge:	4.4 x 2.0m	*(14'4"x6'3")*

This period home incorporates a host of features combining to create a real dream cottage. The Dovecote's appearance certainly conjures up a fairy tale image. One of its favourite features is the beautiful, vaulted dining room which opens to the apex of the second floor. Virtually the whole gable is glazed, creating a feeling of volume and space. The kitchen/ breakfast room incorporates an entire glass wall with glazed panels to the ceiling, allowing light to permeate the whole room. These vast glazed areas provide an interesting contrast to the small, cottagey windows throughout the rest of the house and to the quaint dovecote at the top of the rear gable head.

1906 sq. ft.

The copyright belongs to Kingpost Design Co

Clarendon

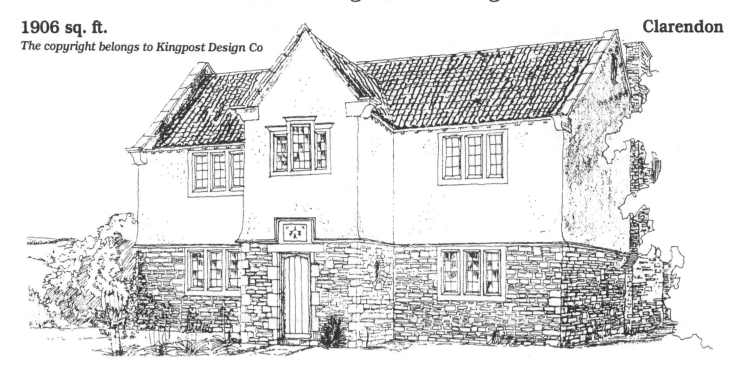

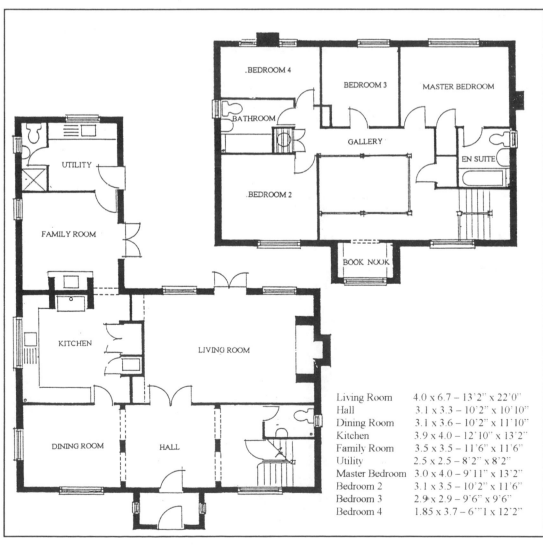

Living Room	4.0 x 6.7	13'2" x 22'0"
Hall	3.1 x 3.3	10'2" x 10'10"
Dining Room	3.1 x 3.6	10'2" x 11'10"
Kitchen	3.9 x 4.0	12'10" x 13'2"
Family Room	3.5 x 3.5	11'6" x 11'6"
Utility	2.5 x 2.5	8'2" x 8'2"
Master Bedroom	3.0 x 4.0	9'11" x 13'2"
Bedroom 2	3.1 x 3.5	10'2" x 11'6"
Bedroom 3	2.9 x 2.9	9'6" x 9'6"
Bedroom 4	1.85 x 3.7	6'"1 x 12'2"

A four bedroomed family house with a galleried dining room/hall divided with brick arches. Double doors lead to a large living room with an inglenook fireplace and more French doors to the garden. The kitchen and family room form the cosy heart of the house with provision for an Aga and a wood burning stove or open fire. Next to the utility room is a toilet with shower, useful for washing muddy dogs and muddy people. Upstairs there is an attractive window alcove, ideal for lining with books and sitting in on rainy afternoons. There are also four good sized bedrooms with the master bedroom being en suite.

165.61 sq. m./1782 sq. ft.   *Copyright refer to Designer Homes*   **The Sandmartin**

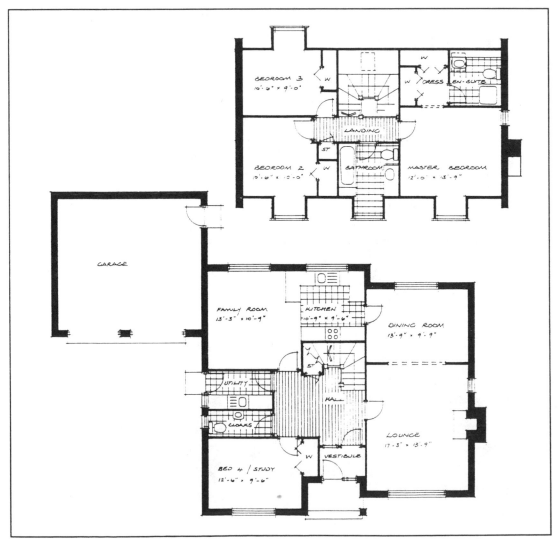

The classic dormer bungalow is able to provide bedrooms in the roof space with one or more bedrooms coming to the ground floor. This ground floor bedroom would be eminently suitable for someone unable to climb the stairs and wishing to occupy the house as a bungalow. At the same time the upper part bedroom accommodation is particularly generous. This house has the added advantage of the family living room area adjoining the kitchen.

181.4 sq. m.

Copyright refer to Designer Homes

Hampton

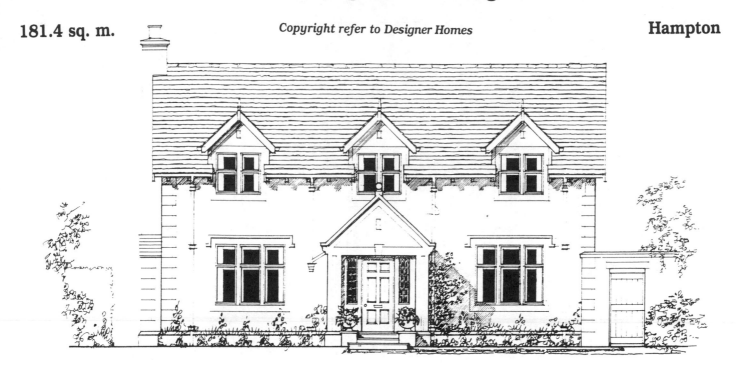

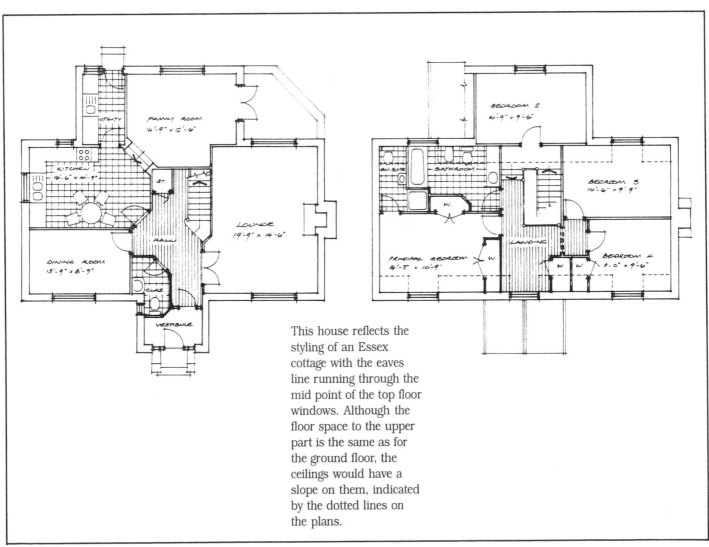

UTILITY

FAMILY ROOM
14'-9" x 12'-6"

KITCHEN
10'-6" x 10'-9"

ST.

LOUNGE
19'-9" x 14'-6"

HALL

DINING ROOM
13'-9" x 8'-9"

CLKS

VESTIBULE

BEDROOM 2
6'-9" x 9'-6"

EN-SUITE

BATHROOM

W

BEDROOM 3
14'-6" x 9'-9"

LANDING

PRINCIPAL BEDROOM
4'-3" x 10'-9"

W

BEDROOM 4
11'-0" x 9'-6"

W W

This house reflects the
styling of an Essex
cottage with the eaves
line running through the
mid point of the top floor
windows. Although the
floor space to the upper
part is the same as for
the ground floor, the
ceilings would have a
slope on them, indicated
by the dotted lines on
the plans.

87.10 sq. m.

Copyright refer to Designer Homes

Teviot

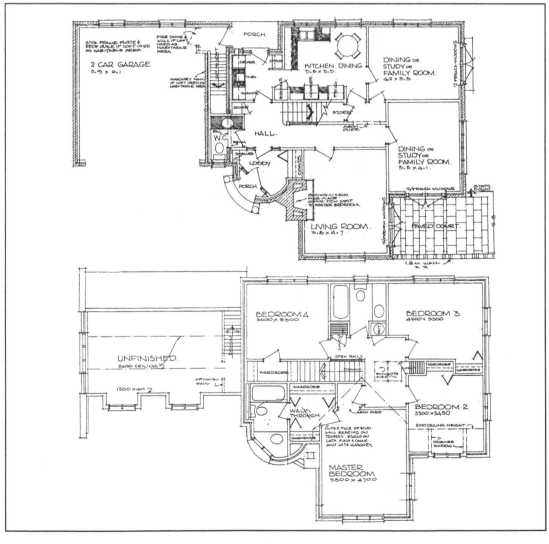

A feature of this book has been that so many of the designers have managed to add interest to otherwise standard floor plan layouts and nowhere is that better illustrated than here. The introduction of the round tower section over the lobby gives this house a character all of its own and closer examination reveals the scope to create semi self contained accommodation for, perhaps, hobbies or games, in the room over the garage.

157.86 sq. m.

Copyright refer to Designer Homes

Lothian

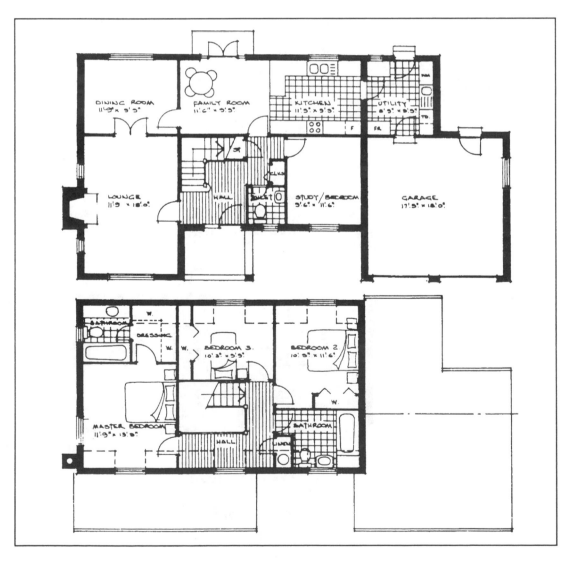

This larger house manages to retain much of the ambiance of the smaller cottage properties that are in another section of this book. Space is available for the provision of a family room as well as for a study and once again one of the bedrooms is brought to the ground floor.

175.1 sq. m.

Copyright refer to
Designer Homes

The Willow Warbler

This is a lovely house with its various architectural features and the cat slide roof that reflects the pitch of the garage roof. For those who want the master bedroom suite to have a degree of privacy, its positioning over the rear facing projection above the living room gives them what they want.

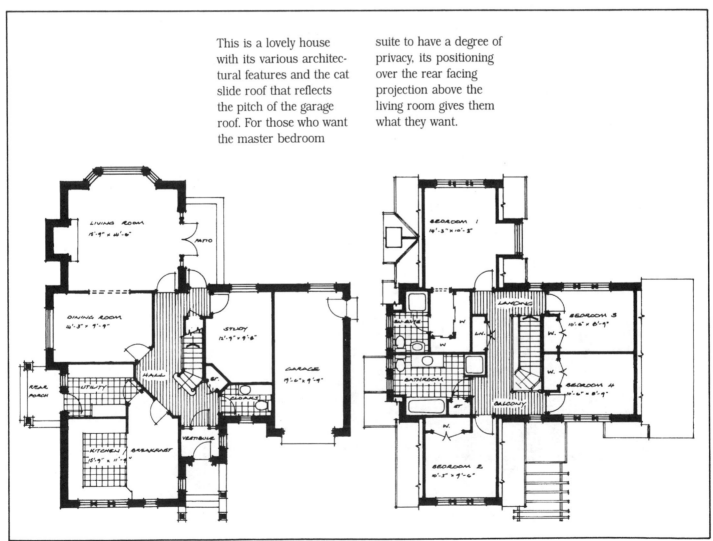

180.6 sq. m./1944 sq.

Copyright refer to Designer Homes

The Goosander

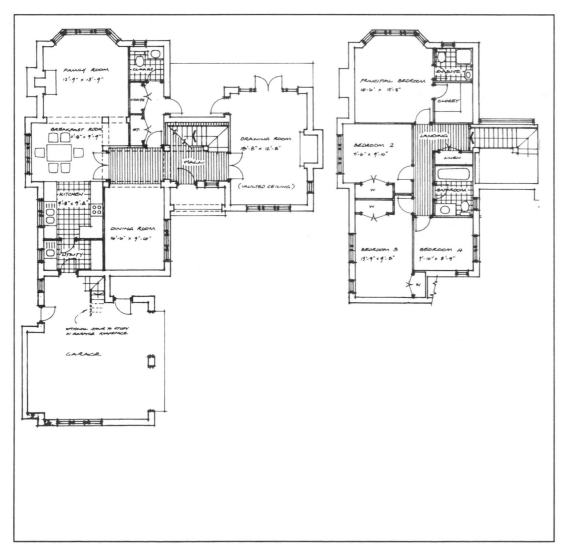

It would have been all too easy to turn this plan form into a fairly basic house type but, once again, the designers have managed to coax out the various architectural features to produce a house design that defies the ordinary. Note the vaulted ceilings to the lounge and the fact that this room is cleverly divorced from the main living sections.

196 sq. m./2110 sq. ft.   *Copyright refer to Designer Homes*   **The Rosefinch**

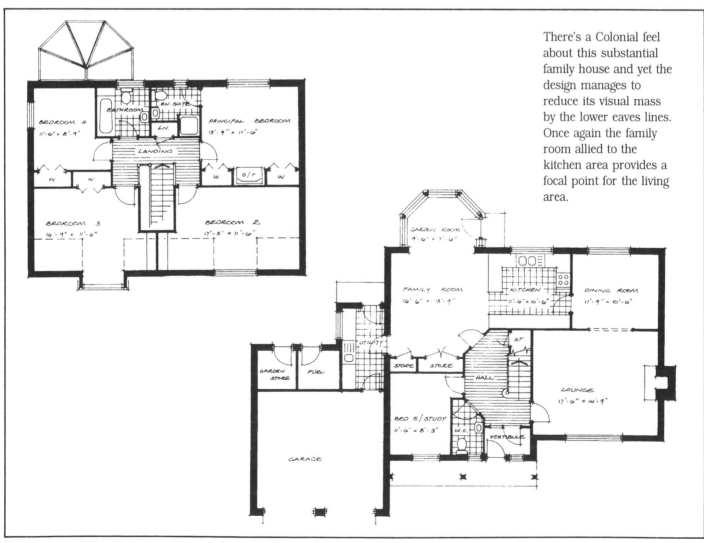

There's a Colonial feel about this substantial family house and yet the design manages to reduce its visual mass by the lower eaves lines. Once again the family room allied to the kitchen area provides a focal point for the living area.

166.2 sq. m./1789 sq. ft.

Copyright refer to Designer Homes

The Brambling

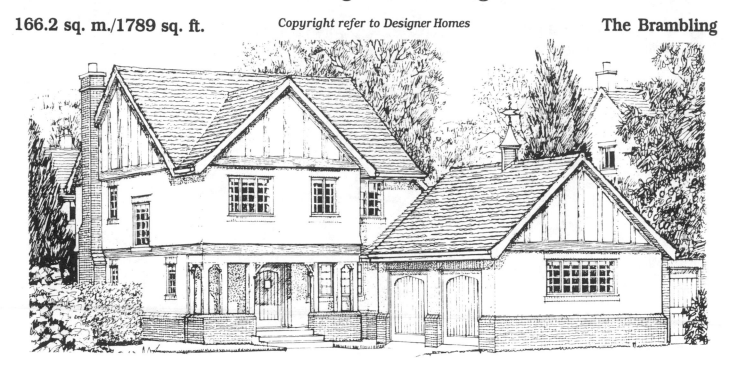

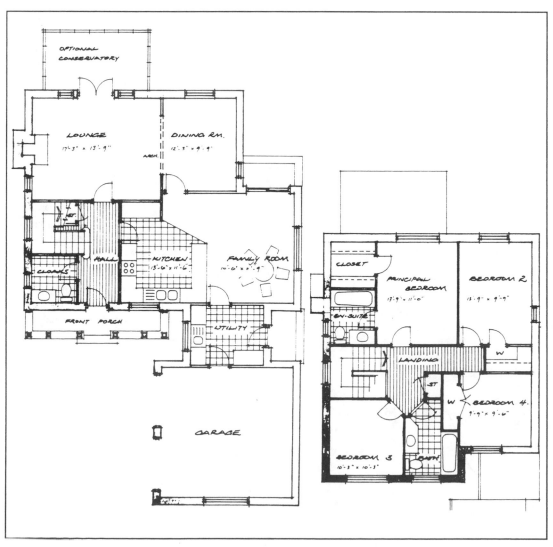

OPTIONAL CONSERVATORY

LOUNGE
17'-3" x 13'-9"

DINING RM.
12'-3" x 9'-9"

ARCH.

HALL

CLOAKS

KITCHEN
13'-6" x 11'-6"

FAMILY ROOM
14'-6" x 11'-9"

FRONT PORCH

UTILITY

GARAGE

CLOSET

PRINCIPAL BEDROOM
13'-9" x 11'-0"

BEDROOM 2
13'-9" x 9'-9"

EN-SUITE

LANDING

W

ST

W

BEDROOM 4.
9'-9" x 9'-6"

BEDROOM 3
10'-3" x 10'-3"

BATH

This is a large family house that has obviously been designed to fit on a plot where the width is limited. Bringing the garage to the front of the house and linking it to the main body of the accommodation by means of the utility room, adds interest and scale to the front elevation.

167.42 sq.m./1799 sq.ft.

The copyright belongs to Kingpost Design Co

Bathurst

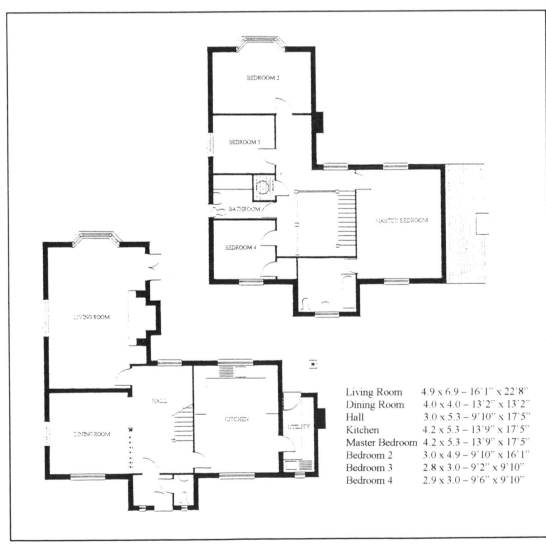

A stylish house particularly suitable for a rural site. The dining room is separated from the hall by a carved oak screen, giving a feeling of spaciousness on entry. The living room has a large inglenook fireplace and an elegant bay window looking into the garden. The master bedroom has a dual aspect with a generous en suite bathroom. The dramatic galleried landing below the vaulted ceiling to the hall gives access to three further generously sized bedrooms.

Living Room	4.9 x 6.9 –	16'1" x 22'8"
Dining Room	4.0 x 4.0 –	13'2" x 13'2"
Hall	3.0 x 5.3 –	9'10" x 17'5"
Kitchen	4.2 x 5.3 –	13'9" x 17'5"
Master Bedroom	4.2 x 5.3 –	13'9" x 17'5"
Bedroom 2	3.0 x 4.9 –	9'10" x 16'1"
Bedroom 3	2.8 x 3.0 –	9'2" x 9'10"
Bedroom 4	2.9 x 3.0 –	9'6" x 9'10"

91.87 sq. m.

Copyright refer to Designer Homes

DH-1

An imposing house, the like of which can be seen on many a self build plot. Once more the fourth bedroom is brought to the ground floor, allowing greater space to be given to the master bedroom on the first floor and providing versatility to the living arrangements.

1826 sq. ft./169 sq. m.

The copyright belongs to Custom Homes

Shropshire

A classic four bedroomed house where as much of the available space as possible has been used to the advantage of the main accommodation. All of the bedrooms end up as having very generous proportions and the major reception rooms have gone for size rather than greater numbers.

1870 sq. ft./174 sq. m.   *The copyright belongs to Custom Homes*   **Rye**

There are only three bedrooms in this quite large house but they are all of a fairly generous size, as are the ground floor reception rooms. If the decision is made to build a house of this size with only three bedrooms then care must be taken regarding the eventual market value but there is no doubt that many self builders make this conscious choice.

1820 sq. ft./169 sq. m.

The copyright belongs to Custom Homes

Colchester

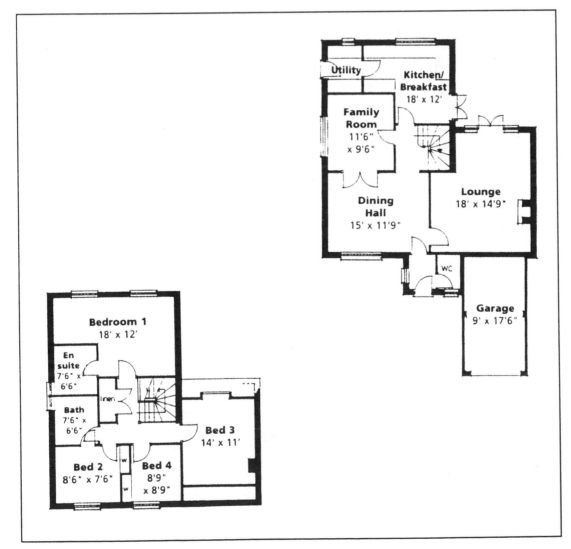

Another house where the designers have cleverly added extra interest to the principal elevation by the use of additional and introduced gables mixed in with hipped roof projections. The increasingly popular dining hall gives further scope to the internal ground floor layout, especially when combined with the internal enclosed staircase giving access to the well proportioned bedroom accommodation.

Houses 2001 – 2500 sq. ft.

When one gets to these sizes, the scope for accommodation really begins to take off. No longer does the hallway, if it is to be impressive, have to be gained at the expense of accommodation elsewhere and its design, usually linked into the upper part gallery, by an equally impressive staircase, can start to become an important architectural feature of the home. The study, which in smaller houses, often meant a slightly smaller lounge, can be replaced or even supplemented by a family room without the need to skimp on the other main ground floor accommodation, and the breakfast area can often be properly divided as a separate section of the kitchen/living area.

Bedrooms can all have room for washing facilities at the very least, with the possibility of en suite shower rooms to more than one of the secondary bedrooms. If the size of all of the bedrooms doesn't have to be too big then there's probably room to expand the number to five or even more bedrooms, or there may be room to designate one of the other bedrooms as a guest suite with its own en suite facilities and a small dressing/sitting area.

Whilst not yet of the size to be considered as an architectural unit in its own right, the dwelling can, nevertheless, start to assert itself on the landscape by means of individual design features.

Contributors in this section:

ASBA Timothy Mostyn
ASBA Julian Owen Associates
ASBA Andrew Smith Associates
Border Oak
Custom Homes
Design & Materials Ltd.
Designer Homes
Kingpost Design Co
Potton Ltd.
Scandia-Hus

2443 sq. ft./227 sq. m.   *The copyright belongs to Scandia-Hus*   **Wealdon**

Master Bedroom:	3.8 x 5.2m *(12'4"x16'10")*	Kitchen:	3.8 x 2.2m *(12'3"x8'0")*
Bedroom 2:	4.0 x 3.4m *(13'1"x11'1")*	Dining/Family Room:	4.4 x 3.6m *(14'4"x11'8")*
Bedroom 3:	3.3 x 4.0m *(10'10"x13'1")*	Sitting Room:	6.0 x 5.8m *(19'6"x19'0")*
Bedroom 4:	3.5 x 2.4m *(11'3"x7'9")*	Study/Bedroom 5:	3.3 x 4.8m *(10'8"x15'9")*

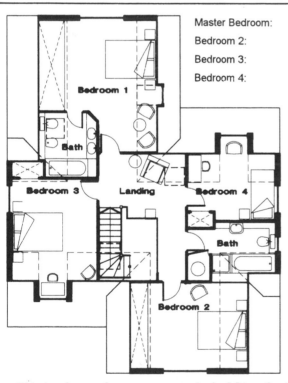

This is a home of distinction and character with its seven bedrooms and four bathrooms provides ample space for even the largest family. The impressive dining hall is fit for a formal banquet and can be overlooked from the first floor gallery and charming tower bay lounge. The lower level sitting room is spacious enough to accommodate even the most ambitious social gathering with large sliding doors affording direct access onto the patio. This area forms a natural site for a Scandia-Hus sun room, which can be added to any design. The integral double garage may be converted into a self-contained granny annex, office, snooker room or even an indoor swimming pool.

2368 sq. ft./220 sq. m. *The copyright belongs to Scandia-Hus* **Halland**

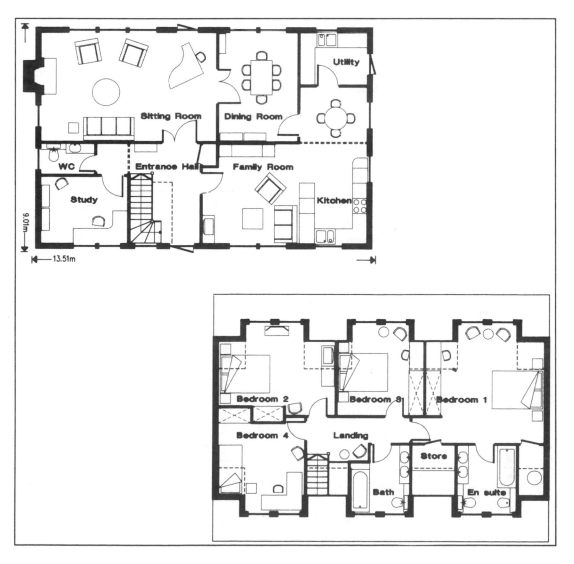

The hipped roof and dormer windows gives the Halland an authentic Sussex feel. Depending on the external finishes, it can blend in with the local vernacular anywhere. On the ground floor, a large kitchen/breakfast/family room creates an attractive L-shaped open-plan living area. The light, spacious sitting room and dining room provide ample space for entertaining, with large picture windows facing the rear garden. This chalet has four large bedrooms. The master bedroom has an en-suite bathroom, and all are generously equipped with wardrobes and storage areas. The sloping first floor ceilings add character and charm and the dormers provide cosy seating areas.

2164 sq. ft./201 sq. m.   *The copyright belongs to Scandia-Hus*   **Courtfield**

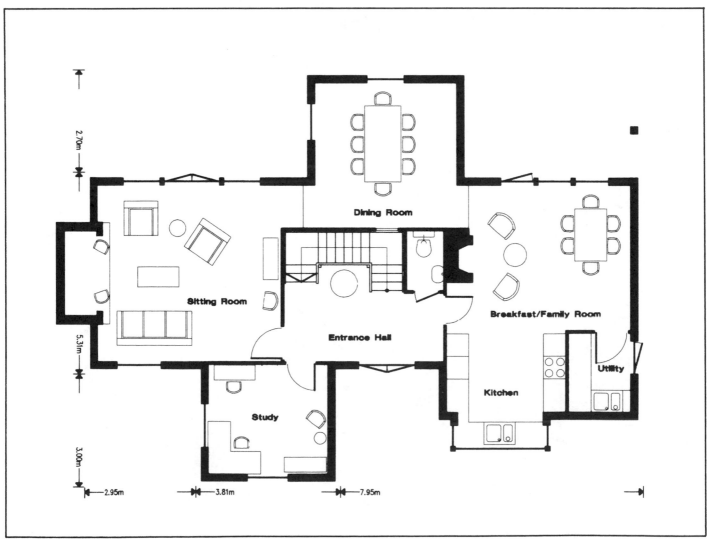

GROUND FLOOR

Kitchen:	3.2 x 2.1m *(10'4"x6'9")*
Dining Room:	3.7 x 3.8m *(12'2"x12'3")*
Sitting Room:	4.9 x 5.0m *(15'10"x16'4")*
Breakfast/Family Room:	4.9 x 3.9m *(15'7"x12'7")*
Study:	3.2 x 2.8m *(12'2"x9'3")*

FIRST FLOOR

Master Bedroom:	3.5 x 4.7m *(11'3"x15'6")*
Bedroom 2:	3.7 x 3.8m *(12'2"x12'3")*
Bedroom 3:	3.2 x 2.8m *(10'4"x9'3")*
Bedroom 4:	3.1 x 2.4m *(10'2"x8'4")*
Landing Lounge:	4.1 x 3.5m *(13'5x11'4")*

This period design incorporates chimneys, two-storey projections, dormers, a kitchen window bay and a covered loggia: all features which contribute to the traditional look of this family home. The wide recessed entrance porch leads into a large hall with an elegant ash staircase, and the higher-level dining room is connected through arches to the sitting room and the breakfast room, providing an open, yet individual feel to each area. The sitting room features a large inglenook fire place and provision has been made in the family room for a wood burner or open fire to suit individual tastes and requirements.

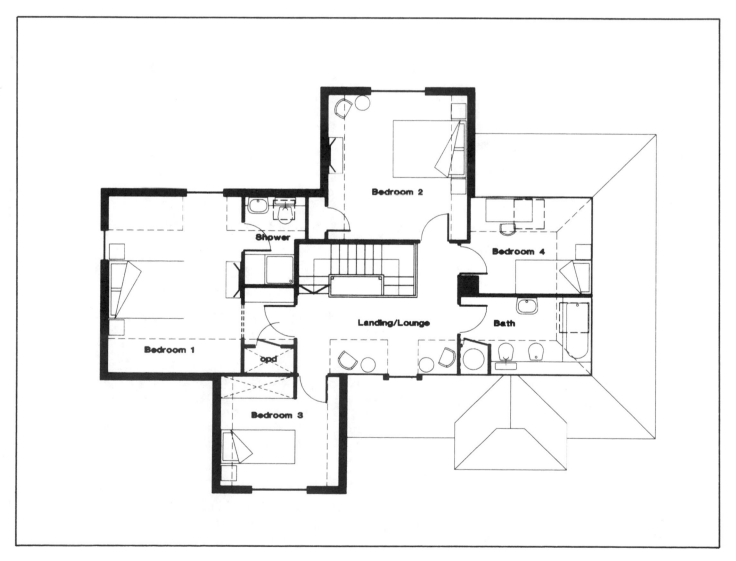

2094 sq. ft./195 sq. m.

The copyright belongs to Scandia-Hus

Dalsland

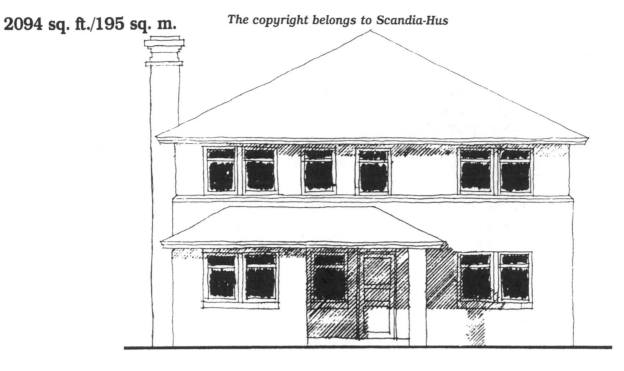

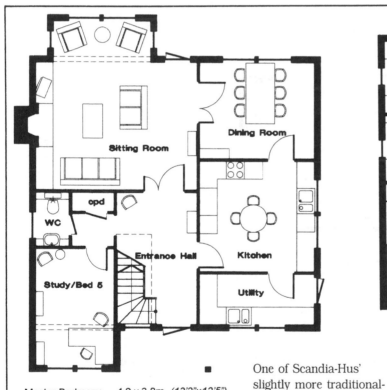

Master Bedroom:	4.0 x 3.8m	(13'2"x12'5")
Bedroom 2:	3.3 x 4.8m	(10'10"x15'8")
Bedroom 3:	3.3 x 3.8m	(10'10"x12'6")
Bedroom 4:	2.7 x 3.2m	(8'10"x10'7")
Kitchen:	3.7 x 3.7m	(12'3"x12'3")
Dining Room:	3.7 x 3.3m	(12'3"x10'10")
Sitting Room:	5.5 x 5.6m	(17'11"x18'4")
Study/Bedroom 5:	2.7 x 3.8m	(8'10"x12'5")

One of Scandia-Hus' slightly more traditional-looking designs, the Dalsland is a modern four bedroom house which will easily blend with neighbouring properties of a more conventional appearance. Through the covered entrance porch, a spacious hall leads to well proportioned ground floor accommodation comprising a large sitting room with an attractive bay, a separate dining room, a spacious family kitchen and utility room as well as a ground floor bedroom or study. The first floor features three double and one single bedroom, the master bedroom with its own a separate dressing area and en-suite bathroom.

2196 sq. ft./204 sq. m.

The copyright belongs to Scandia-Hus

The Tithe Barn

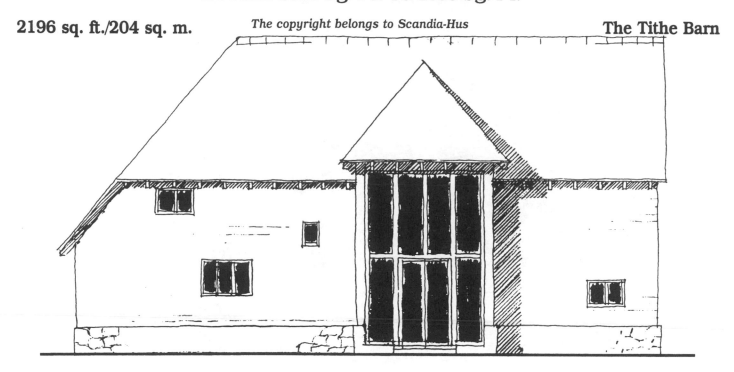

Kitchen: 3.1 x 2.2m *(10'2"x7'3")*

Dining Room: 4.8 x 3.3m *(15'8"x10'8")*

Sitting Room: 4.8 x 6.0m *(15'7"x19'9")*

Family Room: 4.7 x 3.9m *(15'3" x 12'9")*

Study: 3.7 x 2.6m *(12'2"x8'4")*

Master Bedroom: 3.5 x 4.8m *(11'4"x15'10")*

Bedroom 2: 3.8 x 2.0m *(12'8"x6'8")*

Bedroom 3: 2.7 x 2.6m *(8'10"x8'4")*

Bedroom 4: 2.7 x 4.7m *(9'0"x15'2")*

The insulation properties, quality, low-maintenance and speed of construction of the Tithe Barn would put any barn conversion to shame. When completed, you would be forgiven for believing that this is indeed a converted old barn. Its authentic exterior belies the technology, quality and energy-efficiency which lie behind its façade. The Tithe Barn provides generous family accommodation including a large sitting room and separate family room, a spacious kitchen and dining room as well as 5 bedrooms. Its interior layout is both interesting and practical with lots of windows providing a light and open atmosphere.

2088 sq. ft.

The copyright belongs to Kingpost Design Co

Boston

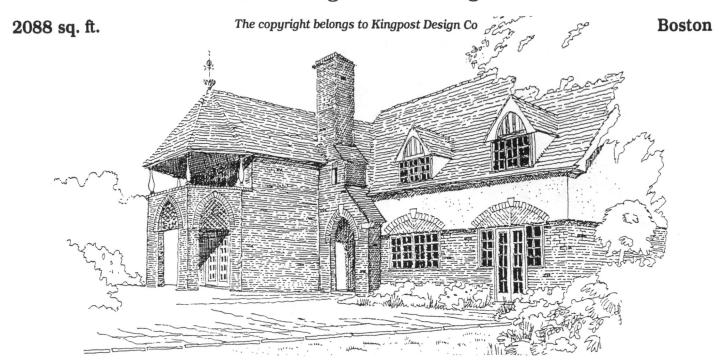

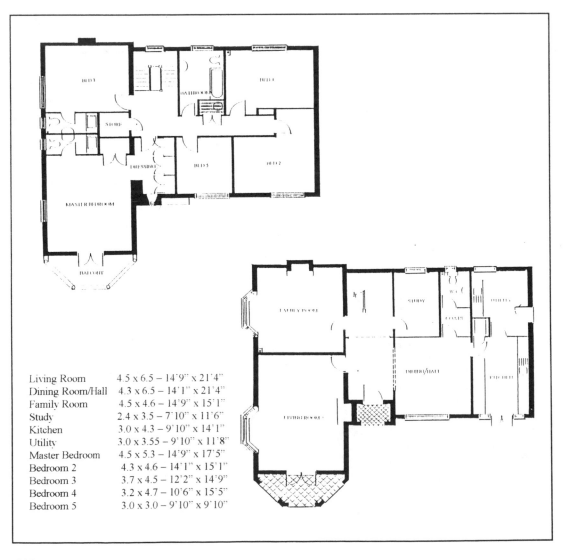

Living Room	4.5 x 6.5 – 14'9" x 21'4"
Dining Room/Hall	4.3 x 6.5 – 14'1" x 21'4"
Family Room	4.5 x 4.6 – 14'9" x 15'1"
Study	2.4 x 3.5 – 7'10" x 11'6"
Kitchen	3.0 x 4.3 – 9'10" x 14'1"
Utility	3.0 x 3.55 – 9'10" x 11'8"
Master Bedroom	4.5 x 5.3 – 14'9" x 17'5"
Bedroom 2	4.3 x 4.6 – 14'1" x 15'1"
Bedroom 3	3.7 x 4.5 – 12'2" x 14'9"
Bedroom 4	3.2 x 4.7 – 10'6" x 15'5"
Bedroom 5	3.0 x 3.0 – 9'10" x 9'10"

A Victorian style house specifically designed for a plot where the front of the house has to face south. The living room opens through French doors onto a loggia beneath Venetian style arches and double doors from the kitchen allow food and drink to be easily carried out to the sunny terrace at the front. Upstairs there are two en suite shower rooms and the master bedroom has a dressing area with generous wardrobe accommodation and an elegant balcony above the loggia.

2135 sq. ft.

The copyright belongs to Kingpost Design Co

Maldon

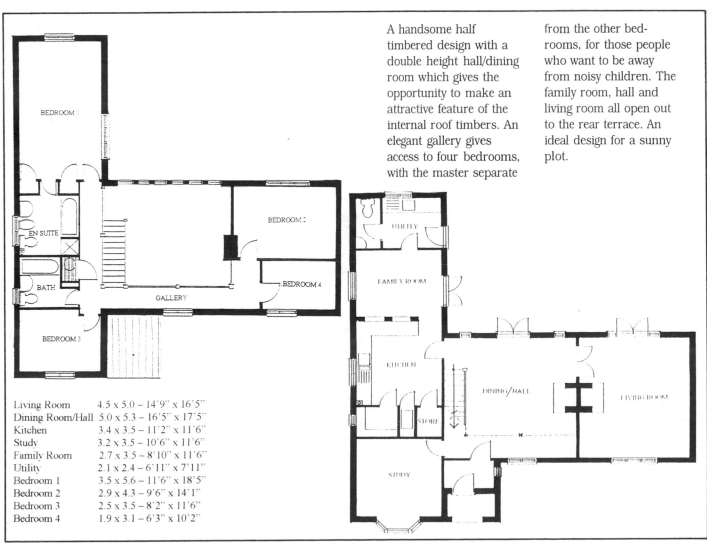

A handsome half timbered design with a double height hall/dining room which gives the opportunity to make an attractive feature of the internal roof timbers. An elegant gallery gives access to four bedrooms, with the master separate from the other bedrooms, for those people who want to be away from noisy children. The family room, hall and living room all open out to the rear terrace. An ideal design for a sunny plot.

Living Room	4.5 x 5.0 – 14'9" x 16'5"
Dining Room/Hall	5.0 x 5.3 – 16'5" x 17'5"
Kitchen	3.4 x 3.5 – 11'2" x 11'6"
Study	3.2 x 3.5 – 10'6" x 11'6"
Family Room	2.7 x 3.5 – 8'10" x 11'6"
Utility	2.1 x 2.4 – 6'11" x 7'11"
Bedroom 1	3.5 x 5.6 – 11'6" x 18'5"
Bedroom 2	2.9 x 4.3 – 9'6" x 14'1"
Bedroom 3	2.5 x 3.5 – 8'2" x 11'6"
Bedroom 4	1.9 x 3.1 – 6'3" x 10'2"

2078 sq. ft.

The copyright belongs to Kingpost Design Co

Morton

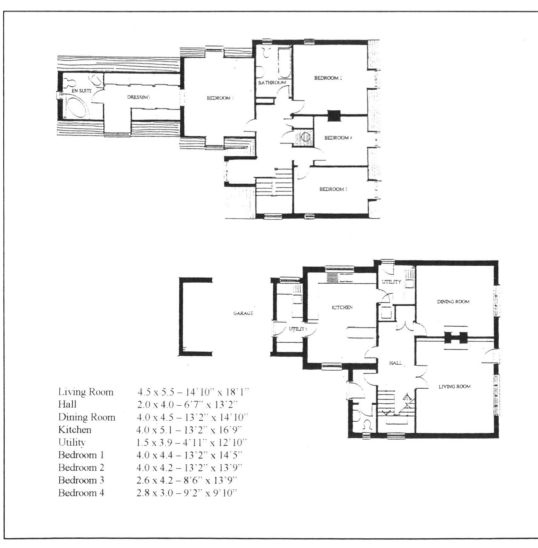

An attractive and practical home in the Cotswold style. The roof space of the ample garage is cleverly utilised to provide a walk through wardrobe and an en suite bathroom for the master bedroom. Three other bedrooms provide spacious accommodation for a growing family. The garage can also be accessed directly from the house through the utility room.

Living Room	4.5 x 5.5 – 14'10" x 18'1"
Hall	2.0 x 4.0 – 6'7" x 13'2"
Dining Room	4.0 x 4.5 – 13'2" x 14'10"
Kitchen	4.0 x 5.1 – 13'2" x 16'9"
Utility	1.5 x 3.9 – 4'11" x 12'10"
Bedroom 1	4.0 x 4.4 – 13'2" x 14'5"
Bedroom 2	4.0 x 4.2 – 13'2" x 13'9"
Bedroom 3	2.6 x 4.2 – 8'6" x 13'9"
Bedroom 4	2.8 x 3.0 – 9'2" x 9'10"

2200 sq. ft.

The copyright belongs to Kingpost Design Co

Bristol

This elegant Regency style house is designed very much with the surrounding gardens in mind, each room looking into its own unique courtyard. The canopies are designed to keep the strong summer sun out of the airy living room while allowing the winter sun in. The conservatory is similarly protected and is designed to be used the whole year round.

Living Room	4.2 x 5.6 – 13'10" x 18'5"
Hall	3.0 x 4.5 – 9'10" x 14'10"
Dining Room	3.5 x 5.6 – 11'6" x 18'5"
Kitchen	3.3 x 3.6 – 10'10" x 11'10"
Conservatory	4.0 x 7.8 – 13'2" x 25'7"
Bedroom 1	3.8 x 4.5 – 12'6" x 14'9"
Bedroom 2	3.7 x 4.0 – 12'2" x 13'2"
Bedroom 3	3.0 x 4.3 – 9'10" x 14'1"
Bedroom 4/Study	2.5 x 3.4 – 8'2" x 11'2"
Bedroom 5	2.6 x 3.0 – 8'6" x 9'10"

191 sq.m./2060 sq.ft.

The copyright belongs to Kingpost Design Co

Moat House

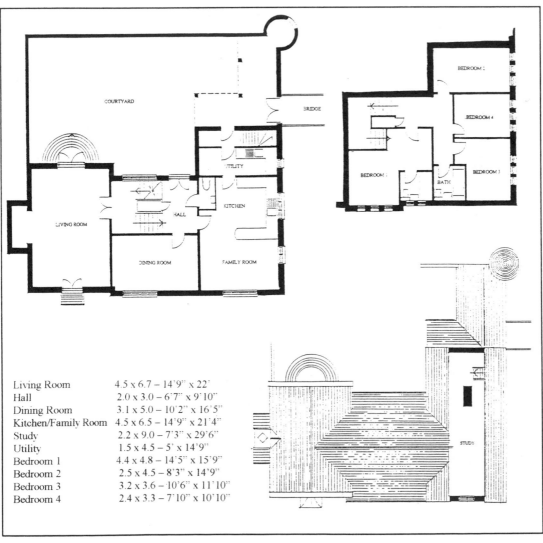

A classic gem of a country house featuring a full range of features that are associated with a house of this type. They include a manorial hall that is the full height of the house and incorporates a minstrels gallery. The bedroom windows are set just above water level to take full advantage of the restful dappled light reflections.

Living Room	4.5 x 6.7 – 14'9" x 22'
Hall	2.0 x 3.0 – 6'7" x 9'10"
Dining Room	3.1 x 5.0 – 10'2" x 16'5"
Kitchen/Family Room	4.5 x 6.5 – 14'9" x 21'4"
Study	2.2 x 9.0 – 7'3" x 29'6"
Utility	1.5 x 4.5 – 5' x 14'9"
Bedroom 1	4.4 x 4.8 – 14'5" x 15'9"
Bedroom 2	2.5 x 4.5 – 8'3" x 14'9"
Bedroom 3	3.2 x 3.6 – 10'6" x 11'10"
Bedroom 4	2.4 x 3.3 – 7'10" x 10'10"

2150 sq. ft.

45 ft. x 21 ft.

*The copyright belongs to
Design & Materials Ltd.*

Banbury

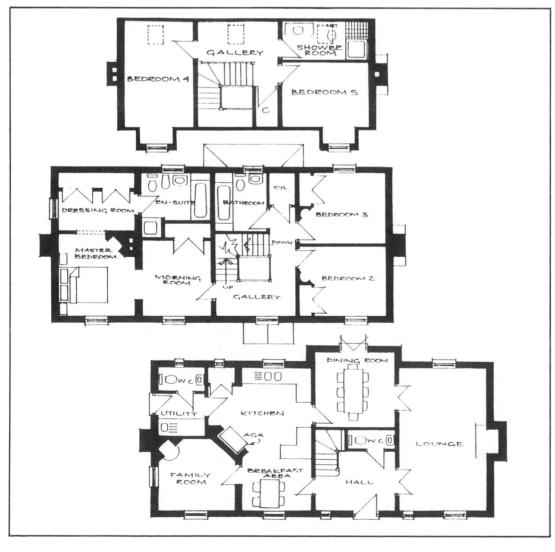

This traditional country house which was designed for the editor of a leading magazine has well planned accommodation on three floors. The centrepiece of the design is the superb master bedroom suite which includes an open fire, dressing room, full bathroom and separate morning room. The spacious kitchen and breakfast area incorporates an Aga range and is linked to the comfortable family room which includes a real fire. Although shown here in stone, it would look equally good in almost any combination of external materials.

2400 sq. ft.

Vale of Clwyd House

This house has traditional brick detailing, stone window sills and Welsh slates in the roof. There are well lit spacious day rooms, four bedrooms and three bathrooms. Loft trusses allow the huge roof space to be utilised for hobbies as well as storage. The double garage includes a workbench with sink and power points and is linked to the house via an oak framed covered way. The house is well insulated and fitted with a condensing boiler and underfloor heating and has an excellent SAP energy rating.

2425 sq. ft.

The copyright belongs to ASBA
Andrew Smith Associates

Tower House

This formal house in the suburbs combines modern and traditional forms to blend in with its Edwardian and 1930's neighbours. It features simple geometrical shapes with several rooms being perfect squares. One bedroom extends up into the tower with a dramatic high ceiling. There is a small courtyard to bring the light into the centre of the house. This has been glazed over to form a winter garden.

237

2250 sq. ft.

68 ft. x 38 ft.

Ruthven

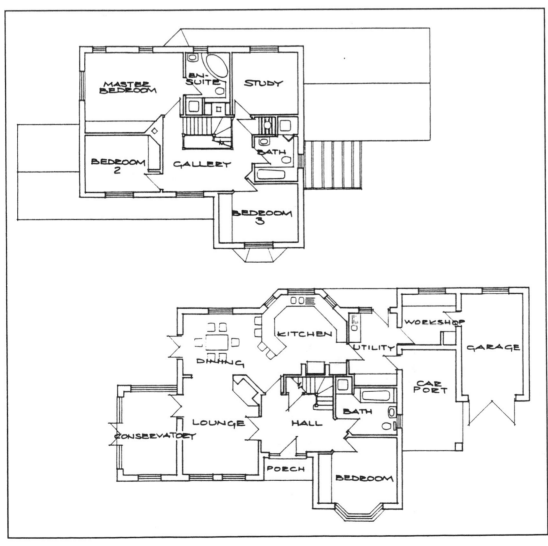

This beautiful Edwardian style house provides marvellous family accommodation. The kitchen/dining/lounge are open plan and the arrangement of the car port and garage is both functional and attractive.

2275 sq. ft.

50 ft. x 40 ft.

The copyright belongs to Design & Materials Ltd.

Amersham

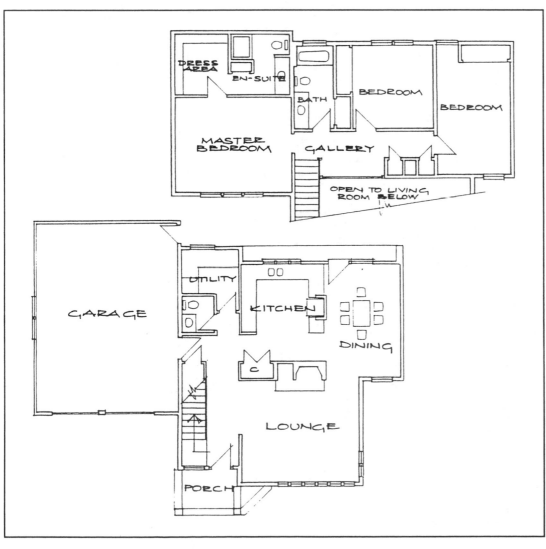

This house has a wonderfully spacious and light feel to its main living area which is galleried and open to the kitchen and dining rooms. A generous double garage is also incorporated.

2250 sq. ft.

46 ft. x 51 ft.

The copyright belongs to Design & Materials Ltd.

Wickford

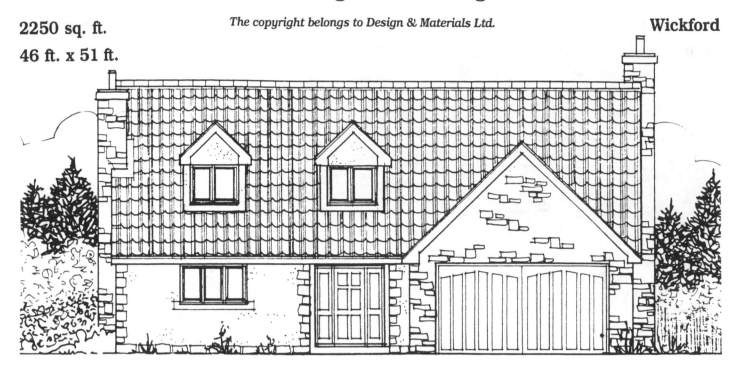

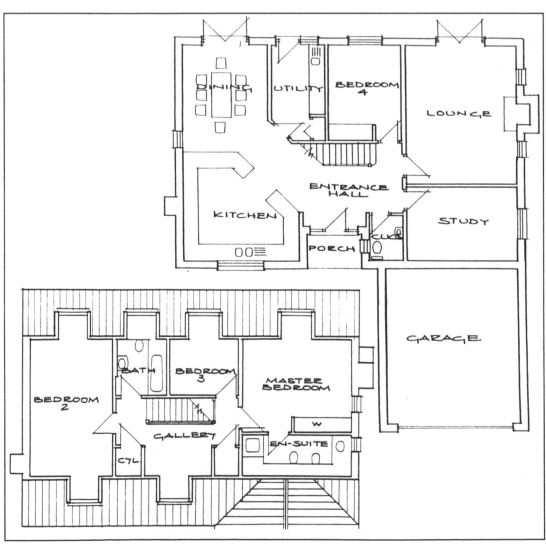

A spacious dormer bungalow, with a double garage, which can be built on a plot of around fifty feet wide. The ridge height, often a big issue with planners, is not too high and overall the design provides very comfortable family accommodation.

2100 sq. ft.

61 ft. x 32 ft.

The copyright belongs to Design & Materials Ltd.

Birchgrove

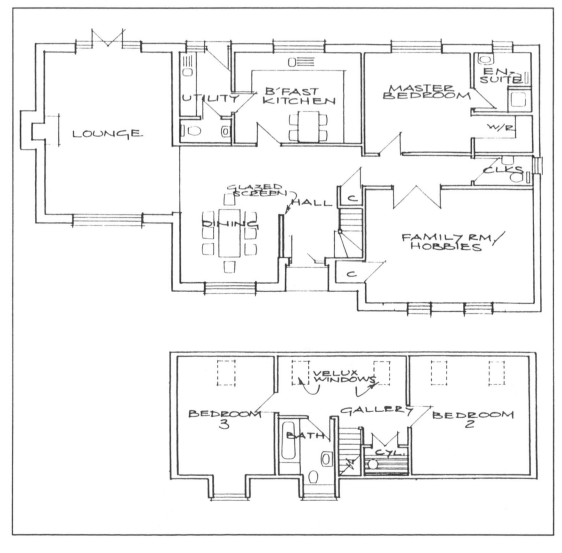

LOUNGE

UTILITY

B'FAST KITCHEN

MASTER BEDROOM

EN-SUITE

W/R

CLKS

GLAZED SCREEN

HALL

C

DINING

FAMILY RM/ HOBBIES

C

VELUX WINDOWS

BEDROOM 3

GALLERY

BEDROOM 2

BATH

CYL.

This well planned dormer has the main bedroom suite downstairs and includes a big family room which could be converted to extra bedrooms for the larger family. The lounge, dining area and hall are open plan.

2045 sq. ft./190 sq. m.

Croft Farm

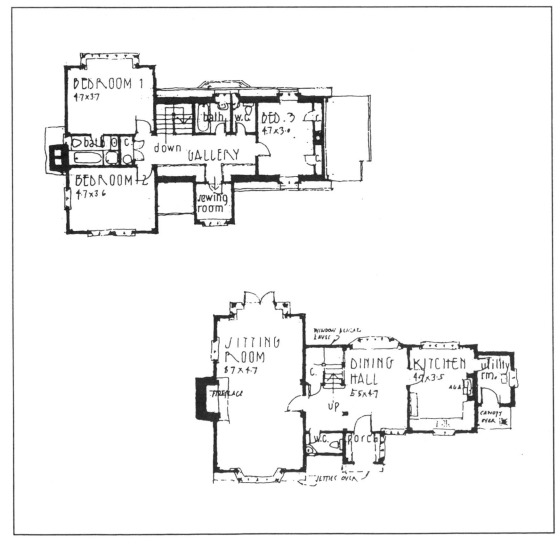

The apparently simple and straightforward plan form of this design belies its inherent elegance. Herringbone brickwork in the panels, as opposed to the more usual render, impart a sense of evolution. This, along with the two storey porch, adds a touch of genteel flamboyance, an indication perhaps of good times in the house's history. The dining hall, with its sweeping bay window, and long gallery over, form a welcoming entrance, a space of shadow play and dust motes.

215 sq. m.

The copyright belongs to Border Oak

Byton Hall

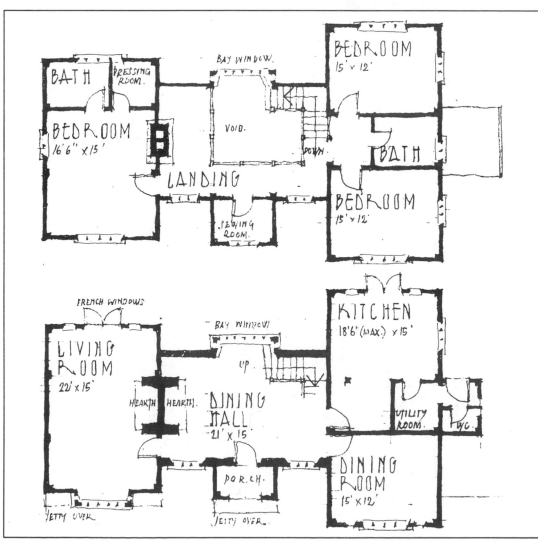

A small manor house, echoing an Elizabethan Manor. A massive oak frame with jetties, close studding, carved bargeboards and exuberant detailing on the front elevation. It has a simple and rustic rear elevation. A massive central dining hall with inglenook and hearth. A two storey high space with leaded windows to flood the room with light. A well-proportioned living room and a practical kitchen - a place to dwell. A panelled dining room - a room in which to impress. A lazy staircase leading a master bedroom with vaulted ceiling. Arched braces frame the lobby which offers access to two further bedrooms and a family bathroom above the kitchen wing.

2340 sq. ft./223 sq. m.

The copyright belongs to Border Oak

Kings Pyon House

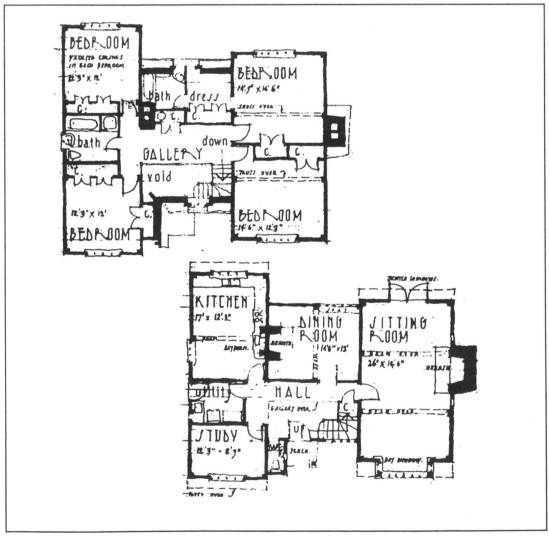

This house, with its close studding and wide swept curved braces, demonstrates the epitome of oak framing, where structure is both function and decoration. It is a house with a heart, a core, the hall, with its gallery over, from which everything else radiates, a home for the Christmas tree, or the mote flecked rays of a high July sun imprinting the barred shadow of the dormer window on the flagstone floor.

203 sq. m.

The copyright belongs to Border Oak

Pencombe Farmhouse

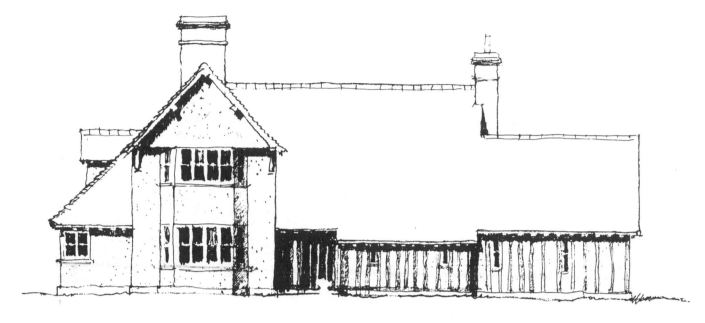

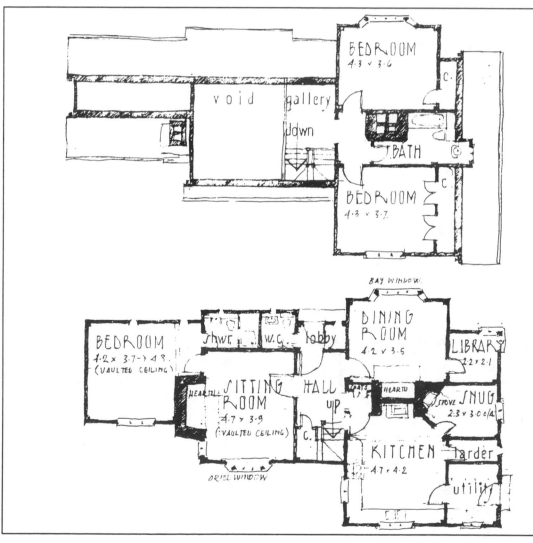

BEDROOM
4·3 × 3·6

void   gallery

↓dwn

c

BATH

c

BEDROOM
4·3 × 3·7

BAY WINDOW

BEDROOM
4·2 × 3·7 → 4·8
(VAULTED CEILING)

shwr   W.C.   lobby

DINING
ROOM
4·2 × 3·5

LIBRARY
2·2 × 2·1

HEARTH   SITTING
ROOM
4·7 × 3·9
(VAULTED CEILING)

HALL

UP

HEARTH

STOVE SNUG
2·3 × 3·0 c/a

C.

KITCHEN
4·7 × 4·2

larder

utility

ORIEL WINDOW

A building with history, a farm with a story to tell. A seemingly random collection of rooms, brings new surprises. A building that defies description and its attractions can only be hinted at by a simple list. A library with corner window detail, a cosy snug with eccentrically placed fireplace, a larder, inglenooks, ground floor bedrooms and vaulted ceilings, shower rooms, single storey sitting rooms with stone inglenooks and oriel windows, creaking staircases, delinquent oak floors, resilient flagstones and a discordant sense of order in the two first floor bedrooms. A home for an individual; a contest for eccentricity between the house and the owner.

192 sq. m.

The copyright belongs to Border Oak

The Elms

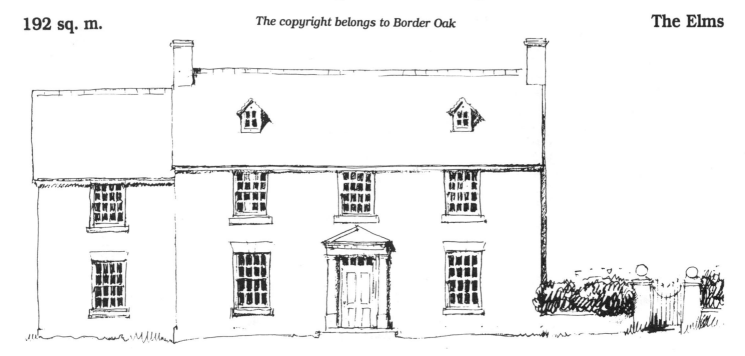

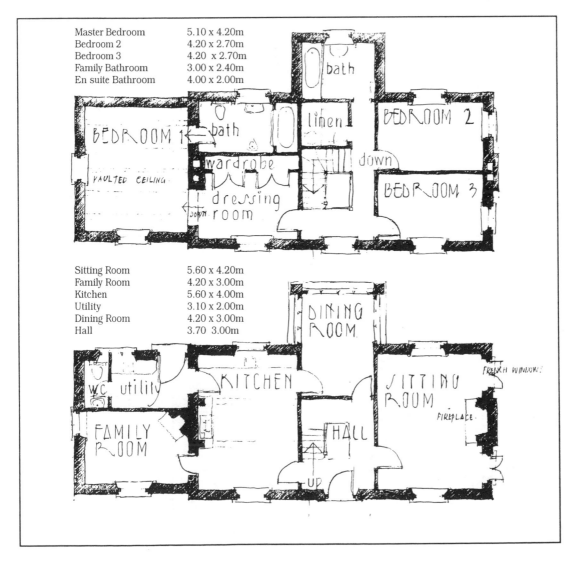

Master Bedroom	5.10 x 4.20m
Bedroom 2	4.20 x 2.70m
Bedroom 3	4.20 x 2.70m
Family Bathroom	3.00 x 2.40m
En suite Bathroom	4.00 x 2.00m

Sitting Room	5.60 x 4.20m
Family Room	4.20 x 3.00m
Kitchen	5.60 x 4.00m
Utility	3.10 x 2.00m
Dining Room	4.20 x 3.00m
Hall	3.70 3.00m

An impressive entrance hall with imposing staircase and gallery provides access to well-proportioned rooms with high ceilings and sash windows, plaster coverings and panelled doors. The dining room, glazed on three sides, is delightful. A farmhouse kitchen with inglenook recess, central beams and bacon hook welcomes animated family discussion around the scrubbed top table. The adjacent family room is a place to relax. The master bedroom with its vaulted ceiling with massive oak beams invites comparison with the cathedral-like space of the threshing barn. The dressing room and en suite bathroom confirm the appreciation of creature comforts.

218 sq. m.

Brunel House

The copyright belongs to Border Oak

Sitting Room	8.10 x 4.20m
Kitchen	4.50 x 4.20m
Utility	2.80 x 2.10m
Dining Room	4.20 x 3.80m
Hall	3.00 x 2.60m
Master Bed	4.20 x 4.10m
Bedroom 2	4.20 x 2.80m
Bedroom 3	4.70 x 4.20m
Bedroom 4	4.20 x 3.20m
Bedroom 5	3.40 x 2.70m
Family Bathrm	2.70 x 2.70m
En suite Shower	3.00 x 1.40m
Study	3.90 x 2.80m

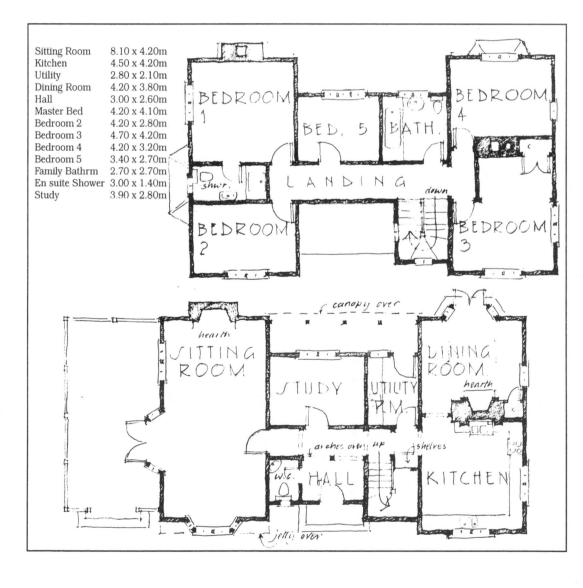

This well proportioned home has a natural air of spaciousness, generous circulation spaces and large well proportioned reception rooms and bedrooms, which reinforce the beauty and ambiance of this home. Unique and attractive detailing includes the stairtower, verandah, bay windows with French doors accessing terraces and decks, Victorian fireplaces, aga recess, panelled rooms, ornate plaster coving, etc. A wide choice of external treatments is available. The Brunel House is illustrated with rendered ground floor elevations and tile hanging to the first floor. Ornate pierced bargeboards with decorative finials complete the picture.

215 sq. m.

The copyright belongs to Border Oak

Saffron Manor

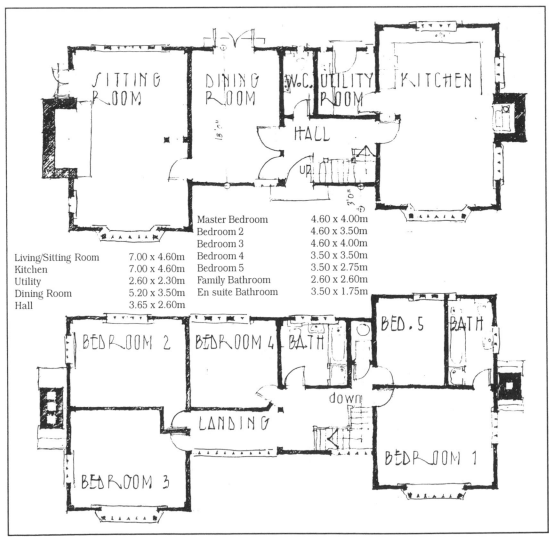

Living/Sitting Room	7.00 x 4.60m
Kitchen	7.00 x 4.60m
Utility	2.60 x 2.30m
Dining Room	5.20 x 3.50m
Hall	3.65 x 2.60m

Master Bedroom	4.60 x 4.00m
Bedroom 2	4.60 x 3.50m
Bedroom 3	4.60 x 4.00m
Bedroom 4	3.50 x 3.50m
Bedroom 5	3.50 x 2.75m
Family Bathroom	2.60 x 2.60m
En suite Bathroom	3.50 x 1.75m

The silver-grey, weather-beaten oak and the soft reassuring hues of the earth combine in this simple perspective layout. Double jetties provide refuge for oriel windows, continuous strip windows intrigue and delight. Massive inglenooks constructed in handmade soft orange/red brickwork provide a focus to the principal rooms and a solid base to the exteriors. Terracotta clay tiles soften the outline. Inside the straight line is banished. Oak walls, oak chamber joists, ledged and boarded doors with blacksmith made fittings meet suddenly curved panels to confirm the organic feel of the building that has evolved over the Century with a quiet dignity. A celebration of the art of the oak frame.

220 sq. m.

The copyright belongs to Border Oak

Staunton Farmhouse

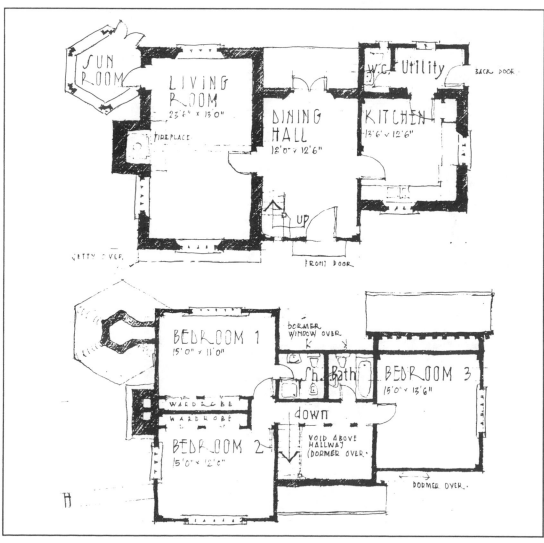

A coming together of sandstone and oak. Heavy defensive ground floor stone walls are topped with an authentic oak frame complete with overhanging jetty and catslide roof to the entrance. The windows and ground floor openings have splayed reveals which allow maximum daylight to enter. The light that enters is graduated and more gentle. An octagonal sunroom and a utility and cloakroom have been added, again respecting the traditions of the region with horizontal weatherboarding to the utility room and clay tiles to the sunroom. An unfussy staircase leads to an attractive gallery. A straightforward honest farmhouse.

2431 sq. ft./226 sq. m.

The copyright belongs to Custom Homes

Arizona

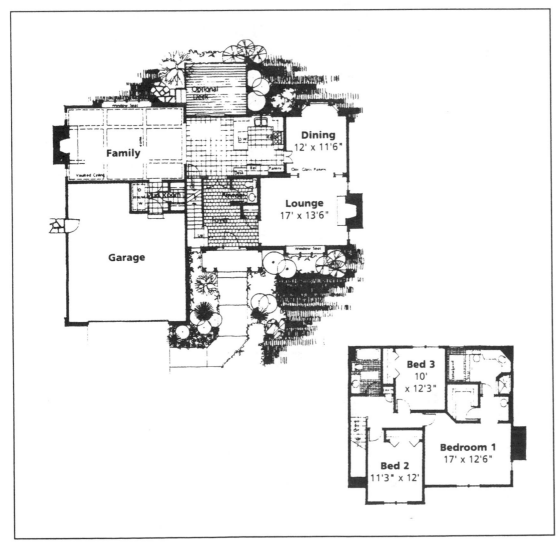

A modest house that, nevertheless, still creates an impression and has within it the seeds of flexibility so important for our ever changing lives.

2420 sq. ft.

The copyright belongs to Custom Homes

Balmoral Range

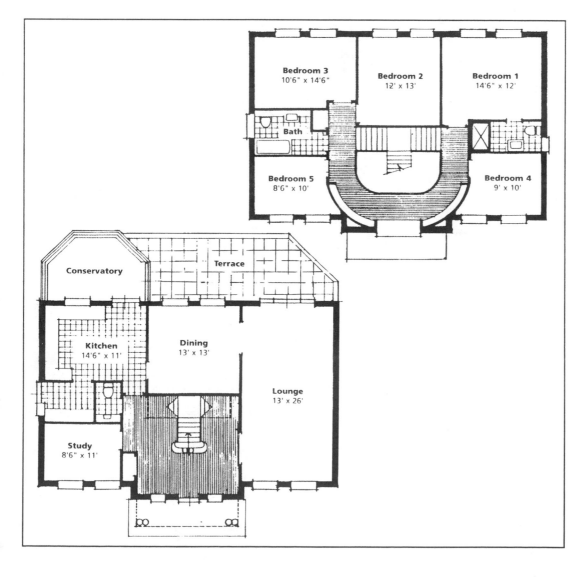

This is from a range of houses by this designer where the key is flexibility in external appearance. The accommodation layout to this design and the plan form lend themselves to adaption without any loss of individuality. Note the exciting staircase arrangement.

2420 sq. ft./245 sq. m.

The copyright belongs to Custom Homes

Priory

The secret of design is in bringing all of the proper elements together to show a pleasing and attractive home. The through lounge in this house is an important and much loved feature.

2255 sq. ft.

The copyright belongs to Custom Homes

Finchampstead

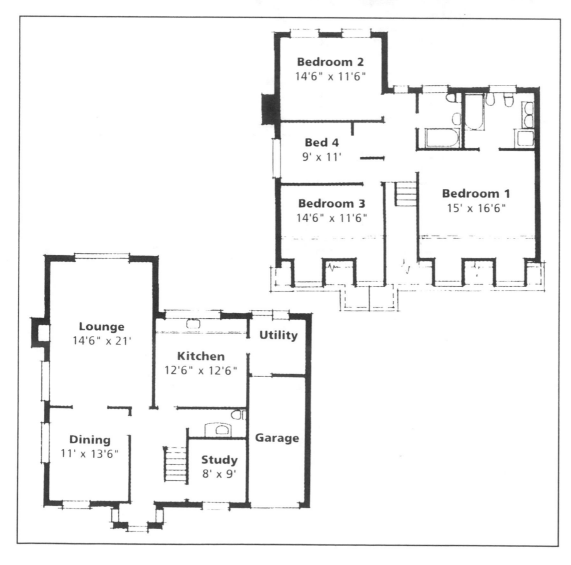

Bedroom 2
14'6" x 11'6"

Bed 4
9' x 11'

Bedroom 3
14'6" x 11'6"

Bedroom 1
15' x 16'6"

Lounge
14'6" x 21'

Utility

Kitchen
12'6" x 12'6"

Dining
11' x 13'6"

Garage

Study
8' x 9'

Simple straightforward family accommodation is the feature of this family home. The 4th bedroom at the side means that the elevation wouldn't be able to go close to a boundary but some minor rearrangements would get over that problem.

The copyright belongs to Potton Ltd.

186.51 sq. m.

14.4m x 13m

95-077

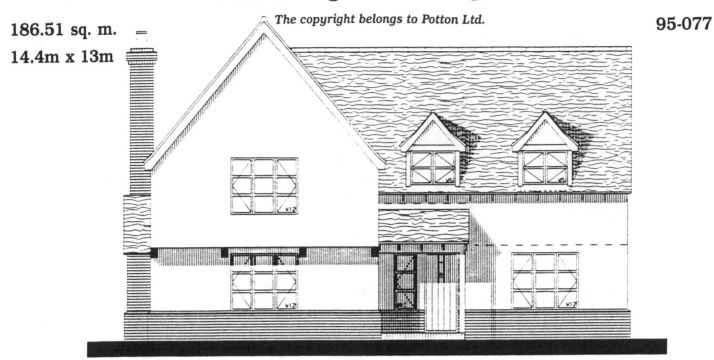

Study	2.82 x 4.26m/9'3" x 14'0"
Kitchen	4.77 x 5.44m/15'8" x 17'10"
Utility	3.17 x 2.26m/10'5" x 7'5"
Living Room	5.81 x 8.94m/19'1" x 29'4"
Dining Room	4.88 x 4.00m/16'0" x 13'1"
WC	1.71 x 2.51m/5'7" x 8'3"
Master Bed	5.81 x 6.66m/19'1" x 21'10"
En suite	3.22 x 3.54m/10'7" x 11'7"
Bedroom 2	3.01 x 4.53m/9'10" x 14'10"
En suite 2	3.01 x 1.19m/9'10" x 3'11"
Bathroom	2.21 x 3.44m/7'3" x 11'3"
Bedroom 3	6.61 x 3.98m/21'8" x 13'1"
Bedroom 4	3.45 x 3.54m/11'4" x 11'7"

A dormer style family home with carefully arranged accommodation. For those who insist on the dining room adjoining the kitchen an simple change of names would provide this.

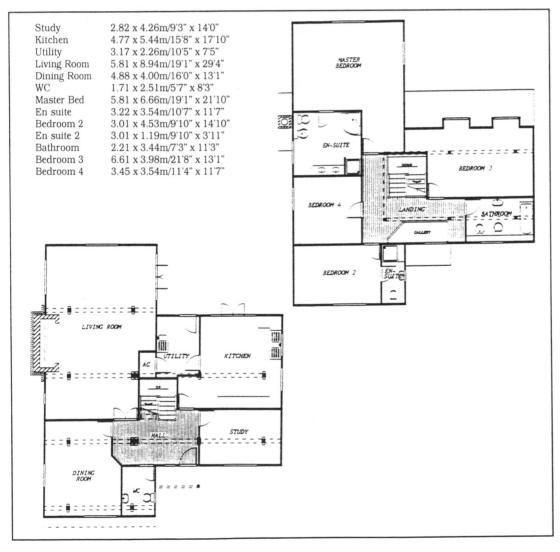

254

266.51 sq. m.

6.30m x 16.35m

The copyright belongs to Potton Ltd.

Music Room	4.62 x 5.19m/15'2" x 17'1"
Living Room	4.62 x 6.04m/15'2" x 19'10"
Dining Hall	5.66 x 6.02m/18'7" x 19'9"
Kitchen	4.06 x 4.62m/13'4" x 15'2"
Utility	1.80 x 3.24m/5'11" x 10'8"
WC	1.80 x 1.10m/5'11" x 3'7"
Garage	5.42 x 5.93m/17'9" x 19'5"
Bedroom 1	5.36 x 4.62m/17'7" x 15'2"
En suite	2.99 x2.05m/9'10" x 6'9"
Storage	3.40 x 7.82m/11'2" x 25'8"
Bathroom	2.28 x 3.19m/7'6" x 10'6"
Bedroom 2	5.28 x 4.62m/17'4" x 15'2"
Bedroom 3	4.62 x 3.31m/15'2" x 10'10"
Bedroom 4	2.53 x 3.20m/8'4" x 10'6"

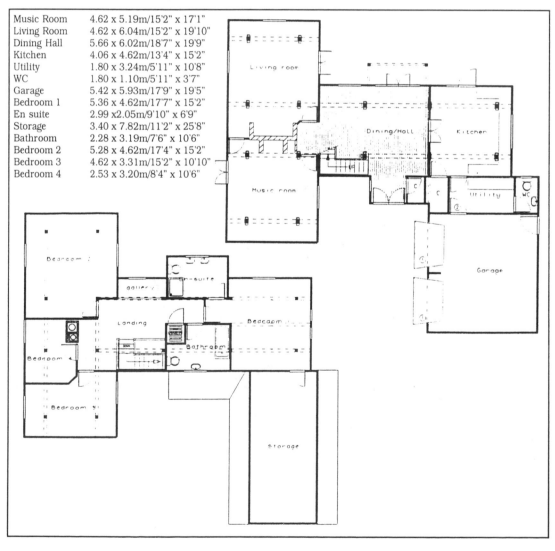

This design has over-tones of a chapel conversion from this elevation with very few windows looking forward. Once again the dining hall gives scope to the accommodation layout.

107.31 sq. m.

11.47m x 12.67m

The copyright belongs to Potton Ltd.

97-033

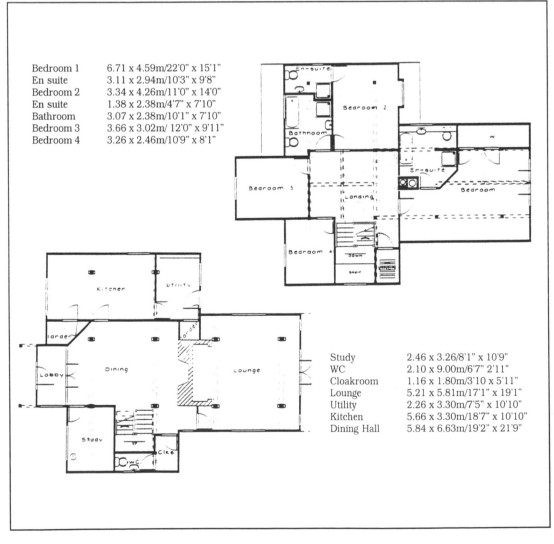

Bedroom 1	6.71 x 4.59m/22'0" x 15'1"
En suite	3.11 x 2.94m/10'3" x 9'8"
Bedroom 2	3.34 x 4.26m/11'0" x 14'0"
En suite	1.38 x 2.38m/4'7" x 7'10"
Bathroom	3.07 x 2.38m/10'1" x 7'10"
Bedroom 3	3.66 x 3.02m/ 12'0" x 9'11"
Bedroom 4	3.26 x 2.46m/10'9" x 8'1"

Study	2.46 x 3.26/8'1" x 10'9"
WC	2.10 x 9.00m/6'7" 2'11"
Cloakroom	1.16 x 1.80m/3'10 x 5'11"
Lounge	5.21 x 5.81m/17'1" x 19'1"
Utility	2.26 x 3.30m/7'5" x 10'10"
Kitchen	5.66 x 3.30m/18'7" x 10'10"
Dining Hall	5.84 x 6.63m/19'2" x 21'9"

The dining hall is becoming increasingly popular, especially if entered via a lobby/entrance porch as with this house. The scope this gives for the accommodation layout can be truly appreciated here.

107.31 sq. m.

8.47m x 12.67m

The copyright belongs to Potton Ltd.

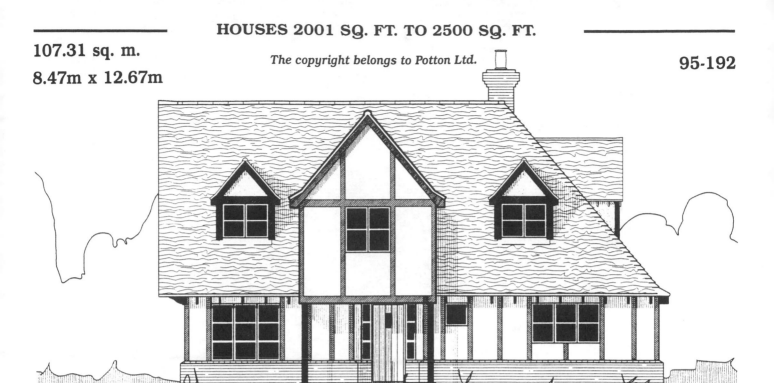

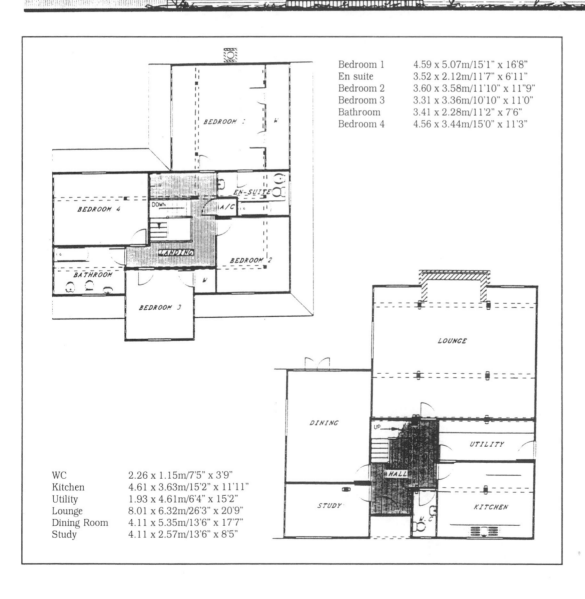

Bedroom 1	4.59 x 5.07m/15'1" x 16'8"
En suite	3.52 x 2.12m/11'7" x 6'11"
Bedroom 2	3.60 x 3.58m/11'10" x 11"9"
Bedroom 3	3.31 x 3.36m/10'10" x 11'0"
Bathroom	3.41 x 2.28m/11'2" x 7'6"
Bedroom 4	4.56 x 3.44m/15'0" x 11'3"

A house in the cottage style is what made the name of this company - with clever use of roof planes, low eaves and carefully thought out and interesting family accommodation. For a house of this complexity, very little space is wasted.

WC	2.26 x 1.15m/7'5" x 3'9"
Kitchen	4.61 x 3.63m/15'2" x 11'11"
Utility	1.93 x 4.61m/6'4" x 15'2"
Lounge	8.01 x 6.32m/26'3" x 20'9"
Dining Room	4.11 x 5.35m/13'6" x 17'7"
Study	4.11 x 2.57m/13'6" x 8'5"

204.20 sq. m.
14.27m x 14.31m

The copyright belongs to Potton Ltd.

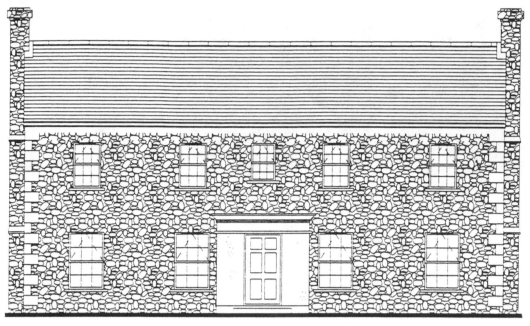

Dining Room	5.81 x 5.71m/19'1" x 18'9"
WC	1.20 x 2.32m/3'11" x 7'7"
Larder	1.20 x 1.45m/3'11" x 4'9"
Kitchen	5.81 x 5.71m/19'1" x 18'9"
Utility	2.21 x 2.45m/7'3" x 8'0"
Drawing Rm	5.81 x 5.71m/19'1" x 18'9"
Master Bed	5.81 x 5.71m/19'1" x 18'9"
En suite	2.20 x 3.16m/7'3" x 10'5"
Bedroom 3	4.92 x 3.16m/16'2" x 10'5"
Bedroom 4	4.52 x 2.55m/14'10" x 8'5"
Bathroom	3.49 x 2.32m/11'5" x 7'7"
Study	3.40 x 2.50m/11'2" x 8'3"
Attic storage	4.00 x 3.95m/13'1" x 13'0"

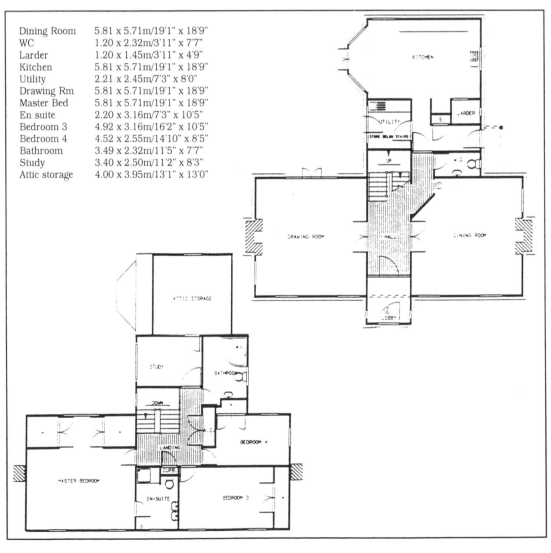

Houses in the style of the old rectories had one drawback in that they achieved their long low symmetrical look by failing to provide very much accommodation inside. The designers have therefore provided this by the carefully designed and proportioned rear projection that leaves the main section free to house the principal living rooms.

279.22 sq. m.

17.3m x 16.1m

98-049

Dining Room	3.75 x 4.79m
Living Room	6.91 x 4.79m
Family Room	3.94 x 3.92m
Kitchen	5.12 x 3.55m
Utility	1.80 x 2.38m
Study	2.70 x 3.55m
Garage	5.44 x 5.48m
Bedroom 1	4.79 x 5.49m
En suite	2.00 x 3.78m
Bedroom 2	5.53 x 4.10m
En suite 2	1.38 x 3.39m
Bedroom 3	2.59 x 3.92m
Bedroom 4	3.82 x 3.55m
Bathroom	2.32 x 3.55m
Bedroom 5	2.70 x 3.55m

This is a lovely family house that would grace many a plot. The garage is not illustrated on the plans but would normally be situated beneath the second bedroom suite.

10.28m x 16.92m
173.93 sq. m.

The copyright belongs to Potton Ltd.

98-048

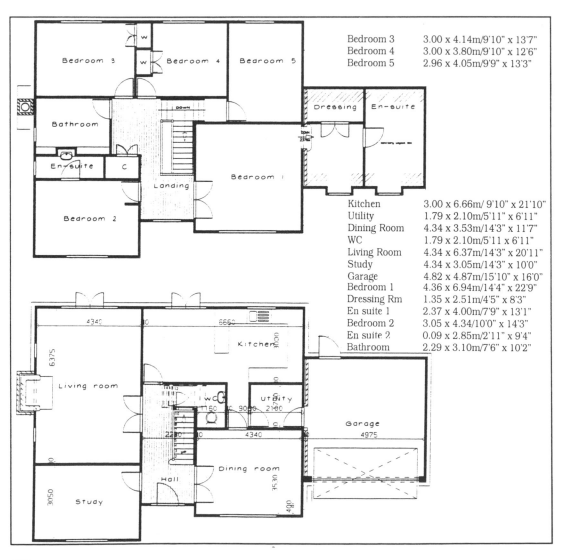

Bedroom 3	3.00 x 4.14m/9'10" x 13'7"
Bedroom 4	3.00 x 3.80m/9'10" x 12'6"
Bedroom 5	2.96 x 4.05m/9'9" x 13'3"

Kitchen	3.00 x 6.66m/ 9'10" x 21'10"
Utility	1.79 x 2.10m/5'11" x 6'11"
Dining Room	4.34 x 3.53m/14'3" x 11'7"
WC	1.79 x 2.10m/5'11 x 6'11"
Living Room	4.34 x 6.37m/14'3" x 20'11"
Study	4.34 x 3.05m/14'3" x 10'0"
Garage	4.82 x 4.87m/15'10" x 16'0"
Bedroom 1	4.36 x 6.94m/14'4" x 22'9"
Dressing Rm	1.35 x 2.51m/4'5" x 8'3"
En suite 1	2.37 x 4.00m/7'9" x 13'1"
Bedroom 2	3.05 x 4.34m/10'0" x 14'3"
En suite 2	0.09 x 2.85m/2'11" x 9'4"
Bathroom	2.29 x 3.10m/7'6" x 10'2"

The offset double frontage progresses well to the set back garage leading the eye across and into the design. The five bedrooms and the wealth of ancillary dressing and en-suite rooms highlight generous ground floor family

167.60 sq. m.

14.60m x 11.48m

The copyright belongs to Potton Ltd.

98-047

Bedroom 1	5.11 x 5.24m/16'9" x 17'2"
Dressing Rm	3.14 x 2.31m/10'4" x 7'7"
En suite	2.31 x 2.01m/7'7" x 6'7"
Bedroom 2	4.00 x 4.62m/13'1" x 15'2"
En suite 2	2.22 x 3.53m/7'3" x 11'7"
Bedroom 3	3.00 x 4.00m/9'10" x 13'1"
Bedroom 4	2.77 x 4.22m/9'1" x 13'10"
Bedroom 5	3.00 x 3.60m/9'10" x 11'10"
Bathroom	2.01 x 3.12m/6'7" x 10'3"

Living Room	7.71 x 4.00m/25'4" x 13'1"
Dining Room	3.45 x 4.87m/11'4" x 16'0"
Kitchen	3.91 x 4.22m/12'10" x 13'10"
Utility	1.60 x 2.10m/5'3" x 6'11"
WC	1.00 x 2.10m/3'3" x 6'11"
Study	2.79 x 5.24m/9'2" x 17'2"
Garage	5.11 x 5.24m/16'9" x 17'2"

The design wraps itself around the entrance arrangements with the garage doors looking across the frontage and providing visual interest to the whole facade. Superb five bedroomed accommodation completes this excellent family home.

2110 sq. ft./48 ft. x 43 ft. *The copyright belongs to ASBA Julian Owen Associates*   **Alexandra**

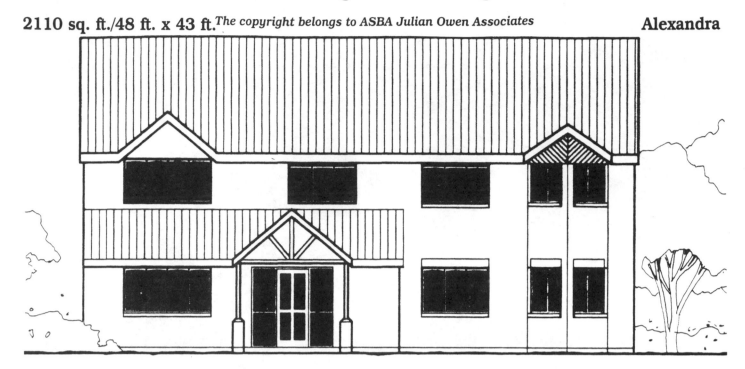

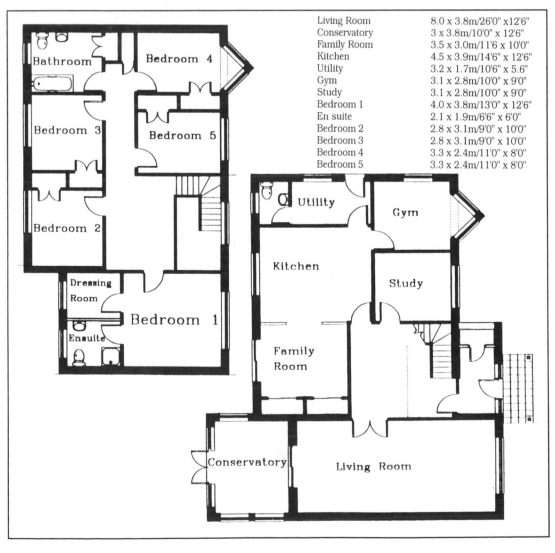

Living Room	8.0 x 3.8m/26'0" x12'6"
Conservatory	3 x 3.8m/10'0" x 12'6"
Family Room	3.5 x 3.0m/11'6 x 10'0"
Kitchen	4.5 x 3.9m/14'6" x 12'6"
Utility	3.2 x 1.7m/10'6" x 5.6"
Gym	3.1 x 2.8m/10'0" x 9'0"
Study	3.1 x 2.8m/10'0" x 9'0"
Bedroom 1	4.0 x 3.8m/13'0" x 12'6"
En suite	2.1 x 1.9m/6'6" x 6'0"
Bedroom 2	2.8 x 3.1m/9'0" x 10'0"
Bedroom 3	2.8 x 3.1m/9'0" x 10'0"
Bedroom 4	3.3 x 2.4m/11'0" x 8'0"
Bedroom 5	3.3 x 2.4m/11'0" x 8'0"

On top of the 5 bed-rooms and built-in gym the house has been designed for use be a professional person who works from home. Crucially, the study is accessed directly from the main hall, allowing clients and others to visit without trespassing into the domestic part of the house. A generous landing has been provided, for fitting out with built in storage.

288.34 sq. m.
14.84m x 19.43m

97-259

Dining Room	5.00 x 5.70m/16'5" x 18'8"
Sitting Room	5.00 x 6.00m/16'5" x 19'8"
Kitchen/	
Breakfast	5.00 x 4.00m/16'5" x 13'1"
Utility	3.00 x 2.40m/9'10" x 7'10"
Study	3.00 x 3.00m/9'10" x 9'10"
Garage	5.00 x 4.91m/16'5" x 16'1"
Master Bed	5.70 x 4.11m/18'8" x 13'6"
En suite	1.95 x 3.11m/6'5" x 13'10"
Bathroom	3.71 x 2.81m/12'2" x 9'3"
Bedroom 3	2.45 x 5.00m/8'1" x 16'5"
Bedroom 4	2.45 x 5.00m/8'1" x 16'5"

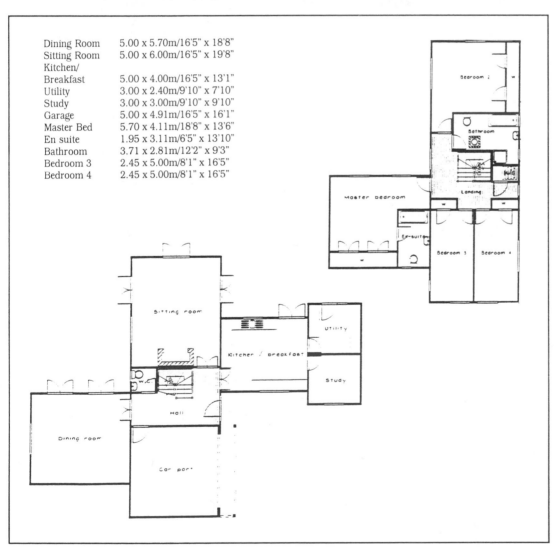

Additive development is a feature of many rural properties and it is a clever designer that manages to create an entirely new design that reflects this style. That this has been properly achieved here, there can be no doubt.

309.05 sq. m.

20.70m x 14.93m

The copyright belongs to Potton Ltd.

97-258

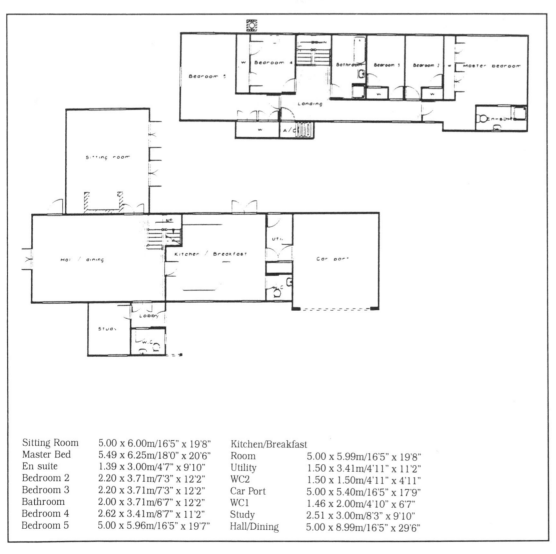

One could be forgiven for thinking that this was a cottage/barn conversion from this illustration and in truth it's in those very same situations that this clever design would find most favour.

Sitting Room	5.00 x 6.00m/16'5" x 19'8"	Kitchen/Breakfast		
Master Bed	5.49 x 6.25m/18'0" x 20'6"	Room	5.00 x 5.99m/16'5" x 19'8"
En suite	1.39 x 3.00m/4'7" x 9'10"	Utility	1.50 x 3.41m/4'11" x 11'2"
Bedroom 2	2.20 x 3.71m/7'3" x 12'2"	WC2	1.50 x 1.50m/4'11" x 4'11"
Bedroom 3	2.20 x 3.71m/7'3" x 12'2"	Car Port	5.00 x 5.40m/16'5" x 17'9"
Bathroom	2.00 x 3.71m/6'7" x 12'2"	WC1	1.46 x 2.00m/4'10" x 6'7"
Bedroom 4	2.62 x 3.41m/8'7" x 11'2"	Study	2.51 x 3.00m/8'3" x 9'10"
Bedroom 5	5.00 x 5.96m/16'5" x 19'7"	Hall/Dining	5.00 x 8.99m/16'5" x 29'6"

The copyright belongs to Potton Ltd.

150.04 sq. m.

12.21m x 12.40m

Sunroom	3.51 x 3.95m/11'6" x 13'0"
Kitchen	5.76 x 5.81m/18'11" x 19'1"
Utility	2.46 x 2.40m/8'1" x 7'11"
WC	0.90 x 1.96m/2'11" x 6'5"
Dining/Hall	6.80 x 7.26m/22'4" x 23'10"
Study	3.86 x 2.26m/12'8" x 7'5"
Living Room	4.86 x 5.81m/15'11" x 19'1"
Bedroom 1	4.59 x 5.16m/15'1" x 16'11"
En suite	2.30 x 2.40m/7'7" x 7'11"
Wardrobe	2.20 x 2.40m/7'3" x 7'11"
Bedroom 2	3.08 x 4.86m/10'1" x 15'11"
Bedroom 3	2.70 x 4.86m/8'10" x 15'11"
Bathroom	2.75 x 3.86m/9'0" x 12'8"
Bedroom 4	2.97 x 3.86m/9'9" x 12'8"

The front elevation of this large home belies the wealth of accommodation that lies behind the front door. The kitchen and sunroom arrangement would be nothing short of wonderful.

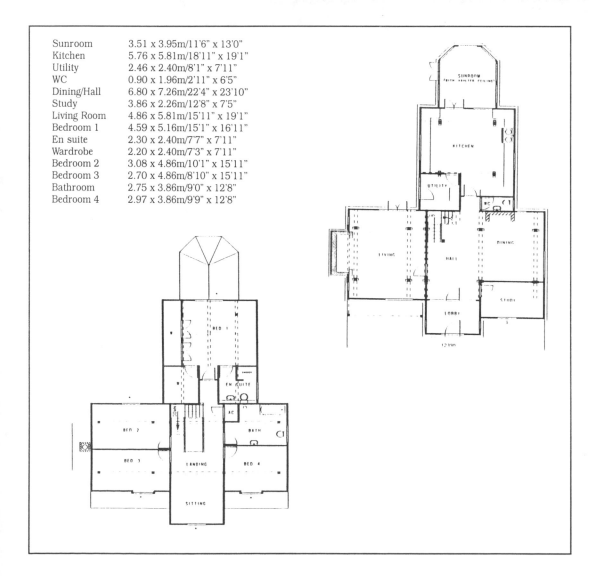

251.81 sq. m.

16.09m x 15.65m

92-090

Study	4.41 x 3.33m/14'6" x 10'10"
Dining Room	4.19 x 3.51m/13'9" x 11'6"
Kitchen/Breakfast	
Area	6.66 x 5.81m/21'10" x 19'1"
Utility	2.53 x 3.26m/8'4" x 10'9"
WC1	1.50 x 1.28m/4'11"x 4'2"
Store 1	1.28 x 1.51m/4'2" x 4'11"
Lounge	6.91 x 6.51m/22'8" x 21'4"
Store 2	1.30 x 1.10m/4'3" x 3'7"
WC2	1.01 x 2.26m/3'4" x 7'5"
Bedroom 1	5.81 x 6.66m/19'1" x 21'10"
En suite	1.85 x 3.12m/6'1" x 10'3"
Bedroom 2	7.01 x 4.59m/23'0" x 15'1"
En suite 2	1.86 x 3.19m/6'1" x 10'6"
Bathroom	3.93 x 2.68m/12'11" x 8'10"
Bedroom 3	4.08 x 2.68m/13'5" x 8'10"
Bedroom 4	3.09 x 3.04m/10'2" x 10'0"

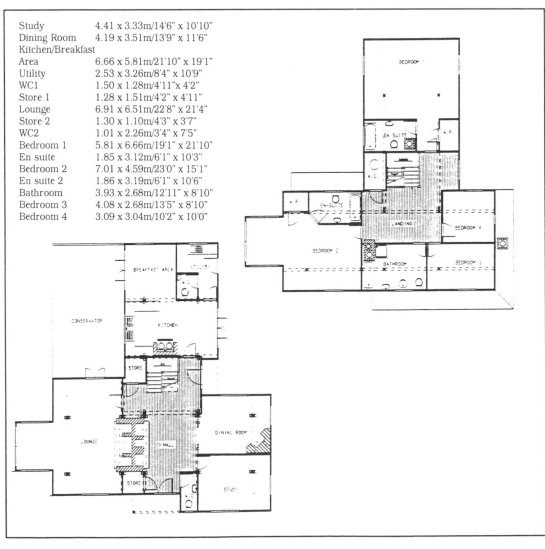

The interesting feature of this design is the fact that so many of the different living activities are confined to separate blocks of accommodation within the room layout. The dayroom accommodation is at the rear adjoining the conservatory with the lounge kept separate.

213 sq. m.

Copyright refer to Designer Homes

Strathbane

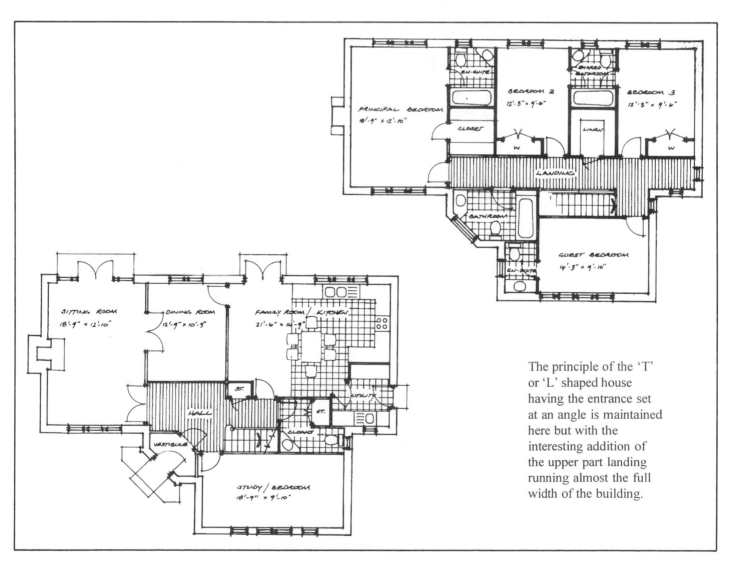

PRINCIPAL BEDROOM
18'·9" x 12'·10"

EN-SUITE

CLOSET

BEDROOM 2
12'·3" x 9'·6"

SHARED BATHROOM

LINEN

BEDROOM 3
12'·3" x 9'·6"

W

W

LANDING

BATHROOM

GUEST BEDROOM
14'·3" x 9'·10"

EN-SUITE

SITTING ROOM
18'·9" x 12'·10"

DINING ROOM
12'·9" x 10'·5"

FAMILY ROOM / KITCHEN
21'·6" x 14'·9"

ST.

HALL

UTILITY

CT.

CLOAKS

VESTIBULE

STUDY / BEDROOM
18'·9" x 9'·10"

The principle of the 'T' or 'L' shaped house having the entrance set at an angle is maintained here but with the interesting addition of the upper part landing running almost the full width of the building.

267

209.6 sq. m.

Copyright refer to Designer Homes

Cotswold

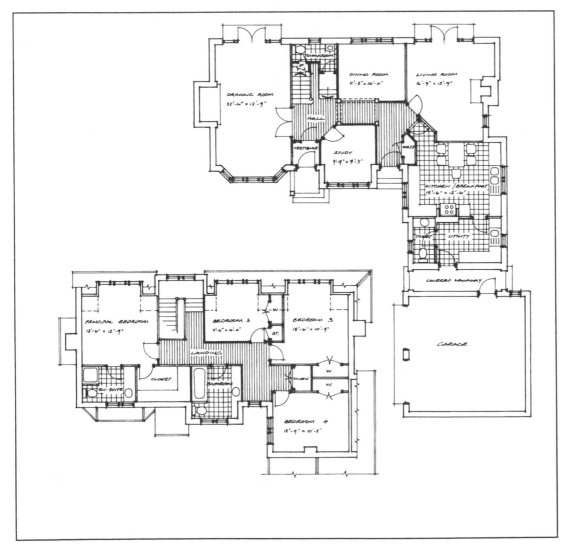

Varied roof planes and a combination of low eaves lines and steeply pitched forward projecting gables give this lovely family house a character all of its own right down to the double entrance arrangement.

2001 sq. ft.

Copyright refer to Designer Homes

Seafield

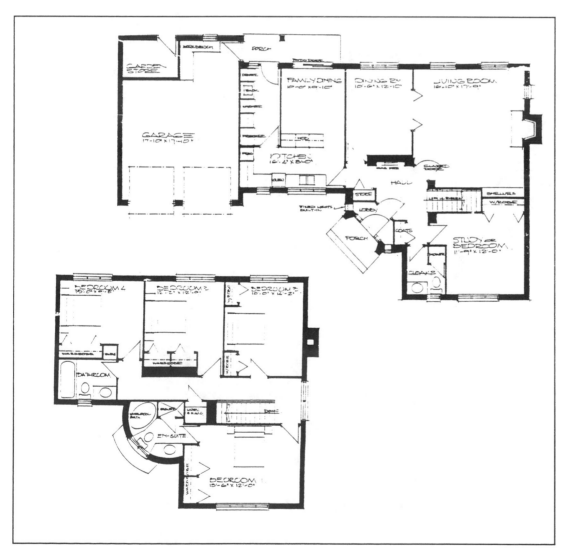

This is another house where the entrance arrangements are the principal feature of the design but, on this house, the feature is expanded into the tower above the porch and hall.

2150 sq. ft.
Copyright refer to Designer Homes
Annandale

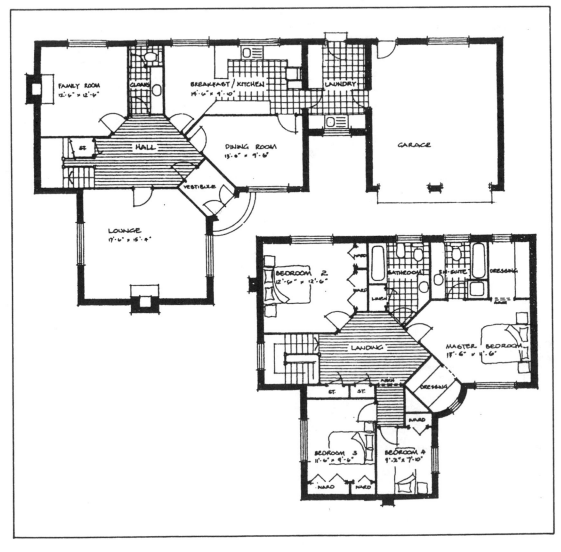

The offset nature of the entrance and hallway allow an interesting and exciting internal arrangement of the rooms to both floors that would certainly impress.

187.74 sq. m.

Copyright refer to Designer Homes

Athol

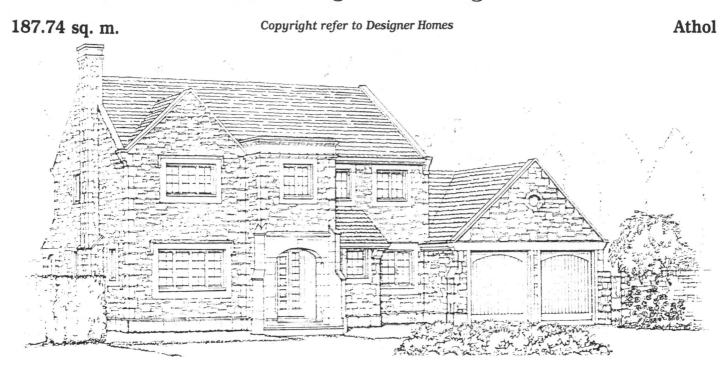

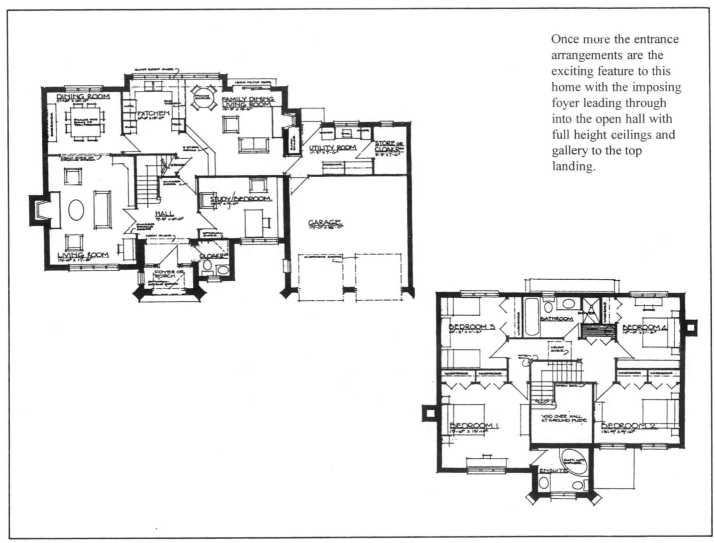

Once more the entrance arrangements are the exciting feature to this home with the imposing foyer leading through into the open hall with full height ceilings and gallery to the top landing.

271

189.48 sq. m.

Copyright refer to Designer Homes

Argyll

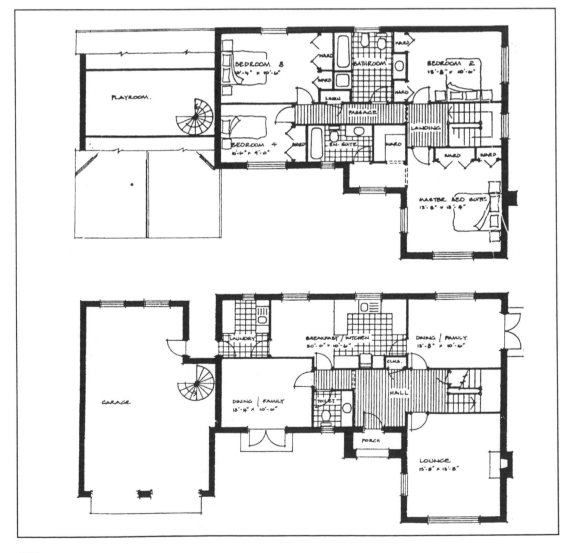

The addition of the self contained playroom over the garage transforms this home. Family life depends so much on flexibility of accommodation requirement and provision and this house has it all.

219.7 sq. m./2364 sq. ft.   *Copyright refer to Designer Homes*   **Denholm**

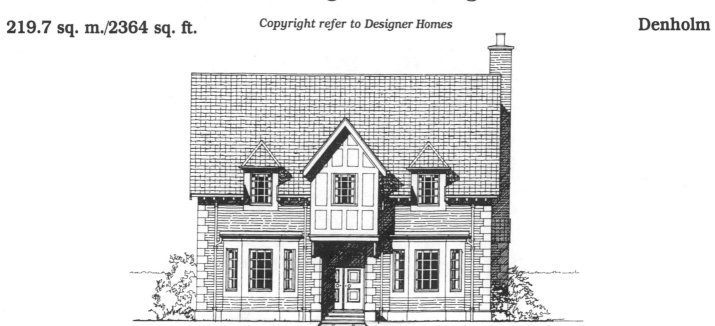

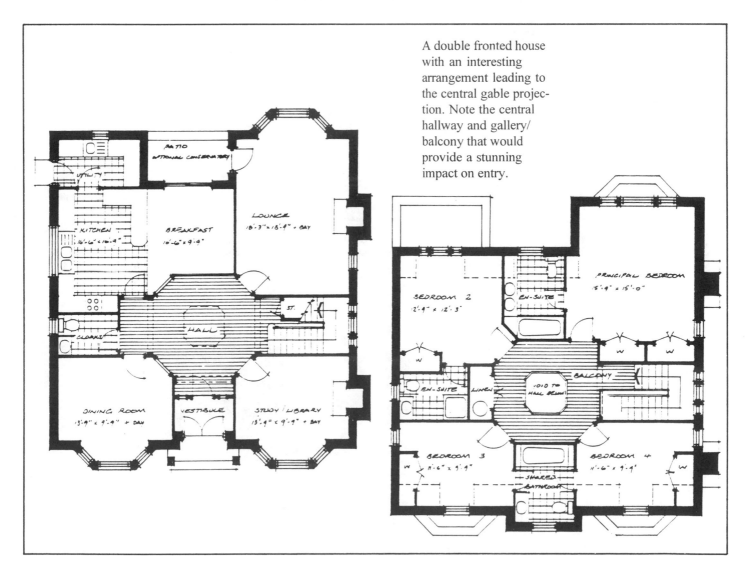

A double fronted house with an interesting arrangement leading to the central gable projection. Note the central hallway and gallery/balcony that would provide a stunning impact on entry.

192.5 sq. m./2072 sq. ft.   *Copyright refer to Designer Homes*   **The Puffin**

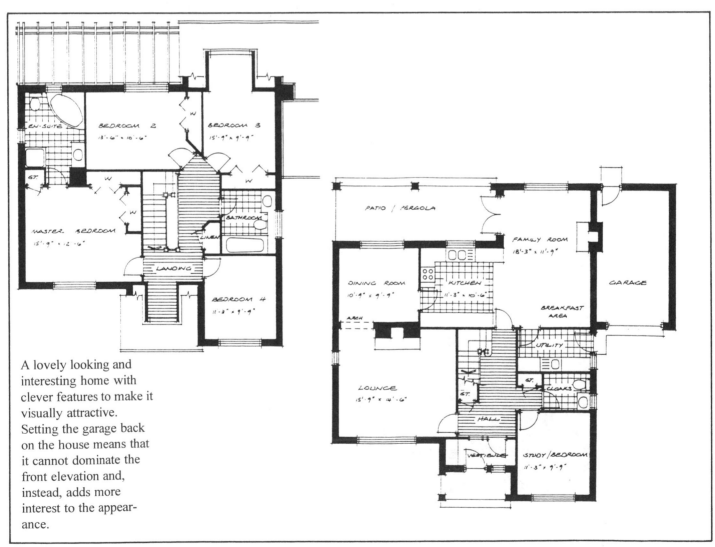

A lovely looking and interesting home with clever features to make it visually attractive. Setting the garage back on the house means that it cannot dominate the front elevation and, instead, adds more interest to the appearance.

210.9 sq. m./2270 sq. ft.   *Copyright refer to Designer Homes*   **The Goldfinch**

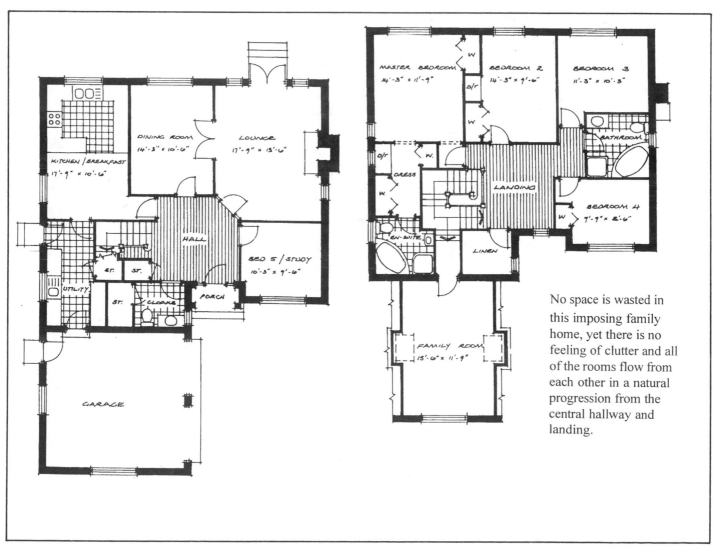

No space is wasted in this imposing family home, yet there is no feeling of clutter and all of the rooms flow from each other in a natural progression from the central hallway and landing.

275

201.92 sq. m.

The Nuthatch

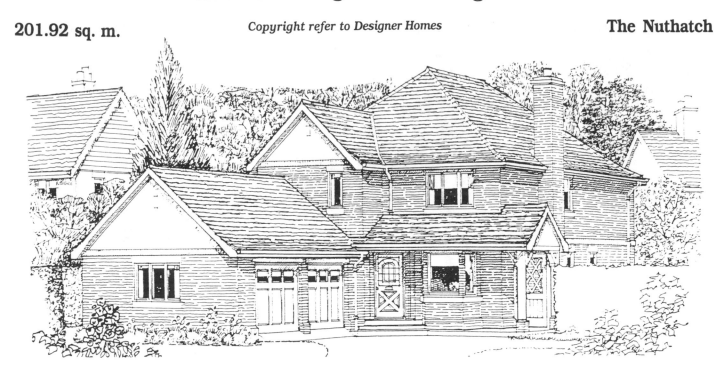

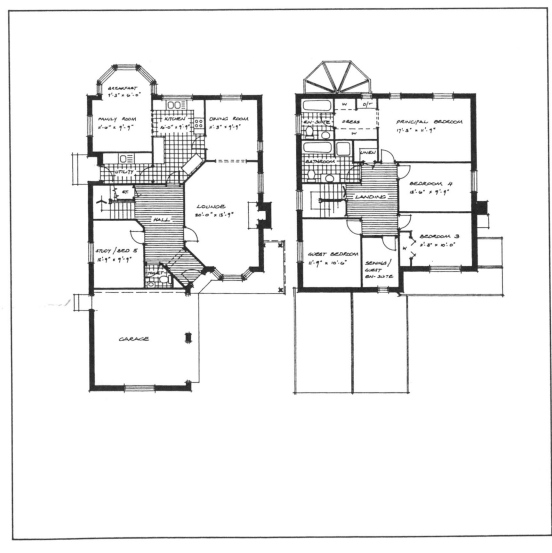

This is a design that would suit the corner plot hived off from the house next door where many of the major rooms would want to look away into the garden without intruding on the accommodation or visual amenity space of the surrounding homes.

215 sq. m.

Copyright refer to Designer Homes

The Greenfinch

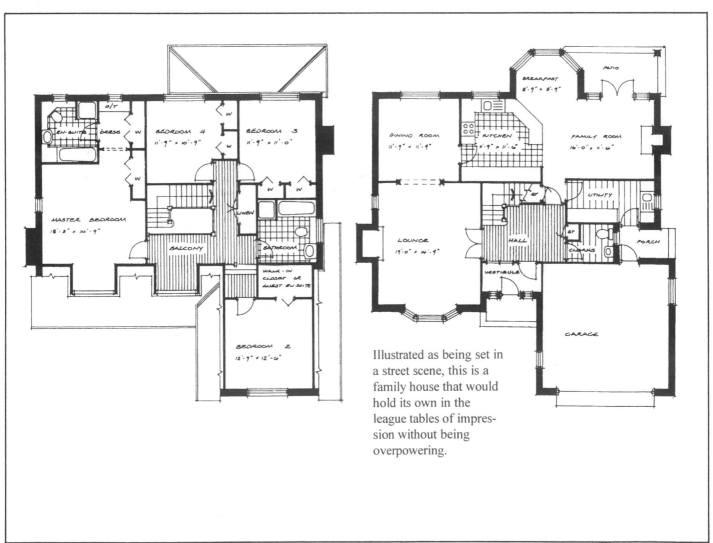

Illustrated as being set in a street scene, this is a family house that would hold its own in the league tables of impression without being overpowering.

215.2 sq. m.

Woodcroft

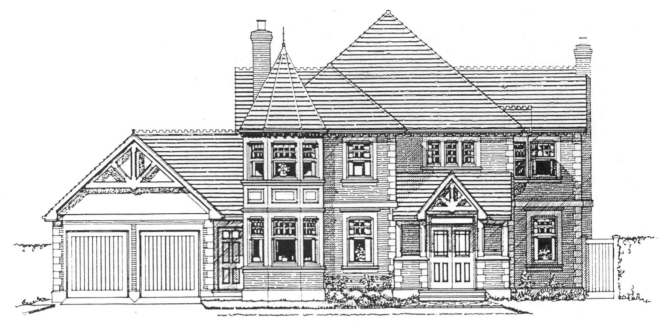

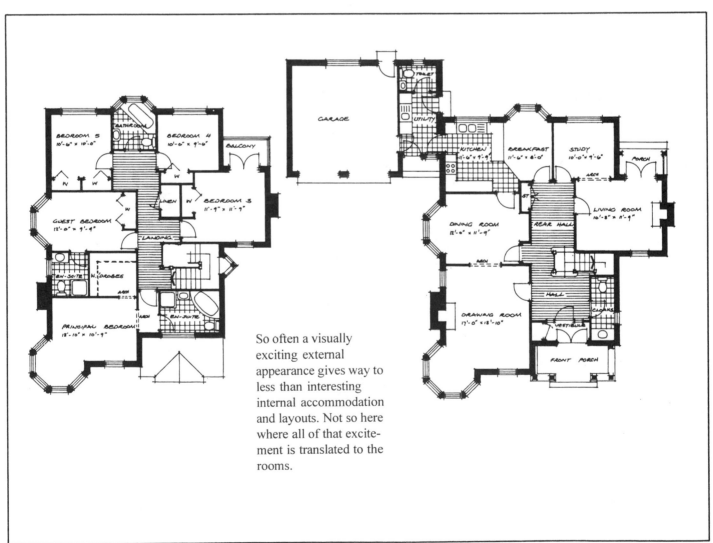

So often a visually exciting external appearance gives way to less than interesting internal accommodation and layouts. Not so here where all of that excitement is translated to the rooms.

2145 sq. ft./199sq. m.

The copyright belongs to Custom Homes

Lacock

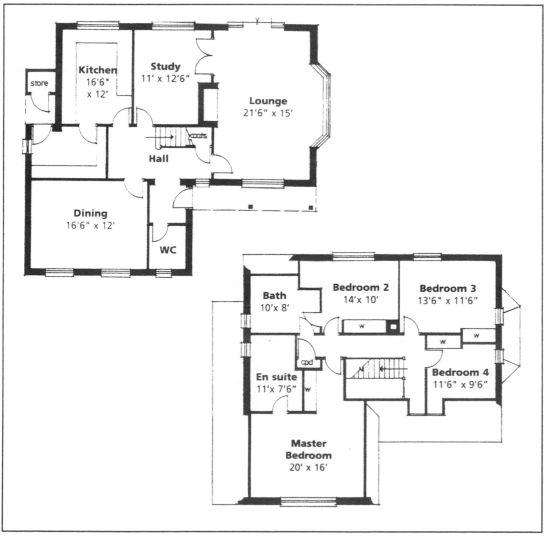

Kitchen
16'6"
x 12'

Study
11' x 12'6"

store

Lounge
21'6" x 15'

coats

Hall

Dining
16'6" x 12'

WC

Bath
10'x 8'

Bedroom 2
14'x 10'

Bedroom 3
13'6" x 11'6"

w

En suite
11'x 7'6"

w

cpd

Bedroom 4
11'6" x 9'6"

w   w

**Master
Bedroom**
20' x 16'

The accommodation in
this lovely family house
lends itself to a plot
where there are views to
be enjoyed in at least
three directions. The
sizes of all of the rooms
are generous with even
the smallest bedroom
capable of being a double
one.

2085 sq. ft./194 sq. m.

The copyright belongs to Custom Homes

Wadhurst

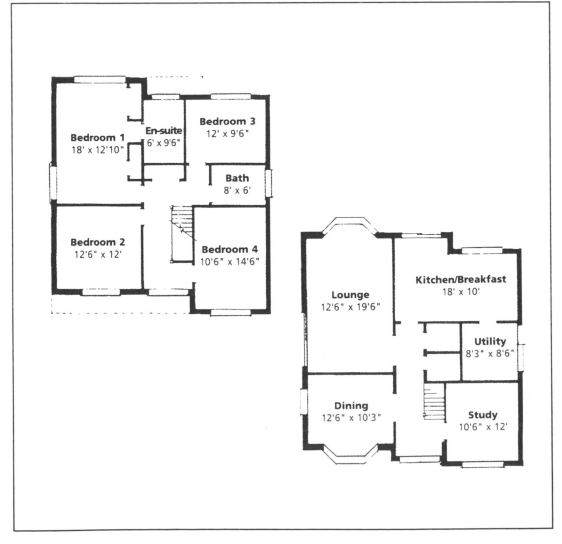

Bedroom 1
18' x 12'10"

En-suite
6' x 9'6"

Bedroom 3
12' x 9'6"

Bath
8' x 6'

Bedroom 2
12'6" x 12'

Bedroom 4
10'6" x 14'6"

Lounge
12'6" x 19'6"

Kitchen/Breakfast
18' x 10'

Utility
8'3" x 8'6"

Dining
12'6" x 10'3"

Study
10'6" x 12'

The partial hipped ends of the main roof coupled with the use of Tudor boarding and bricks place this illustration firmly in the Sussex camp but the innovative floor layout and design could just as easily be adapted to other regional styles.

2112 sq. ft./196 sq. m.

The copyright belongs to Custom Homes

Regency

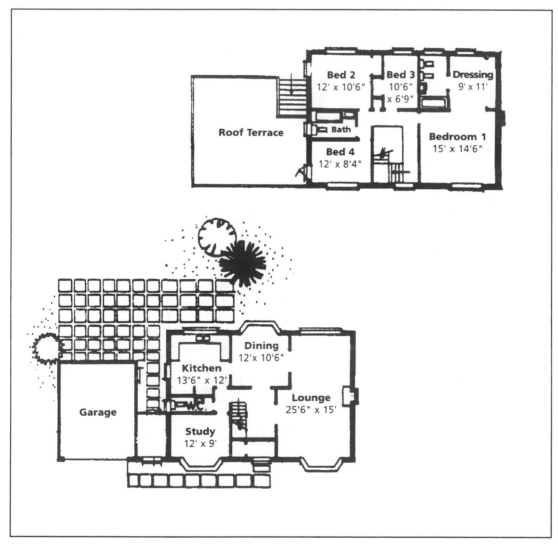

A classic looking house with echoes of the period after which it is named. The roof terrace is obviously optional but would make a welcome and interesting feature.

2062 sq. ft./191 sq. m.

The copyright belongs to Custom Homes

Craig

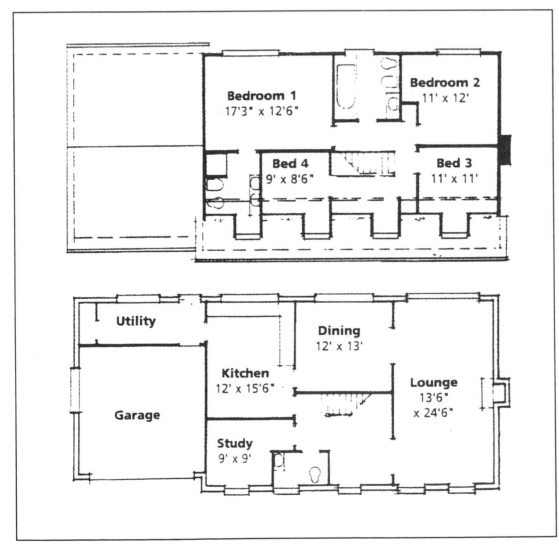

Bedroom 1
17'3" x 12'6"

Bedroom 2
11' x 12'

Bed 4
9' x 8'6"

Bed 3
11' x 11'

Utility

Dining
12' x 13'

Kitchen
12' x 15'6"

Lounge
13'6" x 24'6"

Garage

Study
9' x 9'

A typical dormer style house that by its very simplicity and the symmetry of the dormer arrangements manages to impress.

2062 sq. ft./191 sq. m. *The copyright belongs to Custom Homes* **Ashford**

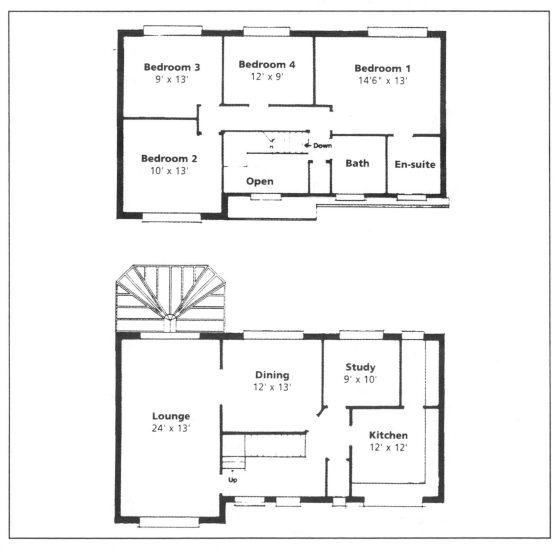

A house for the wide plot, where the roof line to the main house section has been brought down at the eaves to prevent its height being overpowering. Once more the master suite takes up a fairly large proportion of the upper part.

2035 sq. ft./189 sq. m.   *The copyright belongs to Custom Homes*   **Sevenoaks**

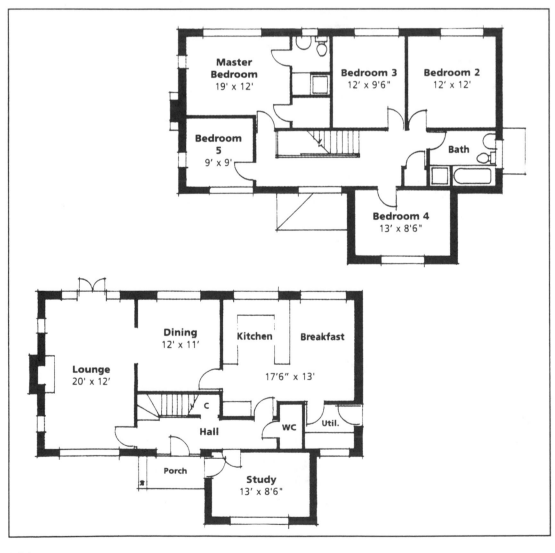

The beauty of this five bedroomed house is the long and well lit hallway and upper gallery giving a feel of light and space upon entering. Interesting elevational features and the hipped main roof reduce the visual mass of the building.

2035 sq. ft./189 sq. m.

The copyright belongs to Custom Homes

Monmouth

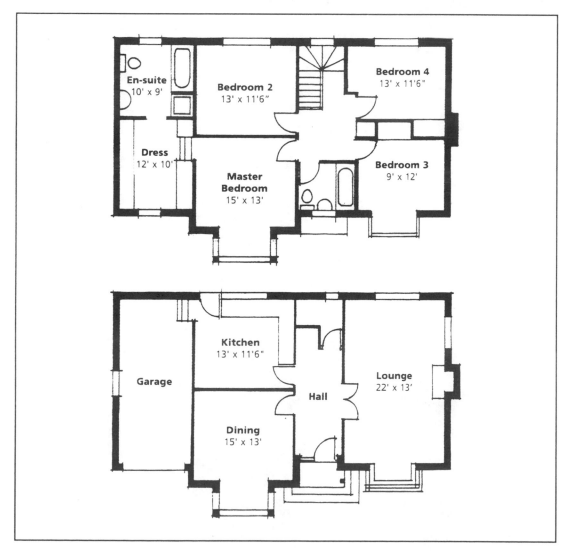

A Victorian influenced four bedroomed family house with the added attraction of the en-suite and dressing room accommodation serving the master bedroom.

Houses 2501 – 3000 sq. ft.

This category of house has been introduced in this book so as to create a division between these houses and the seriously large houses that grace the section on houses above 3000 sq. ft.

When you get up to these sizes, the scope for design, from both an internal as well as an external point of view, is greatly increased and the architect or designer can really begin to let rip with providing all that most would ever want in their new home.

There is scope for even further designations of rooms and, as such, many of the houses that we have categorised in the sections on homes with granny flats, offices or playrooms could, equally well, have found a place in this section.

Modern family life can be a stressful affair, what with televisions, computers and sound systems. Houses of this size give the opportunity for some sort of division between the generations, sufficient often, for everybody to live together under one roof without disturbing the other members of the family. Care does need to be taken to see that rooms above and below each other are compatible, and, for instance, it's absolutely no use providing the kids with their own lounge if it's directly below your bedroom and you find it difficult to sleep to the sound of an extended base.

Contributors in this section:

ASBA Julian Owen Associates
Border Oak
Custom Homes
Design & Materials Ltd.
Designer Homes
Kingpost Design Co
Potton Ltd.
Scandia-Hus

270 sq. m.

The copyright belongs to Border Oak

Westhope Court

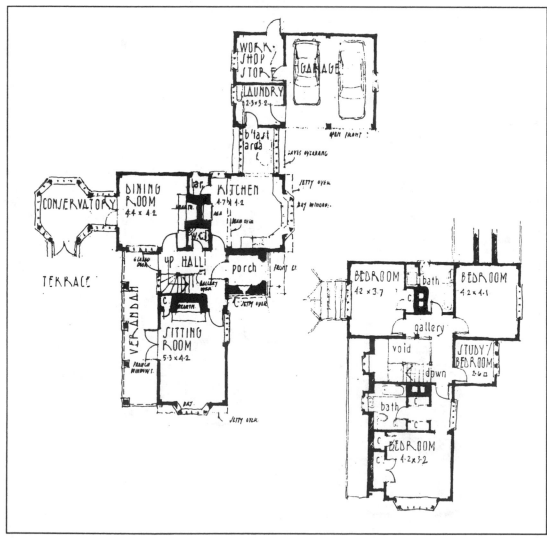

A design that seems to have been inspired by a maze! Every turning presents a range of options, a sense of discovery. A building that demands a garden and grounds to compliment and to emphasise its unusual and intriguing nature for rounders, sunrooms and conservatories, present spaces and the margins between the shelter and security of a massive oak frame and the freedom and soul of an English garden. Inglenooks, jetties, and oriel windows combine in riotous harmony. A house which celebrates life.

260 sq. m.

The copyright belongs to Border Oak

Kimbolton House

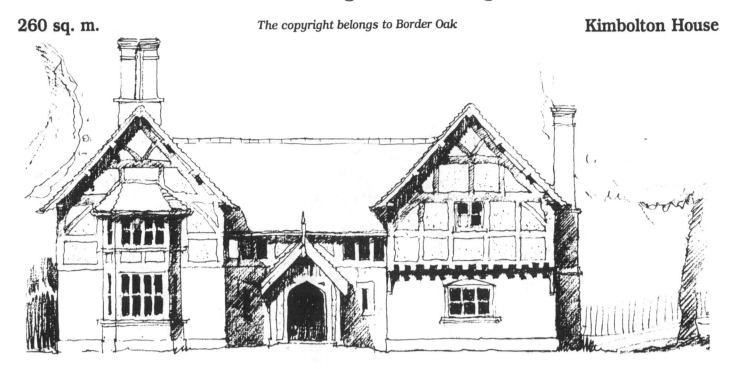

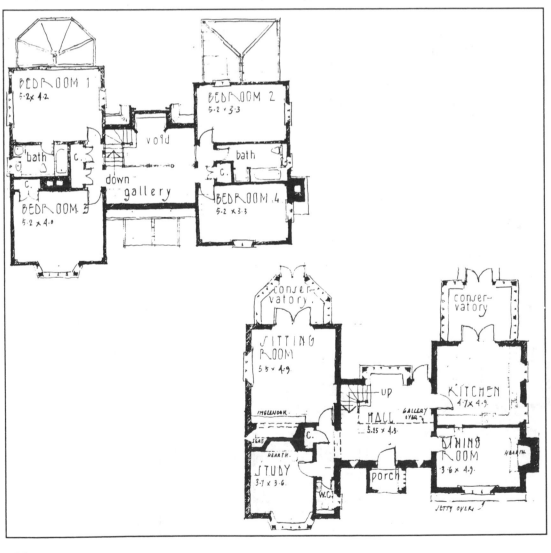

A deceptively simple design with the entrance hall and circulation spaces placed centrally giving easy access to both wings which are divided into well-proportioned bays/rooms. The ground floor is constructed in masonry (brickwork or stone), the first floor in heavy oak framing with traditional detailing allowing the use of overhanging jetties. The steeply pitched roof provides useful attic space which can be converted to additional accommodation with access via a hidden staircase in the area occupied by the cupboards between bedrooms 1 and 3.

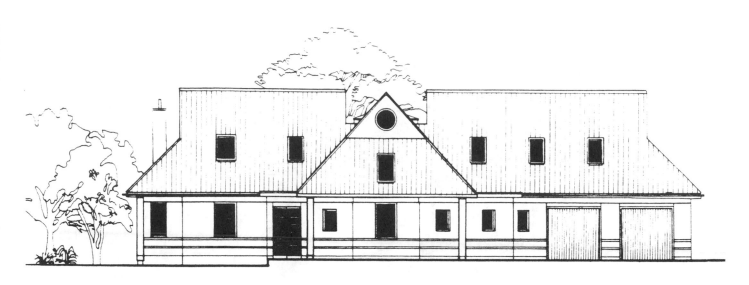

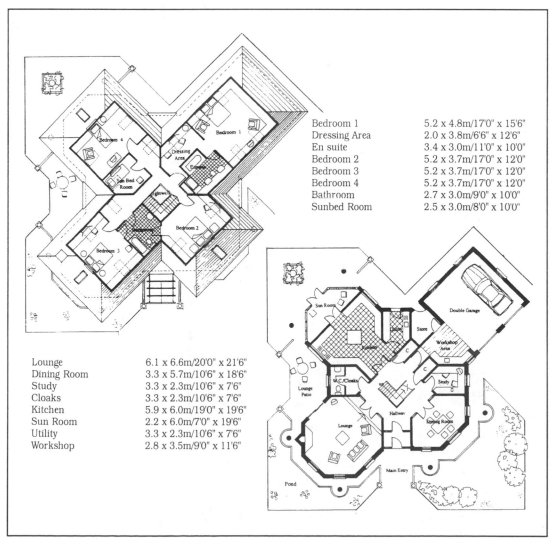

Bedroom 1	5.2 x 4.8m/17'0" x 15'6"
Dressing Area	2.0 x 3.8m/6'6" x 12'6"
En suite	3.4 x 3.0m/11'0" x 10'0"
Bedroom 2	5.2 x 3.7m/17'0" x 12'0"
Bedroom 3	5.2 x 3.7m/17'0" x 12'0"
Bedroom 4	5.2 x 3.7m/17'0" x 12'0"
Bathroom	2.7 x 3.0m/9'0" x 10'0"
Sunbed Room	2.5 x 3.0m/8'0" x 10'0"

Lounge	6.1 x 6.6m/20'0" x 21'6"
Dining Room	3.3 x 5.7m/10'6" x 18'6"
Study	3.3 x 2.3m/10'6" x 7'6"
Cloaks	3.3 x 2.3m/10'6" x 7'6"
Kitchen	5.9 x 6.0m/19'0" x 19'6"
Sun Room	2.2 x 6.0m/7'0" x 19'6"
Utility	3.3 x 2.3m/10'6" x 7'6"
Workshop	2.8 x 3.5m/9'0" x 11'6"

This house has been designed for a modern appearance but using traditional forms of construction, for cost effectiveness. The whole first floor is 'room in the roof', to be constructed from standard attic trusses, also a very economical way of building. At the heart of the house is a staircase, top lit by a pyramidal rooflight. The ground floor rooms are octagonal which adds to the contemporary feel of the design.

2730 sq. ft.

The copyright belongs to ASBA Julian Owen Associates

Parkway

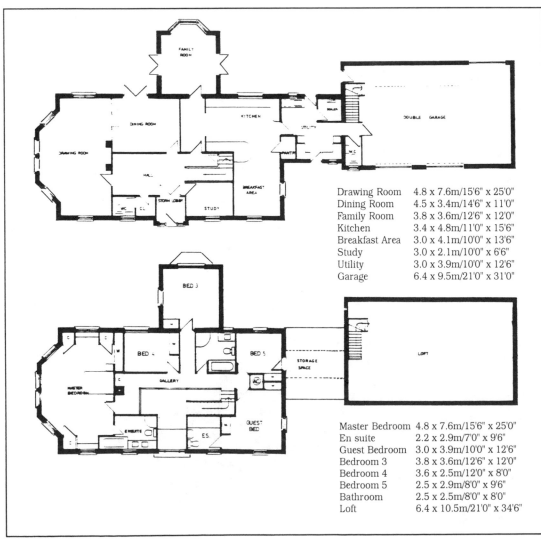

Drawing Room	4.8 x 7.6m/15'6" x 25'0"	
Dining Room	4.5 x 3.4m/14'6" x 11'0"	
Family Room	3.8 x 3.6m/12'6" x 12'0"	
Kitchen	3.4 x 4.8m/11'0" x 15'6"	
Breakfast Area	3.0 x 4.1m/10'0" x 13'6"	
Study	3.0 x 2.1m/10'0" x 6'6"	
Utility	3.0 x 3.9m/10'0" x 12'6"	
Garage	6.4 x 9.5m/21'0" x 31'0"	

Master Bedroom	4.8 x 7.6m/15'6" x 25'0"	
En suite	2.2 x 2.9m/7'0" x 9'6"	
Guest Bedroom	3.0 x 3.9m/10'0" x 12'6"	
Bedroom 3	3.8 x 3.6m/12'6" x 12'0"	
Bedroom 4	3.6 x 2.5m/12'0" x 8'0"	
Bedroom 5	2.5 x 2.9m/8'0" x 9'6"	
Bathroom	2.5 x 2.5m/8'0" x 8'0"	
Loft	6.4 x 10.5m/21'0" x 34'6"	

Designed for construction in stone, this design has an elegant front facade, and a large hall/gallery, affording a double height space as the house is entered through the front door. Wide bay windows add character to the principal rooms, and space for future expansion is provided over the garage.

15.95m x 14.09m
224.74 sq. m.

The copyright belongs to Potton Ltd.

97-307

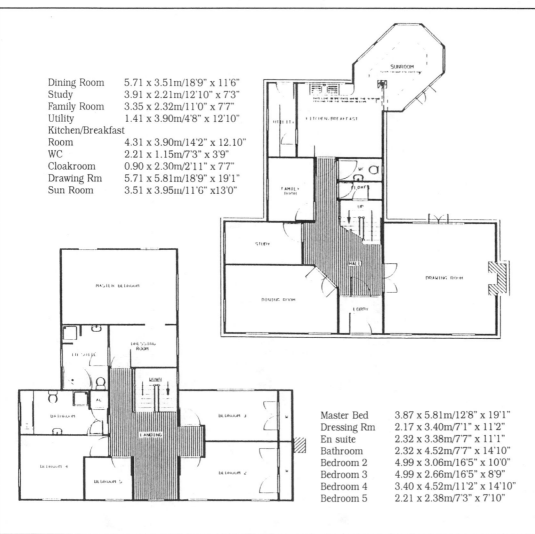

Dining Room	5.71 x 3.51m/18'9" x 11'6"
Study	3.91 x 2.21m/12'10" x 7'3"
Family Room	3.35 x 2.32m/11'0" x 7'7"
Utility	1.41 x 3.90m/4'8" x 12'10"
Kitchen/Breakfast	
Room	4.31 x 3.90m/14'2" x 12.10"
WC	2.21 x 1.15m/7'3" x 3'9"
Cloakroom	0.90 x 2.30m/2'11" x 7'7"
Drawing Rm	5.71 x 5.81m/18'9" x 19'1"
Sun Room	3.51 x 3.95m/11'6" x13'0"

Master Bed	3.87 x 5.81m/12'8" x 19'1"
Dressing Rm	2.17 x 3.40m/7'1" x 11'2"
En suite	2.32 x 3.38m/7'7" x 11'1"
Bathroom	2.32 x 4.52m/7'7" x 14'10"
Bedroom 2	4.99 x 3.06m/16'5" x 10'0"
Bedroom 3	4.99 x 2.66m/16'5" x 8'9"
Bedroom 4	3.40 x 4.52m/11'2" x 14'10"
Bedroom 5	2.21 x 2.38m/7'3" x 7'10"

The symmetry to the street scene gives way, on the rear elevations of this magnificent house, to interesting projections that allow for the extension of the accommodation into another league. The master suite takes up almost the whole of the upper part of the rear projection and the clever offsetting of the conservatory allows for views from, to and past it from many of the main rooms.

The copyright belongs to Potton Ltd.

206.06 sq. m.

14.39m x 14.32m

96-086

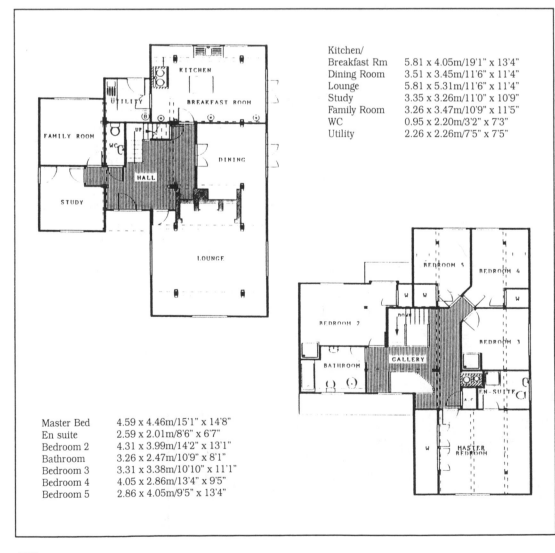

Kitchen/		
Breakfast Rm	5.81 x 4.05m/19'1" x 13'4"	
Dining Room	3.51 x 3.45m/11'6" x 11'4"	
Lounge	5.81 x 5.31m/11'6" x 11'4"	
Study	3.35 x 3.26m/11'0" x 10'9"	
Family Room	3.26 x 3.47m/10'9" x 11'5"	
WC	0.95 x 2.20m/3'2" x 7'3"	
Utility	2.26 x 2.26m/7'5" x 7'5"	

Master Bed	4.59 x 4.46m/15'1" x 14'8"
En suite	2.59 x 2.01m/8'6" x 6'7"
Bedroom 2	4.31 x 3.99m/14'2" x 13'1"
Bathroom	3.26 x 2.47m/10'9" x 8'1"
Bedroom 3	3.31 x 3.38m/10'10" x 11'1"
Bedroom 4	4.05 x 2.86m/13'4" x 9'5"
Bedroom 5	2.86 x 4.05m/9'5" x 13'4"

A compact looking house that, nevertheless, hides a wealth of accommodation, including 5 good sized bedrooms, amongst which is a generous master suite. Downstairs there is a family room as well as a study and the size of the kitchen means it can truly be used as a living area.

184.64 sq. m.
12.40m x 14.89m

The copyright belongs to Potton Ltd.

97-192

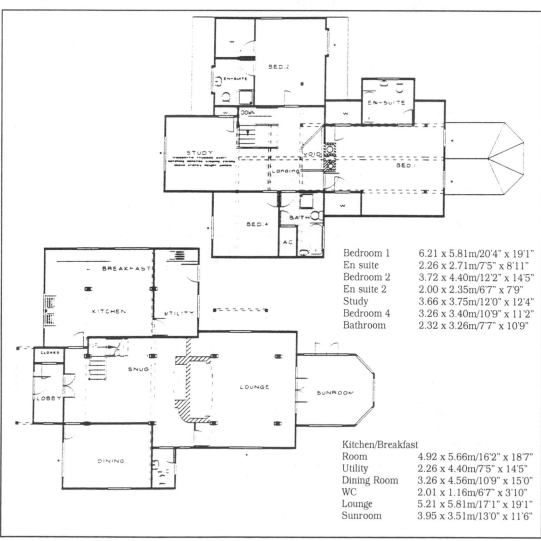

Bedroom 1	6.21 x 5.81m/20'4" x 19'1"
En suite	2.26 x 2.71m/7'5" x 8'11"
Bedroom 2	3.72 x 4.40m/12'2" x 14'5"
En suite 2	2.00 x 2.35m/6'7" x 7'9"
Study	3.66 x 3.75m/12'0" x 12'4"
Bedroom 4	3.26 x 3.40m/10'9" x 11'2"
Bathroom	2.32 x 3.26m/7'7" x 10'9"

Kitchen/Breakfast Room	4.92 x 5.66m/16'2" x 18'7"
Utility	2.26 x 4.40m/7'5" x 14'5"
Dining Room	3.26 x 4.56m/10'9" x 15'0"
WC	2.01 x 1.16m/6'7" x 3'10"
Lounge	5.21 x 5.81m/17'1" x 19'1"
Sunroom	3.95 x 3.51m/13'0" x 11'6"

As drawn, this house could well fit on a relatively narrow plot, with the entrance to the front, but a simple rearrangement of the front door within the lobby would render this design suitable for a much wider plot. Clever use of the accommodation and the layout of the internal hall as a snug means that this space need not be wasted and the study to the upper part could just as easily become the 4th bedroom.

186.96 sq. m.

11.29m x 16.56m

The copyright belongs to Potton Ltd.

96-199

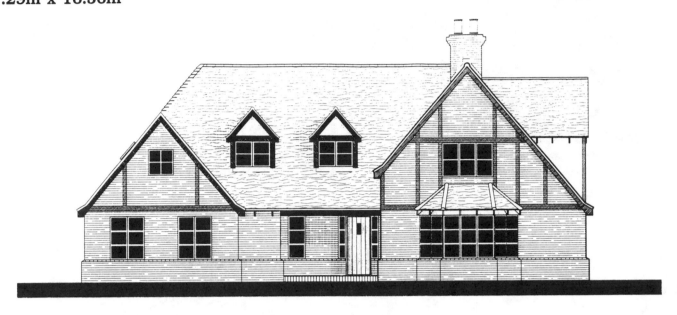

Lounge	6.91 x 5.58m/22'8" x 18'4"
Family Room	5.33 x 5.86m/17'6" x 19'3"
Kitchen	4.56 x 5.68m/15'0" x 18'8"
Sunroom	4.29 x 4.63m/14'1" x 15'2"
Utility	3.31 x 3.91m/10'10" x 12'10"
Wine Cellar	2.81 x 2.86m/9'3" x 9'5"
Dining Room	5.66 x 5.01m/18'7" x 16'5"
WC	1.36 x 2.26m/4'6" x 7'5"

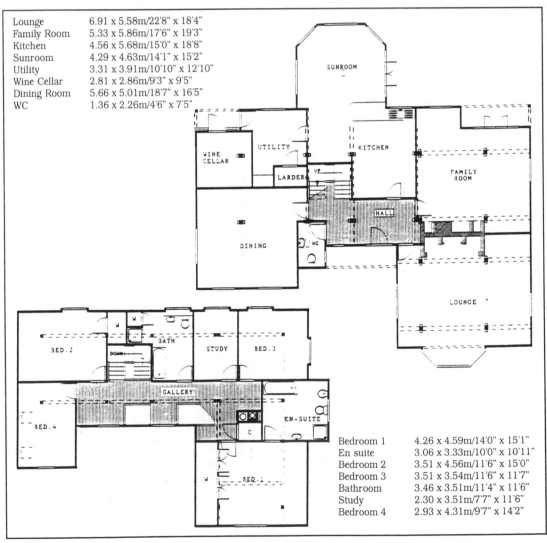

Bedroom 1	4.26 x 4.59m/14'0" x 15'1"
En suite	3.06 x 3.33m/10'0" x 10'11"
Bedroom 2	3.51 x 4.56m/11'6" x 15'0"
Bedroom 3	3.51 x 3.54m/11'6" x 11'7"
Bathroom	3.46 x 3.51m/11'4" x 11'6"
Study	2.30 x 3.51m/7'7" x 11'6"
Bedroom 4	2.93 x 4.31m/9'7" x 14'2"

This could, just as easily, have been described as a five bedroomed house. Downstairs the room between the lounge and the kitchen area has been described as the family room, but if your lifestyle preferred, then it could just as easily swap functions with the dining room. The hallway has taken up a much smaller proportion of the ground floor than is usual on houses of this size.

194.37 sq. m.

11.34m x 17.14m

The copyright belongs to Potton Ltd.

94-073

Master Bed	5.15 x 5.61m/16'11" x 18'5"
Dressing Rm	3.75 x 2.00m/12'4" x 6'7"
En suite	3.06 x 3.96m/10'1" x 13'0"
Study	2.00 x 2.25m/6'7" x 7'5"
Bedroom 3	2.85 x 5.15m/9'4" x 16'11"
En suite/	
Bathroom	2.17 x 3.65m/7'1" x 12'0"
Bedroom 2	5.15 x 5.85m/16'11" x 19'2"
Bedroom 4	2.76 x 4.11m/9'1" x 13'6"
Bedroom 5	3.51 x 4.11m/11'6" x 13'6"

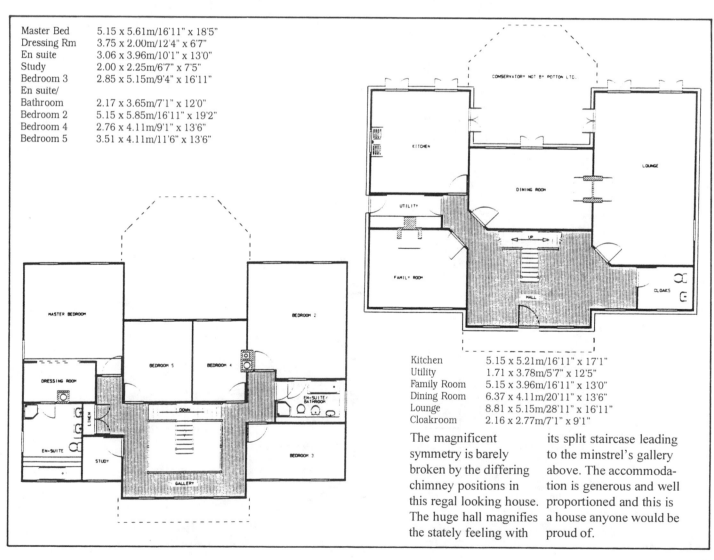

Kitchen	5.15 x 5.21m/16'11" x 17'1"
Utility	1.71 x 3.78m/5'7" x 12'5"
Family Room	5.15 x 3.96m/16'11" x 13'0"
Dining Room	6.37 x 4.11m/20'11" x 13'6"
Lounge	8.81 x 5.15m/28'11" x 16'11"
Cloakroom	2.16 x 2.77m/7'1" x 9'1"

The magnificent symmetry is barely broken by the differing chimney positions in this regal looking house. The huge hall magnifies the stately feeling with its split staircase leading to the minstrel's gallery above. The accommodation is generous and well proportioned and this is a house anyone would be proud of.

285.93 sq. m.
13.38m x 21.37m

The copyright belongs to Potton Ltd.

98-017

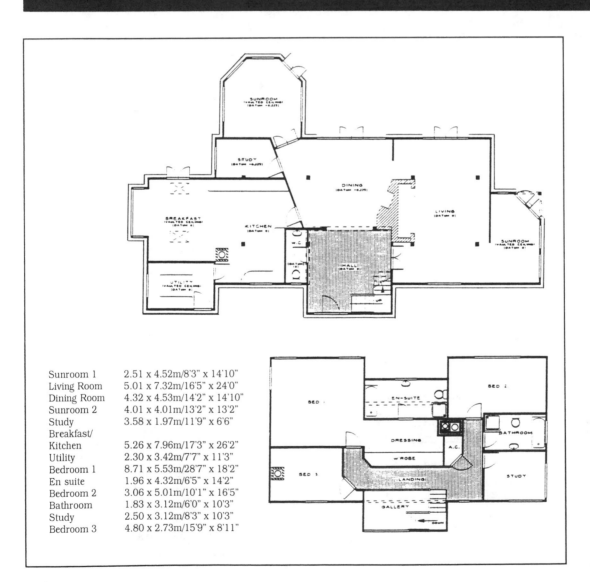

Reminiscent of a barn conversion this is, nevertheless, a well thought out modern house that doesn't need to compromise in order to provide the proper progression and layout of rooms. Once more there is a conscious division between general and more formal living rooms.

Sunroom 1	2.51 x 4.52m/8'3" x 14'10"
Living Room	5.01 x 7.32m/16'5" x 24'0"
Dining Room	4.32 x 4.53m/14'2" x 14'10"
Sunroom 2	4.01 x 4.01m/13'2" x 13'2"
Study	3.58 x 1.97m/11'9" x 6'6"
Breakfast/ Kitchen	5.26 x 7.96m/17'3" x 26'2"
Utility	2.30 x 3.42m/7'7" x 11'3"
Bedroom 1	8.71 x 5.53m/28'7" x 18'2"
En suite	1.96 x 4.32m/6'5" x 14'2"
Bedroom 2	3.06 x 5.01m/10'1" x 16'5"
Bathroom	1.83 x 3.12m/6'0" x 10'3"
Study	2.50 x 3.12m/8'3" x 10'3"
Bedroom 3	4.80 x 2.73m/15'9" x 8'11"

171.36 sq. m.

13.60m x 12.60m

The copyright belongs to Potton Ltd.

95-218

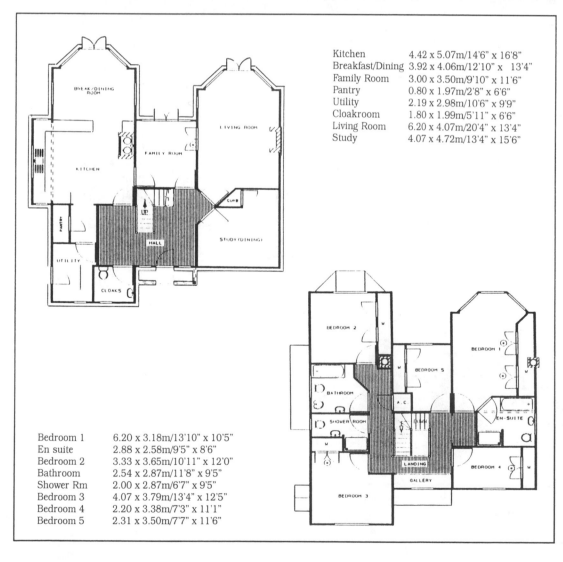

Kitchen	4.42 x 5.07m/14'6" x 16'8"	
Breakfast/Dining	3.92 x 4.06m/12'10" x	13'4"
Family Room	3.00 x 3.50m/9'10" x 11'6"	
Pantry	0.80 x 1.97m/2'8" x 6'6"	
Utility	2.19 x 2.98m/10'6" x 9'9"	
Cloakroom	1.80 x 1.99m/5'11" x 6'6"	
Living Room	6.20 x 4.07m/20'4" x 13'4"	
Study	4.07 x 4.72m/13'4" x 15'6"	

Bedroom 1	6.20 x 3.18m/13'10" x 10'5"
En suite	2.88 x 2.58m/9'5" x 8'6"
Bedroom 2	3.33 x 3.65m/10'11" x 12'0"
Bathroom	2.54 x 2.87m/11'8" x 9'5"
Shower Rm	2.00 x 2.87m/6'7" x 9'5"
Bedroom 3	4.07 x 3.79m/13'4" x 12'5"
Bedroom 4	2.20 x 3.38m/7'3" x 11'1"
Bedroom 5	2.31 x 3.50m/7'7" x 11'6"

At first sight the plain, almost Victorian façade of this house, broken only by generous bays and one forward projecting gable, belies the complex shape of the structure when viewed on plan. The two rear facing gables divide the accommodation neatly between general living, and the more formal reception areas and the upper part provides 5 bedrooms, two of which have en-suite facilities.

182.99 sq. m.

10.11m x 18.10m

97-001

Kitchen	3.88 x 3.31m/12'9" x 10'10"
Breakfast/Family	3.88 x 4.50m/12'9" x 14'9"
Utility	1.70 x 3.15m/5'7" x 10'4"
WC	2.09 x 2.09m/6'10" x 6'10"
Dining Room	4.53 x 3.88m/14'10" x 12'9"
Lounge	3.88 x 6.82m/12'9" x 22'4"
Study	3.20 x 3.88m/10'6" x 12'9"

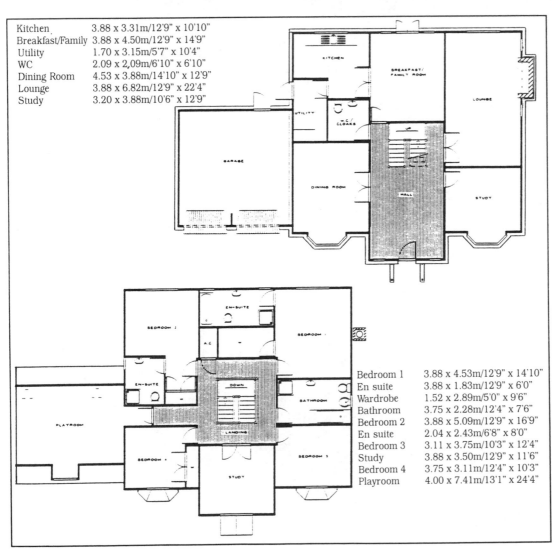

Bedroom 1	3.88 x 4.53m/12'9" x 14'10"
En suite	3.88 x 1.83m/12'9" x 6'0"
Wardrobe	1.52 x 2.89m/5'0" x 9'6"
Bathroom	3.75 x 2.28m/12'4" x 7'6"
Bedroom 2	3.88 x 5.09m/12'9" x 16'9"
En suite	2.04 x 2.43m/6'8" x 8'0"
Bedroom 3	3.11 x 3.75m/10'3" x 12'4"
Study	3.88 x 3.50m/12'9" x 11'6"
Bedroom 4	3.75 x 3.11m/12'4" x 10'3"
Playroom	4.00 x 7.41m/13'1" x 24'4"

The massive area of the hallway to this house will appeal to many, even more so when they see that the space repeated to the upper floor is used for the provision of the study that could just as easily be described as the 5th bedroom. This, in combination with the playroom above the garage, makes for an extremely adaptable and extensive family house.

163.03 sq. m.
12.57m x 12.97m

97-015

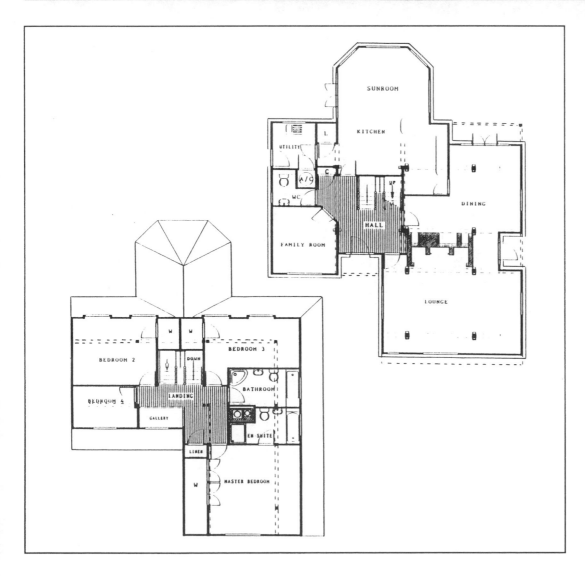

Although only a relatively small proportion of the space to both floors has been taken up with the hallway and landing, the imposing staircase will give a luxurious feeling to this family home. Interesting shapes and dog legs in the partition walling will allow for the proper placing and display of furniture and pictures. The kitchen/breakfast room in combination with the sunroom is an important feature.

245 sq. m.   *The copyright belongs to Border Oak*   **Pendragon Court**

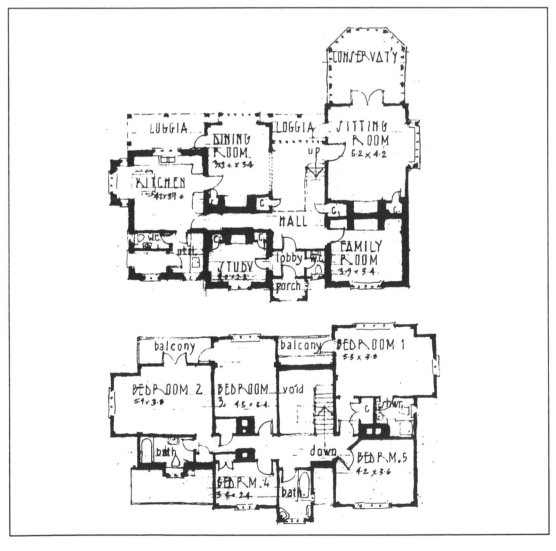

A design with no concessions to practicality or economics. A design and layout that obeys specific requirements of the owner and makes no concessions to slavish practicality. Cupolas, eccentrically placed chimney stacks, balconies, steps, staircases, gables, dormers, loggias, and grottos tumble together and provide an intrinsic charm. A showcase for the skills of a master builder but a difficult project for the intrepid selfbuilder.

255 sq. m.

The copyright belongs to Border Oak

Culmington Court

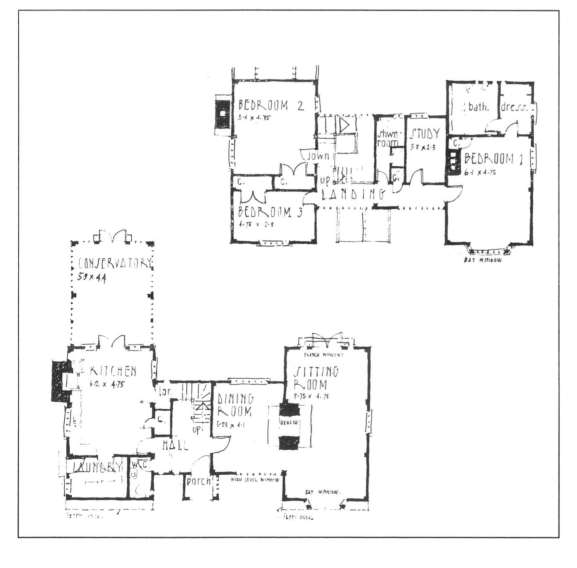

A traditional oak framed house with close and vertical studs or posts. The framing is prevalent in Suffolk and Essex but can be found throughout England. Close framing was demonstration of the wealth of the owner and is often found on the street-side elevation only. Unusual features include an open porch resembling the entrance porch of rural churches, a galleried hallway with vaulted ceilings, magnificent master bedroom wing with vaulted ceilings and generally proportioned dressing room and bathroom, a sitting room with adjacent dining room, both sharing an internal inglenook and fireplace, a magnificent kitchen with French doors leading to a conservatory with feature oak trusses.

2766 sq. ft./257 sq. m.

The copyright belongs to Scandia-Hus

Lappland

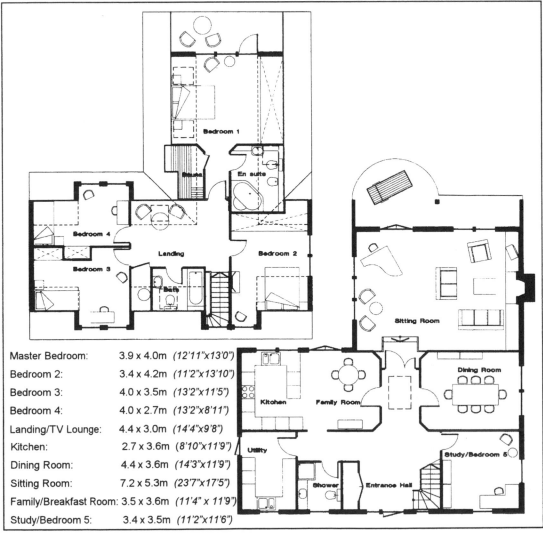

Master Bedroom:	3.9 x 4.0m	*(12'11"x13'0")*
Bedroom 2:	3.4 x 4.2m	*(11'2"x13'10")*
Bedroom 3:	4.0 x 3.5m	*(13'2"x11'5")*
Bedroom 4:	4.0 x 2.7m	*(13'2"x8'11")*
Landing/TV Lounge:	4.4 x 3.0m	*(14'4"x9'8")*
Kitchen:	2.7 x 3.6m	*(8'10"x11'9")*
Dining Room:	4.4 x 3.6m	*(14'3"x11'9")*
Sitting Room:	7.2 x 5.3m	*(23'7"x17'5")*
Family/Breakfast Room:	3.5 x 3.6m	*(11'4" x 11'9")*
Study/Bedroom 5:	3.4 x 3.5m	*(11'2"x11'6")*

This home typifies the original Scandia-Hus designs and, throughout the past two decades, has become something of a Scandia-Hus 'trademark'. The impression you get as you enter the spacious hall, accentuated by shafts of light filtering from the first-floor roof light, and continue down the steps into the split-level sitting room, is of a stylish and spacious family home. The open-tread pine staircase and galleried first-floor landing lounge lend the Lappland a distinctive Scandinavian atmosphere, further enhanced by the first-floor sauna and timbered gable-head balcony.

2595 sq. ft.

Chiddingstone

Master Bedroom:	3.3 x 4.6m	*(10'10"x15'2")*
Bedroom 2:	3.4 x 2.7m	*(11'0"x9'0")*
Bedroom 3:	3.4 x 2.7m	*(11'0"x9'0")*
Bedroom 4:	3.0 x 4.9m	*(9'9"x16'1")*
Bedroom 5:	3.4 x 4.9m	*(11'2"x16'1")*
Landing/Sitting Area:	5.2 x 2.1m	*(11'9"x6'9")*
Sun Room(Optional):	3.6 x 3.4m	*(11'9"x11'1")*

Kitchen:	3.1 x 3.6m	*(10'1"x11'9")*
Dining Hall:	6.6 x 3.8m	*(21'6"x12'3")*
Sitting Room:	4.8 x 5.9m	*(15'7"x19'4")*
Study :	3.6 x 2.1m	*(11'9"x6'10")*

This is one of the show houses featured at the Scandia-Hus Show Centre in East Grinstead, Sussex. The feeling of space that greets you as you enter this home has to be seen to be appreciated. The view through the dining room, via glazed double doors, to the lower level sitting room and on to the sunroom is stunning. Like several of the Scandia-Hus chalet designs, the Chiddingstone can be equipped initially as a single-storey home, leaving the option to finish the first floor at a later stage to accommodate future requirements, and the optional sunroom can be added to any design.

2700 sq. ft.

52 ft. x 29 ft.

The copyright belongs to Design & Materials Ltd.

Earlswood

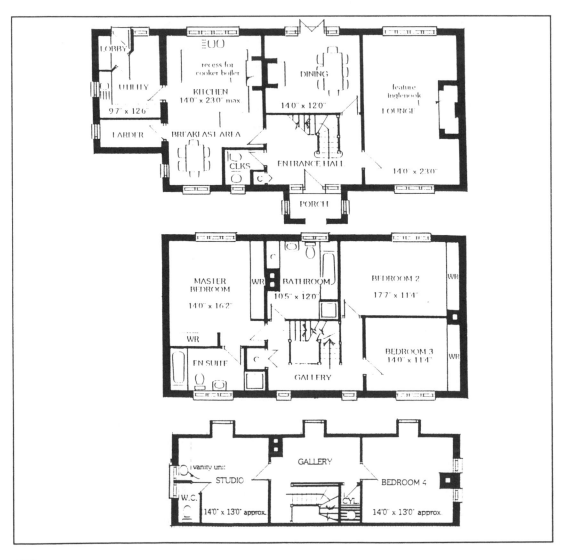

As you can see from the elevations the third storey is not evident from the front of the house. This can sometimes make all the difference when negotiating the planning permission. Overall the design provides outstanding accommodation in a format typical of houses of this ilk.

The copyright belongs to Design & Materials Ltd.

2700 sq. ft. 51 ft. x 41 ft.

Woldingham

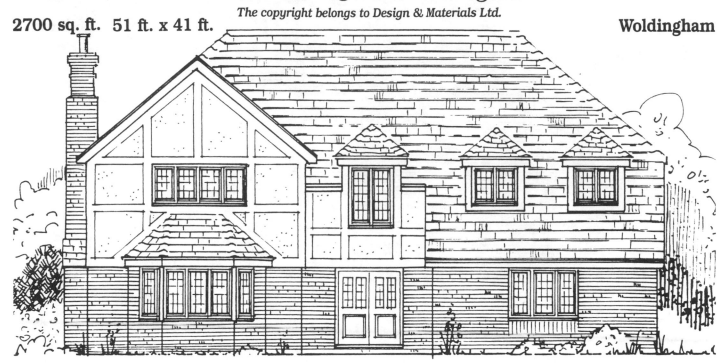

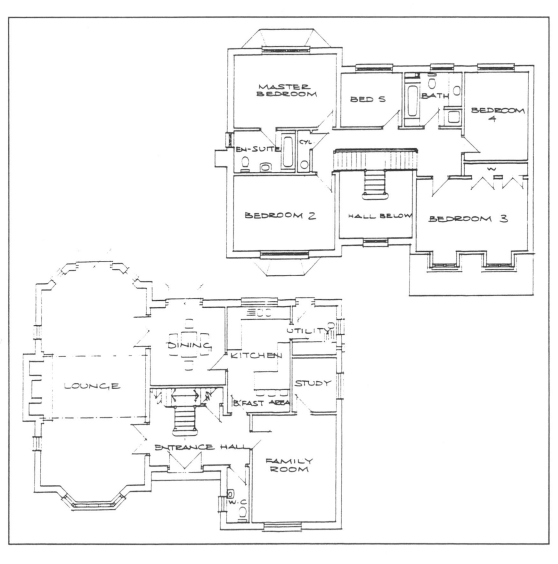

This impressive family home includes a lounge with two bay windows and a big inglenook. There is a separate family room, breakfast kitchen and feature split staircase with gallery open to the hall below.

305

The copyright belongs to Design & Materials Ltd.

2550 sq. ft.

48 ft. x 39 ft.

Melbourne

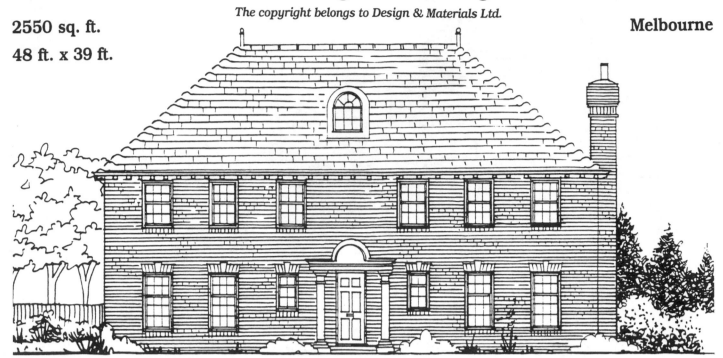

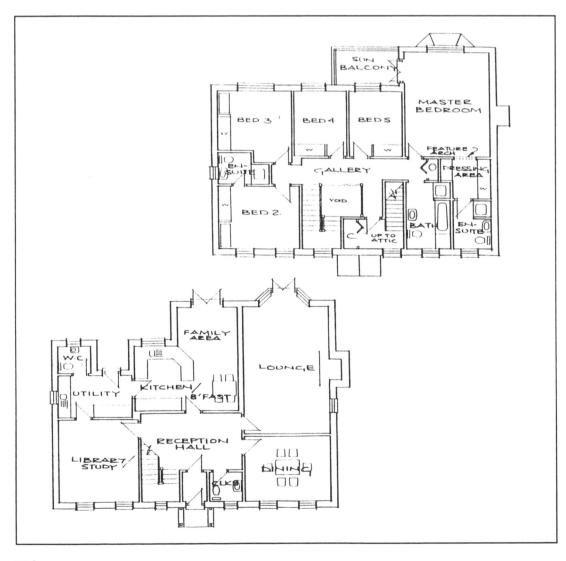

This magnificent period house provides a high standard of accommodation. Interesting design features include a walk-in bay to the lounge and a master bedroom complete with dressing room and sun balcony.

2750 sq. ft.
43 ft. x 39 ft.

The copyright belongs to Design & Materials Ltd.

Cairnsmore

This classic three storey house is illustrated here in the Scottish vernacular but would be equally at home almost anywhere. Both the dining and lounge have open fires and all the main rooms are well proportioned.

2840 sq. ft.

The copyright belongs to Kingpost Design Co

Norton

Hall	8'2" x 23'8"
Living Room	13'2" x 19'9"
Dining Room	11'2" x 14'1"
Family Room	11'2" x 17'1"
Kitchen	11'6" x 18'4"
Utility	7'7" x 11'6"
Master Bed	11'6" x 16'5"
Bedroom 2	11'2" x 13'2"
Bedroom 3	11'2" x 14'1"
Bedroom 4	9'10" x 13'2"
Bedroom 5	8'2" x 9'10"
Book Nook	4'7" x 8'3"

An impressive five bedroomed house which provides comfortable and well planned accommodation for the larger family. Downstairs the large and welcoming hall provides direct access to all the main rooms. The living room, dining room and family room are all provided with fireplaces, perfect for large family gatherings at Christmas! Upstairs there are two en suite bathrooms, a cosy book nook looking out near the main entrance, and the fifth bedroom could perhaps be used for a study.

254.5 sq. m./2739 sq. ft.

Copyright refer to Designer Homes

Canterbury

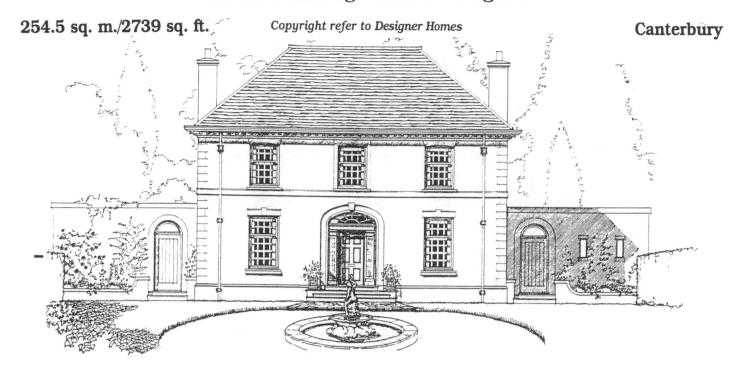

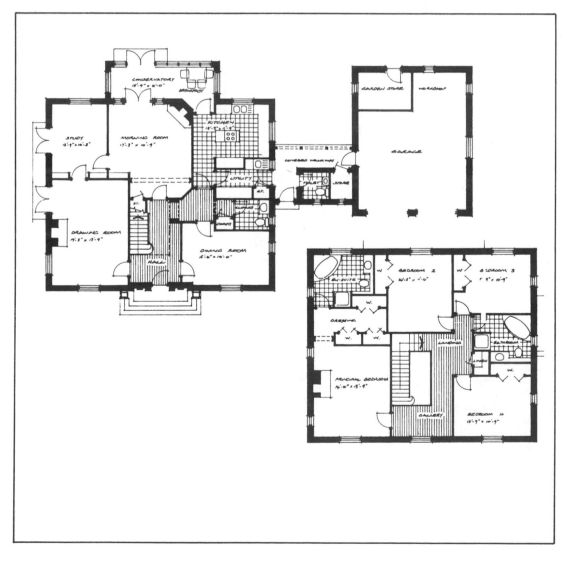

Symmetry is the guiding factor in this design which is illustrated in a setting that seeks to maintain it. The garage will serve to take away some of the balance but with careful treatment should enhance the main building. The hallway and upper part landing and gallery are an important feature of this house and would add a great deal to its feeling of light and space.

2585 sq. ft./240 sq. m.

The copyright belongs to Custom Homes

Limpsfield

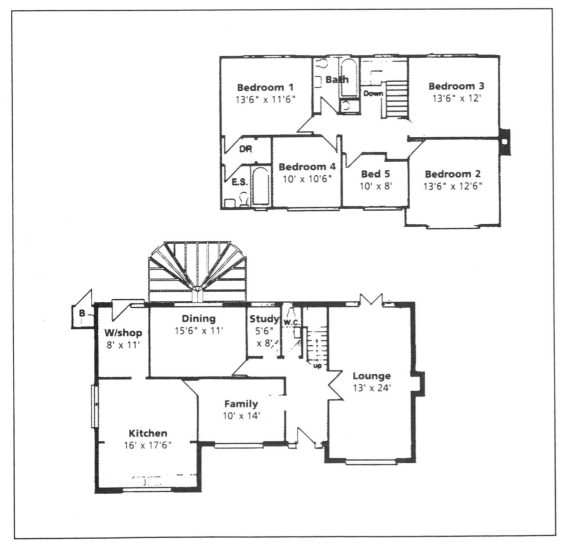

Bedroom 1
13'6" x 11'6"

Bath

Down

Bedroom 3
13'6" x 12'

DR

E.S.

Bedroom 4
10' x 10'6"

Bed 5
10' x 8'

Bedroom 2
13'6" x 12'6"

W/shop
8' x 11'

Dining
15'6" x 11'

Study
5'6"
x 8'

w.c.

B

up

Lounge
13' x 24'

Family
10' x 14'

Kitchen
16' x 17'6"

This is a house for the wider plot where its presence on the street can be fully stated. The extensive accommodation to the ground floor is reflected in the scope and availability of the upper part accommodation with 5 good sized bedrooms off a well lit landing.

2640 sq. ft./245 sq. m.

The copyright belongs to Custom Homes

Buxton

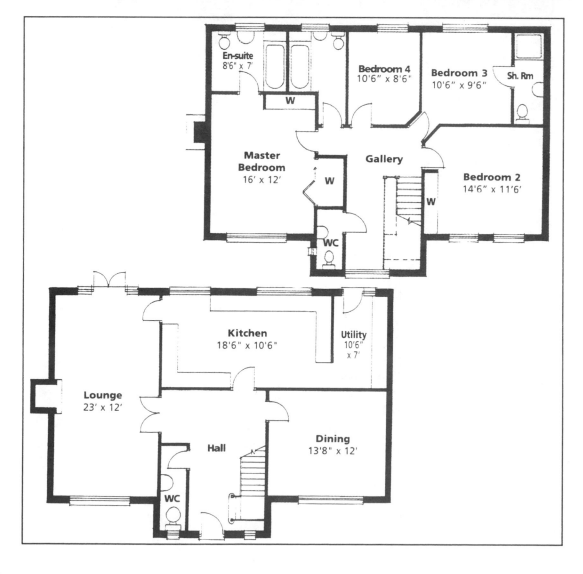

En-suite
8'6" x 7'

Bedroom 4
10'6" x 8'6"

Bedroom 3
10'6" x 9'6"

Sh. Rm

W

Master
Bedroom
16' x 12'

Gallery

W

Bedroom 2
14'6" x 11'6'

W

WC

Kitchen
18'6" x 10'6"

Utility
10'6"
x 7'

Lounge
23' x 12'

Hall

Dining
13'8" x 12'

WC

A compact and cost
effective shape belies the
wealth of accommoda-
tion within this large
family home. The
forward projection of the
entrance porch and hall
allows a feeling of
spaciousness on entry
and this is reflected in
the size and scope of the
accommodation.

311

2640 sq. ft./245 sq. m.

The copyright belongs to Custom Homes

Cheltenham

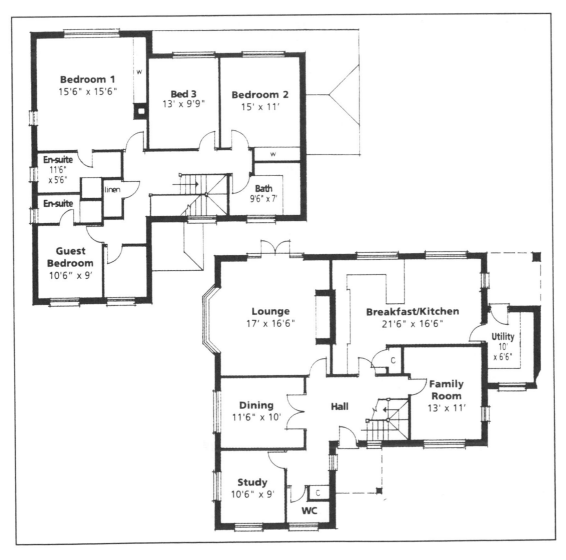

An imposing and varied house that displays interesting roof planes and shapes to all elevations. The accommodation is extensive with two of the upper part bedrooms having en-suite facilities and the possibility, by the addition of a door, of the downstairs study doubling up as a ground floor bedroom and en-suite.

251 sq. m./2701 sq. ft.

Copyright refer to Designer Homes

Malvern

This is a lovely family house that has a timeless elegance to its complex appearance. Just a short mental wander through the rooms will not fail to impress.

Houses over 3000 sq. ft.

For most would be selfbuilders the houses that follow in this category can only be a distant dream. For others, as the plans themselves bear testament, they are only too real and there are a significant number of really big houses built by self or individual builders every year.

Although they obviously have to reflect the local style, particularly in respect of the choice of external materials, many of the really big houses can be considered as architectural units in their own right which means that they, in a way, create their own architectural environment. As the majority also occupy significantly large and often well screened plots this means that they don't always have to conform to all of the nuances of local architectural detail which, in any event, might not translate to their scale. The innovations and the free expression of design that these dwellings are often able to impart can often, however, be translated downwards into houses that are much smaller.

Contributors in this section:

Border Oak
Custom Homes
Design & Materials Ltd.
Designer Homes
Kingpost Design Co
Potton Ltd.
Scandia-Hus
Swedish Homes

355 sq. m.

The copyright belongs to Border Oak

Deangate House

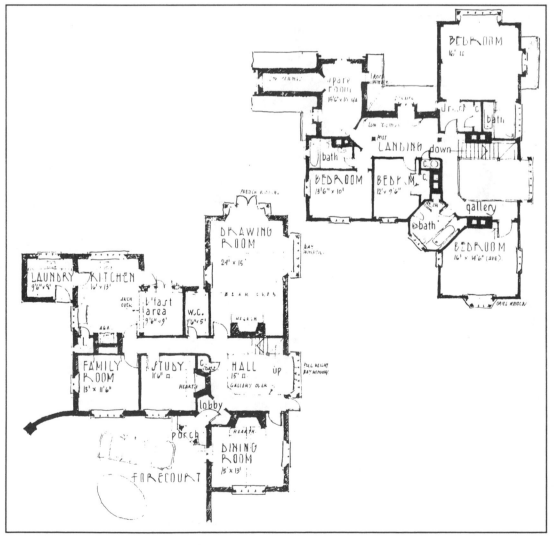

A design which draws inspiration from the works of Lutchins and reflects the architecture of the Southern Counties. A forest of chimney stacks, the exuberance of the hexagonal two storey entrance porch, the interplay of masonry, half-timbering and tile hanging; elements of a more genteel era, often cruelly categorised as the stockbroker 'Tudor'. Two storey hallway with galleries and a bay window with a bank of leaded lights flood the building with sunlight. The bay window and the French windows of the drawing invite the cry 'Anyone for tennis?'.

400 sq. m.

The copyright belongs to Border Oak

Dinmore Hall

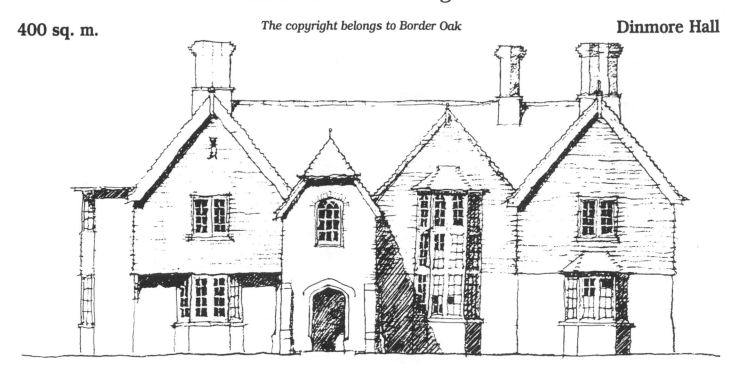

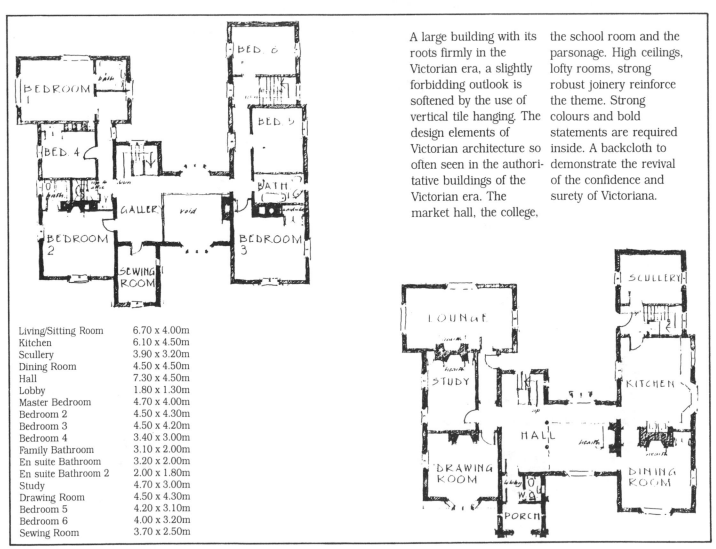

A large building with its roots firmly in the Victorian era, a slightly forbidding outlook is softened by the use of vertical tile hanging. The design elements of Victorian architecture so often seen in the authoritative buildings of the Victorian era. The market hall, the college, the school room and the parsonage. High ceilings, lofty rooms, strong robust joinery reinforce the theme. Strong colours and bold statements are required inside. A backcloth to demonstrate the revival of the confidence and surety of Victoriana.

Living/Sitting Room	6.70 x 4.00m
Kitchen	6.10 x 4.50m
Scullery	3.90 x 3.20m
Dining Room	4.50 x 4.50m
Hall	7.30 x 4.50m
Lobby	1.80 x 1.30m
Master Bedroom	4.70 x 4.00m
Bedroom 2	4.50 x 4.30m
Bedroom 3	4.50 x 4.20m
Bedroom 4	3.40 x 3.00m
Family Bathroom	3.10 x 2.00m
En suite Bathroom	3.20 x 2.00m
En suite Bathroom 2	2.00 x 1.80m
Study	4.70 x 3.00m
Drawing Room	4.50 x 4.30m
Bedroom 5	4.20 x 3.10m
Bedroom 6	4.00 x 3.20m
Sewing Room	3.70 x 2.50m

4890 sq. ft.

The copyright belongs to Kingpost Design Co

Rendcombe

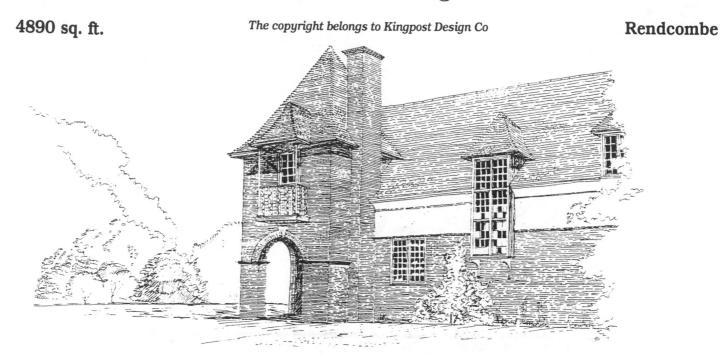

Master Bed	16'5" x 19'9"
Sitting Rm	10'10" x 13'6"
Bedroom 2	10'6" x 19'9"
Bedroom 3	11'6" x 16'5"
Guest Bed	14'5" x 19'9"
Study	11'6" x 11'6"

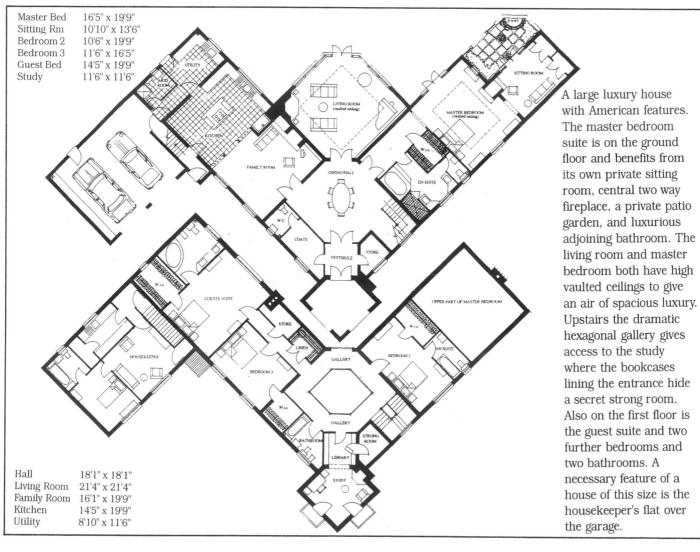

Hall	18'1" x 18'1"
Living Room	21'4" x 21'4"
Family Room	16'1" x 19'9"
Kitchen	14'5" x 19'9"
Utility	8'10" x 11'6"

A large luxury house with American features. The master bedroom suite is on the ground floor and benefits from its own private sitting room, central two way fireplace, a private patio garden, and luxurious adjoining bathroom. The living room and master bedroom both have high vaulted ceilings to give an air of spacious luxury. Upstairs the dramatic hexagonal gallery gives access to the study where the bookcases lining the entrance hide a secret strong room. Also on the first floor is the guest suite and two further bedrooms and two bathrooms. A necessary feature of a house of this size is the housekeeper's flat over the garage.

426.01 sq. m.

20.01m x 21.29m

98-004

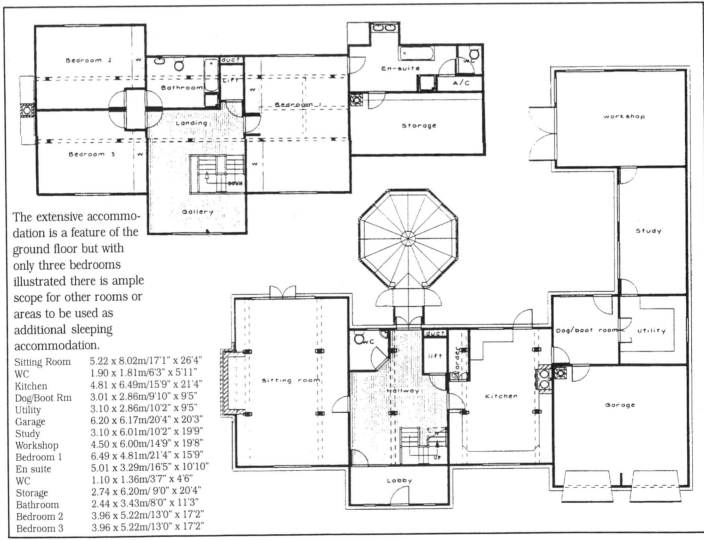

The extensive accommodation is a feature of the ground floor but with only three bedrooms illustrated there is ample scope for other rooms or areas to be used as additional sleeping accommodation.

Sitting Room	5.22 x 8.02m/17'1" x 26'4"
WC	1.90 x 1.81m/6'3" x 5'11"
Kitchen	4.81 x 6.49m/15'9" x 21'4"
Dog/Boot Rm	3.01 x 2.86m/9'10" x 9'5"
Utility	3.10 x 2.86m/10'2" x 9'5"
Garage	6.20 x 6.17m/20'4" x 20'3"
Study	3.10 x 6.01m/10'2" x 19'9"
Workshop	4.50 x 6.00m/14'9" x 19'8"
Bedroom 1	6.49 x 4.81m/21'4" x 15'9"
En suite	5.01 x 3.29m/16'5" x 10'10"
WC	1.10 x 1.36m/3'7" x 4'6"
Storage	2.74 x 6.20m/ 9'0" x 20'4"
Bathroom	2.44 x 3.43m/8'0" x 11'3"
Bedroom 2	3.96 x 5.22m/13'0" x 17'2"
Bedroom 3	3.96 x 5.22m/13'0" x 17'2"

562.65 sq. m.

18.28m x 30.78m

The copyright belongs to Potton Ltd.

96-089

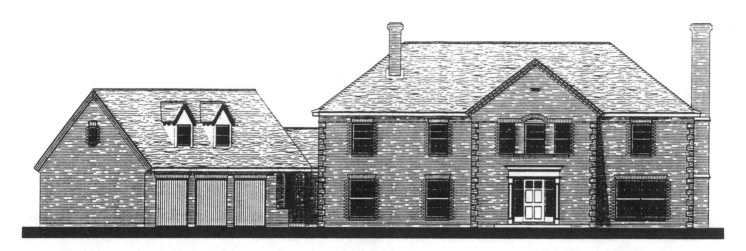

A gracefully proportioned house where the principle of off setting the garage/ancillary accommodation adds interest and comfort to the entrance facade.

Although denoted as a games room, there's ample scope for the space above the garage to become a self contained unit.

544.20 sq. m.

21.97m x 24.77m

97-172

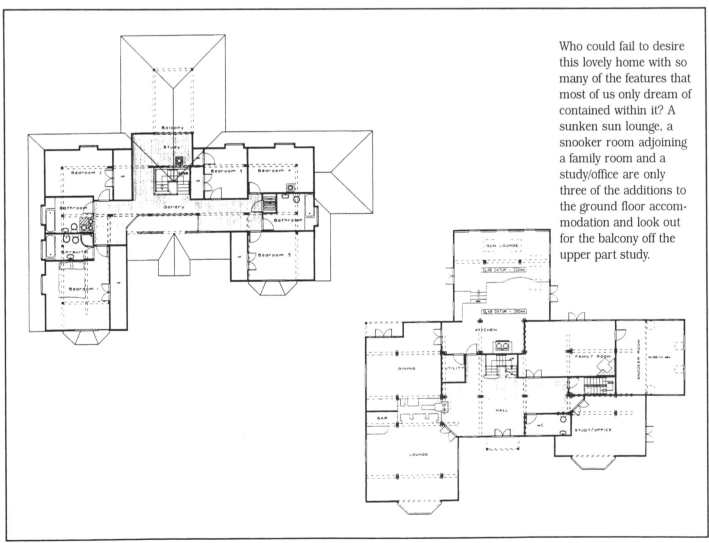

Who could fail to desire this lovely home with so many of the features that most of us only dream of contained within it? A sunken sun lounge, a snooker room adjoining a family room and a study/office are only three of the additions to the ground floor accommodation and look out for the balcony off the upper part study.

14.29m x 15.78m
225.50 sq. m.

The copyright belongs to Potton Ltd.

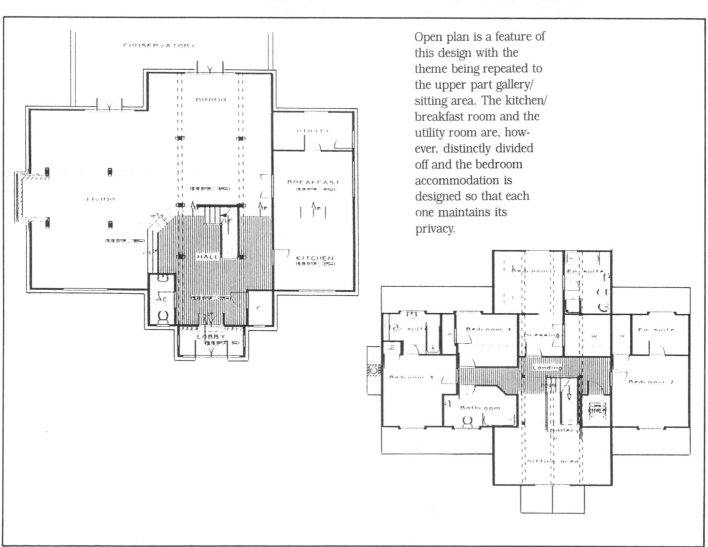

Open plan is a feature of this design with the theme being repeated to the upper part gallery/ sitting area. The kitchen/ breakfast room and the utility room are, however, distinctly divided off and the bedroom accommodation is designed so that each one maintains its privacy.

398.56 sq. m.

15.08m x 26.43m

The copyright belongs to Potton Ltd.

96-015

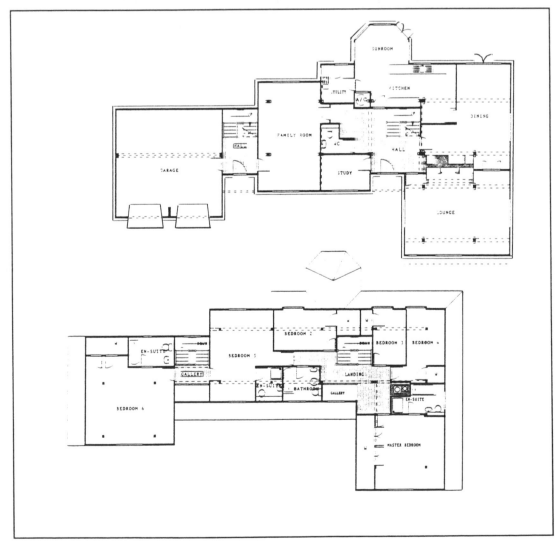

A six bedroomed house where, once again, the accommodation over the garage is more or less self contained, allowing its use by either semi-detached members of the family or possibly staff. A mental walk through the main living accommodation will not fail to delight.

The copyright belongs to Potton Ltd.

16.87m x 20.88m
352.25 sq. m.

Although similar to some of the other homes by this company, this one serves to illustrate that not everything has to be in straight lines and that interest can be gained by off setting accommodation at an angle. The self contained nature of the bedroom over the garage could well prove attractive to those with noisy teenage children.

3410 sq. ft.

Tenterden

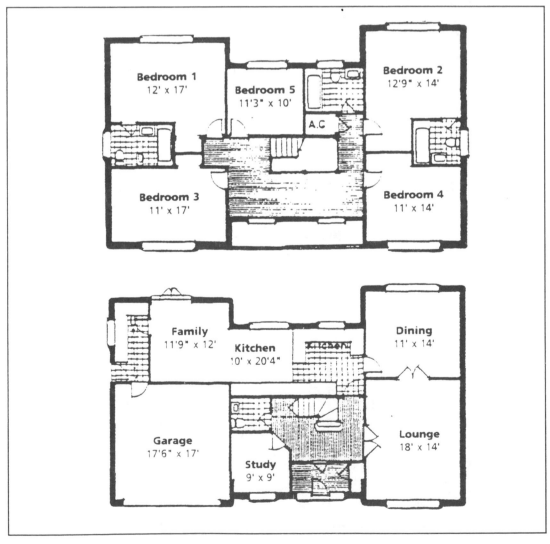

This house proclaims its importance and its architectural antecedents but, having said that, a simple change of external materials could place it in another genre. Once again the entrance foyer, hall and gallery are a feature of the house.

3465 sq. ft./313 sq. m.

The copyright belongs to Custom Homes

Grange

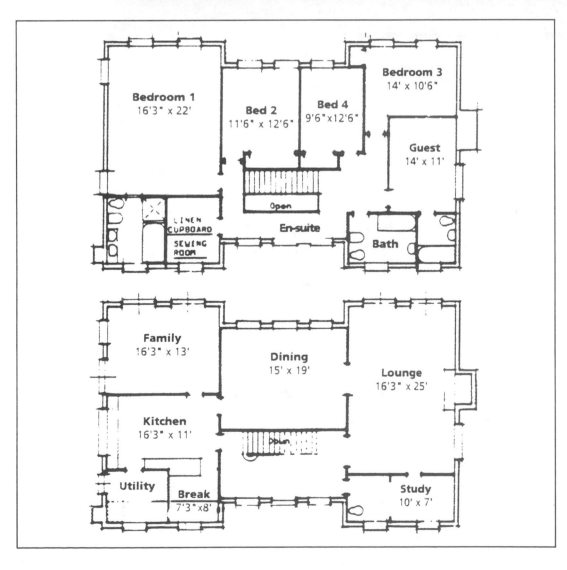

Bedroom 1
16'3" x 22'

Bed 2
11'6" x 12'6"

Bed 4
9'6"x12'6"

Bedroom 3
14' x 10'6"

Guest
14' x 11'

LINEN CUPBOARD

SEWING ROOM

Open

En-suite

Bath

Family
16'3" x 13'

Dining
15' x 19'

Lounge
16'3" x 25'

Kitchen
16'3" x 11'

Open

Utility

Break
7'3" x 8'

Study
10' x 7'

An imposing looking modern house harking back to earlier and grander times with the double fronted accommodation reached by way of a large entrance foyer. Four good sized bedrooms with their own ancillary accommodation are augmented by the addition of a guest suite with its own en-suite facilities.

3564 sq. ft./331 sq. m.

The copyright belongs to Custom Homes

Dorchester

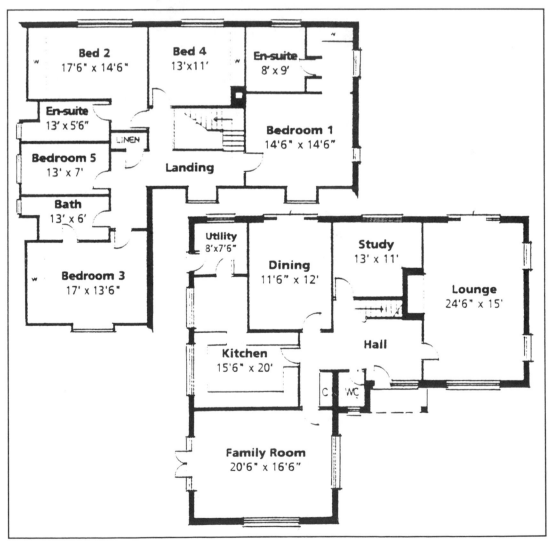

In plan form this is a large modern house with the accommodation appropriate to present day life. It has been illustrated in cottage format with a thatched roof but could just as easily be built in more conventional materials and styling.

3965 sq. ft./368 sq. m.

The copyright belongs to Custom Homes

Weybridge

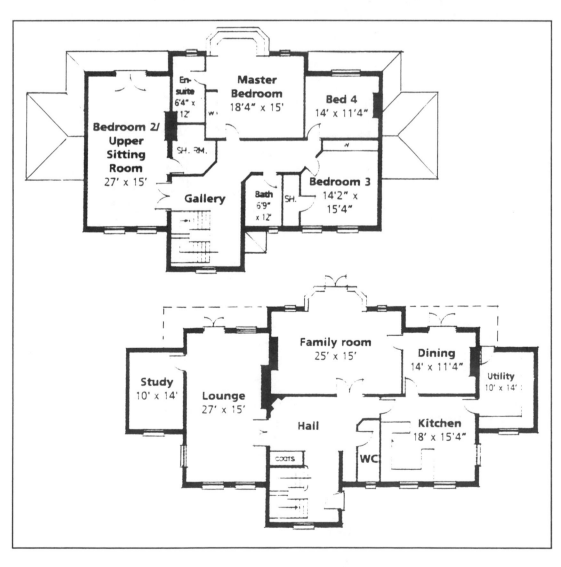

The family room is the central feature of the ground floor accommodation for this imposing family house that could well grace its namesake town. The full height mezzanine window in the entrance area is another feature that gives character to the external appearance.

4136 sq. ft./384 sq. m.

The copyright belongs to Custom Homes

Eton

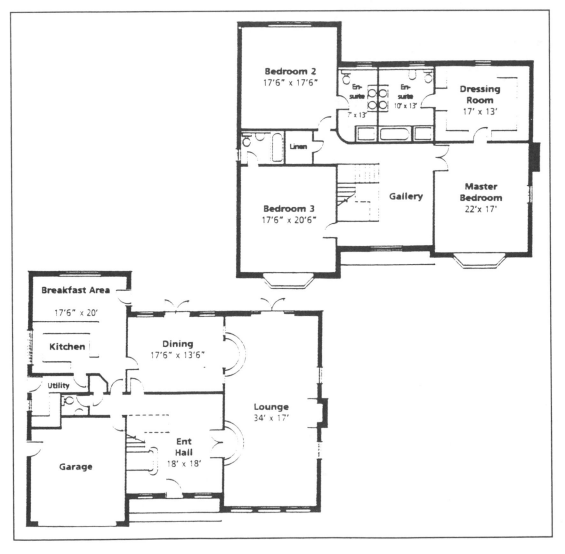

Bedroom 2
17'6" x 17'6"

En-suite
7' x 13'

En-suite
10' x 13'

Dressing Room
17' x 13'

Linen

Bedroom 3
17'6" x 20'6"

Gallery

Master Bedroom
22' x 17'

Breakfast Area
17'6" x 20'

Kitchen

Dining
17'6" x 13'6"

Utility

Lounge
34' x 17'

Ent Hall
18' x 18'

Garage

The arched heads of the windows, repeated in the arch over the gallery window, and the eyebrow features to the bedroom windows, give a distinctive character to this large house. Although illustrated as having only three bedrooms, quite simple rearrangement of the accommodation could create four.

585 sq. m.

The copyright belongs to Border Oak

Luston Manor

Living/sitting room	6.80 x 4.90m
Family Room	5.00 x 4.30m
Kitchen	6.20 x 4.50m
Dining Room	5.20 x 4.50m
Hall	5.70 x 4.50m
Garage	7.00 x 7.00m
Sitting Room 2 (Annex)	6.40 x 4.20m
Kitchen 2 (Annex)	3.00 x 2.40m
Bedroom 5	5.60 x 3.40m
Bedroom 6 (Annex)	4.80 x 3.80m
Sewing Room	3.30 x 2.80m
En suite Shower	1.80 x 1.50m
En suite Shower 2	2.70 x 1.70m

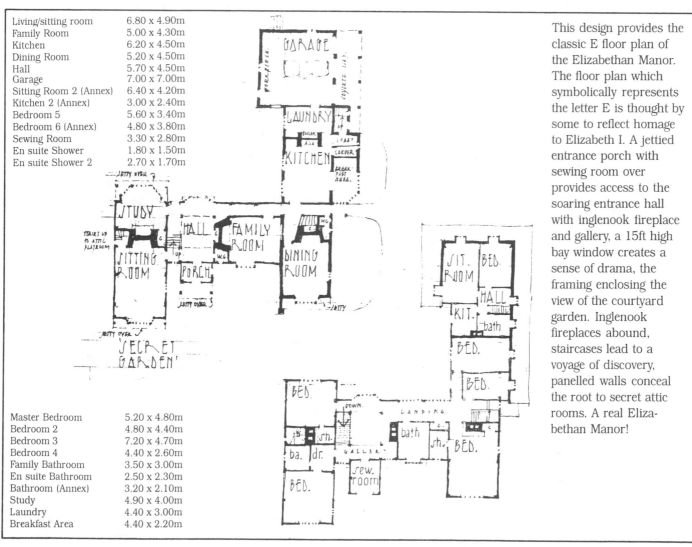

Master Bedroom	5.20 x 4.80m
Bedroom 2	4.80 x 4.40m
Bedroom 3	7.20 x 4.70m
Bedroom 4	4.40 x 2.60m
Family Bathroom	3.50 x 3.00m
En suite Bathroom	2.50 x 2.30m
Bathroom (Annex)	3.20 x 2.10m
Study	4.90 x 4.00m
Laundry	4.40 x 3.00m
Breakfast Area	4.40 x 2.20m

This design provides the classic E floor plan of the Elizabethan Manor. The floor plan which symbolically represents the letter E is thought by some to reflect homage to Elizabeth I. A jettied entrance porch with sewing room over provides access to the soaring entrance hall with inglenook fireplace and gallery, a 15ft high bay window creates a sense of drama, the framing enclosing the view of the courtyard garden. Inglenook fireplaces abound, staircases lead to a voyage of discovery, panelled walls conceal the root to secret attic rooms. A real Elizabethan Manor!

380 sq. m.

The copyright belongs to Border Oak

Howitzer Hall

Sitting Room	9.00 x 8.00m	Family Bathroom	3.20 x 3.00m
Kitchen	6.80 x 3.80m	Family Bathroom	2.50 x 2.00m
Utility	3.00 x 3.00m	En suite Bathroom	3.50 x 1.50m
Dining Room	7.00 x 3.80m	Study	3.80 x 3.40m
Hall	9.80 x 3.80m	Breakfast Area	3.80 x 3.40m
Master Bedroom	8.00 x 8.00m	Garage	6.20 x 5.40m
Bedroom 2	7.00 x 3.80m	En suite Shower	3.50 x 1.50m
Bedroom 3	7.00 x 3.80m	En suite Shower 2	2.50 x 1.50m
Bedroom 4	7.00 x 3.80m	Sewing Room	6.80 x 4.00m

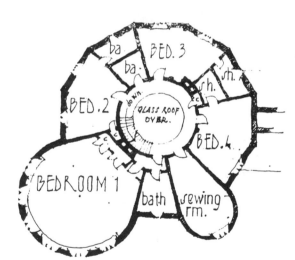

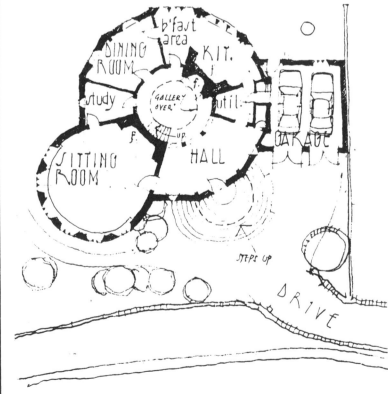

A voyage into the bizarre. A design to sit atop an existing concrete gun emplacement under rocky shore, a defensive structure built in masonry with Harling (Scottish roughcast) external elevations, circular steps grudgingly permit entry to hallway with a view to a circular gallery, awash with the grey light which filters through the central atrium. Twin stacks rise from massive fireplaces. The sitting room and master bedroom command a panoramic view. An unusual home, but surprisingly efficient in layout. An interesting proposal for the planners.

295 sq. m.

The copyright belongs to Border Oak

Carolina Court

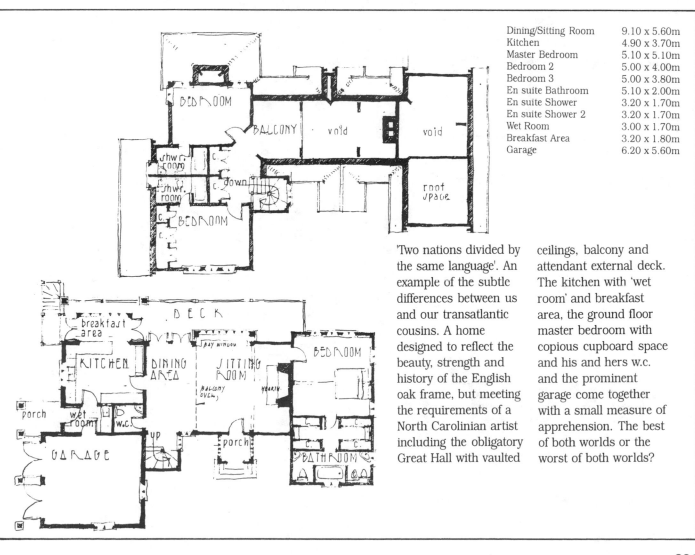

Dining/Sitting Room	9.10 x 5.60m
Kitchen	4.90 x 3.70m
Master Bedroom	5.10 x 5.10m
Bedroom 2	5.00 x 4.00m
Bedroom 3	5.00 x 3.80m
En suite Bathroom	5.10 x 2.00m
En suite Shower	3.20 x 1.70m
En suite Shower 2	3.20 x 1.70m
Wet Room	3.00 x 1.70m
Breakfast Area	3.20 x 1.80m
Garage	6.20 x 5.60m

'Two nations divided by the same language'. An example of the subtle differences between us and our transatlantic cousins. A home designed to reflect the beauty, strength and history of the English oak frame, but meeting the requirements of a North Carolinian artist including the obligatory Great Hall with vaulted ceilings, balcony and attendant external deck. The kitchen with 'wet room' and breakfast area, the ground floor master bedroom with copious cupboard space and his and hers w.c. and the prominent garage come together with a small measure of apprehension. The best of both worlds or the worst of both worlds?

305 sq. m.

The Parsonage

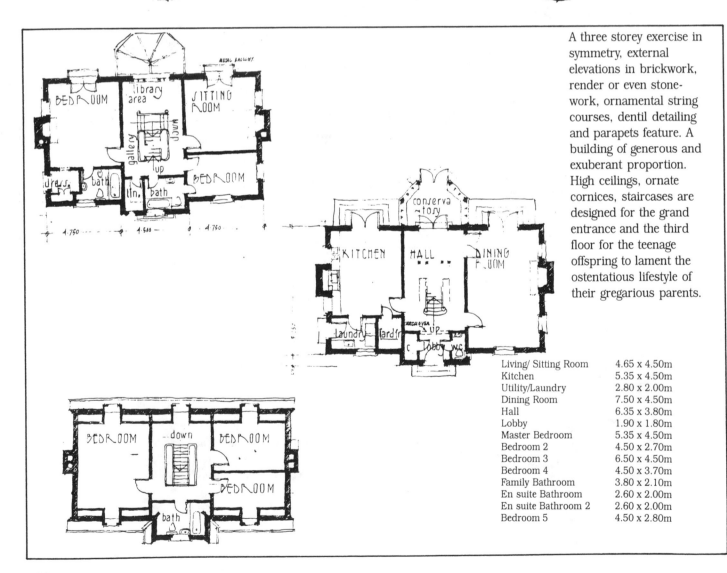

A three storey exercise in symmetry, external elevations in brickwork, render or even stonework, ornamental string courses, dentil detailing and parapets feature. A building of generous and exuberant proportion. High ceilings, ornate cornices, staircases are designed for the grand entrance and the third floor for the teenage offspring to lament the ostentatious lifestyle of their gregarious parents.

Living/ Sitting Room	4.65 x 4.50m
Kitchen	5.35 x 4.50m
Utility/Laundry	2.80 x 2.00m
Dining Room	7.50 x 4.50m
Hall	6.35 x 3.80m
Lobby	1.90 x 1.80m
Master Bedroom	5.35 x 4.50m
Bedroom 2	4.50 x 2.70m
Bedroom 3	6.50 x 4.50m
Bedroom 4	4.50 x 3.70m
Family Bathroom	3.80 x 2.10m
En suite Bathroom	2.60 x 2.00m
En suite Bathroom 2	2.60 x 2.00m
Bedroom 5	4.50 x 2.80m

366 sq. m.

The copyright belongs to Border Oak

Hickstead Hall

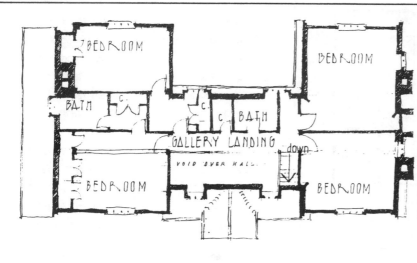

A home designed for a racehorse trainer, a family that like to entertain with some exuberance, hence the gigantic dining hall with French doors to the patio and bedrooms which make no concessions to the limitations of conventional modern living. The ground floor bed sitting room pro-vides accommodation for stable girls. A study to conduct the day-to-day business of a busy stud farm and perhaps examine the form of fillies. A verandah provides a vantage point for the trainer and the owner to view their investment being put through its paces.

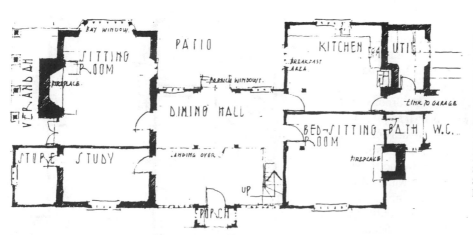

Sitting Room	6.40 x 5.00m
Kitchen	5.50 x 5.00m
Utility	3.50 x 2.20m
Dining Room/Hall	7.40 x 6.70m
Master Bedroom	5.50 x 4.50m
Bedroom 2	5.50 x 3.80m
Bedroom 3	6.00 x 5.50m
Bedroom 4	5.50 x 4.50m
Family Bathroom	2.50 x 2.30m
En suite Bathroom	3.30 x 2.10m
Bathroom	2.15 x 1.90m
Study	5.00 x 3.20m
Store	3.35 x 2.35m
Bed-sitting Room	5.50 x 5.40m

4553 sq. ft./423 sq. m.

The copyright belongs to Scandia-Hus

Sandhamn

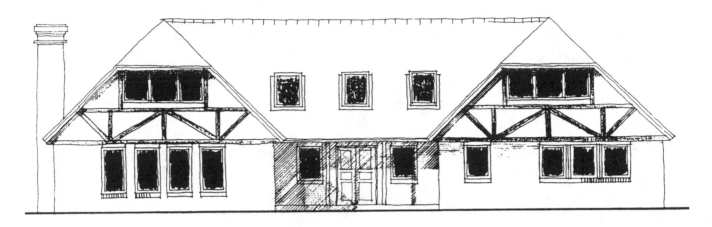

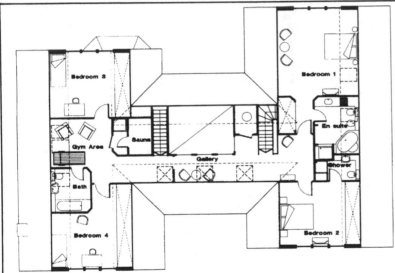

Kitchen:	3.7 x 3.9m *(12'0"x12'8")*
Breakfast Room:	3.5 x 5.1m *(11'7"x16'9")*
Dining Hall:	4.9 x 3.6m *(16'2"x11'11")*
Sitting Room:	7.2 x 5.8m *(23'7"x19'1")*
Family Room:	7.2 x 4.5m *(23'7"x14'11")*
Library:	4.2 x 2.8m *(13'8"x9'2")*
Study :	2.4 x 2.7m *(7'9"x8'11")*
Master Bedroom:	5.0 x 5.1m *(16'3"x16'10")*
Bedroom 2:	4.0 x 4.0m *(13'1"x13'1")*
Bedroom 3:	4.0 x 4.0m *(13'1"x13'1")*
Bedroom 4:	4.1 x 4.6m *(13'6"x15'0")*
Bedroom 5	4.7 x 3.4m *(15'7"x11'0")*
Relaxation/Exercise Area:	3.8 x 3.0m *(12'7"x9'10")*

Large and prestigious, the Sandhamn is a magnificent example of Scandia-Hus' potential. From the impressive entrance you look through three arches into the galleried dining hall, which progresses down to the spacious sitting room. Wide patio doors open to the garden, and the sheltered courtyard. Everyday living can be accommodated within the family room, linked to the bay-windowed breakfast room through the rear hall. The back stairs lead to the children's bedroom wing with its own sauna and exercise area. Four double bedrooms will sleep family and guests in comfort, with space for a granny annex or fifth bedroom and study on the ground floor.

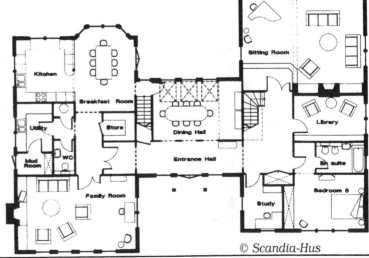

© *Scandia-Hus*

3046 sq. ft./283 sq. m.

The copyright belongs to Scandia-Hus

Millstone

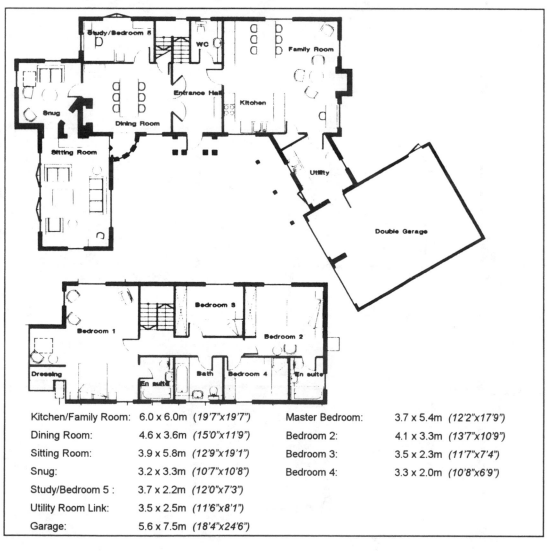

Kitchen/Family Room:	6.0 x 6.0m	*(19'7"x19'7")*
Dining Room:	4.6 x 3.6m	*(15'0"x11'9")*
Sitting Room:	3.9 x 5.8m	*(12'9"x19'1")*
Snug:	3.2 x 3.3m	*(10'7"x10'8")*
Study/Bedroom 5 :	3.7 x 2.2m	*(12'0"x7'3")*
Utility Room Link:	3.5 x 2.5m	*(11'6"x8'1")*
Garage:	5.6 x 7.5m	*(18'4"x24'6")*

Master Bedroom:	3.7 x 5.4m	*(12'2"x17'9")*
Bedroom 2:	4.1 x 3.3m	*(13'7"x10'9")*
Bedroom 3:	3.5 x 2.3m	*(11'7"x7'4")*
Bedroom 4:	3.3 x 2.0m	*(10'8"x6'9")*

This is a new design but you could be forgiven for thinking that this Kentish farmhouse was built 100 years ago. The design of this rambling family home caters for the wide interests of a busy family. It has a large farmhouse kitchen and family room with a cosy fire at one end. The sitting room with a cathedral ceiling, snug and the dining room all benefit from a central 'three-way' fireplace and, although each room forms a separate area, they can open up to form a generous space for entertaining. The semi-circular tower joining the dining and sitting rooms, the angled utility room which links the house with the garage, porches and chimneys are special features.

335

3315 sq. ft./308 sq. m.

The copyright belongs to Scandia-Hus

Stonehurst

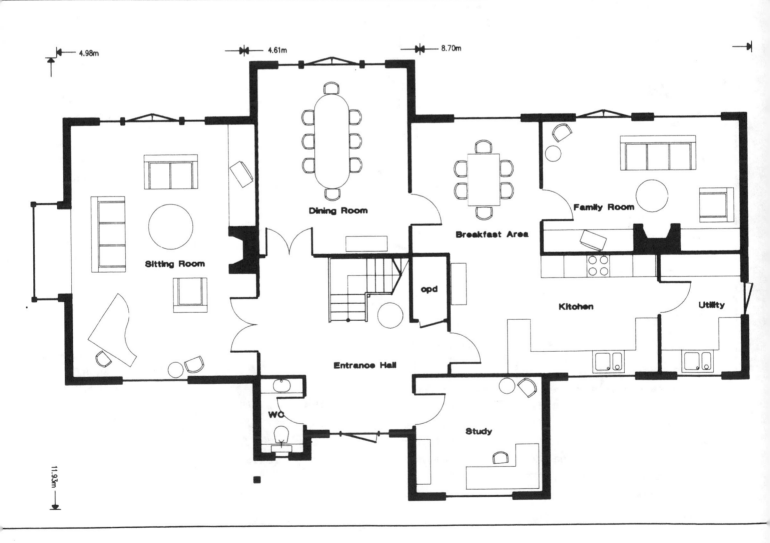

4.98m 4.61m 8.70m

11.93m

Sitting Room

Dining Room

Breakfast Area

Family Room

opd

Kitchen

Utility

Entrance Hall

WC

Study

This traditional design incorporates everything a large family could possibly want; five double bedrooms – two with en-suite facilities – a spacious first floor landing/sitting room, and ample cupboard space. The ground floor features three reception rooms – one with an inglenook fire - a large kitchen, a separate breakfast room and a comfortable study. As the exterior finishes of all Scandia-Hus homes are 'cosmetic' only, with the structure being carried by the timber frame, your home can be finished externally in brick, stone, tile-hanging, weather boarding, render or any combination to suit your individual taste.

GROUND FLOOR

Kitchen:	5.4 x 3.1m	*(17'7"x10'3")*
Breakfast Room:	3.4 x 3.4m	*(11'2"x11'2")*
Dining Room:	4.0 x 4.9m	*(13'0"x16'0")*
Sitting Room:	4.9 x 6.7m	*(16'0"x21'10")*
Family Room:	5.1 x 3.4m	*(16'10"x11'2")*
Study:	3.4 x 3.0m	*(11'2"x10'0")*

FIRST FLOOR

Master Bedroom:	4.4 x 4.5m	*(14'4"x14'8")*
Bedroom 2:	3.3 x 3.8m	*(10'10"x12'4")*
Bedroom 3:	3.9 x 3.0m	*(12'9"x10'0")*
Bedroom 4:	3.4 x 3.1m	*(11'1"x10'1")*
Bedroom 5:	3.5 x 2.3m	*(11'6"x7'7")*
Landing/Seating Area:	5.1 x 5.5m	*(16'8"x16'5")*

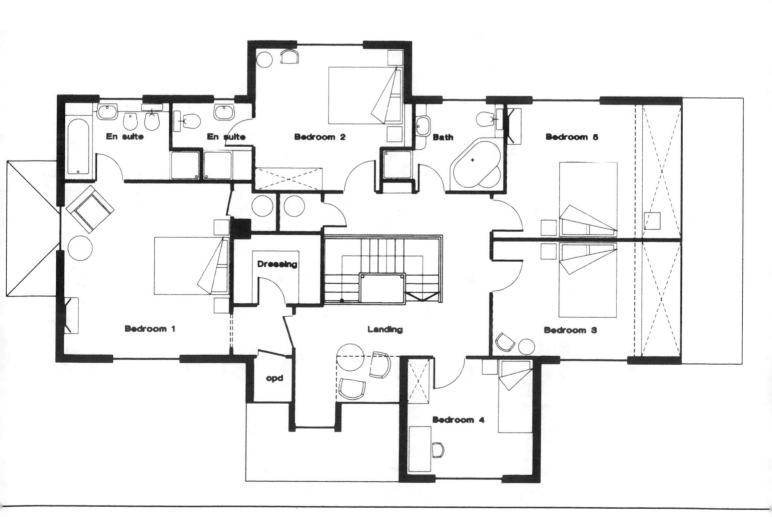

3046 sq. ft./283 sq. m.

The copyright belongs to Scandia-Hus

Linden

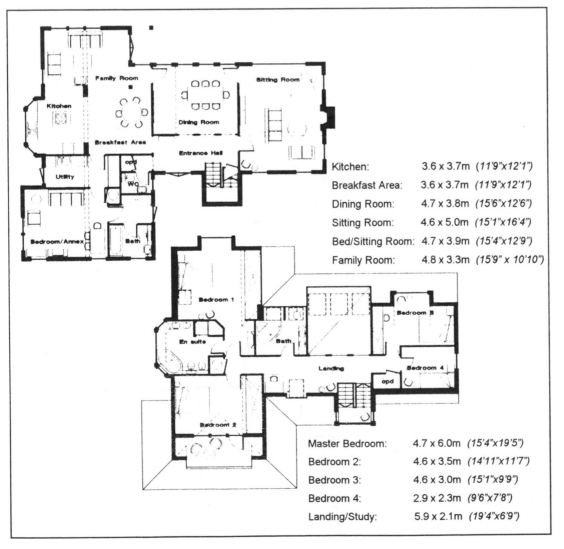

Kitchen:	3.6 x 3.7m	*(11'9"x12'1")*
Breakfast Area:	3.6 x 3.7m	*(11'9"x12'1")*
Dining Room:	4.7 x 3.8m	*(15'6"x12'6")*
Sitting Room:	4.6 x 5.0m	*(15'1"x16'4")*
Bed/Sitting Room:	4.7 x 3.9m	*(15'4"x12'9")*
Family Room:	4.8 x 3.3m	*(15'9" x 10'10")*

Master Bedroom:	4.7 x 6.0m	*(15'4"x19'5")*
Bedroom 2:	4.6 x 3.5m	*(14'11"x11'7")*
Bedroom 3:	4.6 x 3.0m	*(15'1"x9'9")*
Bedroom 4:	2.9 x 2.3m	*(9'6"x7'8")*
Landing/Study:	5.9 x 2.1m	*(19'4"x6'9")*

The Linden abounds with innovative ideas. This spacious home offers four bedrooms – the master bedroom has an oriel window and window seat and a luxurious bathroom. The second bedroom has a roof balcony and the galleried landing area is large enough to house a study, sewing room or hobby area. The open-plan kitchen/breakfast area, overlooking the indoor garden, is combined with a family room with access to the patio and garden. It also features a separate dining hall and sitting room with an inglenook fire and patio doors. The ground floor annex is practically self-contained, offering privacy and convenience for a resident grandparent or au-pair.

3475 sq. ft. 59 ft. x 65 ft.
The copyright belongs to
Design & Materials Ltd.

Alverton

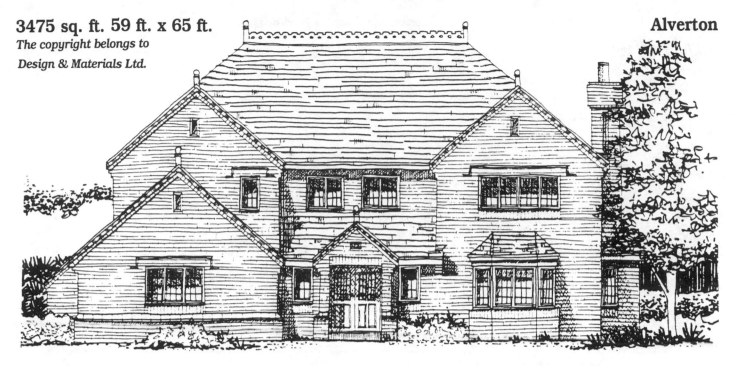

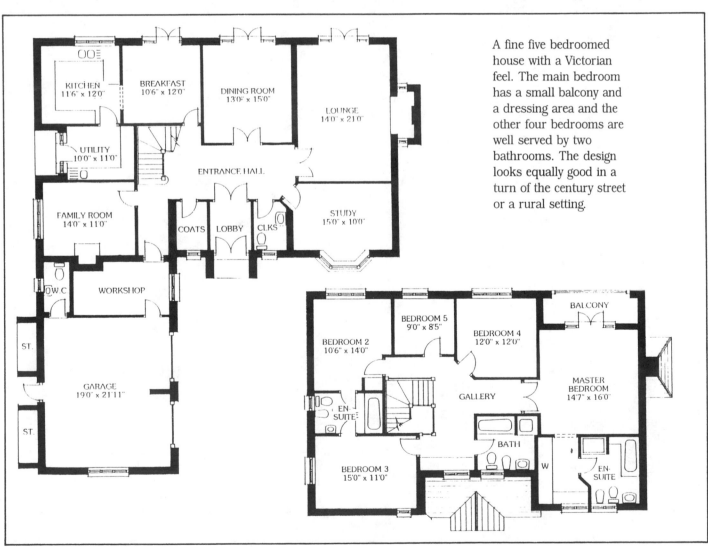

KITCHEN
11'6" x 12'0"

BREAKFAST
10'6" x 12'0"

DINING ROOM
13'0" x 15'0"

LOUNGE
14'0" x 21'0"

UTILITY
10'0" x 11'0"

ENTRANCE HALL

FAMILY ROOM
14'0" x 11'0"

COATS   LOBBY   CLKS

STUDY
15'0" x 10'0"

W.C.   WORKSHOP

ST.

GARAGE
19'0" x 21'11"

ST.

BEDROOM 2
10'6" x 14'0"

BEDROOM 5
9'0" x 8'5"

BEDROOM 4
12'0" x 12'0"

BALCONY

EN-SUITE

GALLERY

MASTER BEDROOM
14'7" x 16'0"

BATH

W

EN-SUITE

BEDROOM 3
15'0" x 11'0"

A fine five bedroomed
house with a Victorian
feel. The main bedroom
has a small balcony and
a dressing area and the
other four bedrooms are
well served by two
bathrooms. The design
looks equally good in a
turn of the century street
or a rural setting.

3200 sq. ft.
80 ft. x 31 ft.

The copyright belongs to Design & Materials Ltd.

Carnforth

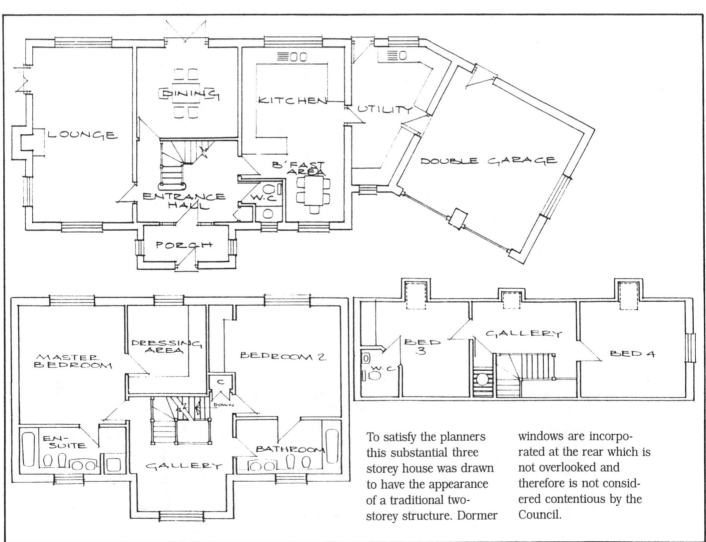

To satisfy the planners this substantial three storey house was drawn to have the appearance of a traditional two-storey structure. Dormer windows are incorporated at the rear which is not overlooked and therefore is not considered contentious by the Council.

3010 sq. ft.

63 ft. x 41 ft.

The copyright belongs to Design & Materials Ltd.

Milhampton

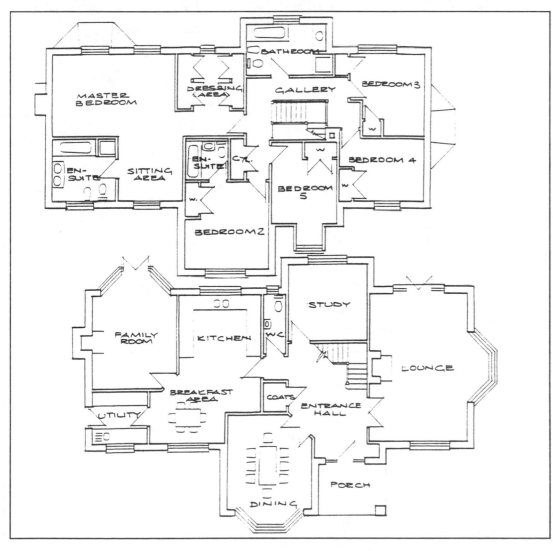

A very impressive country house with well proportioned rooms throughout. The master bedroom has a sitting area, en suite and dressing room.

341

The copyright belongs to Design & Materials Ltd.

3050 sq. ft.

53 ft. x 52 ft.

Langholm

This attractive family home has a definite rural feel. The outstanding design feature is the big entrance hall and upper gallery with split stair-case. There is a large country-style kitchen and a private guest suite over the garage.

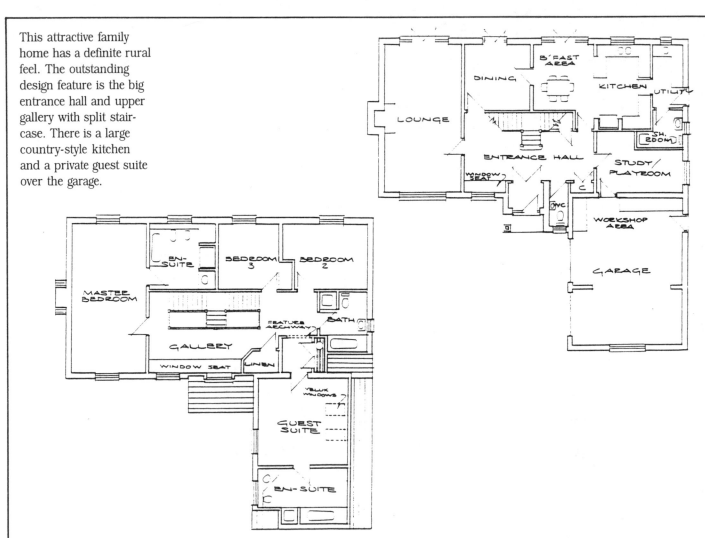

The copyright belongs to Design & Materials Ltd.

5200 sq. ft.
68 ft. x 49 ft.

Belhaven

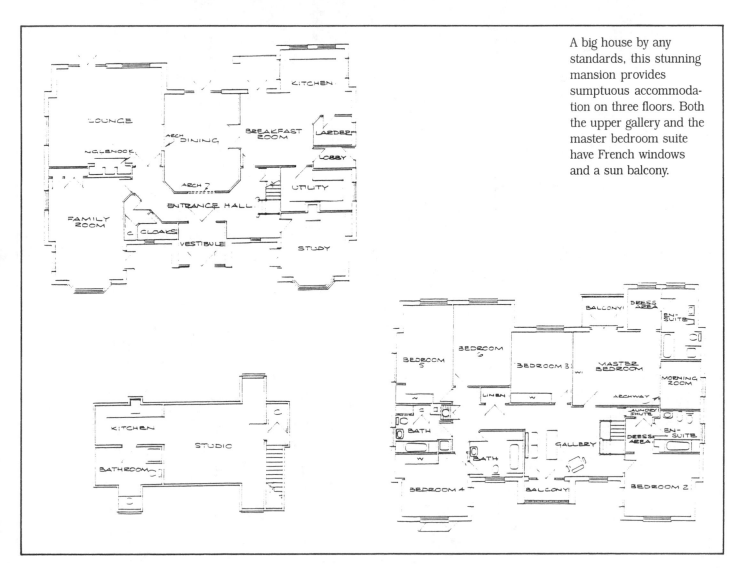

A big house by any standards, this stunning mansion provides sumptuous accommodation on three floors. Both the upper gallery and the master bedroom suite have French windows and a sun balcony.

343

6250 sq. ft.

81 ft. x 102 ft.

Bathampton

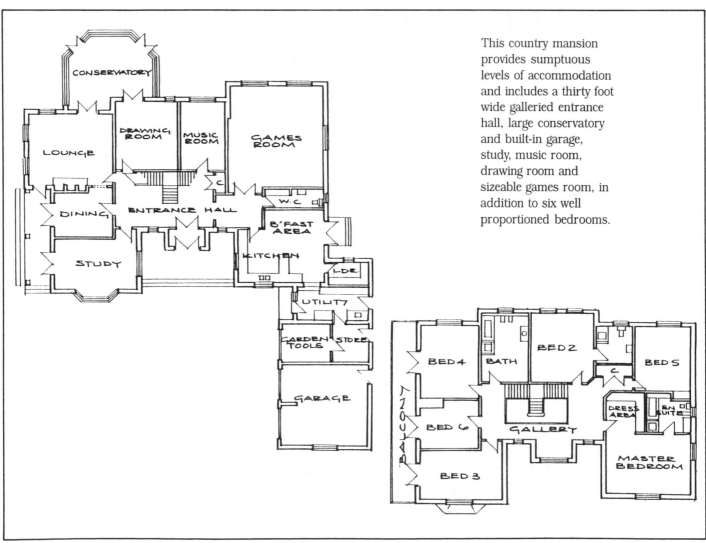

This country mansion provides sumptuous levels of accommodation and includes a thirty foot wide galleried entrance hall, large conservatory and built-in garage, study, music room, drawing room and sizeable games room, in addition to six well proportioned bedrooms.

3063 sq. ft./285 sq. m.

The copyright belongs to Kingpost Design Co

Campden

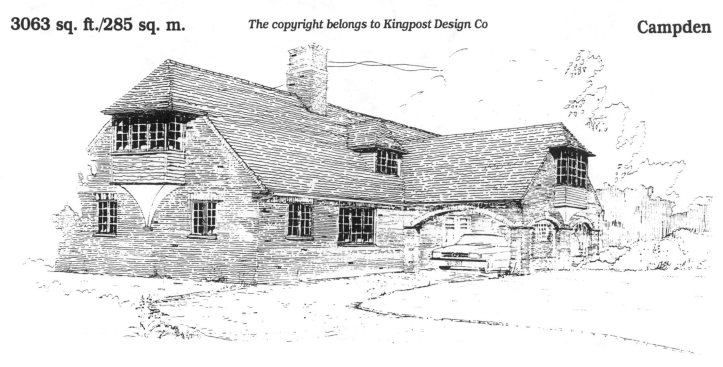

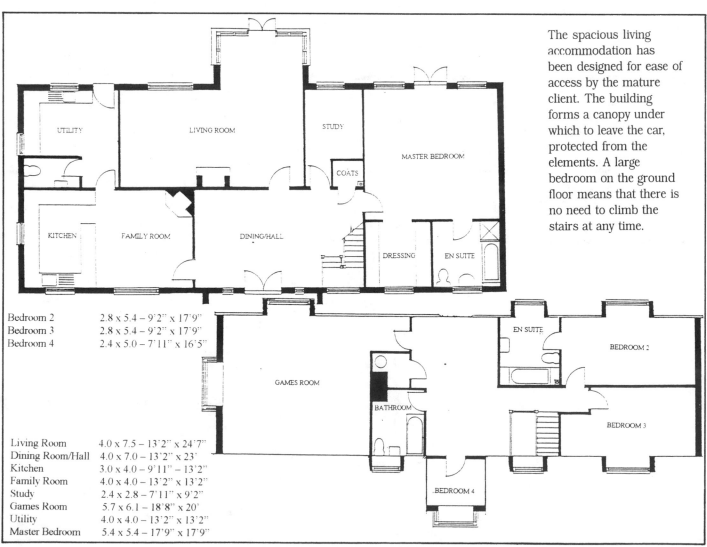

The spacious living accommodation has been designed for ease of access by the mature client. The building forms a canopy under which to leave the car, protected from the elements. A large bedroom on the ground floor means that there is no need to climb the stairs at any time.

Bedroom 2	2.8 x 5.4 – 9'2" x 17'9"
Bedroom 3	2.8 x 5.4 – 9'2" x 17'9"
Bedroom 4	2.4 x 5.0 – 7'11" x 16'5"

Living Room	4.0 x 7.5 – 13'2" x 24'7"
Dining Room/Hall	4.0 x 7.0 – 13'2" x 23'
Kitchen	3.0 x 4.0 – 9'11" – 13'2"
Family Room	4.0 x 4.0 – 13'2" x 13'2"
Study	2.4 x 2.8 – 7'11" x 9'2"
Games Room	5.7 x 6.1 – 18'8" x 20'
Utility	4.0 x 4.0 – 13'2" x 13'2"
Master Bedroom	5.4 x 5.4 – 17'9" x 17'9"

2789 sq. ft./260 sq. m.

The copyright belongs to Kingpost Design Co

Buckland

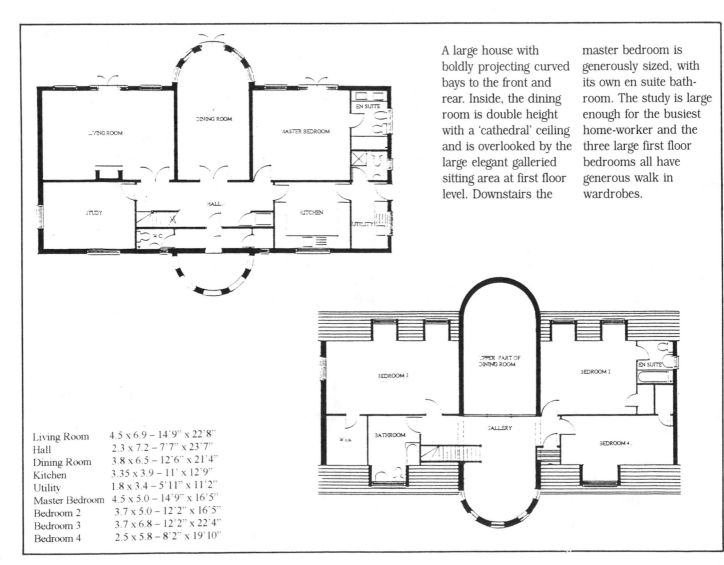

A large house with boldly projecting curved bays to the front and rear. Inside, the dining room is double height with a 'cathedral' ceiling and is overlooked by the large elegant galleried sitting area at first floor level. Downstairs the master bedroom is generously sized, with its own en suite bathroom. The study is large enough for the busiest home-worker and the three large first floor bedrooms all have generous walk in wardrobes.

Living Room	4.5 x 6.9 – 14'9" x 22'8"
Hall	2.3 x 7.2 – 7'7" x 23'7"
Dining Room	3.8 x 6.5 – 12'6" x 21'4"
Kitchen	3.35 x 3.9 – 11' x 12'9"
Utility	1.8 x 3.4 – 5'11" x 11'2"
Master Bedroom	4.5 x 5.0 – 14'9" x 16'5"
Bedroom 2	3.7 x 5.0 – 12'2" x 16'5"
Bedroom 3	3.7 x 6.8 – 12'2" x 22'4"
Bedroom 4	2.5 x 5.8 – 8'2" x 19'10"

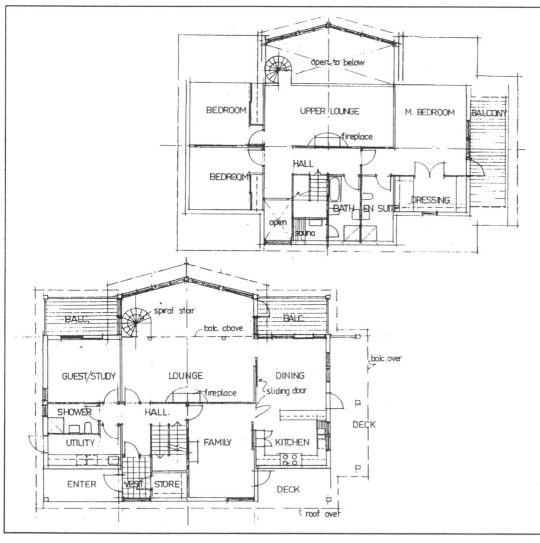

An exciting home where cathedral ceilings and galleried upper lounge areas give a marvellous feeling of space and light, undoubtedly borrowing from the ideals of Scandinavian design.

3028 sq. ft.

The copyright belongs to Kingpost Design Co

Prestbury

Living Room	4.6 x 6.0 – 15'1" x 19'9"
Hall	3.0 x 7.8 – 9'10" x 25'7"
Dining Room	4.0 x 4.6 – 13'2" x 15'1"
Kitchen	3.5 x 5.1 – 11'6" x 16'9"
Family Room	4.5 x 5.0 – 14'9" x 16'5"
Study	3.0 x 3.0 – 9'10" x 9'10"
Garden Room	3.0 x 3.0 – 9'10" x 9'10"
Utility	1.9 x 3.6 – 6'3" x 11'10"
Master Bedroom	4.0 x 4.5 – 13'2" x 14'9"
Bedroom 2	3.4 x 5.0 – 11'2" x 16'5"
Bedroom 3	4.6 x 5.0 – 15'1" x 16'5"
Bedroom 4	2.3 x 4.6 – 7'7" x 15'1"
Bedroom 5	2.3 x 3.5 – 7'7" x 11'6"

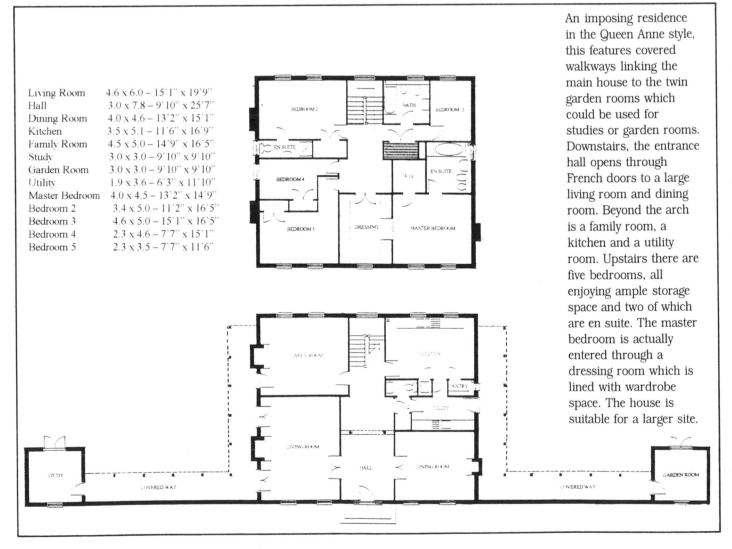

An imposing residence in the Queen Anne style, this features covered walkways linking the main house to the twin garden rooms which could be used for studies or garden rooms. Downstairs, the entrance hall opens through French doors to a large living room and dining room. Beyond the arch is a family room, a kitchen and a utility room. Upstairs there are five bedrooms, all enjoying ample storage space and two of which are en suite. The master bedroom is actually entered through a dressing room which is lined with wardrobe space. The house is suitable for a larger site.

350 sq. m./3762 sq. ft.

Copyright refer to Designer Homes

Lytham

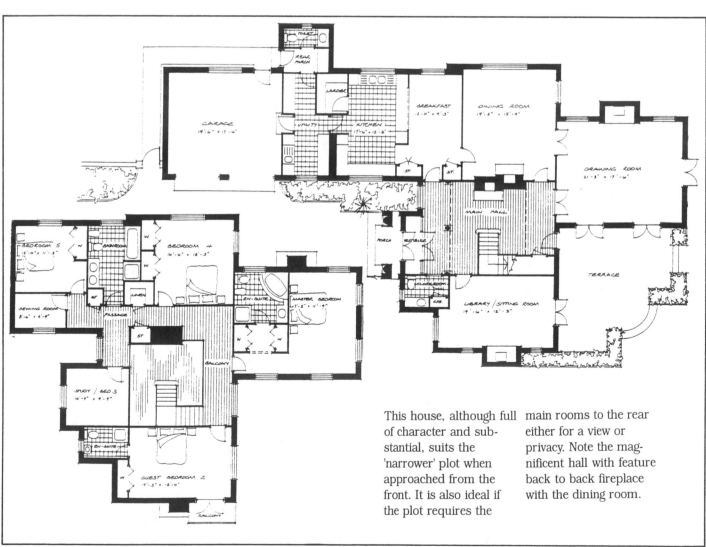

This house, although full of character and substantial, suits the 'narrower' plot when approached from the front. It is also ideal if the plot requires the main rooms to the rear either for a view or privacy. Note the magnificent hall with feature back to back fireplace with the dining room.

337.26 sq. m./3629 sq. ft.   *Copyright refer to Designer Homes*   **Marlow**

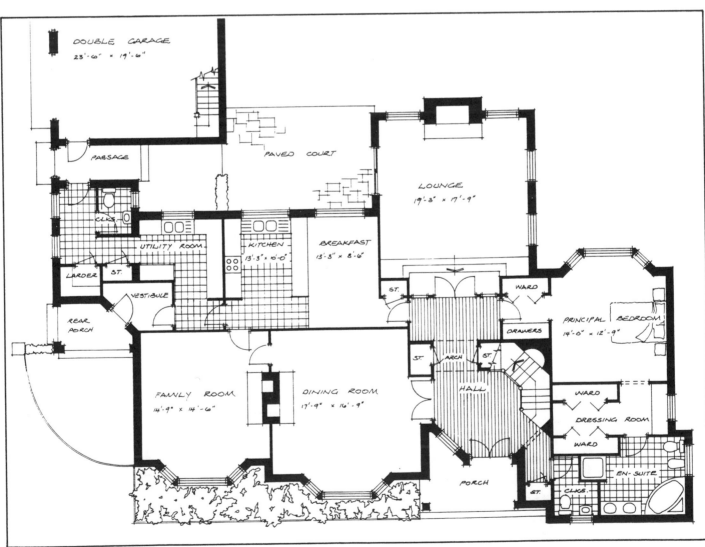

DOUBLE GARAGE
23'-6" × 19'-6"

PASSAGE

PAVED COURT

LOUNGE
19'-3" × 17'-9"

CLKS.

UTILITY ROOM

KITCHEN
13'-3" × 10'-0"

BREAKFAST
13'-3" × 8'-6"

LARDER   ST.

ST.

WARD

VESTIBULE

DRAWERS

PRINCIPAL BEDROOM
14'-0" × 12'-9"

REAR PORCH

ST.   ARCH   ST.

WARD

FAMILY ROOM
14'-9" × 14'-6"

DINING ROOM
17'-9" × 16'-9"

HALL

DRESSING ROOM

WARD

PORCH

ST.

CLKS.

EN-SUITE

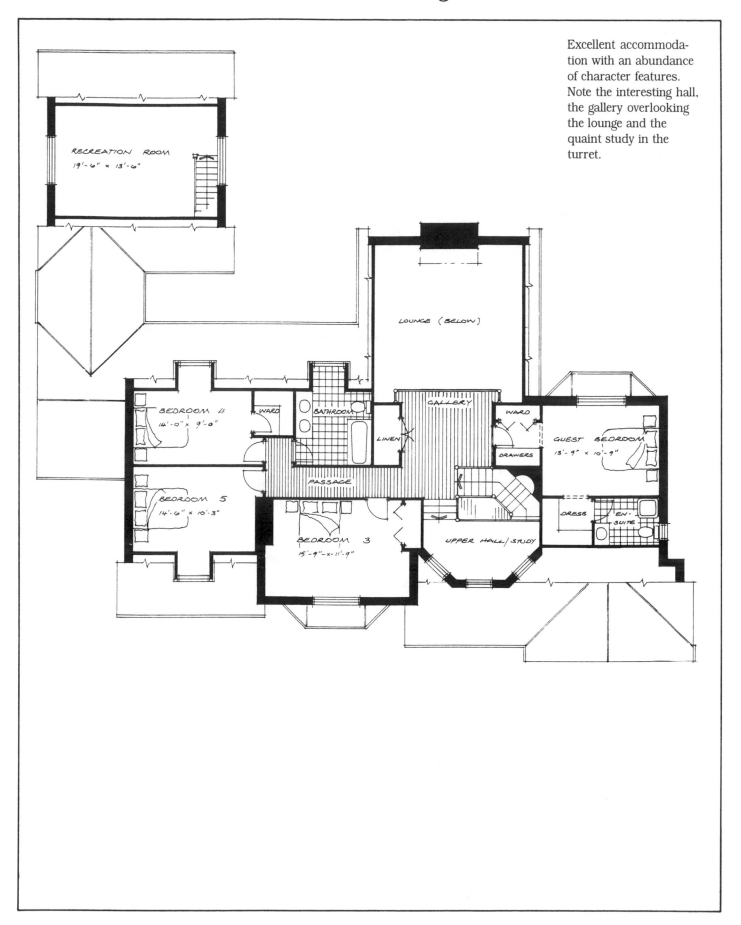

RECREATION ROOM
19'-6" x 13'-6"

Excellent accommodation with an abundance of character features. Note the interesting hall, the gallery overlooking the lounge and the quaint study in the turret.

LOUNGE (BELOW)

BEDROOM 4
14'-0" x 9'-0"

WARD

BATHROOM

GALLERY

WARD

LINEN

DRAWERS

GUEST BEDROOM
13'-9" x 10'-9"

BEDROOM 5
14'-6" x 10'-3"

PASSAGE

BEDROOM 3
15'-9" x 11'-9"

UPPER HALL/STUDY

DRESS

EN-SUITE

414.1 sq. m./4457 sq. ft.

Copyright refer to Designer Homes

Warwick

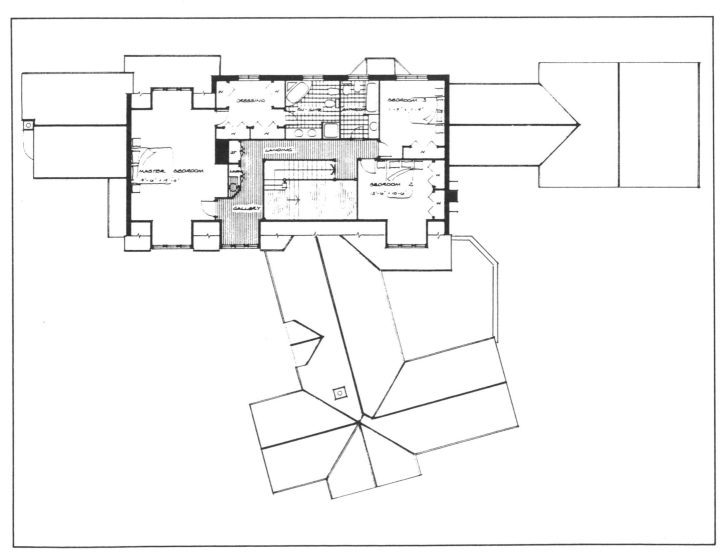

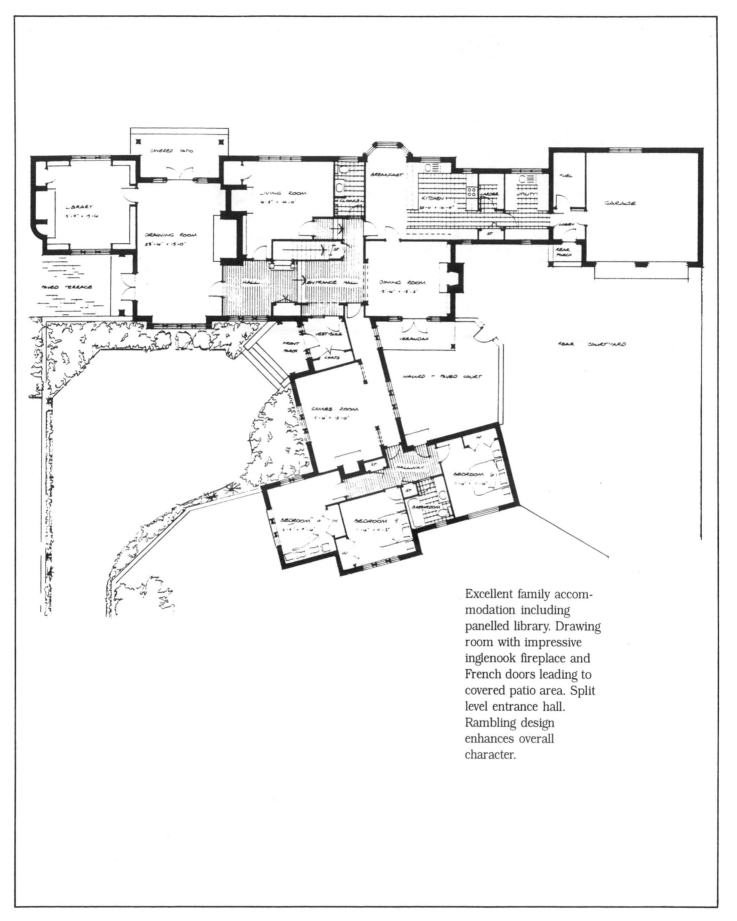

Excellent family accommodation including panelled library. Drawing room with impressive inglenook fireplace and French doors leading to covered patio area. Split level entrance hall. Rambling design enhances overall character.

Copyright refer to Designer Homes

480.7 sq. m./5174 sq. ft.

Sunningdale

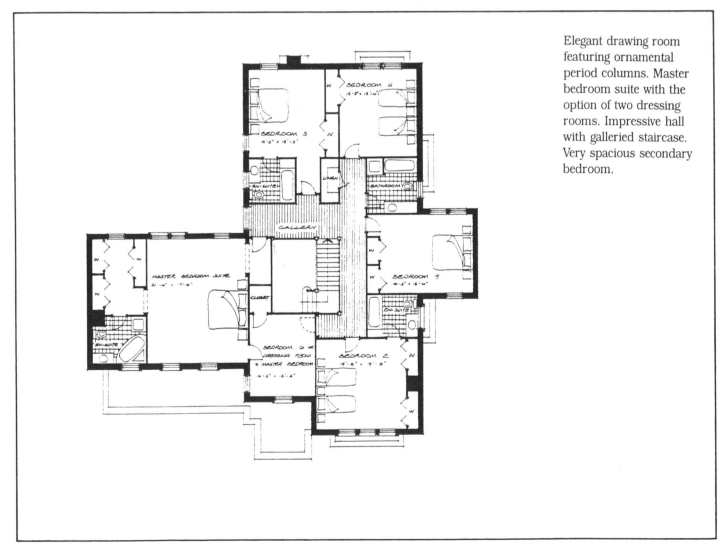

Elegant drawing room featuring ornamental period columns. Master bedroom suite with the option of two dressing rooms. Impressive hall with galleried staircase. Very spacious secondary bedroom.

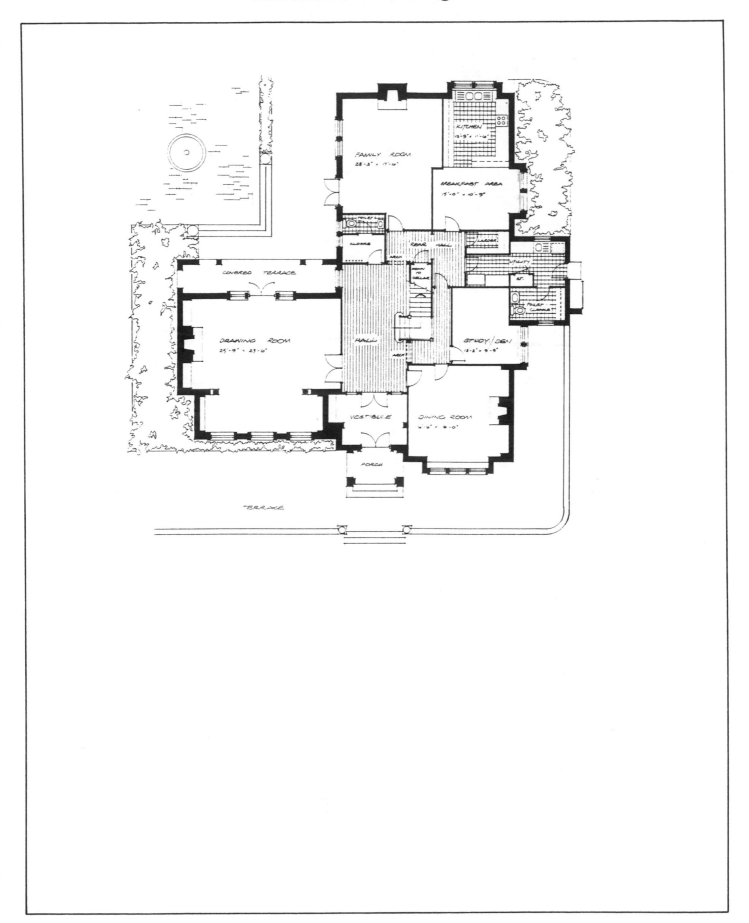

357 sq. m./3840 sq. ft.

Waterford

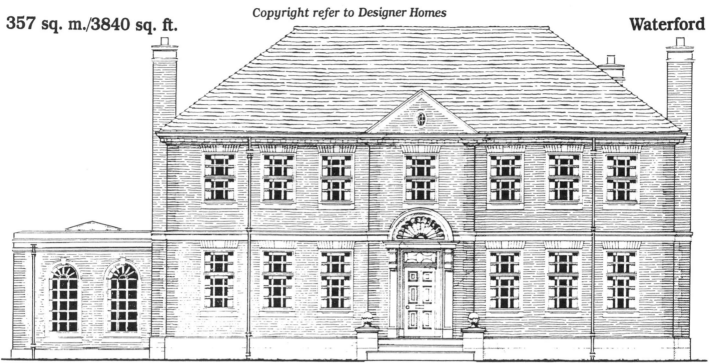

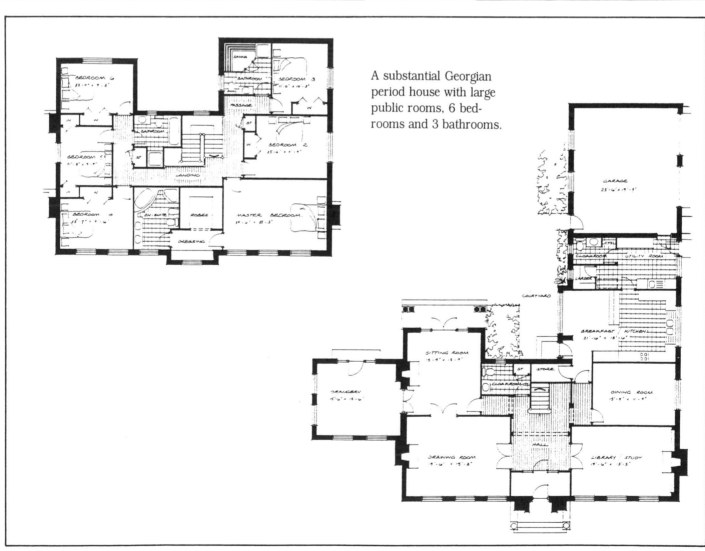

A substantial Georgian period house with large public rooms, 6 bedrooms and 3 bathrooms.

3300 sq. ft./306 sq. m

The copyright belongs to Custom Homes

Malvern

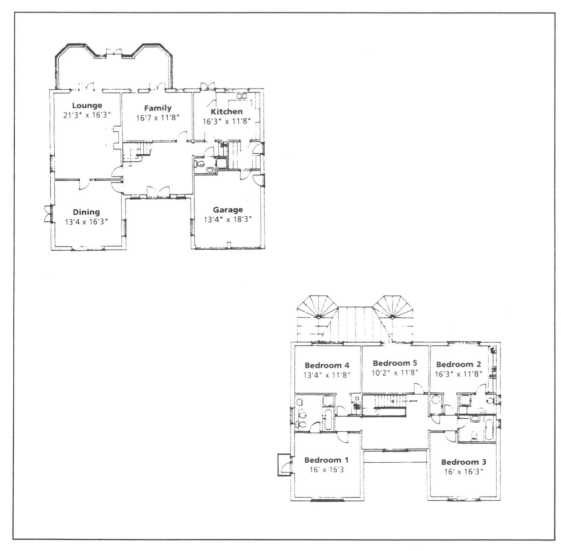

A symmetrically double fronted house with the generous family accommodation grouped around and entered from the centrally situated hallway and landing. From a family perspective it can often save many arguments to have bedrooms evenly sized.

3168 sq. ft./294 sq. m.

The copyright belongs to Custom Homes

Carlisle

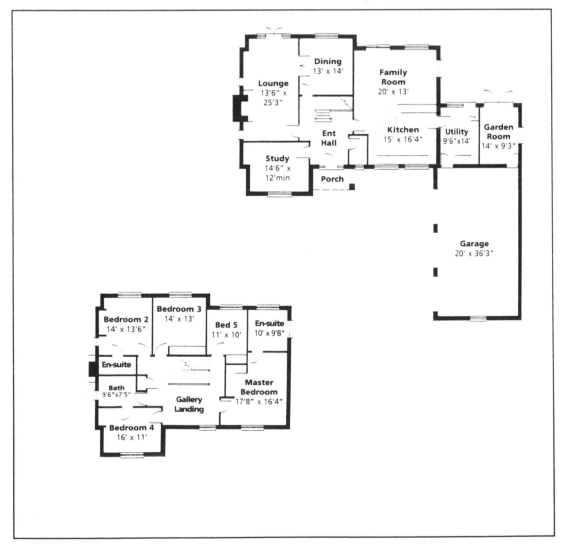

The slope of the roof over the porch leads the eye down and the partial hips of the main roofs reduce the mass of this large house which, even then, would need to be set on a generous plot. The garden room is a useful feature that could also find other uses and the large open plan kitchen/family room means that day to day living can be separated from more formal occasions.

3025 sq. ft./281 sq. m.

The copyright belongs to Custom Homes

Letchworth

Bed 2
19'6"x16'

Bed 4
11'6"x12'

Bed 3
23' x12'

C

C

Gallery

Bedroom 1
16'6" x 19'

Dining
16' x 12'

Study
7' x 9'

Kitchen
13'6"
x12'6"

Utility
9'6" x 8'

Garden
Room

Garage

Drawing
Room
19' x 16'

The catslide roof at the garage end of this family house brings the eye down and reduces the visual bulk of the house, something that might be important in many planning situations. The gallery to the upper part is particularly well lit.

Copyright refer to Designer Homes

Tewkesbury

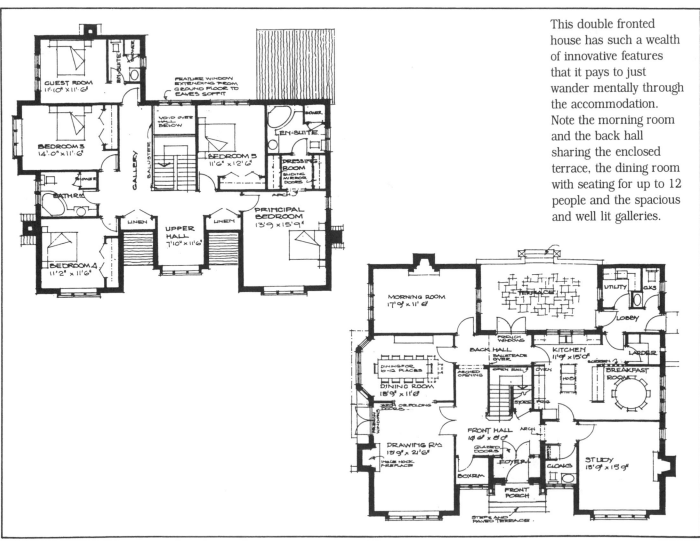

GUEST ROOM
11'10" x 11'6"

FEATURE WINDOW
EXTENDING FROM
GROUND FLOOR TO
EAVES SOFFIT

EN-SUITE

VOID OVER
HALL
BELOW

EN-SUITE

BEDROOM 3
14'0" x 11'6"

GALLERY

BALUSTER

SHOWER

BEDROOM 5
11'6" x 12'6"

DRESSING
ROOM
SLIDING
MIRROR
DOORS

BATH RM

LINEN

UPPER
HALL
7'10" x 11'6"

LINEN

PRINCIPAL
BEDROOM
13'9" x 15'9"

BEDROOM 4
11'2" x 11'6"

This double fronted
house has such a wealth
of innovative features
that it pays to just
wander mentally through
the accommodation.
Note the morning room
and the back hall
sharing the enclosed
terrace, the dining room
with seating for up to 12
people and the spacious
and well lit galleries.

MORNING ROOM
17'9" x 11'6"

TERRACE

UTILITY

CLKS

LOBBY

FRENCH
WINDOWS

BACK HALL
BALUSTRADE
OVER

KITCHEN
11'9" x 15'0"

LARDER

DINING FOR
10-12 PLACES

ARCHED
OPENING

OPEN RAIL

OVEN

BREAKFAST
ROOM

DINING ROOM
18'9" x 11'6"

STORE RM

BI-FOLDING
DOORS

FRONT HALL
14'6" x 8'0"

ARCH

FRENCH
WINDOWS

DRAWING RM
18'9" x 21'6"

GLAZED
DOORS

STUDY
15'9" x 15'9"

INGLE NOOK
FIREPLACE

FOYER

CLOAKS

BOX RM

FRONT
PORCH

STEPS AND
PAVED TERRACE

Homes for narrow sites

Most people think of a narrow site in terms of its width from side to side relative to its frontage but it can, of course, equally apply to a site where there is a longer frontage but a restricted depth to the plot.

All houses suitable for a restricted site have to be very carefully designed and there are some very clever innovations on the pages that follow.

The temptation will always be to build right up to the boundaries but, quite apart from the fact that the planners will be concerned to stop you doing that, it isn't always the best way of overcoming the problem. At least one side should be one metre from the boundary and consideration has to be given to the fact that foundations spread beyond the walls of the house so that, unless they are to encroach on your neighbour's land, even a wall that goes up close to the boundary may well have to actually stop short of it. If things can be arranged so that a metre is left on both sides then the overall benefit to the appearance of the house is greatly increased.

The garage is, once again, the bit that will cause the greatest headaches in design terms and it's difficult to avoid it becoming the dominant architectural feature of the design in a plot with a narrow frontage. If the depth of the plot compensates the narrowness of the width, it might be beneficial to consider the garage as being detached towards the front of the site and, if the width of the plot is sufficient, this will always look better positioned with the garage door looking across the width, rather than into the road.

Contributors in this section:

ASBA Julian Owen Associates
Custom Homes
Design & Materials Ltd.
Designer Homes
Kingpost Design Co
Potton Ltd.
Scandia-Hus

2175 sq. ft.
44 ft. x 32 ft.

The copyright belongs to Design & Materials Ltd.

Oakfield

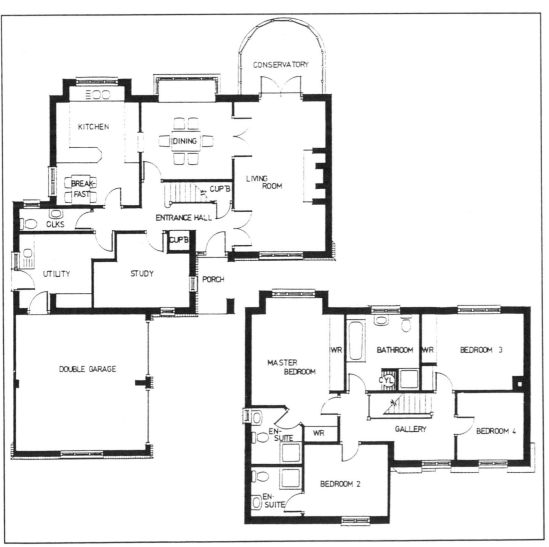

Here we have a really outstanding family home, shown here in the Tudor style. Many interesting features have been incorporated into the design and the overall feeling is one of character and style. The conservatory can be added, after if initial funds are limited. The design looks good in brick, render or stone. It requires a 50' plot and is ideal for infill and looks good in any materials.

The copyright belongs to Design & Materials Ltd.

1800 sq. ft.

44 ft. x 33 ft.

Abercastle

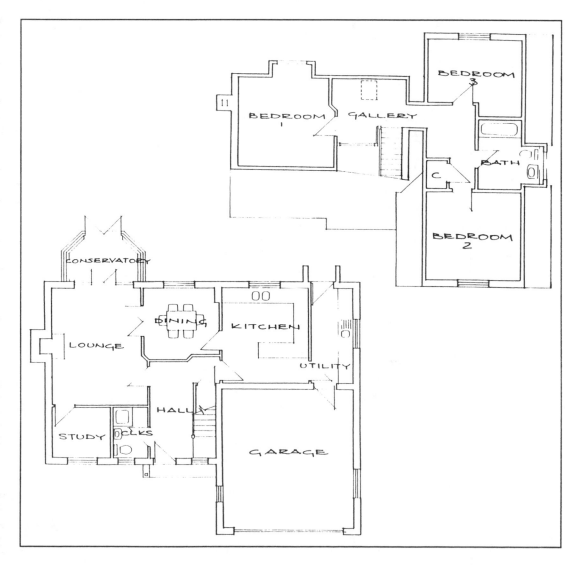

A compact and cost effective chalet bungalow that provides well planned and comfortable family accommodation. The ridge height is relatively low making the design very suitable for narrow infill plots between existing low rise houses.

363

1550 sq. ft.

27 ft. x 33 ft.

Winscombe

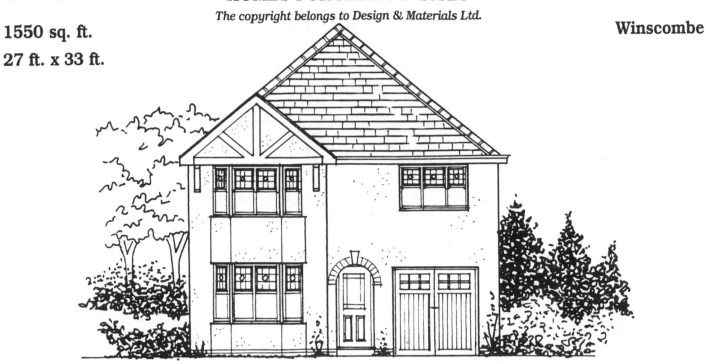

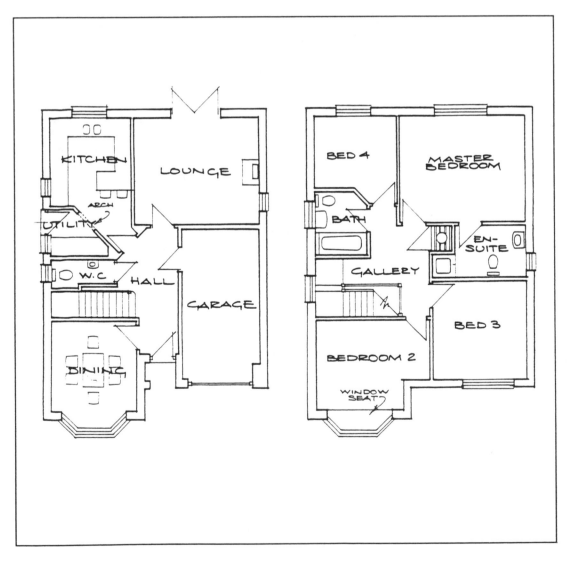

KITCHEN

LOUNGE

ARCH

UTILITY

W.C.

HALL

GARAGE

DINING

BED 4

MASTER BEDROOM

BATH

EN-SUITE

GALLERY

BED 3

BEDROOM 2

WINDOW SEAT

This town house is ideal for narrow infill plots and, with appropriate external materials, could be built almost anywhere. It provides comfortable and cost effective family accommodation.

1350 sq. ft.

34 ft. x 31 ft.

Crofton

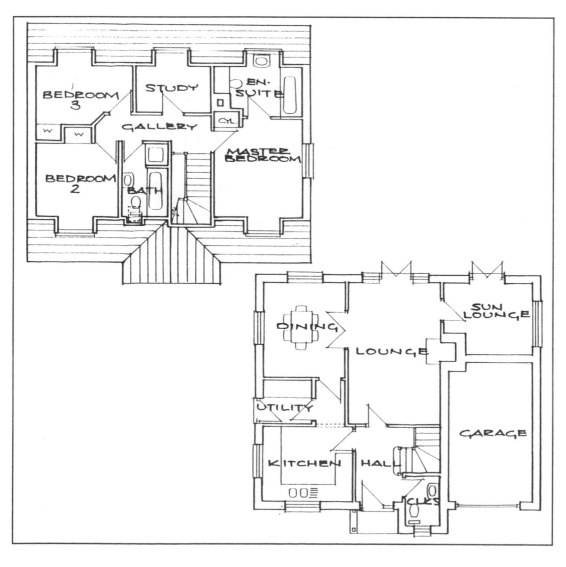

This pretty cottage would be ideal for a village infill plot. Accommodation includes a spacious lounge, separate sun room, two bathrooms and a small study.

1650 sq. ft.

30 ft. x 39 ft.

The copyright belongs to Design & Materials Ltd.

Melksham

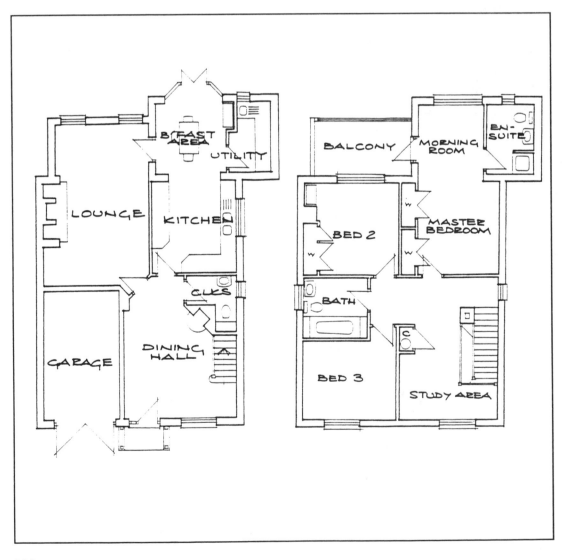

Creating a spacious family home on a narrow site is no easy task but this design succeeds. Features include a dining hall and master bedroom with morning room and balcony.

1034 sq. ft./96 sq. m.

The copyright belongs to Custom Homes

Timsbury

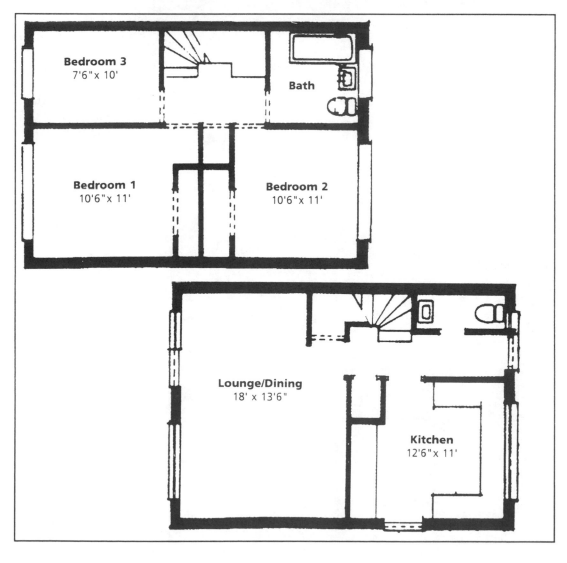

Bedroom 3
7'6" x 10'

Bath

Bedroom 1
10'6" x 11'

Bedroom 2
10'6" x 11'

Lounge/Dining
18' x 13'6"

Kitchen
12'6" x 11'

This is a house designed for a site that is narrow in its depth rather than its width and in addition it seeks to confine all windows to the front or the side elevations. Sites of this nature often come up as areas that were once occupied by railway lines or as narrow tongues of land alongside a road or lane.

367

1440 sq. ft./134 sq. m.

The copyright belongs to Custom Homes

Tibberton

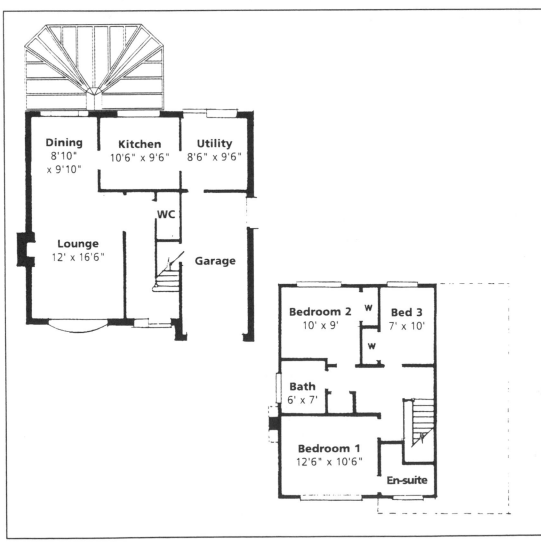

Dining
8'10"
x 9'10"

Kitchen
10'6" x 9'6"

Utility
8'6" x 9'6"

WC

Lounge
12' x 16'6"

Garage

Bedroom 2
10' x 9'

W

Bed 3
7' x 10'

W

Bath
6' x 7'

Bedroom 1
12'6" x 10'6"

En-suite

A pleasant little family house, capable of fitting onto a narrow plot with ease. Only three bedrooms are available but in spite of that, much of the accommodation that one would expect in a far larger house is provided.

2077 sq. ft.

The copyright belongs to Kingpost Design Co

Fairford

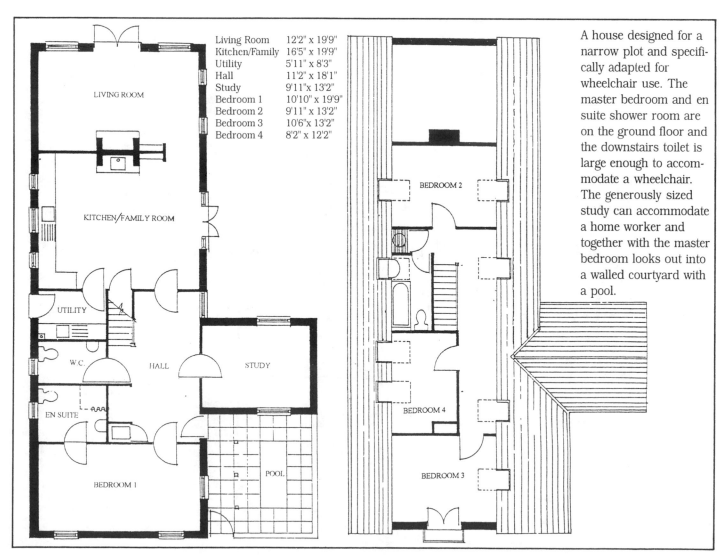

Living Room	12'2" x 19'9"
Kitchen/Family	16'5" x 19'9"
Utility	5'11" x 8'3"
Hall	11'2" x 18'1"
Study	9'11" x 13'2"
Bedroom 1	10'10" x 19'9"
Bedroom 2	9'11" x 13'2"
Bedroom 3	10'6" x 13'2"
Bedroom 4	8'2" x 12'2"

LIVING ROOM

KITCHEN/FAMILY ROOM

UTILITY

W.C.

HALL

STUDY

EN SUITE

BEDROOM 1

POOL

BEDROOM 2

BEDROOM 4

BEDROOM 3

A house designed for a narrow plot and specifically adapted for wheelchair use. The master bedroom and en suite shower room are on the ground floor and the downstairs toilet is large enough to accommodate a wheelchair. The generously sized study can accommodate a home worker and together with the master bedroom looks out into a walled courtyard with a pool.

225.38 sq. m.

10.82m x 20.83m

97-155

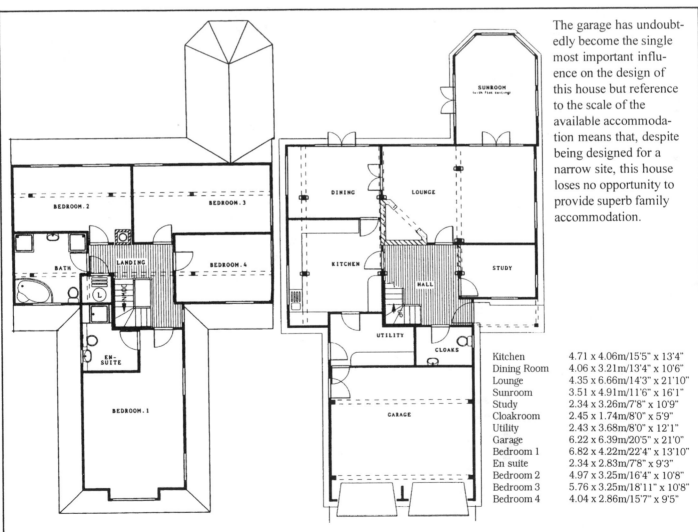

The garage has undoubtedly become the single most important influence on the design of this house but reference to the scale of the available accommodation means that, despite being designed for a narrow site, this house loses no opportunity to provide superb family accommodation.

Kitchen	4.71 x 4.06m/15'5" x 13'4"
Dining Room	4.06 x 3.21m/13'4" x 10'6"
Lounge	4.35 x 6.66m/14'3" x 21'10"
Sunroom	3.51 x 4.91m/11'6" x 16'1"
Study	2.34 x 3.26m/7'8" x 10'9"
Cloakroom	2.45 x 1.74m/8'0" x 5'9"
Utility	2.43 x 3.68m/8'0" x 12'1"
Garage	6.22 x 6.39m/20'5" x 21'0"
Bedroom 1	6.82 x 4.22m/22'4" x 13'10"
En suite	2.34 x 2.83m/7'8" x 9'3"
Bedroom 2	4.97 x 3.25m/16'4" x 10'8"
Bedroom 3	5.76 x 3.25m/18'11" x 10'8"
Bedroom 4	4.04 x 2.86m/15'7" x 9'5"

1400 sq. ft.
10.58m x 11.84m

SS102

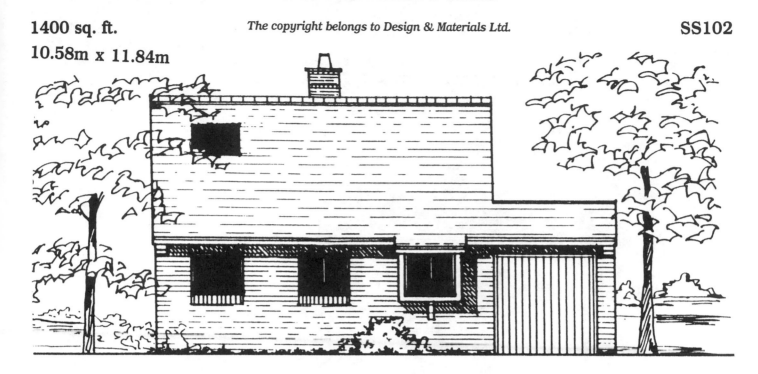

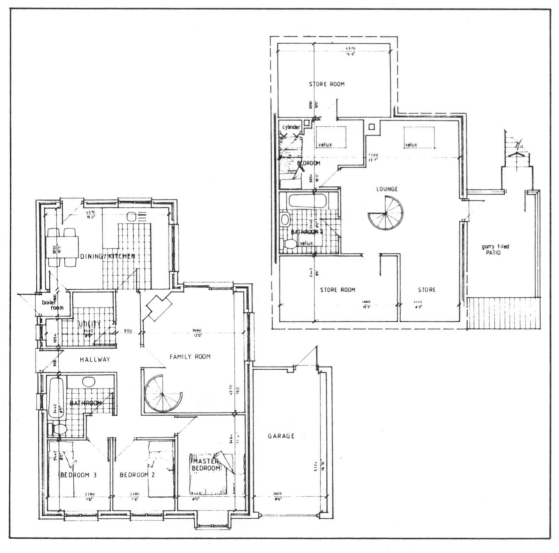

The road elevation of this house gives all of the appearances of being a simple bungalow but the versatility and scope of the accommodation is huge. The layout can either be used as a bungalow with guest accommodation upstairs or else there's scope for the upper part to be self contained with access via the staircase to the patio above the garage.

1289 sq. ft./120 sq. m.
7.79 x 10.42/25' 7" x 34' 2"

The copyright belongs to Design & Materials Ltd.

Shire 118

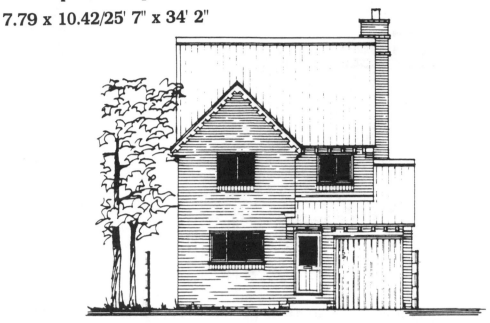

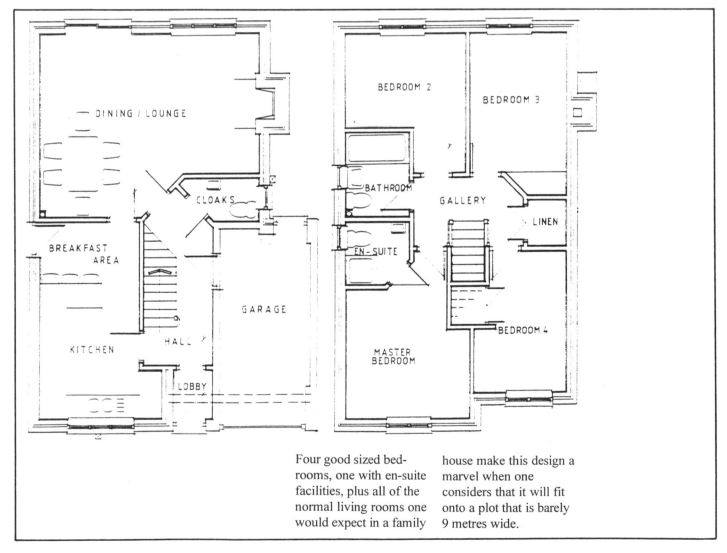

DINING / LOUNGE

CLOAKS

BREAKFAST AREA

GARAGE

KITCHEN

HALL

LOBBY

BEDROOM 2

BEDROOM 3

BATHROOM

GALLERY

LINEN

EN-SUITE

BEDROOM 4

MASTER BEDROOM

Four good sized bedrooms, one with en-suite facilities, plus all of the normal living rooms one would expect in a family house make this design a marvel when one considers that it will fit onto a plot that is barely 9 metres wide.

1477 sq. ft./137 sq. m.

7.57m x 11m

The copyright belongs to

Design & Materials Ltd.

Shire 124

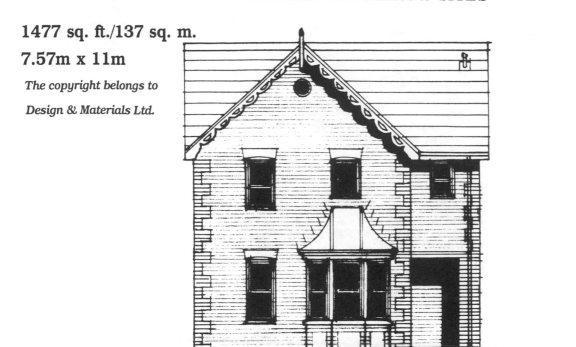

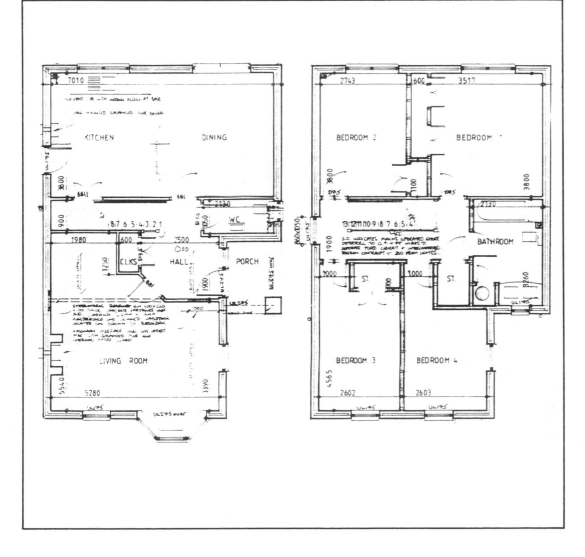

The Victorian influence on this design is fully apparent both from the point of view of the proportions and the detail of the design. The confines of the site mean that the entrance has to be at the side but the forward looking aspect of the porch loses any negative effects of this.

107.6 sq. m.

Copyright refer to Designer Homes

The Flycatcher

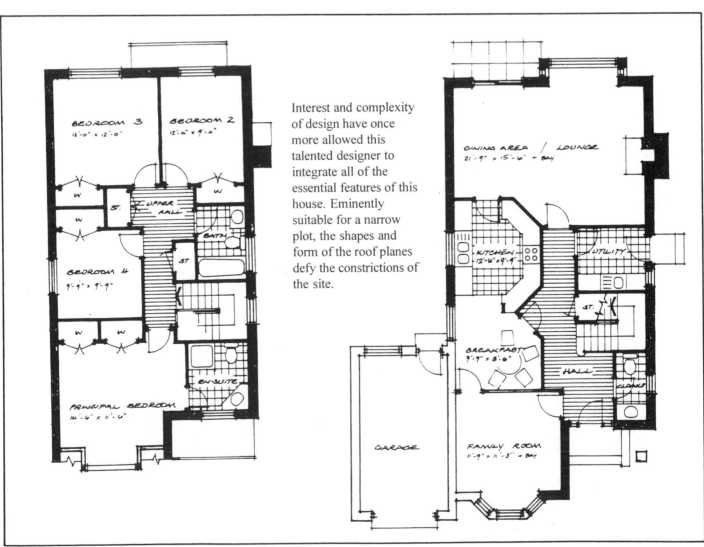

BEDROOM 3
12'-0" x 12'-0"

BEDROOM 2
12'-0" x 9'-6"

W

W

ST.

UPPER HALL

W

BATH

BEDROOM 4
9'-9" x 9'-9"

ST

W

W

EN-SUITE

PRINCIPAL BEDROOM
16'-6" x 11'-6"

Interest and complexity of design have once more allowed this talented designer to integrate all of the essential features of this house. Eminently suitable for a narrow plot, the shapes and form of the roof planes defy the constrictions of the site.

DINING AREA / LOUNGE
21'-9" x 15'-6" + BAY

KITCHEN
12'-6" x 9'-9"

UTILITY

ST.

BREAKFAST
9'-9" x 8'-6"

HALL

GARAGE

FAMILY ROOM
11'-9" x 11'-3" + BAY

154.8 sq. m./1666 sq. ft.

Copyright refer to Designer Homes

Berwick

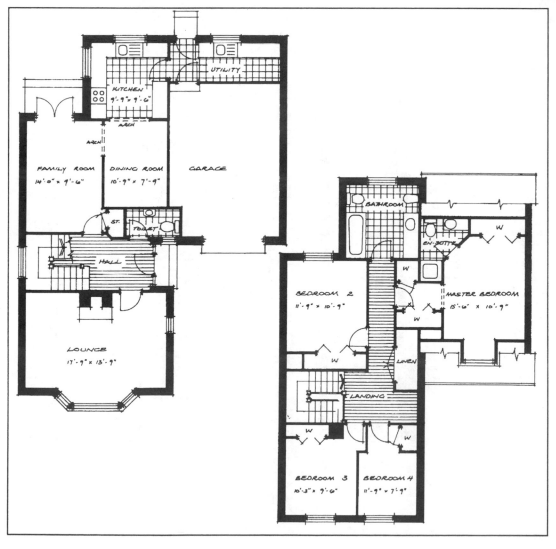

Having the garage set back from the frontage of this house, means that the garage door doesn't have an overriding impact on the elevation whilst still allowing it to add interest. Entrances on the side aren't always popular but this arrangement is, perhaps, an exception with the entrance porch and canopy seeming to be in exactly the right place.

198.7 sq. m.

Copyright refer to Designer Homes

The Sparrowhawk

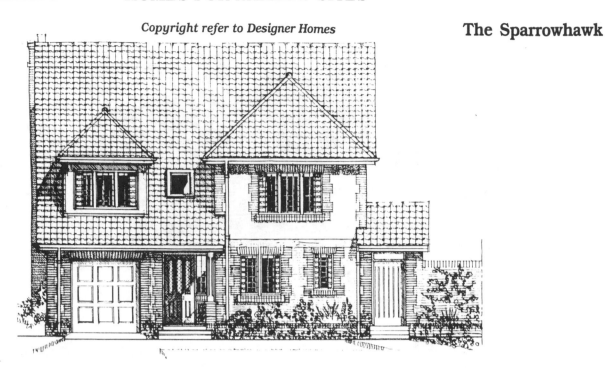

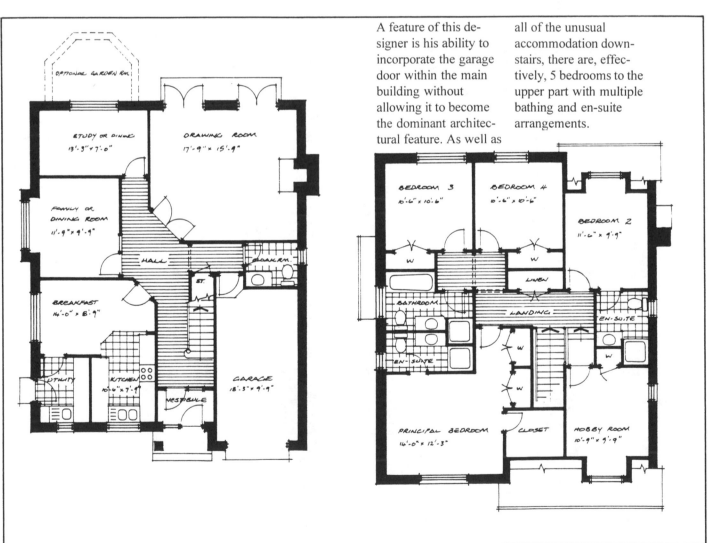

OPTIONAL GARDEN RM.

STUDY OR DINING
13'-3" x 7'-0"

DRAWING ROOM
17'-9" x 15'-9"

FAMILY OR
DINING ROOM
11'-9" x 9'-9"

HALL

CLOAK RM.

ST.

BREAKFAST
14'-0" x 8'-9"

UTILITY

KITCHEN
10'-6" x 7'-9"

VESTIBULE

GARAGE
18'-3" x 9'-9"

BEDROOM 3
10'-6" x 10'-6"

BEDROOM 4
10'-6" x 10'-6"

BEDROOM 2
11'-6" x 9'-9"

W

W

BATHROOM

LINEN

LANDING

EN-SUITE

EN-SUITE

W

W

W

PRINCIPAL BEDROOM
14'-0" x 12'-3"

CLOSET

HOBBY ROOM
10'-9" x 9'-9"

A feature of this designer is his ability to incorporate the garage door within the main building without allowing it to become the dominant architectural feature. As well as all of the unusual accommodation downstairs, there are, effectively, 5 bedrooms to the upper part with multiple bathing and en-suite arrangements.

1800 sq. ft.

The copyright belongs to ASBA
Julian Owen Associates

Blidworth

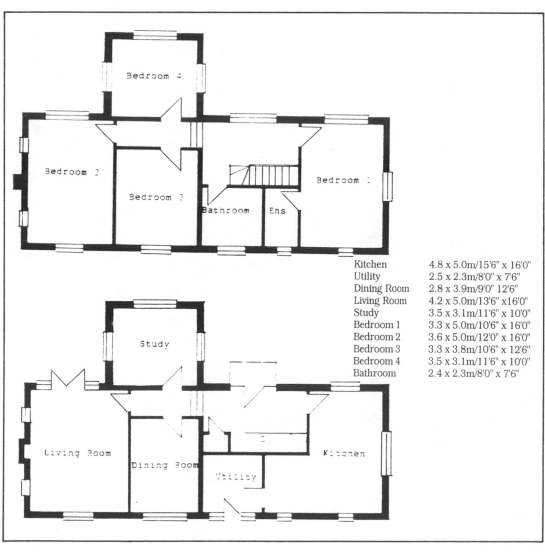

This building has been designed for a narrow site, with an optional extra study/bedroom wing. The end gables have been given parapets, with stone. The longest elevation has been broken up by the introduction of a very slight change in level, and an additional parapet to break the roof line.

Kitchen	4.8 x 5.0m/15'6" x 16'0"
Utility	2.5 x 2.3m/8'0" x 7'6"
Dining Room	2.8 x 3.9m/9'0" 12'6"
Living Room	4.2 x 5.0m/13'6" x16'0"
Study	3.5 x 3.1m/11'6" x 10'0"
Bedroom 1	3.3 x 5.0m/10'6" x 16'0"
Bedroom 2	3.6 x 5.0m/12'0" x 16'0"
Bedroom 3	3.3 x 3.8m/10'6" x 12'6"
Bedroom 4	3.5 x 3.1m/11'6" x 10'0"
Bathroom	2.4 x 2.3m/8'0" x 7'6"

2820 sq. ft.

Thameshouse

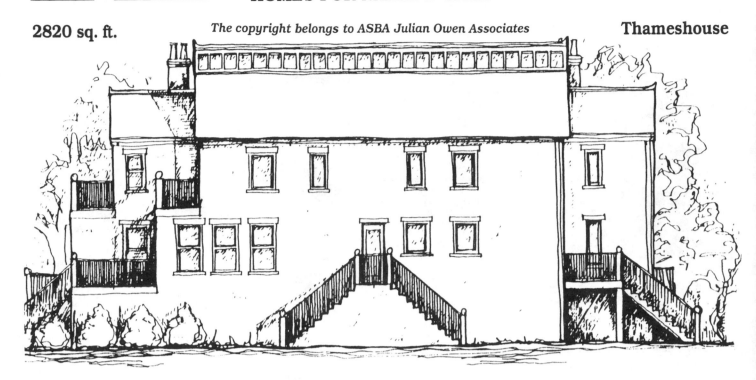

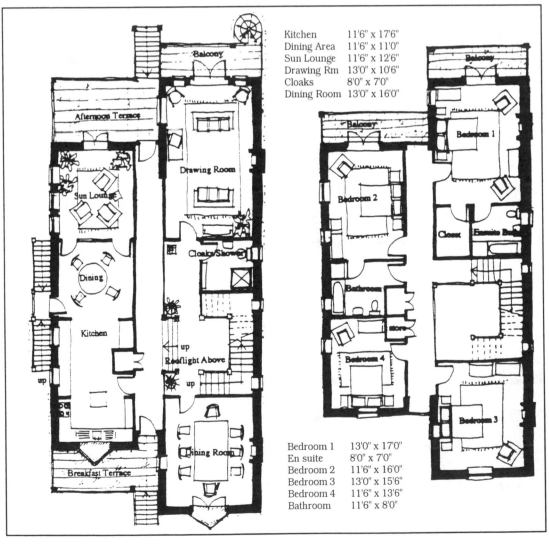

Kitchen	11'6" x 17'6"
Dining Area	11'6" x 11'0"
Sun Lounge	11'6" x 12'6"
Drawing Rm	13'0" x 10'6"
Cloaks	8'0" x 7'0"
Dining Room	13'0" x 16'0"

Bedroom 1	13'0" x 17'0"
En suite	8'0" x 7'0"
Bedroom 2	11'6" x 16'0"
Bedroom 3	13'0" x 15'6"
Bedroom 4	11'6" x 13'6"
Bathroom	11'6" x 8'0"

On a narrow site for its size, this house has a central 'street', running from front to back, with overhead glazing for its full length. Because it was originally designed for construction on the flood plain of a river, the ground floor has been elevated, with a garage tucked away in the basement. The rooms to the rear open out onto balconies and terraces, designed to afford views over the nearby river and catch the evening sun.

2196 sq. ft./204 sq. m.

The copyright belongs to Scandia-Hus

Kungsvik

A well-proportioned home ideal for a narrow site, the Kungsvik shows that you do not need a large plot to live in comfort. In addition to the imposing sitting room, large enough to house a grand piano, there is a spacious dining room and a sizeable family kitchen. The Kungsvik can be supplied with or without the first floor balcony and, in common with all Scandia-Hus chalet designs, offers a choice of dormer roof styles and pitches. The master bedroom has an en-suite shower room and can feature a vaulted, ceiling. Spruce boarding is supplied as standard for the kitchen as with all Scandia-Hus homes, and can be incorporated elsewhere in the house.

1498 sq. ft.

29 ft. x 33 ft.

Linstock

This traditional family house wastes not an inch of space and at only 29ft wide, is ideal for a restricted plot. The kitchen/dining area is open plan and there are four good size bedrooms.

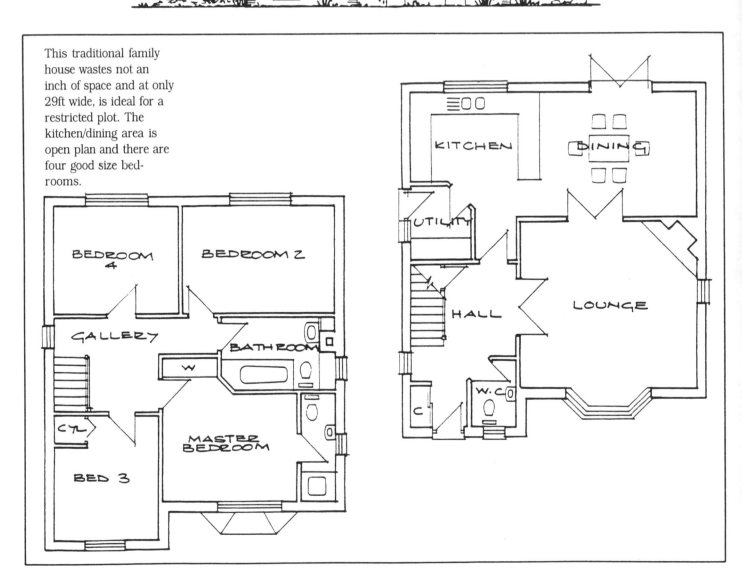

99.59 sq. m.

10.98m x 9.07m

97-327

Kitchen	5.48 x 2.98m/18'0" x 9'6"
Living/	
Dining Area	7.51 x 3.85m/24'8" x 12'8"
WC	2.27 x 9.90m/7'5" x 3'3"
Garage	5.59 x 3.37m/18'4" x 11'1"
Bedroom 1	3.94 x 4.37m/12'11" x 14'4"
En suite	2.27 x 1.86m/7'5" x 6'1"
Bedroom 2	3.45 x 3.05m/11'4" x 10'0"
Bedroom 3	3.20 x 2.85m/10'6" x 9'4"
Bedroom 4	3.44 x 2.27m/11'3" x 7'5"
Bathroom	2.85 x 2.59m/9'4" x 8'6"

The problem that many narrow house designs have is the dominance that the garage door achieves on the front elevation. In this design the effect of this has been mitigated by the clever use of the run over roof of the porch. The design shows four bedrooms and, if the garage wasn't needed, then the space could be used to provide an extra reception room.

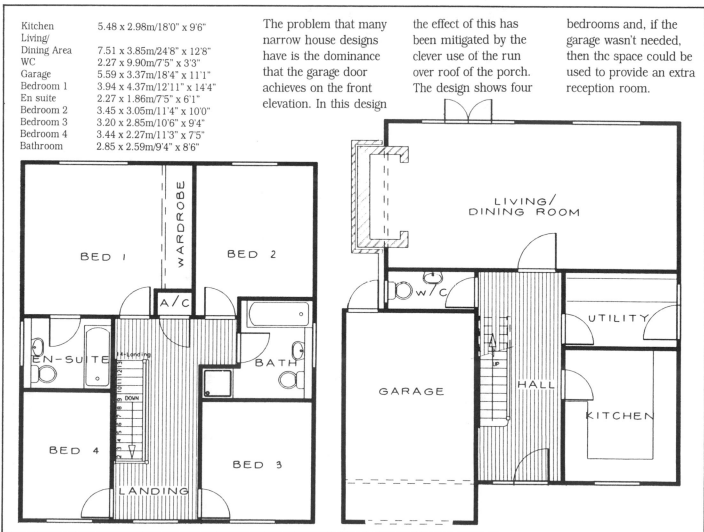

2575 sq. ft.

46 ft. x 47 ft.

Mickleham

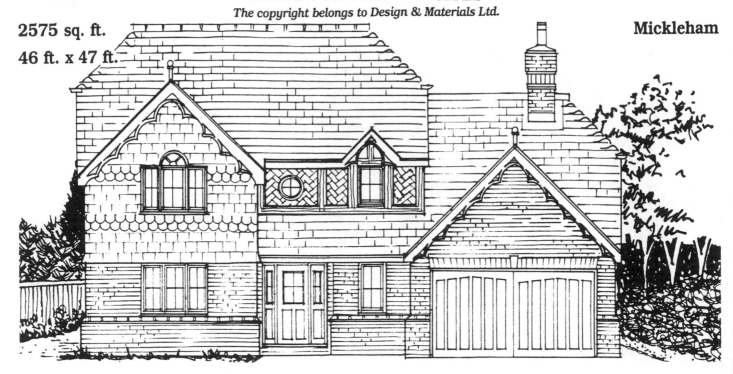

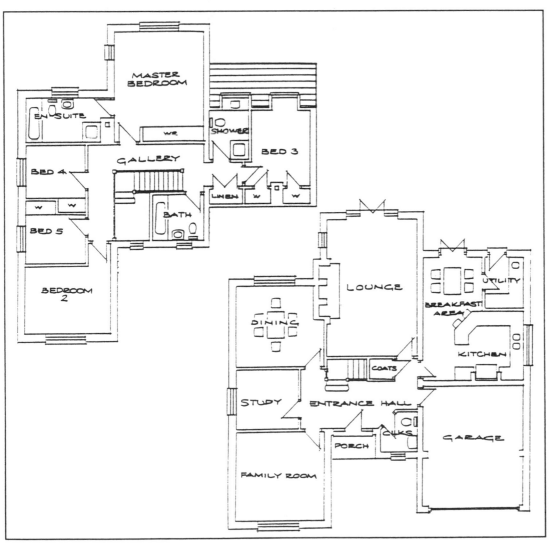

Ideal for plots with limited frontage, this design is only 46 feet wide, yet provides spacious and well planned accommodation for the larger family. Features include hung tiles, finials and filigree bargeboards.

Homes for sloping sites

A steeply sloping site can be a challenge to any designer and you might find that, in order to make a start on the drawing, you first of all need to obtain a detailed levels survey.

Sometimes the levels of the site mean that the design one is looking for is basically the same as one for a level plot but that there may be some makeup or cutting in required. Sometimes the level changes are just sufficient for a change in floor levels to some of the major rooms with the ceiling heights remaining the same. On other sites the changes in level may be so dramatic that there is no option but to consider a multi-levelled design with steps up and down linking each area. At all times the sloping site gives the designer opportunities for innovation and interest that are sometimes lacking on the flat sites.

Designing a house on a sloping site may mean that some walls are wholly or partly below ground level and, if the ground cannot be cut away and retained, then that might, in turn, mean that some of the walls might have to be tanked or made water-proof in much the same way as a basement wall would be treated.

The garage and car parking needs careful consideration. If the road is at the higher level, then the access driveway and garage might have to be retained or, alternatively, the drive might be bridged across to the higher level of the house with the garage at this level. If the road is at the lower level then the garage might well find itself forming the basement or lower level of the house with its rear walls below ground level and, therefore, tanked and retaining.

Contributors in this section:

ASBA Julian Owen Associates
ASBA Reed Architects
Custom Homes
Design & Materials Ltd.
Designer Homes
Scandia-Hus
Swedish Homes

2490 sq. ft. *The copyright belongs to ASBA Julian Owen Associates* **Ashdown**

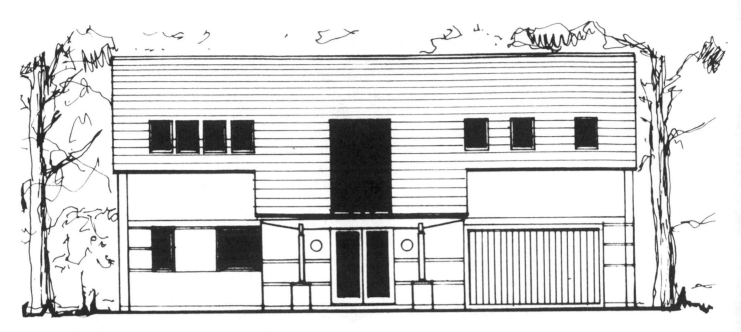

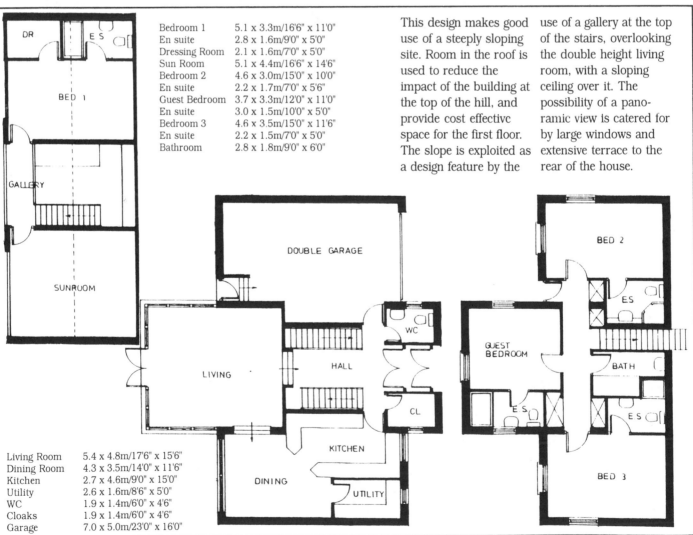

Bedroom 1	5.1 x 3.3m/16'6" x 11'0"
En suite	2.8 x 1.6m/9'0" x 5'0"
Dressing Room	2.1 x 1.6m/7'0" x 5'0"
Sun Room	5.1 x 4.4m/16'6" x 14'6"
Bedroom 2	4.6 x 3.0m/15'0" x 10'0"
En suite	2.2 x 1.7m/7'0" x 5'6"
Guest Bedroom	3.7 x 3.3m/12'0" x 11'0"
En suite	3.0 x 1.5m/10'0" x 5'0"
Bedroom 3	4.6 x 3.5m/15'0" x 11'6"
En suite	2.2 x 1.5m/7'0" x 5'0"
Bathroom	2.8 x 1.8m/9'0" x 6'0"

This design makes good use of a steeply sloping site. Room in the roof is used to reduce the impact of the building at the top of the hill, and provide cost effective space for the first floor. The slope is exploited as a design feature by the use of a gallery at the top of the stairs, overlooking the double height living room, with a sloping ceiling over it. The possibility of a panoramic view is catered for by large windows and extensive terrace to the rear of the house.

Living Room	5.4 x 4.8m/17'6" x 15'6"
Dining Room	4.3 x 3.5m/14'0" x 11'6"
Kitchen	2.7 x 4.6m/9'0" x 15'0"
Utility	2.6 x 1.6m/8'6" x 5'0"
WC	1.9 x 1.4m/6'0" x 4'6"
Cloaks	1.9 x 1.4m/6'0" x 4'6"
Garage	7.0 x 5.0m/23'0" x 16'0"

1259 sq. ft.

The copyright belongs to ASBA Reed Architects

Sunnyside

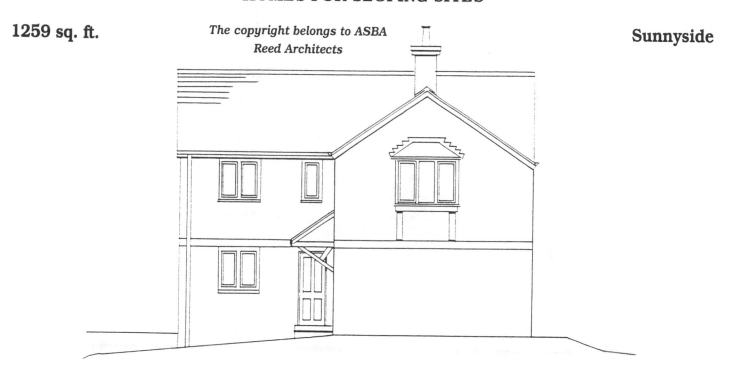

The generous living room with its deep window seat designed to take advantage of the elevated views across and down the valley from a house that can be sited on a steeply sloping site without need for retaining walls. Other features include the landing window, which neatly avoids the lack of light often associated with central staircases, and one of the ground floor bedrooms could easily convert to a home-office with easy access for business visitors away from the family accommodation.

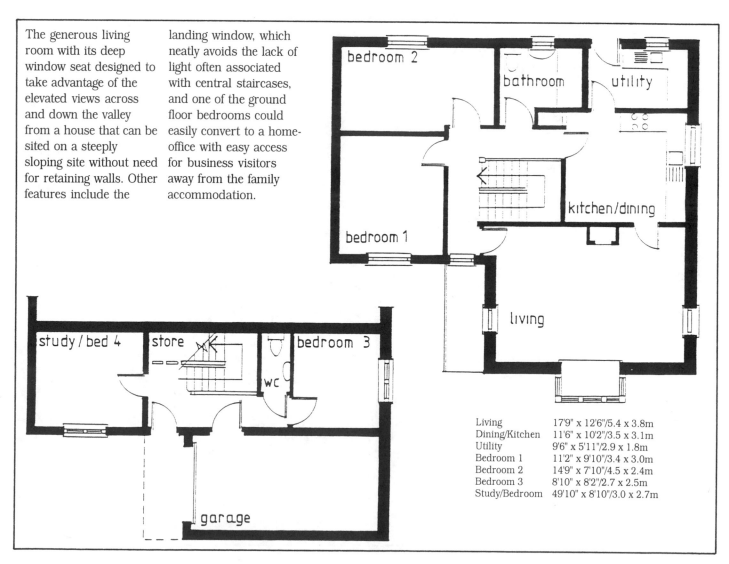

Living	17'9" x 12'6"/5.4 x 3.8m
Dining/Kitchen	11'6" x 10'2"/3.5 x 3.1m
Utility	9'6" x 5'11"/2.9 x 1.8m
Bedroom 1	11'2" x 9'10"/3.4 x 3.0m
Bedroom 2	14'9" x 7'10"/4.5 x 2.4m
Bedroom 3	8'10" x 8'2"/2.7 x 2.5m
Study/Bedroom	49'10" x 8'10"/3.0 x 2.7m

1425 sq. ft./132 sq. m.

The copyright belongs to Custom Homes

Glendower

This is the design that is thought by many to be the original behind the concept of a split level house with the principle living accommodation set as a mezzanine level, roughly halfway between the levels of the rest of the accommodation. It has been emulated and copied but never bettered.

2000 sq. ft.

45 ft. x 57 ft.

The copyright belongs to Design & Materials Ltd.

Thornwood

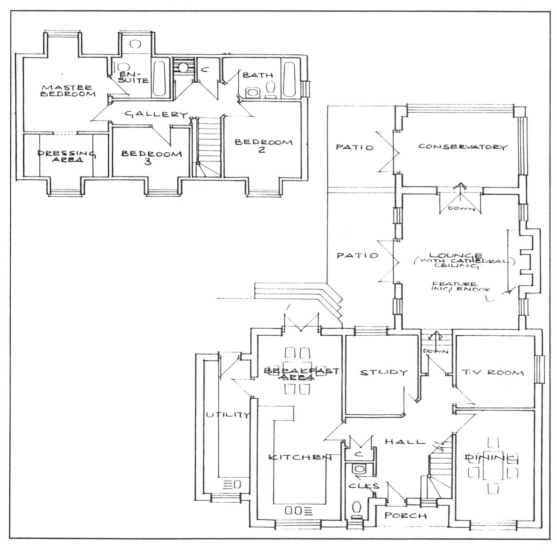

This property is perfect for a sloping country setting and features patios around two sides of the L-shaped ground floor. There is a cathedral lounge and large conservatory.

387

Sturbridge

1775 sq. ft.
34 ft. x 38 ft.

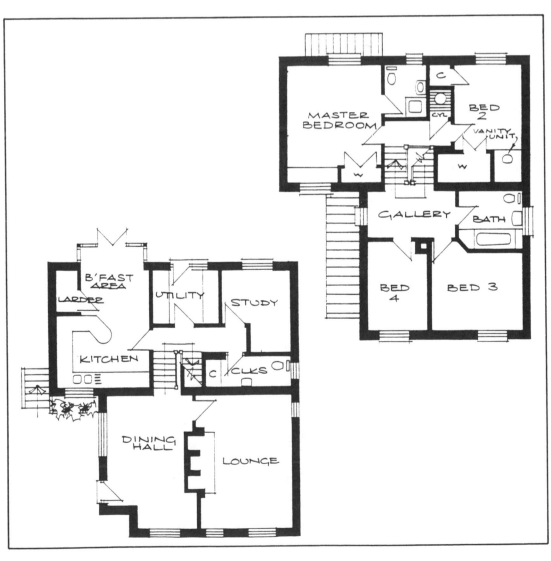

This attractive design was specially drawn for a site that slopes upwards away from the roadside. This creates an interesting internal layout on four different levels! At road level is the lounge with inglenook fireplace and dining hall leading up to the kitchen/breakfast room and study. The next half flight leads to two bedrooms and main bathroom and from there onto the top level.

1850 sq. ft.

52 ft. x 30 ft.

The copyright belongs to Design & Materials Ltd.

Hexham

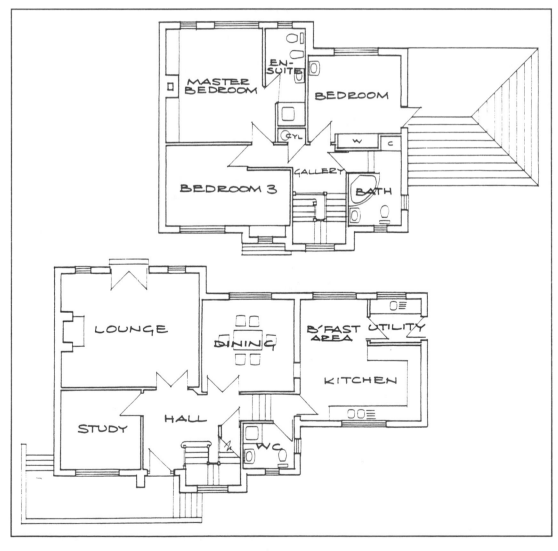

This design illustrates that although sloping sites have their difficulties, they offer the designer and client exciting opportunities that don't exist on level plots. Overall, it provides good family accommodation on three levels.

SWHS5

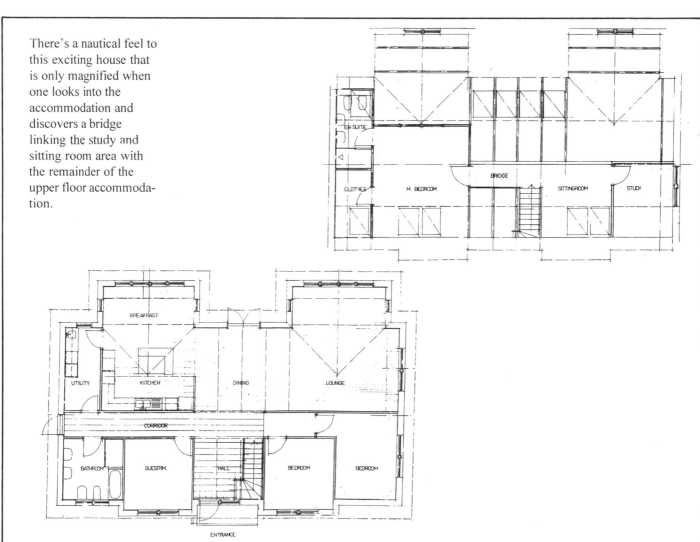

There's a nautical feel to this exciting house that is only magnified when one looks into the accommodation and discovers a bridge linking the study and sitting room area with the remainder of the upper floor accommodation.

EN-SUITE

CLOTHES

M. BEDROOM

BRIDGE

SITTINGROOM

STUDY

BREAKFAST

UTILITY

KITCHEN

DINING

LOUNGE

CORRIDOR

BATHROOM

GUESTRM.

HALL

BEDROOM

BEDROOM

ENTRANCE

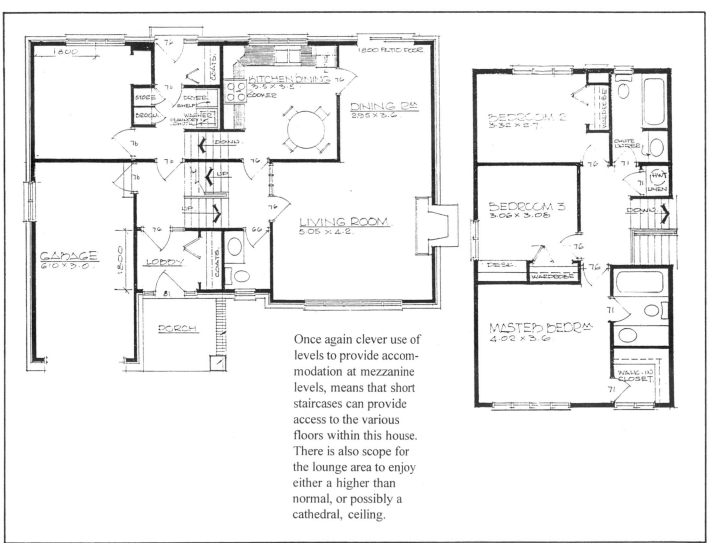

Once again clever use of levels to provide accommodation at mezzanine levels, means that short staircases can provide access to the various floors within this house. There is also scope for the lounge area to enjoy either a higher than normal, or possibly a cathedral, ceiling.

211.14 sq. m.

Copyright refer to Designer Homes

The Capercaillie

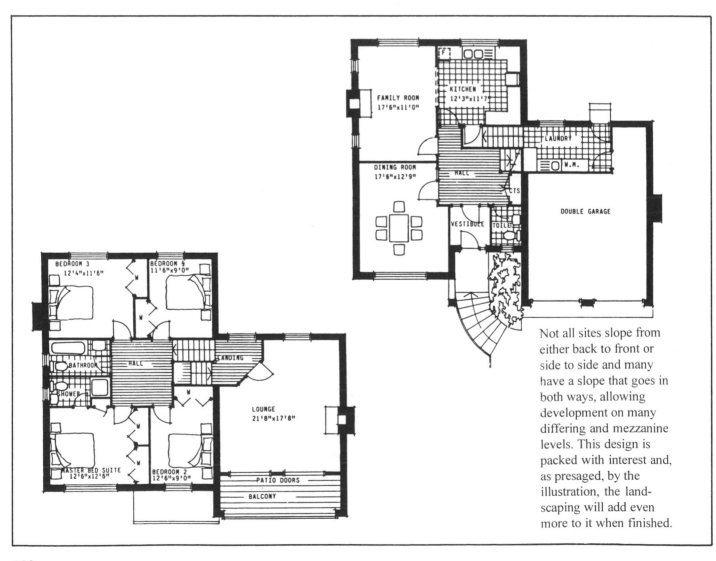

FAMILY ROOM
17'6"x11'0"

KITCHEN
12'3"x11'7"

LAUNDRY

DINING ROOM
17'6"x12'9"

HALL

W.M.

DOUBLE GARAGE

VESTIBULE TOILET

CTS

BEDROOM 3
12'4"x11'6"

BEDROOM 4
11'6"x9'0"

BATHROOM

HALL

LANDING

SHOWER

LOUNGE
21'8"x17'8"

MASTER BED SUITE
12'6"x12'6"

BEDROOM 2
12'6"x9'0"

PATIO DOORS

BALCONY

Not all sites slope from either back to front or side to side and many have a slope that goes in both ways, allowing development on many differing and mezzanine levels. This design is packed with interest and, as presaged, by the illustration, the landscaping will add even more to it when finished.

The Pelican

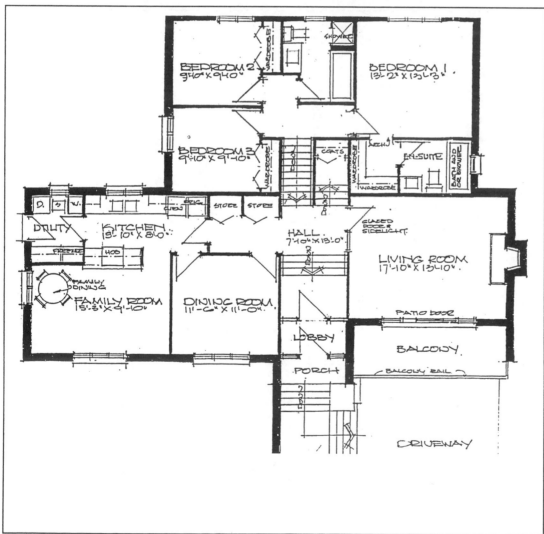

This extensive bungalow design is eminently suitable for the type of site where the land slopes up quite steeply to a relatively flat area where a level plinth can be formed. The garage, at street level, forms the only true basement area and the front part of it is cleverly utilised as a balcony.

1848 sq. ft./ 172 sq. m.   *The copyright belongs to Scandia-Hus*   **Brigworth**

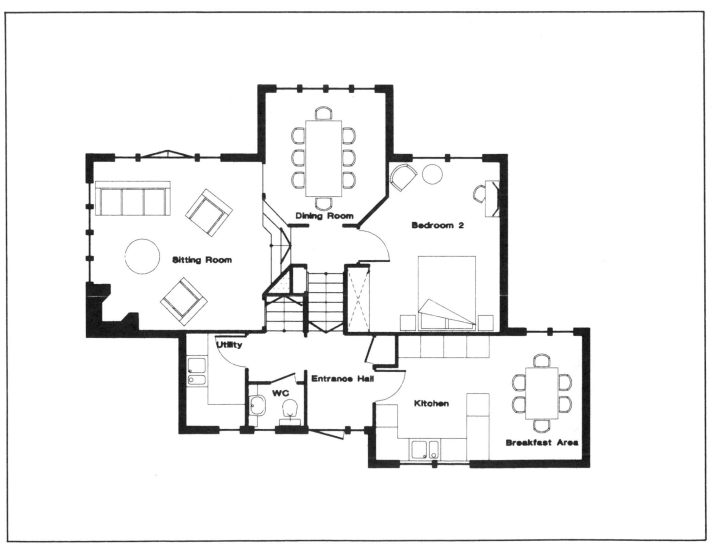

GROUND FLOOR

Kitchen/Breakfast Room:	5.5 x 3.3m	*(17'9"x11'0")*
Dining Room:	3.2 x 3.7m	*(10'5"x12'0")*
Sitting Room:	4.5 x 4.5m	*(14'6"x14'6")*
Bedroom 2:	3.7 x 4.5m	*(12'0"x14'6")*

FIRST FLOOR

Master Bedroom:	3.6 x 4.0m	*(11'7"x13'1")*
Dressing/Sitting Room:	3.0 x 2.5m	*(9'7"x8'2")*
Bedroom 3:	4.5 x 3.6m	*(14'6"x11'6")*
Landing/Study:	3.2 x 2.4m	*(10'5"x7'9")*

This split-level design represents an architect's dream! On five levels, the fenestration is amazing, with picture windows to the living rooms and triangular gable head windows and timbered balconies on two sides. From the entrance, steps lead down to the dining room with a vaulted ceiling. The sitting room leads off the dining room, three steps down, and features an attractive corner fireplace. The kitchen/breakfast area is at the same level as the entrance hall, with steps leading up to the fourth level with two bedrooms and a gallery overlooking the dining room. The top level has a sitting room off the master bedroom, and a landing that can house a study or hobby room.

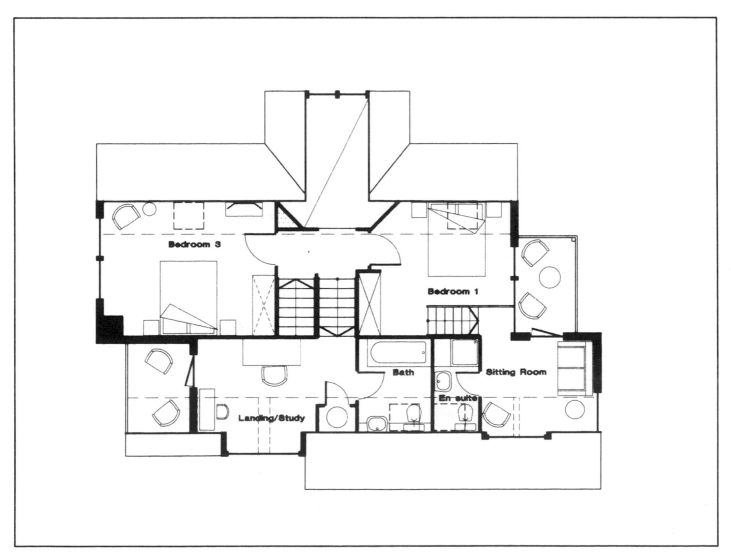

Homes with granny flats

Granny flats can be completely self contained units within, or attached, to the main body of the house or they can be a series of rooms within the house that are set aside for separate occupation but are an integral part of the main accommodation.

I have already discussed granny flats in some detail earlier on in this book and those thoughts are expanded upon in *Building Your Own Home*. Sometimes the annexe can be so self contained as to even have its own front entrance door. Sometimes access can be via a back door or a lobby that it shares with the main house. More often than not access is gained by the annexe and the main house sharing the utility room facilities. Whatever interconnection arrangements there are, thought needs to be given to the possibility of all doors being 2'9" or even 3' feet wide, to facilitate wheelchair access.

One thing that can upset an older person is for the annexe to be situated in the darker or utility area of the property with little or no view of the gardens. Older people might not always want or be able to get out of the house but that doesn't mean that they want to feel shut in with little or no view. Try to arrange the accommodation so that a small garden or courtyard area, that attracts the sun at some time of the day, can be given over to the annexe.

Contributors in this section:

ASBA Reed Architects
Border Oak
Design & Materials Ltd.

265 sq. m.

The copyright belongs to Border Oak

Clungunford House

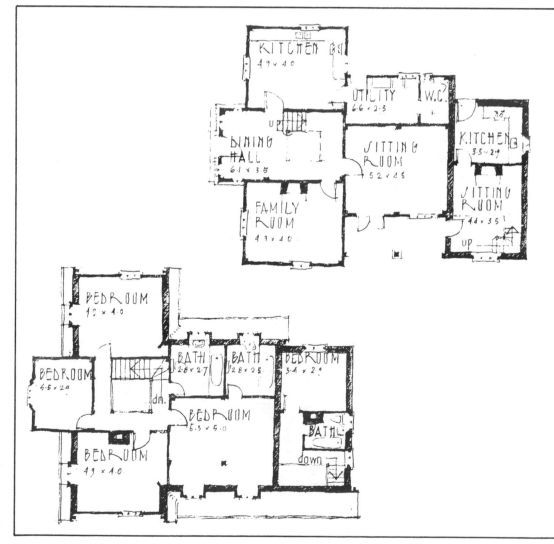

A house which faces in two directions and meets the needs of two very different occupants. On the left a home for the owner of a working farm with a generous utility and cloakroom area, the farmhouse kitchen, the informal family room, generous bedrooms. On the right a "granny annexe" self-contained accommodation for the farmer's widowed mother, an opportunity to be part of an extended family but to retain her dignity and privacy. The verandah works to provide both the connection and separation required. An alliance of half-timbering and masonry and the coexistence of the new and the old on every level.

200 sq. m.

The copyright belongs to Border Oak

Archer House

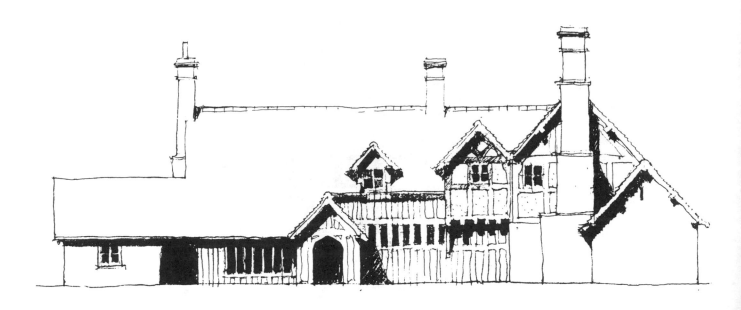

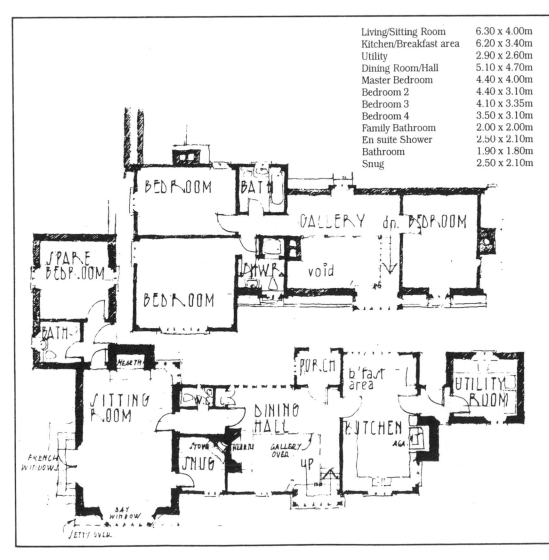

Living/Sitting Room	6.30 x 4.00m
Kitchen/Breakfast area	6.20 x 3.40m
Utility	2.90 x 2.60m
Dining Room/Hall	5.10 x 4.70m
Master Bedroom	4.40 x 4.00m
Bedroom 2	4.40 x 3.10m
Bedroom 3	4.10 x 3.35m
Bedroom 4	3.50 x 3.10m
Family Bathroom	2.00 x 2.00m
En suite Shower	2.50 x 2.10m
Bathroom	1.90 x 1.80m
Snug	2.50 x 2.10m

A quintessential Tudor structure. All the elements and artistry of the Tudor age and a design that has evolved through the centuries with the addition of accommodation reflecting the needs and aspirations of succeeding owners. A small annexe provides independent accommodation for a member of the family or perhaps weekend guests. The farmhouse kitchen with breakfast area, the snug and the utility room make useful and practical contributions to a home which displays practicality and quiet dignity.

190 sq. m.

The copyright belongs to Border Oak

Yeovil Cottage

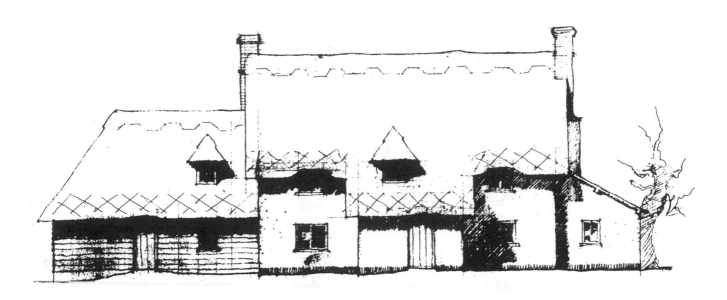

Sitting Room	5.00 x 4.00m
Kitchen	5.00 x 3.75m
Utility	2.20 x 2.00m
Dining Room/Hall	6.90 x 3.40m
Master Bedroom	5.00 x 4.00m
Bedroom 2	3.70 x 3.00m
Bedroom 3	3.70 x 2.40m
Family Bathroom	2.40 x 2.10m
En suite Bathroom	3.70 x 3.50m
Bathroom (Annex)	3.20 x 1.70m
Kitchen 2 (Annex)	4.40 x 3.70m
Shower Room	2.90 x 1.30m

An updated example of the Devon cob cottage. The internal walls are constructed in oak framing and joists providing a wealth of beams. Externally, the soft outlines of the cob cottage is replicated with lime rich render and a tea cosy-like thatched roof. An annexe clad with traditional weather-boarding enhances the property and provides a ground floor bed sitting room with spacious accommodation. The first floor is used for en suite facilities to the master bedroom of the main house, both living units sharing the inglenook chimney stack. Purposemade casement windows with authentic glazing bars provide one of the many touches which reinforce the authenticity and delight the eye.

1900 sq. ft.
41 ft. x 32 ft.

The copyright belongs to Design & Materials Ltd.

Harleston

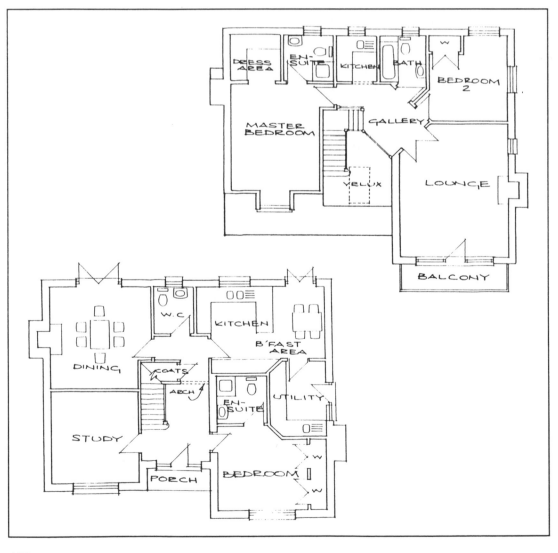

If your plot has good views, or if you are looking for something a little different, then this unusual design should provide plenty of inspiration. The lounge is on the upper floor and includes a vaulted ceiling, feature window and balcony. There is also a bedroom suite for elderly parents on the ground floor.

3600 sq. ft.
65 ft. x 53 ft.

Chesterton

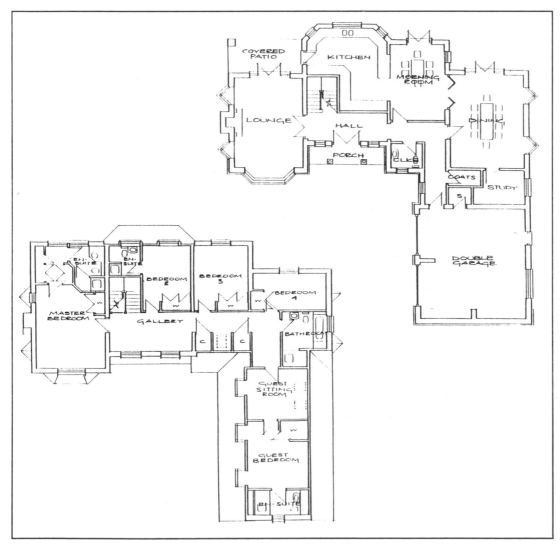

An impressive house for the discerning individual. Main features include a large kitchen with morning room, ten seater dining room and separate annex with sitting room and private bathroom.

2044 sq. ft.

The copyright belongs to ASBA
Reed Architects

Cefn Morfa

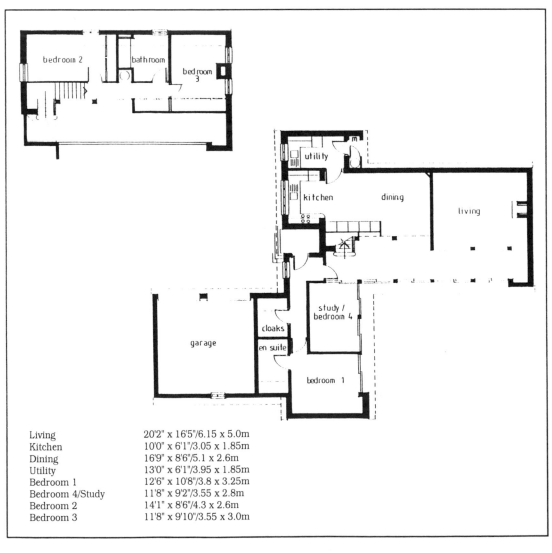

Living	20'2" x 16'5"/6.15 x 5.0m
Kitchen	10'0" x 6'1"/3.05 x 1.85m
Dining	16'9" x 8'6"/5.1 x 2.6m
Utility	13'0" x 6'1"/3.95 x 1.85m
Bedroom 1	12'6" x 10'8"/3.8 x 3.25m
Bedroom 4/Study	11'8" x 9'2"/3.55 x 2.8m
Bedroom 2	14'1" x 8'6"/4.3 x 2.6m
Bedroom 3	11'8" x 9'10"/3.55 x 3.0m

An unusual house designed to take advantage of wide ranging views over the Welsh countryside to the South and West. The galleried landing open to the living accommodation would not suit a family with small children but older families perhaps with relative requiring ground floor, self-contained accommodation would find this a convenient if unconventional house.

Homes with study/office space

Although this accommodation can often double up as, or be converted from a granny annexe, there is not the requirement for a view that I have referred to above and it can therefore be put at the darker or utility end of the house.

If it's just an office to enable a company representative, or a writer, to work from home then all we're really talking about is a room that is set aside for this purpose, that is big enough to contain the necessary office furniture and equipment. If a small business is to be run from home and there is the likelihood of staff being employed then you might like to consider whether you want the work activities spreading into the home environment. In this case the provision of separate toilet accommodation might well be necessary and, if at all possible, a separate entrance should be arranged.

If your business involves having colleagues or clients visiting then consideration needs to be given to where they will sit and, if at all possible, the office should contain a sitting area, or at least be big enough to house your desk with other chairs in front of it.

Contributors in this section:

ASBA Reed Architects
Border Oak
Design & Materials Ltd.

576 sq. m.

The copyright belongs to Border Oak

Dorchester Manor

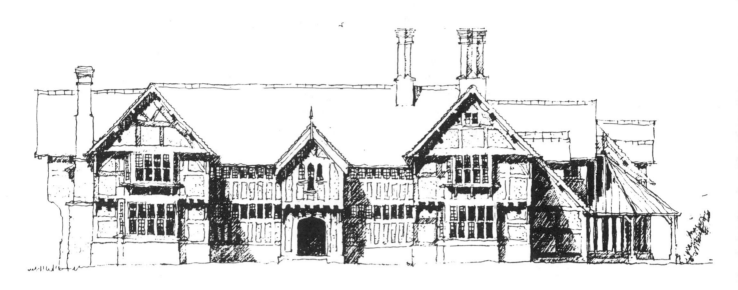

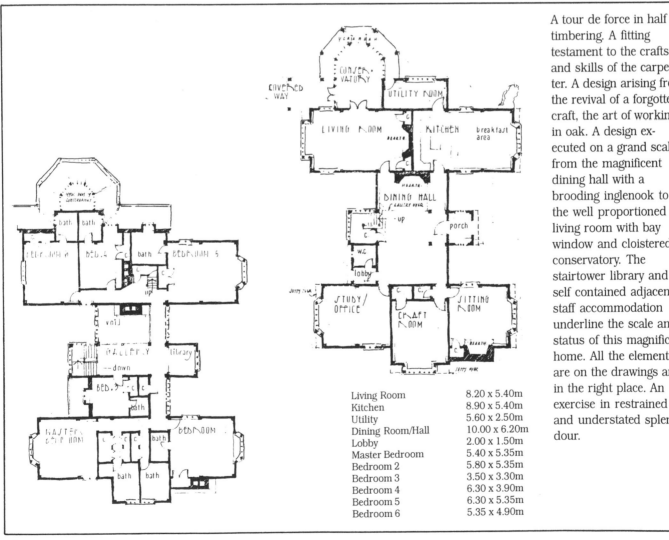

A tour de force in half timbering. A fitting testament to the crafts and skills of the carpenter. A design arising from the revival of a forgotten craft, the art of working in oak. A design executed on a grand scale from the magnificent dining hall with a brooding inglenook to the well proportioned living room with bay window and cloistered conservatory. The stairtower library and self contained adjacent staff accommodation underline the scale and status of this magnificent home. All the elements are on the drawings and in the right place. An exercise in restrained and understated splendour.

Living Room	8.20 x 5.40m
Kitchen	8.90 x 5.40m
Utility	5.60 x 2.50m
Dining Room/Hall	10.00 x 6.20m
Lobby	2.00 x 1.50m
Master Bedroom	5.40 x 5.35m
Bedroom 2	5.80 x 5.35m
Bedroom 3	3.50 x 3.30m
Bedroom 4	6.30 x 3.90m
Bedroom 5	6.30 x 5.35m
Bedroom 6	5.35 x 4.90m

222 sq. m.

The copyright belongs to Border Oak

Dorrington Vicarage

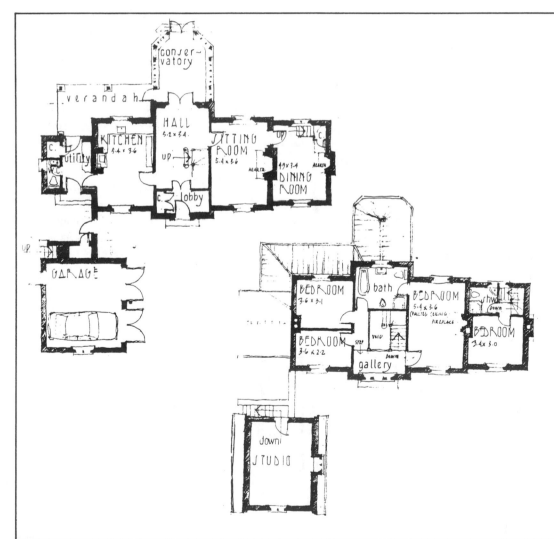

The Vicarage achieves the space massing and detail of this early Victorian forebear and meets the needs of the 20th Century without compromise. Well proportioned rooms with high ceilings nestle together beneath a skin of render, stonework or handmade facing bricks. The authentic door casing, venetian window, sash windows, parapets and even the owl combine successfully. The two storey annexe with lower roofline provides the facility for division for self contained accommodation. The studio over the garage acknowledges the trend for working from home. The verandah and conservatory become part of the house.

157 sq. m. *The copyright belongs to Border Oak* **Broad Oak Farmhouse**

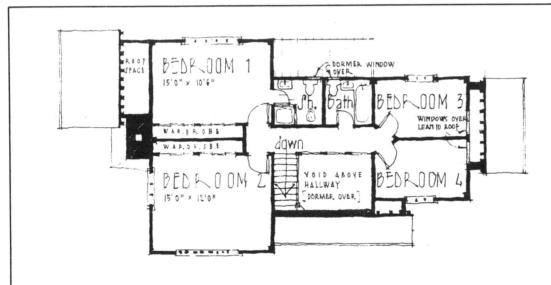

ROOF SPACE

BEDROOM 1
15'0" x 10'6"

DORMER WINDOW OVER

Sh. Bath

BEDROOM 3

WINDOWS OVER LEAN TO ROOF

WARDROBE

WARDROBE

down

BEDROOM 2
15'0" x 12'0"

VOID ABOVE HALLWAY
[DORMER OVER]

BEDROOM 4

An uncluttered and practical design where practicality wins over symmetry. Scale and balance ensure the house is easy on the eye and the study, minstrels gallery and en suite facilities contribute to the enjoyment of the space without diminishing the visual pleasures. A building to enhance and enrich its locale and environment.

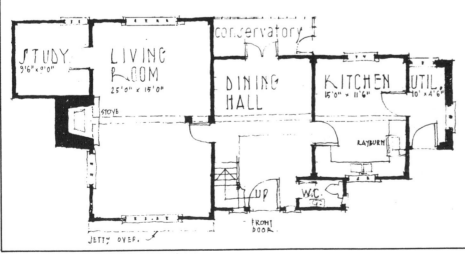

STUDY
9'6" x 9'0"

LIVING ROOM
25'0" x 15'0"

conservatory

DINING HALL

KITCHEN
15'0" x 11'6"

UTIL
10' x 4'6"

STOVE

RAYBURN

UP

W.C.

FRONT DOOR

JETTY OVER.

232 sq. m.

The copyright belongs to Border Oak

Wolbeading Manor

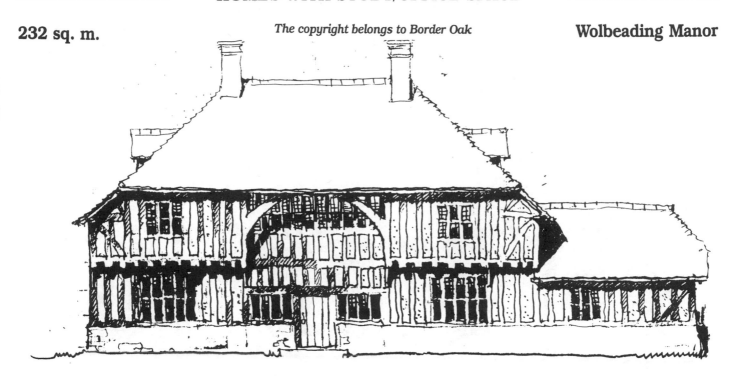

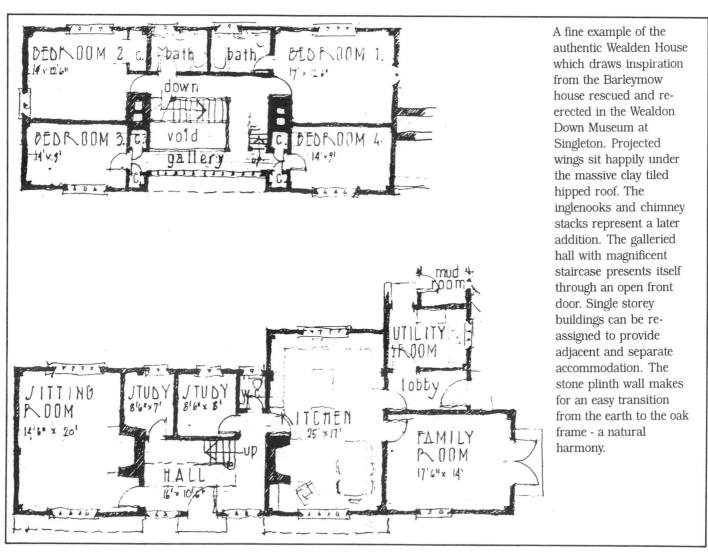

A fine example of the authentic Wealden House which draws inspiration from the Barleymow house rescued and re-erected in the Wealdon Down Museum at Singleton. Projected wings sit happily under the massive clay tiled hipped roof. The inglenooks and chimney stacks represent a later addition. The galleried hall with magnificent staircase presents itself through an open front door. Single storey buildings can be re-assigned to provide adjacent and separate accommodation. The stone plinth wall makes for an easy transition from the earth to the oak frame - a natural harmony.

355 sq. m.

The copyright belongs to Border Oak

Lichfield Manor

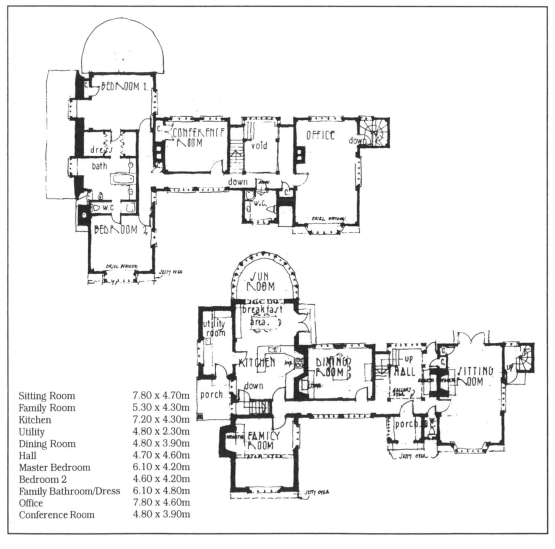

Sitting Room	7.80 x 4.70m
Family Room	5.30 x 4.30m
Kitchen	7.20 x 4.30m
Utility	4.80 x 2.30m
Dining Room	4.80 x 3.90m
Hall	4.70 x 4.60m
Master Bedroom	6.10 x 4.20m
Bedroom 2	4.60 x 4.20m
Family Bathroom/Dress	6.10 x 4.80m
Office	7.80 x 4.60m
Conference Room	4.80 x 3.90m

A classic oak framed manor house in an unusual guise. The thatched roof which is normally more suited to the humble cottage works surprisingly well on a building which would normally be roofed with clay tiles. 3m high ground floor ceilings underline the apparent incongruity of thatch material that normally hugs the contours of the house and the ground. Cotswold stone walls compliment the site and the building. Whilst the building is currently used as offices with conference rooms etc, the transition to a full manor house is simple providing up to five double bedrooms with the usual en suite facilities. A gentle giant.

174 sq. m.   *The copyright belongs to Border Oak*   **Teme Farmhouse**

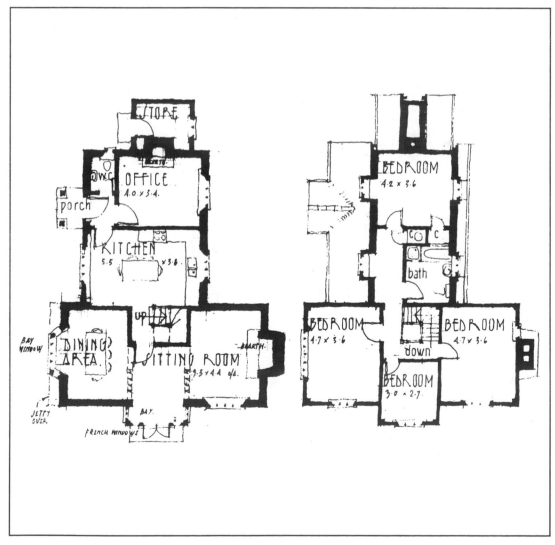

A footprint in a T configuration, one wing in brickwork with full hcight oak frame above, a central bay with gable inglenook at one end and bay window and jetty at the other end acting as a visual balance. The cross wing of greater span but lower eaves height has a more modest appearance and houses the farmhouse kitchen and the farm office and store. The entrance porch position allows the office and cloakroom to be used without disturbance to the family home. An ideal design for a busy farm or to work from home without loss of family privacy. Traditional dormers, simple large chimney stacks and a weatherboarded outbuilding round off the composition.

1625 sq. ft.

52 ft. x 40 ft.

Helston 'Studio'

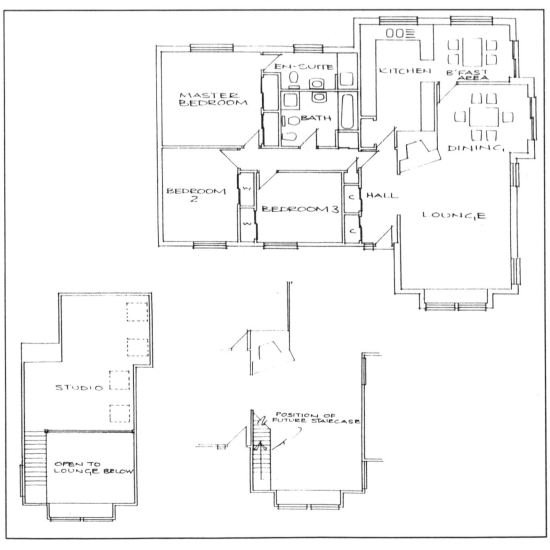

Combining traditional and contemporary ideas, the open-plan arrangement of the living area is enhanced by a high cathedral ceiling which provides the option to convert the upper floor into a studio.

2900 sq. ft.
65 ft. x 46 ft.

The copyright belongs to Design & Materials Ltd. **Pevensey 'Dentists Surgery'**

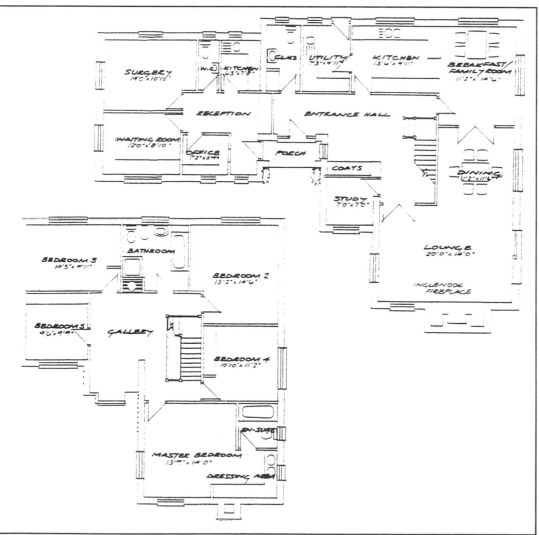

SURGERY 14'0" x 10'10"

W.C.

KITCHEN 10'3" x 7'8"

CLKS

UTILITY 7'3" x 4'11"

KITCHEN 13'6" x 9'11"

BREAKFAST/ FAMILY ROOM 11'2" x 14'6"

RECEPTION

ENTRANCE HALL

WAITING ROOM 12'0" x 8'10"

OFFICE 7'2" x 5'4"

PORCH

COATS

DINING 11'2" x 11'6"

STUDY 7'0" x 7'0"

LOUNGE 20'0" x 14'0"

INGLENOOK FIREPLACE

BEDROOM 3 14'5" x 4'11"

BATHROOM

BEDROOM 2 13'2" x 14'6"

BEDROOM 5 9'6" x 9'0"

GALLERY

BEDROOM 4 10'10" x 11'2"

EN-SUITE

MASTER BEDROOM 13'7" x 14'0"

DRESSING AREA

This interesting design, illustrated here in stock bricks, plain tiles with tile hanging and casement windows, would be ideal for a doctor or dentist who wanted to work from home. The design combined a large two storey family house with a single storey annex housing the surgery. At the heart of the house is a large reception hall with upper gallery leading to a beautiful master bedroom suite, four further bedrooms and a big family bathroom. The lounge/dining is open plan and includes an inglenook fireplace and double doors to the breakfast room.

1870 sq. ft./174 sq. m.

The copyright belongs to Border Oak

Stoke Lacy Farmhouse

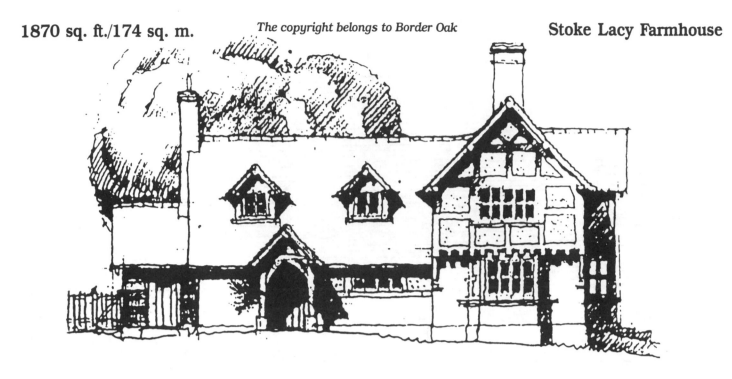

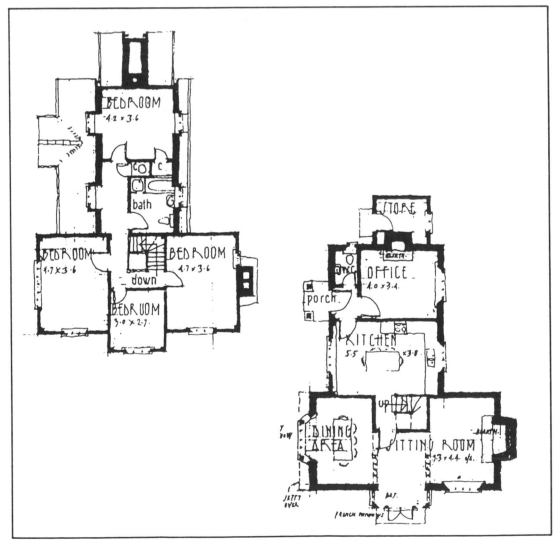

This house, with its combination of mellow brick and oak framing, demonstrates the marrying of elements, the stolid, stoical farmer, planted in the earth, functional and unfancy, and his wife, apple cheeked and whimsical, linen tablecloths and spices, seeing the dance in things. The house can encompass both elements, and, in so doing, becomes more, becomes both friend and shelter.

2260 sq. ft.

The copyright belongs to ASBA
Reed Architects

Herongate

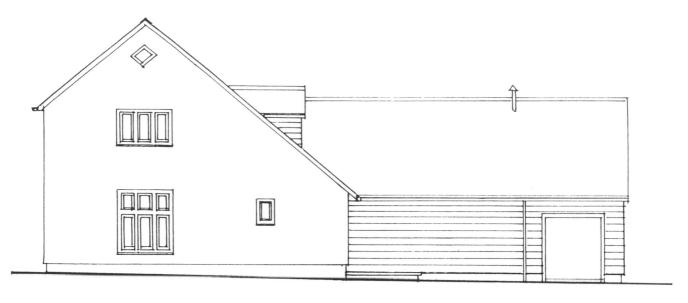

Sitting	29'10" x 19'8"/9.1 x 6.0m
Dining/Kitchen	19'4" x 15'1"/5.9 x 4.6m
Study	19'4" x 12'6"/5.9 x 3.8m
Utility	11'2" x 7'10"/3.4 x 2.4m
Bedroom 1	13'1" x 11'10"/4.0 x 3.6m
Bedroom 2	11'10" x 9'2"/3.6 x 2.8m
Bedroom 3	12'10" x 9'2"/3.9 x 2.8m
Bedroom 4	11'2" x 9'2"/3.4 x 2.8m

The principal room of this family house is a vaulted oak framed barn through which the staircase rises, first to a gallery, then to the bedroom accommodation. A long range of full-height windows take advantage of southerly views. The home-office is directly accessible from the entrance lobby and keeps business visitors away from family life. It has a low-cilled north facing window to give good light for drawing. If not used for a business it could be used as a generous dining room. Higher than average ceiling heights in the office and kitchen are lowered over the ancillary accommodation to provide a zone for services.

413

Homes with play/rumpus rooms

In Canada and Australia, most houses have what is called a rumpus room that can double up as a storage room or a playroom. The designs illustrated in this category could just as easily have been placed in many of the other categories, but we decided to create a separate category, more to promote the idea of a hobbies area within the home than for any other reason. Swimming pools and billiards rooms apart, there are many other areas where the provision of a separate games/hobbies room can make a huge difference to the enjoyment of your new home and its design and layout will be dictated by your chosen usage.

If roof voids to either house or garage are to be converted to hobbies areas, do make sure that their future use is reflected in the original design and in the form of construction. Expecting a standard attic truss, or timber floor joists that have not been beefed up, to support a full size billiard table might be too much.

Contributors in this section:

ASBA David H. Anderson
ASBA Julian Owen Associates
ASBA Reed Architects
Border Oak
Custom Homes
Design & Materials Ltd.
Kingpost Design Co
Potton Ltd.

375 sq. m.

The copyright belongs to Border Oak

Brambley Farm

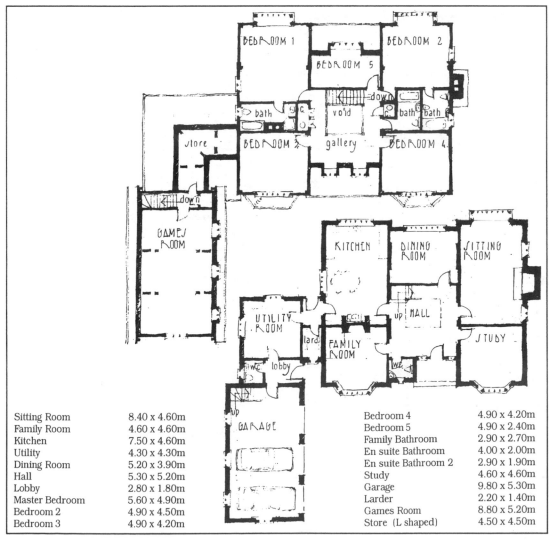

Sitting Room	8.40 x 4.60m	Bedroom 4	4.90 x 4.20m
Family Room	4.60 x 4.60m	Bedroom 5	4.90 x 2.40m
Kitchen	7.50 x 4.60m	Family Bathroom	2.90 x 2.70m
Utility	4.30 x 4.30m	En suite Bathroom	4.00 x 2.00m
Dining Room	5.20 x 3.90m	En suite Bathroom 2	2.90 x 1.90m
Hall	5.30 x 5.20m	Study	4.60 x 4.60m
Lobby	2.80 x 1.80m	Garage	9.80 x 5.30m
Master Bedroom	5.60 x 4.90m	Larder	2.20 x 1.40m
Bedroom 2	4.90 x 4.50m	Games Room	8.80 x 5.20m
Bedroom 3	4.90 x 4.20m	Store (L shaped)	4.50 x 4.50m

A central cross wing with long and low catslide roofs result in an unusual, almost rectilinear, floorplan. The first dormers provide light to a large and spacious entrance hall with perimeter gallery. The kitchen commands equal status with the sitting room, the dining room separates these competing areas. The triple garage and internal staircase can house a granny flat, staff accommodation and playroom or a den. The garage block is constructed simply with soft orange/red facing bricks and vertical tile hanging. The masonry and half timbering of the house is balanced and appropriate.

4220 sq. ft.

The copyright belongs to ASBA Julian Owen Associates

The Manor

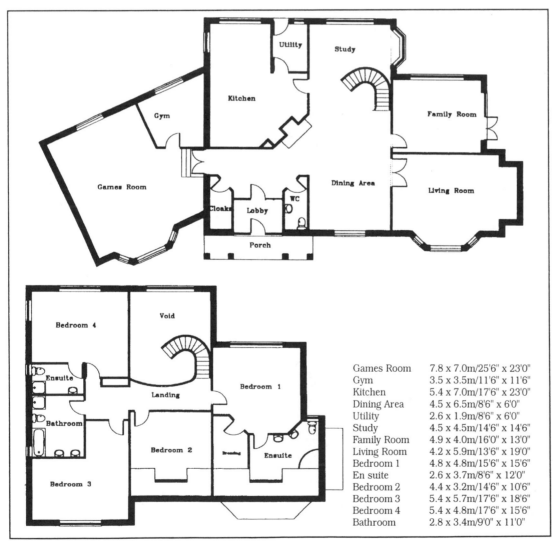

Games Room	7.8 x 7.0m/25'6" x 23'0"
Gym	3.5 x 3.5m/11'6" x 11'6"
Kitchen	5.4 x 7.0m/17'6" x 23'0"
Dining Area	4.5 x 6.5m/8'6" x 6'0"
Utility	2.6 x 1.9m/8'6" x 6'0"
Study	4.5 x 4.5m/14'6" x 14'6"
Family Room	4.9 x 4.0m/16'0" x 13'0"
Living Room	4.2 x 5.9m/13'6" x 19'0"
Bedroom 1	4.8 x 4.8m/15'6" x 15'6"
En suite	2.6 x 3.7m/8'6" x 12'0"
Bedroom 2	4.4 x 3.2m/14'6" x 10'6"
Bedroom 3	5.4 x 5.7m/17'6" x 18'6"
Bedroom 4	5.4 x 4.8m/17'6" x 15'6"
Bathroom	2.8 x 3.4m/9'0" x 11'0"

Designed to suggest a large, 'barn-like' farm-house, this house combines eclectic traditional details, with some complex roof shapes to add interest and entertainment to the elevations. On the ground floor the free-flowing spaces accentu-ate the large scale of the rooms, finishing with a swirling staircase up to a first floor gallery at the rear. A double height window onto the study also affords views from the gallery across this space and out to the rear garden.

2266 sq. ft./210 sq. m.

The copyright belongs to Custom Homes

Windermere

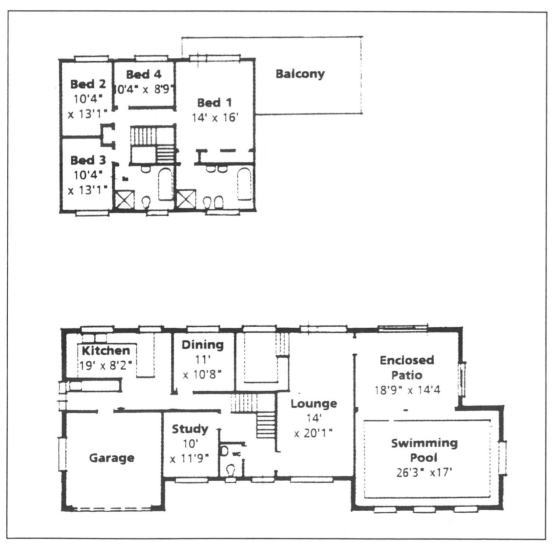

The swimming pool is an integral part of the main house and the inclusion of the enclosed patio area would make this part of the design a focal point within it. The large balcony enhances the relatively small size of the upper part accommodation and there's scope for the upper part to be extended over the kitchen and garage accommodation.

417

439.38 sq. m.

21.98 x 19.99m

96-333

The swimming pool for this large family house in an integral part of the accommodation and, as such, this whole area could well be treated and thought of as part and parcel of the living arrangements. The area to the front of the pool could be used as either a sitting area or given over to changing or showering and toilet facilities.

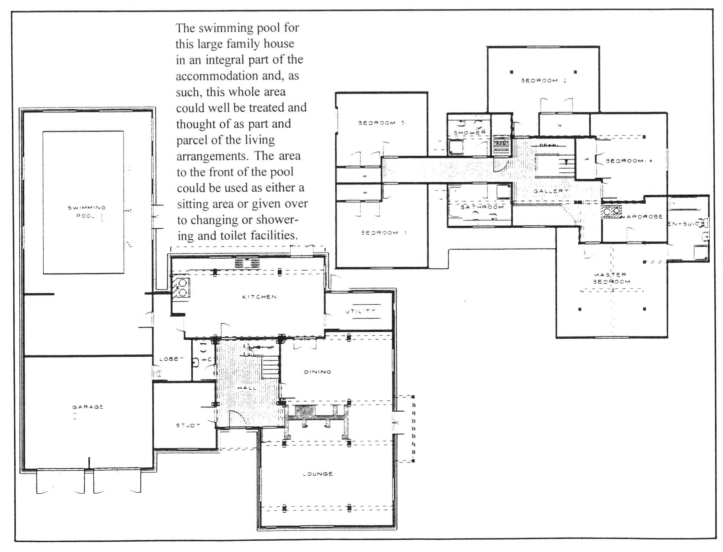

7700 sq. ft./715 sq. m.

The copyright belongs to Custom Homes

Sandringham

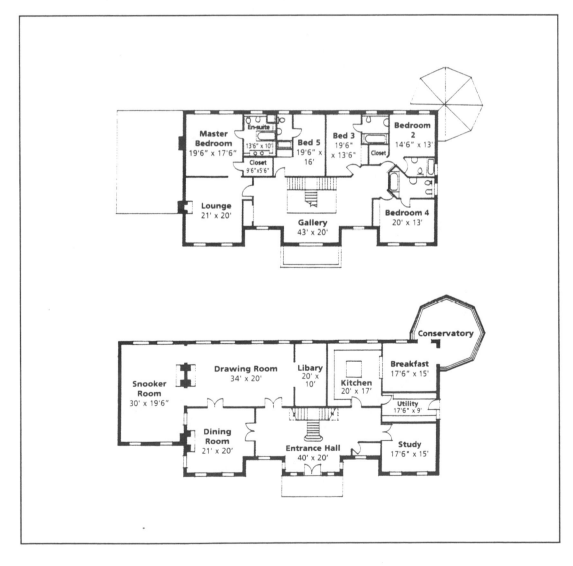

Master
Bedroom
19'6" x 17'6"

En-suite
13'6" x 10'

Closet
9'6"x5'6"

Bed 5
19'6" x
16'

Bed 3
19'6"
x 13'6"

Closet

Bedroom
2
14'6" x 13'

Lounge
21' x 20'

Gallery
43' x 20'

Bedroom 4
20' x 13'

Conservatory

Snooker
Room
30' x 19'6"

Drawing Room
34' x 20'

Libary
20' x
10'

Kitchen
20' x 17'

Breakfast
17'6" x 15'

Utility
17'6" x 9'

Dining
Room
21' x 20'

Entrance Hall
40' x 20'

Study
17'6" x 15'

Symmetry with additive development, both in terms of the bungalow section housing the snooker room and the seven sided conservatory, combine to make this a magnificent and imposing residence.

250 sq. m.
The copyright belongs to Border Oak
Worthen Court

Essentially a full oak frame with a third storey over the kitchen wing and masonry to the ground floor of the sitting room. Close framing, strip windows, the ornate entrance porch and jetties are the main ingredients. The outbuildings make the difference. A cobbled courtyard is surrounded by a house, utility room and an open-sided wagon shed for storage of vintage cars. Offices exist above the garage and playrooms in the attic of the kitchen wing.

Sitting Room	6.80 x 4.20m
Family Room	3.90 x 3.90m
Kitchen	5.80 x 3.90m
Utility	3.70 x 2.30m
Hall	5.40 x 4.50m
Master Bedroom	5.20 x 4.70m
Bedroom 2	3.90 x 3.40m
Bedroom 3	3.90 x 2.70m
Bedroom 4	3.00 x 2.90m
Family Bathroom	2.70 x 2.20m
En suite Bathroom	2.50 x 2.50m
En suite Shower	2.90 x 1.60m
Study	2.00 x 2.00m
Garage	9.80 x 5.00m
Workshop	3.80 x 3.50m

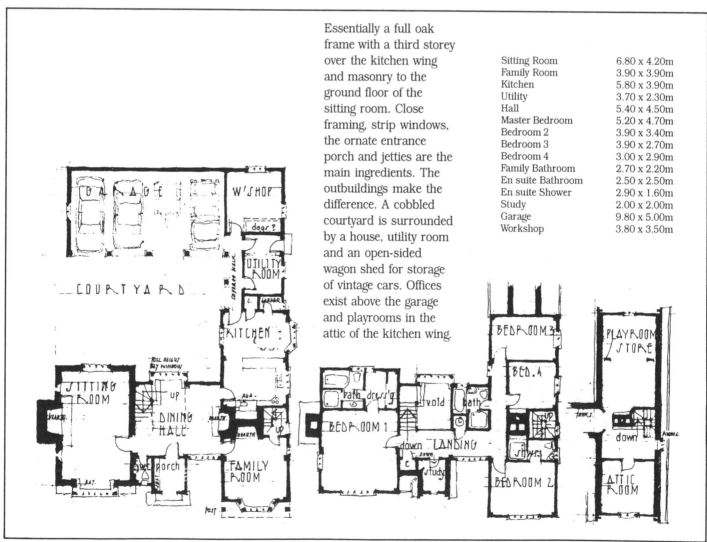

180 sq. m.

The copyright belongs to Border Oak

Kobe Cottage

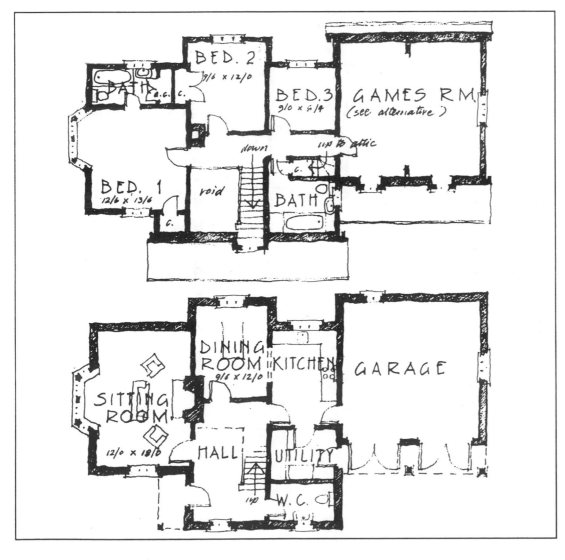

The appreciation of English vernacular architecture knows no boundaries. This design was developed for a Japanese housebuilder and is based on the use of modern softwood structural framing with applied claddings (brick slips and vertical tile hanging). A design able to withstand seismic forces and capable of being transported across the world in containers. Wide eaves, hip roofs and sash windows provide the decoration, stressed skin structural framing, exceptional insulation levels and securely fixed tiles and claddings deal with the practicalities.

242 sq. m.

The copyright belongs to Border Oak

Brook Cottage

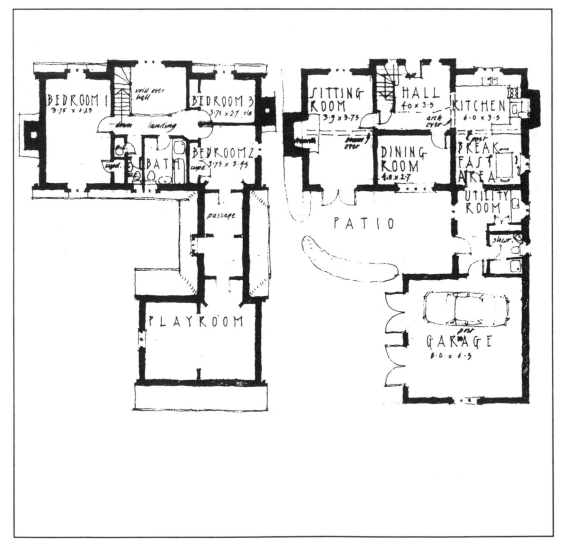

A design for a narrow site. A two storey hallway with minstrels' gallery, a farmhouse kitchen with breakfast area, utility room and ground floor shower, a sitting room with inglenook, three bedrooms, family bathroom and a secret passage to a first floor playroom. External elevations i.e. the brickwork or render under a pantilled roof; a design of the Norfolk/Suffolk area.

328 sq. m./3527 sq.

The copyright belongs to ASBA David H. Anderson

Buntons Hill Farm

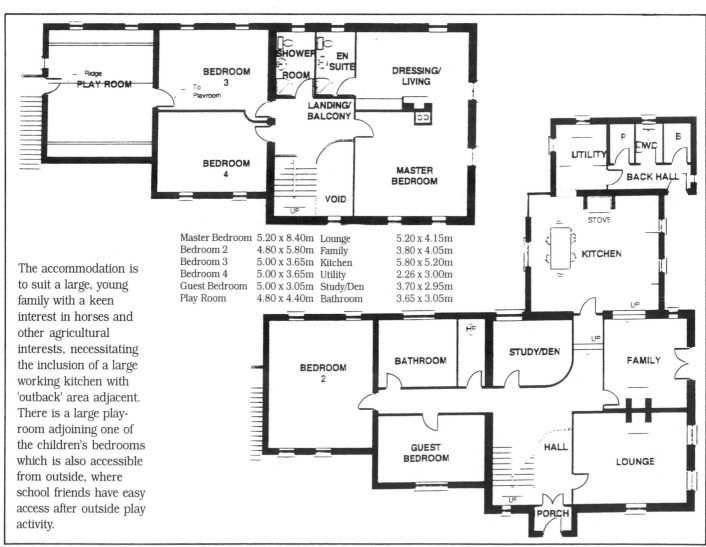

Master Bedroom	5.20 x 8.40m	Lounge	5.20 x 4.15m
Bedroom 2	4.80 x 5.80m	Family	3.80 x 4.05m
Bedroom 3	5.00 x 3.65m	Kitchen	5.80 x 5.20m
Bedroom 4	5.00 x 3.65m	Utility	2.26 x 3.00m
Guest Bedroom	5.00 x 3.05m	Study/Den	3.70 x 2.95m
Play Room	4.80 x 4.40m	Bathroom	3.65 x 3.05m

The accommodation is to suit a large, young family with a keen interest in horses and other agricultural interests, necessitating the inclusion of a large working kitchen with 'outback' area adjacent. There is a large playroom adjoining one of the children's bedrooms which is also accessible from outside, where school friends have easy access after outside play activity.

2239 sq. ft.

The copyright belongs to ASBA
Reed Architects

Forden

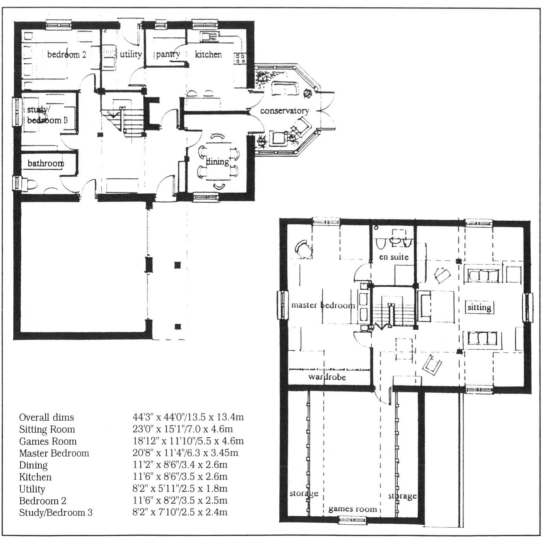

bedroom 2 · utility · pantry · kitchen

study/bedroom 3

bathroom

conservatory

dining

en suite

master bedroom

sitting

wardrobe

storage   storage

games room

This is a house which can be developed gradually. The main block can be constructed before the sun room and garage wing are added at a later date. This main block has a first floor living room which takes advantage of the post and beam construction with open trusses and high ceiling. This house is ideal for sites where the best views are available from a high level.

Overall dims	44'3" x 44'0"/13.5 x 13.4m
Sitting Room	23'0" x 15'1"/7.0 x 4.6m
Games Room	18'12" x 11'10"/5.5 x 4.6m
Master Bedroom	20'8" x 11'4"/6.3 x 3.45m
Dining	11'2" x 8'6"/3.4 x 2.6m
Kitchen	11'6" x 8'6"/3.5 x 2.6m
Utility	8'2" x 5'11"/2.5 x 1.8m
Bedroom 2	11'6" x 8'2"/3.5 x 2.5m
Study/Bedroom 3	8'2" x 7'10"/2.5 x 2.4m

2590 sq. ft.

The copyright belongs to Kingpost Design Co

Oban

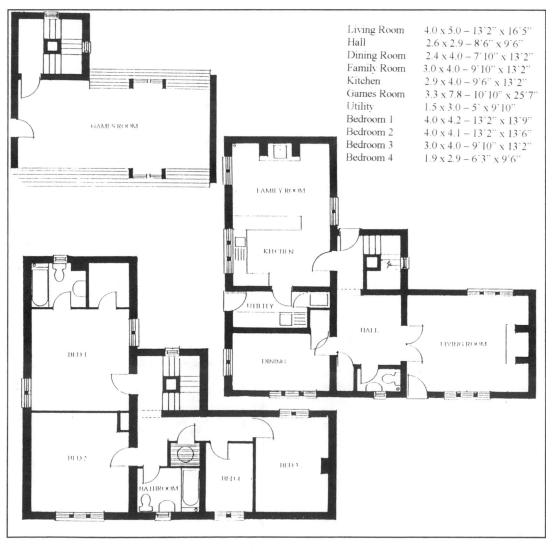

Living Room	4.0 x 5.0 – 13'2" x 16'5"
Hall	2.6 x 2.9 – 8'6" x 9'6"
Dining Room	2.4 x 4.0 – 7'10" x 13'2"
Family Room	3.0 x 4.0 – 9'10" x 13'2"
Kitchen	2.9 x 4.0 – 9'6" x 13'2"
Games Room	3.3 x 7.8 – 10'10" x 25'7"
Utility	1.5 x 3.0 – 5' x 9'10"
Bedroom 1	4.0 x 4.2 – 13'2" x 13'9"
Bedroom 2	4.0 x 4.1 – 13'2" x 13'6"
Bedroom 3	3.0 x 4.0 – 9'10" x 13'2"
Bedroom 4	1.9 x 2.9 – 6'3" x 9'6"

Built in a typical Scottish style the tower provides a focal point leading you to the entrance. Details such as the stepped gable ends add character to this attractive home. Downstairs a large living room opens off the hall as does the spacious kitchen/diner and the study. The attic space is utilised to provide a large playroom and storage space. The plan provides for four bedrooms, the master bedroom having a large walk-in wardrobe.

425

4630 sq. ft.

The copyright belongs to Kingpost Design Co

Stratford

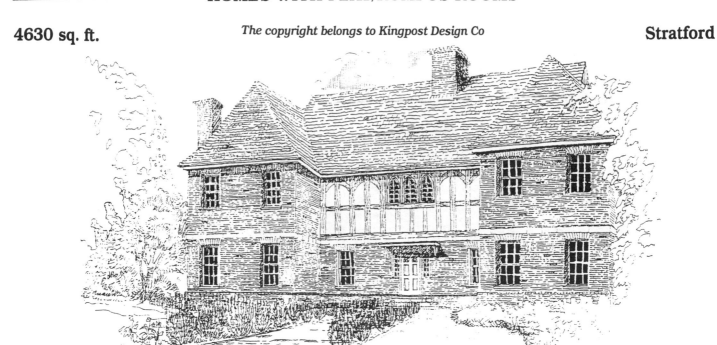

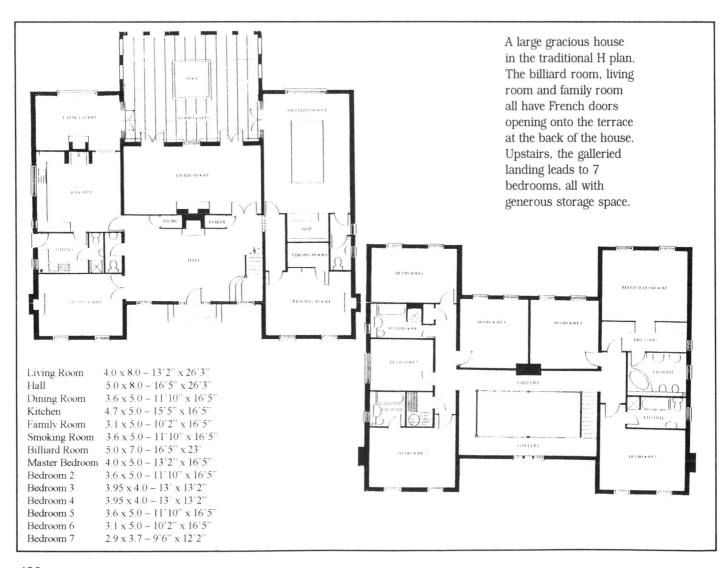

A large gracious house in the traditional H plan. The billiard room, living room and family room all have French doors opening onto the terrace at the back of the house. Upstairs, the galleried landing leads to 7 bedrooms, all with generous storage space.

Living Room	4.0 x 8.0 – 13'2" x 26'3"
Hall	5.0 x 8.0 – 16'5" x 26'3"
Dining Room	3.6 x 5.0 – 11'10" x 16'5"
Kitchen	4.7 x 5.0 – 15'5" x 16'5"
Family Room	3.1 x 5.0 – 10'2" x 16'5"
Smoking Room	3.6 x 5.0 – 11'10" x 16'5"
Billiard Room	5.0 x 7.0 – 16'5" x 23'
Master Bedroom	4.0 x 5.0 – 13'2" x 16'5"
Bedroom 2	3.6 x 5.0 – 11'10" x 16'5"
Bedroom 3	3.95 x 4.0 – 13' x 13'2"
Bedroom 4	3.95 x 4.0 – 13' x 13'2"
Bedroom 5	3.6 x 5.0 – 11'10" x 16'5"
Bedroom 6	3.1 x 5.0 – 10'2" x 16'5"
Bedroom 7	2.9 x 3.7 – 9'6" x 12'2"

2800 sq. ft.

The copyright belongs to Kingpost Design Co

Beckford

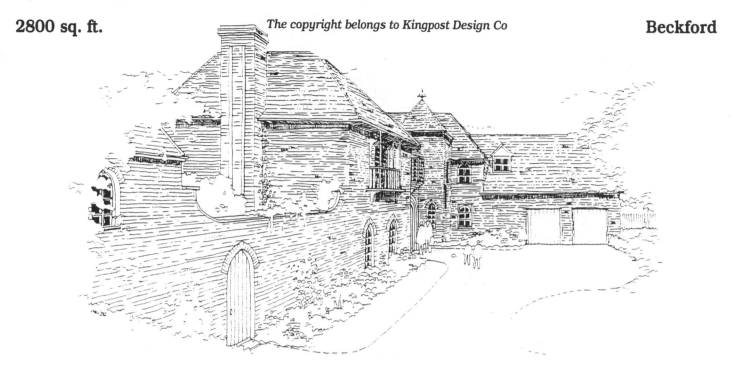

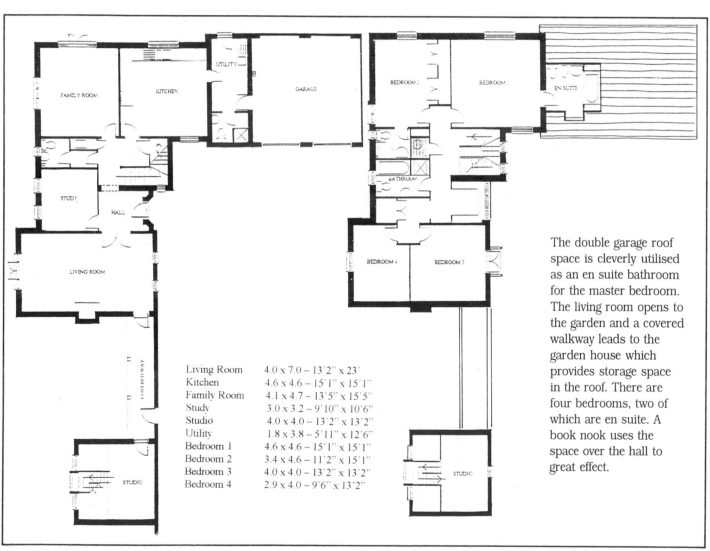

Living Room	4.0 x 7.0 – 13'2" x 23'
Kitchen	4.6 x 4.6 – 15'1" x 15'1"
Family Room	4.1 x 4.7 – 13'5" x 15'5"
Study	3.0 x 3.2 – 9'10" x 10'6"
Studio	4.0 x 4.0 – 13'2" x 13'2"
Utility	1.8 x 3.8 – 5'11" x 12'6"
Bedroom 1	4.6 x 4.6 – 15'1" x 15'1"
Bedroom 2	3.4 x 4.6 – 11'2" x 15'1"
Bedroom 3	4.0 x 4.0 – 13'2" x 13'2"
Bedroom 4	2.9 x 4.0 – 9'6" x 13'2"

The double garage roof space is cleverly utilised as an en suite bathroom for the master bedroom. The living room opens to the garden and a covered walkway leads to the garden house which provides storage space in the roof. There are four bedrooms, two of which are en suite. A book nook uses the space over the hall to great effect.

2900 sq. ft.
36 ft. x 58 ft.

Bridgewater

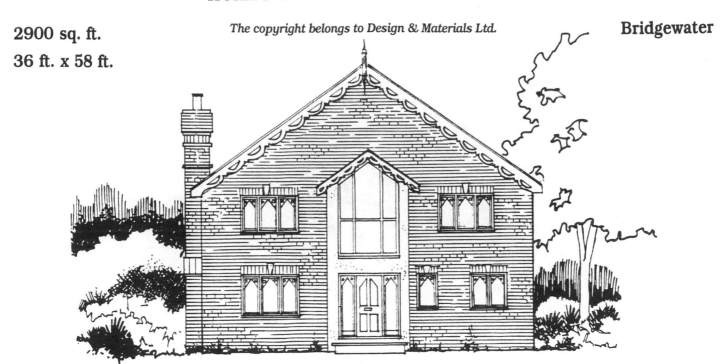

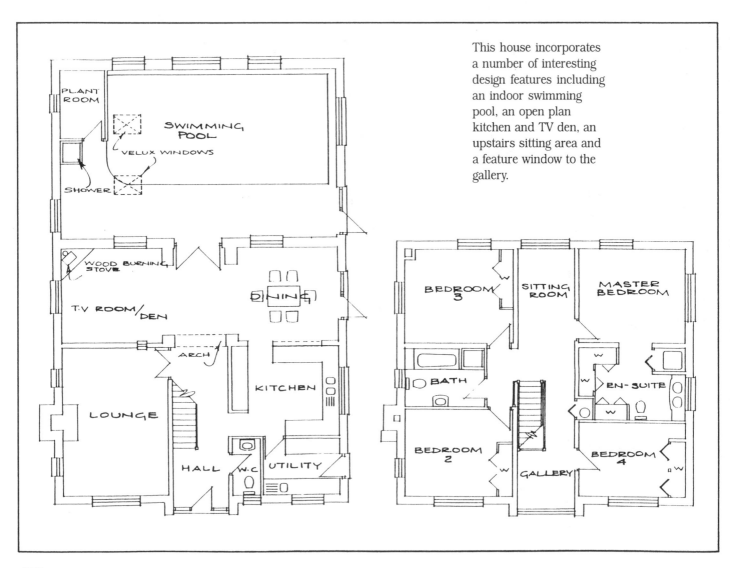

This house incorporates a number of interesting design features including an indoor swimming pool, an open plan kitchen and TV den, an upstairs sitting area and a feature window to the gallery.

PLANT ROOM

SWIMMING POOL

VELUX WINDOWS

SHOWER

WOOD BURNING STOVE

DINING

T.V ROOM/DEN

ARCH

KITCHEN

LOUNGE

HALL

W.C

UTILITY

BEDROOM 3

SITTING ROOM

MASTER BEDROOM

BATH

EN-SUITE

BEDROOM 2

GALLERY

BEDROOM 4

1650 sq. ft.

32 ft. x 41 ft.

The copyright belongs to Design & Materials Ltd.

Tad Caster

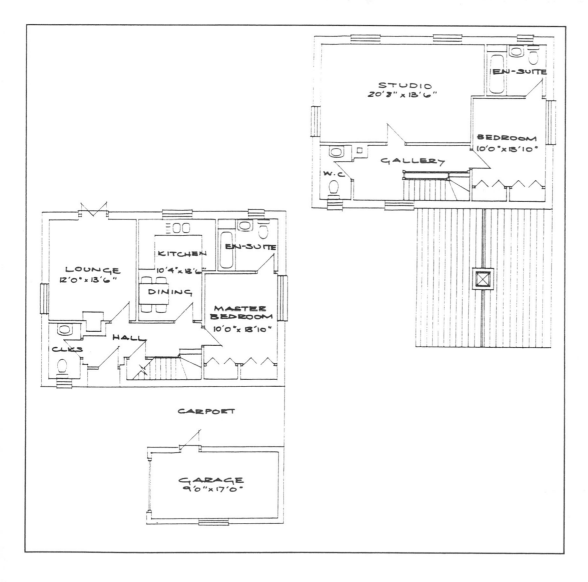

This interesting house is worth considering for infill situations but particularly suitable for a corner plot. The main feature is the spacious, well lit studio on the upper floor, whilst the ground floor provides comfortable, self contained accommodation. The garage is linked to the house by a covered car port. The design is illustrated here in render with brick plinth, quoins and verge detailing pantiles and country bar windows.

2600 sq. ft.
48 ft. x 39 ft.

The copyright belongs to Design & Materials Ltd.

Chiddington

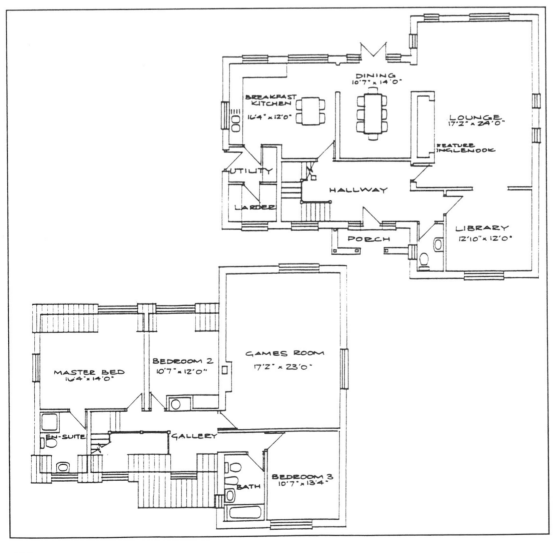

This substantial family home, illustrated here in brick and render, plain tiles and lead casement windows, is designed to provide a free flowing link from the spacious kitchen/breakfast area to the dining room featuring French windows through to the lounge with inglenook fireplace, and on into the library/study. The upper floor arrangement is flexible enough to allow a variety of layouts but in standard form, features an open gallery, three bedrooms and a games room.

3000 sq. ft.
46 ft. x 69 ft.

The copyright belongs to Design & Materials Ltd.

Patchcombe

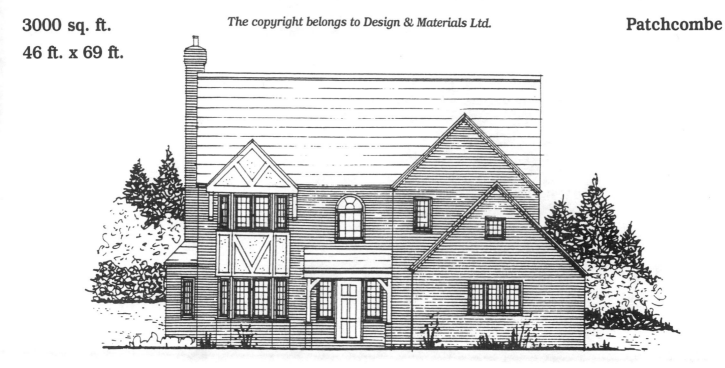

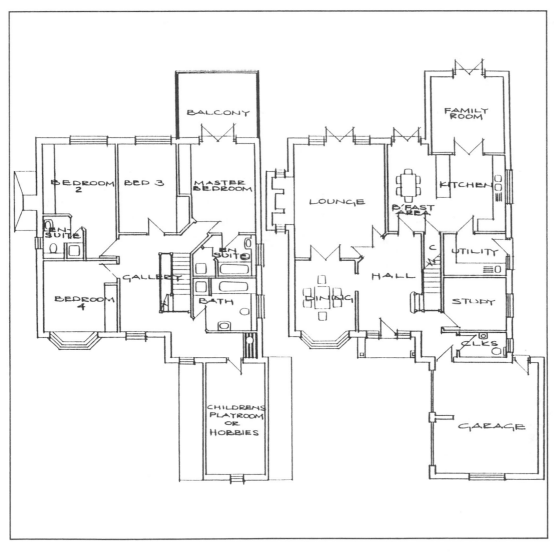

BALCONY

BEDROOM 2

BED 3

MASTER BEDROOM

FAMILY ROOM

KITCHEN

LOUNGE

B'FAST AREA

EN SUITE

EN SUITE

UTILITY

GALLERY

HALL

BEDROOM 4

BATH

DINING

STUDY

CLKS

CHILDRENS PLAYROOM OR HOBBIES

GARAGE

A great family house which could be built on a 50 ft. plot almost anywhere in the county. Main features include a walk-in inglenook fireplace, separate family room, children's play-room over the garage and a sun balcony to the master bedroom.

431

304.88 sq. m.
16.40m x 18.59m

97-234

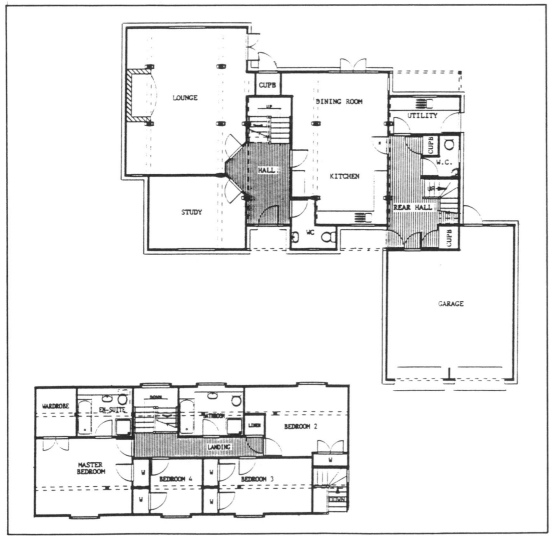

What at first sight is a fairly standard but extensive family house then becomes even more exciting with the addition of the upper, self contained, accommodation over the garage being designated as a playroom. This is approached from the very useful rear hall that, in turn, has its own separate entrance.

3770 sq. ft.

The copyright belongs to ASBA Julian Owen Associates

Grangealea

Lounge	4.2 x 6.5m/13'6" x 21'0"
Sitting Room	.2 x 4.6m/13'6"x 15'0"
Study	3.6 x 3.6m/12'0" x 12'0"
Games Room	8.0 x 6.5m/26'0" x 21'0"
Dining Room	4.3 x 4.8m/15'6" x 14'0"
Kitchen	4.2 x 4.6m/13'6" x 15'0"
Breakfast Area	3.6 x 3.6m/12'0" x 12'0"
Utility	3.6 x 3.6m/12'0" x 12'0"
Bedroom 1	4.2 x 6.0m/13'6" x 19'6"
En suite	2.2 x 2.4m/7'0" x 8'0"
Bathroom	3.0 x 4.7m/10'0" x 15'6"
Bedroom 2	4.1 x 4.1m/13'6" x 13'6"
Bedroom 3	3.4 x 4.7m/11'0" x 15'6"
Bedroom 4	4.2 x 2.6m/13'6" x 8'6"
Bedroom 5	4.2 x 2.6m/13'6" x 8'6"

Created in the Georgian style, this uncompromisingly grand house presents an impressive, symmetrical frontage. The stone portico provides shelter around the entrance area as well as adding to the period feel of the property. Inside, large, high ceilinged rooms are clustered around the centrepiece staircase and gallery. The master bedroom has access to a balcony at the rear of the house, which also form the roof to a fully glazed semicircular bay window to the dining room below.

433

Companies whose designs are featured in this book

The drawings and plans that are reproduced in this book may not be used, copied or reproduced for any purpose without the permission of the copyright holders. The copyright holders are clearly identified on each page where their plans or drawings appear.

Although some of the architectural practices may agree to sell copies of their plans or the right to reproduce them, the majority are available as part of a more comprehensive service.

We would urge you to obtain the company's literature to find out just what each has to offer and the literature will, in all cases, prove helpful with your proposed selfbuild.

ASSOCIATED SELF BUILD ARCHITECTS LTD. (ASBA)
The Archway, 373 Anlaby Road, Hull,
E.Yorkshire, HU3 6AB
Freephone 0800 387310 Fax 01482 576303

BORDER OAK DESIGN & CONSTRUCTION LTD.
Kingsland Sawmills, Kingsland, Leominster,
Herefordshire, HR6 9SF
Telephone 01568 708752 Fax 01568 708295

THE BUNGALOW COMPANY
The Old Foundry, Willow Road, Potton, Sandy,
Beds., SG19 2PP
Telephone 01767 263326 Fax 01767 263311
E-mail: bungalows@potton.co.uk

CUSTOM HOMES LTD.
106 Balcombe Road, Horley, Surrey, RH6 9BW
Telephone 01293 822898 Fax 01293 782229
E-mail: info@customhomes.co.uk

DESIGNER HOMES
Craigover, Maxton, Melrose, Roxburghshire,
Scotland, TD6 0RP
Telephone/fax 01835 823806

DESIGN & MATERIALS LTD.
Lawn Road, Carlton-in-Lindrick, Worksop,
Notts., S81 9LB
Telephone 01909 730333 Fax 01909 730201

KINGPOST DESIGN COMPANY LTD.
17 Kingshill Close, Malvern,
Worcestershire. WR14 2BP
Telephone/fax 01684 566494

POTTON LTD.
The Old Foundry, Willow Road, Potton, Sandy,
Beds., SG19 2PP
Telephone 01767 263300 Fax 01767 263311
E-mail: www.potton.co.uk

SCANDIA-HUS LTD.
Courtfield, Cranston Road, East Grinstead,
Sussex, RH19 3YU
Telephone 01342 327977 01342 315139

THE SWEDISH HOUSE COMPANY LTD.
P.O. Box 130, Crowborough, Sussex, TN6 1ZU
Telephone 01892 665007 Fax 01892 665125

Further information

Books
BUILDING YOUR OWN HOME, Murray Armor/ David Snell, Ebury Press, Ryton Books 01909 591652
PLANS FOR A DREAM HOME, Murray Armor, Ebury Press, Ryton Books 01909 591652
PRACTICAL HOUSEBUILDING, Bob Matthews, J.M.Dent, Ryton Books 01909 591652
THE HOUSEBUILDERS BIBLE, Mark Brinkley, Ryton Books 01909 591652
HOW TO FIND & BUY A BUILDING PLOT, Speer & Dade, Stonepound Books, Ryton Books, 01909 591652
HOW TO GET PLANNING PERMISSION, Speer & Dade, Stonepound Books, Ryton Books, 01909 591652

Magazines
HOMEBUILDING & RENOVATING, 01527 834400
BUILD IT, 0171 837 8727
SELF BUILD, 01283 742950

Useful agencies and associations
THE ASSOCIATION OF SELFBUILDERS, 01604 493757 & 0116 270 8843
ROYAL INSTITUTE OF BRITISH ARCHITECTS (RIBA), 0171 580 5533
ASSOCIATED SELF BUILD ARCHITECTS (ASBA), 0800 387310
ROYAL TOWN PLANNING INSTITUTE, 0171636 9107
PLANNING INSPECTORATE:
ENGLAND - 0117 987 8754
WALES - 0122 282 3308
SCOTLAND - 0131 244 5649
N. IRELAND - 01232 244710
THE BUILDING RESEARCH ESTABLISHMENT (and BRECSU), 01983 664000
HM LAND REGISTRY, 0171 917 8888
NATIONAL RADIOLOGICAL PROTECTION BOARD, 01235 831600
COMMISSION FOR NEWTOWNS, 01908 692692
TIMBER & BRICK INFORMATION COUNCIL, 01923 778136
NATIONAL ENERGY FOUNDATION, 01908 501908

BRICK DEVELOPMENT ASSOCIATION, 01344 885651
THE BRITISH CEMENT ASSOCIATION, 01344 762676
THE CONSERVATORY ASSOCIATION, 01480 458278
SOLAR TRADES ASSOCIATION, 01208 873518
DISABLED LIVING FOUNDATION, 0171 289 6111

Companies and agencies assisting in land finding
PLOTFINDER, 01527 834444
LANDBANK SERVICES, 0118 961 8002
COMMISSION FOR NEWTOWNS, 01908 692692
HM LAND REGISTRY, 0171 917 8888

Exhibitions
THE HOMEBUILDING AND RENOVATING SHOW, run by *Homebuilding & Renovating* magazine. Every spring at the NEC and in early summer at Sandown Park, Surrey 01527 834400
THE SELF BUILD HOMES SHOW, run by *Build It* magazine. Every autumn at Alexandra Palace, London with another major show in Scotland, plus at least 5 regional shows. 0171 837 8727
IDEAL HOMES EXHIBITION, every spring at Earls Court, London.
THE BUILDING CENTRE, 26 Store Street, London, Nr. Goodge Street underground. The Building Bookshop is in the same building.

Self build insurances
DMS SERVICES LTD. 01909 591652 Offering Norwich Union and Guardian insurance policies to selfbuilders and individual builders.
VULCAN INSURANCE. Insurances for conversions and renovations 01909 591652

Warranties
NHBC *Buildmark* and *Solo* 01494 434477
ZURICH *Custombuild* 01252 522000
TRENWICK WILLIS COROON (Forest of Dean Scheme), 0151 625 3883

Manufacturers and suppliers with particularly useful literature

RICHARD BURBRIDGE LTD. Staircases and balustrading etc. 01691 655131

BUTTERLEY BRICK LTD. (Hanson Brick) 0990 258258

CAMAS BUILDING MATERIALS. Reconstituted stone products. 01335 372222

CONDOR PRODUCTS LTD. Septic tanks, cesspools, pumps etc. 01962 863577

FLYGT LTD. Pumps to solve drainage problems. 0115 940 0444

IBSTOCK BRICK CO.LTD. 0171 391 4000

IPPEC HEATING & PLUMBING SYSTEMS. Specialists in underfloor central heating 0121 622 4333

KLARGESTER LTD. Pumps, cesspools, septic tanks and bio-discs to suit all drainage situations. 01296 633000

PILKINGTON GLASS LTD. 01744 28882

REDLAND TILES LTD. 01306 872000

YORKPARK LTD. Boilers & hot water cylinders. 01494 764031

YORK HANDMADE BRICK CO.LTD. 01347 838881

WARMWORLD LTD.Datatherm heating controls. 0117 949 8800

Also by the same authors, **Murray Armor & David Snell**

The new 16th edition of

BUILDING YOUR OWN HOME

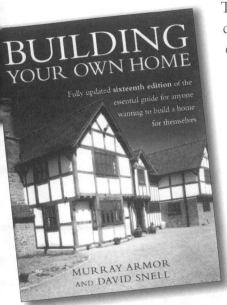

The best selling book ever written on self build and now brought right up to date with over 300 pages packed with advice and information, this is **the** essential book for anyone thinking of building a new home or extending or altering an existing home. This book explains, in clear and precise terms, what is involved in building for yourself, including costs, and carves a way through the maze of conflicting advice and legislation to evaluate all of the available choices without fear or favour. This is the standard handbook for the thousands who build their own homes each year, covering every aspect of finding, evaluating and buying a site, through to the choice of plan to suit your site, your lifestyle and your budget and then on to Planning and Building Regulations approvals. It examines the choices that are available between architects and package companies, brick and block or timber frame, having your hand held or going it alone and gives you the information you need to decide which is best for you. It also shows you how to go about building with either builders or subcontractors and expands upon all of this advice by the inclusion of real-life stories that highlight the achievements and experiences of other self-builders.

Plus

PLANS FOR A DREAM HOME

Murray Armor

Now in its fourth edition, this is a blockbuster
of a book with over 400 plans of homes created for the clients of five of the leading companies working within the self-build field. They vary from five- and six-bedroom houses to small retirement bungalows.

ORDERS BY POST
Ryton Books, Orchard House, Blyth, Worksop, Notts S81 8HF

Please supply books as indicated

Name

Address

Building Your Own Home   £25   ☐
Plans for a Dream Home   £20   ☐   (Both books deduct £2)

p&p free for delivery within the UK. Books despatched within 24 hours

Card No. ☐☐☐☐ ☐☐☐☐ ☐☐☐☐ ☐☐☐☐ ·expiry ☐☐ ☐☐

MASTERCARD/VISA/CHEQUE ORDER
PHONE 01909 591652
FAX 01909 591031
E.Mail:insurance@selfbuild.demon.co.uk

Both of these books are published by Ebury Press Ltd. and are available from all good booksellers or by post from Ryton Books, Orchard House, Blyth, Worksop, S81 8HF. Telephone 01909 591652 for credit card orders. Books despatched within 24 hours together with details of other books and services of interest to would-be self-builders.

INSURANCE

CHOOSE THE RIGHT POLICY TO COVER EVERY ASPECT OF YOUR SELFBUILD PROJECT.

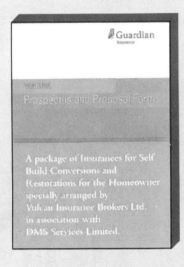 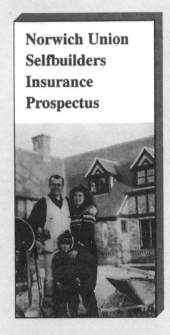 

FOR PROSPECTUSES AND ADVICE FROM AN EXPERT – RING D.M.S. SERVICES LTD.

01909 591652

UNDERWRITTEN BY
NORWICH UNION AND GUARDIAN INSURANCE

DMS Services Ltd., Orchard House, Blyth, Nr. Worksop, Notts. S81 8HF.
Website – http://www.selfbuild.demon.co.uk
Fax: 01909 591031

SELFBUILDERS INSURANCES
ASSESSING YOUR INSURANCE REQUIREMENTS

Guardian Insurance

STANDARD COVER

LIABILITIES   Limit of Liability

A. Employers Liability – *no excess*   £10,000,000

B. Public Liability   £2,000,000
in respect of the site, the natural features on it including trees and the work proposed – *excess of £250 for property damage*

CONTRACT WORKS

C. Contract Works insurance to the value declared in respect of the works and materials for use in the works, with a standard excess of £500

OPTIONAL COVER

PLANT

D. Plant and tools owned by the proposer, cover on the site only with a standard excess of £500

E. Employees tools or plant, cover effective on the site only with a standard excess of £50. (Maximum 2 employees)

F. Plant and tools hired in by the proposer and NOT covered by Hiresafe or other hirers scheme, cover for the whole term of the policy with the standard excess of £500

G. Plant and tools hired in by the proposer and NOT covered by Hiresafe or other hirers scheme, short term cover for a 14 day period. (Phone 01909 591652 to arrange)

CARAVAN

H. Caravan on the site, used as a site hut or temporary dwelling, excess £250

INCREASED PUBLIC LIABILITY LIMITS

J. Increase Public Liability cover for a 14 day period if required by an authority to facilitate a drain connection or similar purpose

K. Public Liability to £1,000,000 and Fire Cover to an agreed value on existing buildings, walls and other structures on the site which are not part of the construction project.

The above cover extends for the duration of the building work or 15 months whichever is the sooner. It applies to mainland UK, C. Isles, IoM, and Shetlands. Rates for N. Ireland exactly double the mainland rates above.

TERRORISM – cover only applies for sum insured on works and plant up to £100,000 total sum insured. If additional cover is required premiums will be quoted.

Public Liability and Employers Liability premiums account for £100 in the premiums below:

INCLUSIVE PREMIUMS

Rebuild Cost Up to £	Premium £	Rebuild Cost Up to £	Premium £
80,000 (min)	395	90,000	432
100,000	469	110,000	506
120,000	543	130,000	580
140,000	617	150,000	654

Premiums for larger sums on application
Premiums INCLUDE Insurance Premium Tax

£2 per £100 of value

value £ [ ]

Cover for £330 each employee, premium £30

£2.50 per £100 of value

value £ [ ]

*The **minimum** total premium for Section D, E & F is £250. It is recommended that proposers requiring this cover telephone 01909 591652 to discuss their requirements*

Premiums will be quoted after consultation

£52 per £1,000 value of caravan. (Does not include cover for personal possessions)

value £ [ ]

REVISED LIMIT OF INDEMNITY
£2,500,000   fixed premium £25
£5,000,000   fixed premium £45
Premiums will be quoted after consultation

If living within 25 metres of the new building deduct 10% from the contract works premium. Refer to 01909 591652 for advice of discounted premium.

If excesses on Sections C, D & F are to be increased to £1000 deduct 10% from contract works premiums. Refer to 01909 591652 for advice of discounted premium.

PREMIUM PAYABLE
(Premiums above are inclusive of Insurance Premium Tax at 4%)

PAYMENT – Please tick as appropriate

☐ Cheque for payment enclosed

☐ Payment to be made by credit card

Card No. [ ][ ][ ][ ] [ ][ ][ ][ ] [ ][ ][ ][ ] [ ][ ][ ][ ] expiry [ ][ ][ ][ ]

ENTER PREMIUM REQUIRED

REBATES

A rebate of the premium will be made as a credit towards the cost of a Buildings and Contents policy for the finished homes arranged by DMS Services Ltd. or its associates if the building work is finished and the new policy arranged

within 6 months   10% of the premium paid for basic selfbuild cover

within 9 months   5% of the premium paid for basic selfbuild cover

Basic selfbuild cover on a home with a £80,000 rebuilding value completed in six months by a selfbuilder living on the site and opting for the increased excess on contract works cover would thus cost only £299 after crediting the rebate.

COMPLETED FORMS AND PREMIUMS SHOULD BE SENT TO DMS SERVICES LTD, ORCHARD HOUSE, BLYTH, WORKSOP, NOTTS. S81 8HF
TEL. 01909 591652 FAX. 01909 591031

SELFBUILDERS INSURANCES

PROPOSAL

Name of proposer: Mr/Mrs/Ms .... Phone number: ....

Full postal address: ....

.... Post Code: ....

Address of property to be insured: ....

....

Name, address and any reference number of any interested party, e.g. Building Society: ....

....

YOUR PROPOSAL

1. Have you made any other proposal for insurance in respect of the risk proposed? **YES/NO**
   If "yes" give details at 10 below.

2. Has any company or underwriter declined your proposal? *If "yes" give details at 10 below.* **YES/NO**

3. Have you been convicted of (or charged but not yet tried with) arson or any offence involving dishonesty of any kind (e.g. fraud, theft, handling stolen goods etc.) *If "yes" give details at 10 below.* **YES/NO**

YOUR PROGRAMME

4(a). Commencing date of insurance ..../.........../.........

4(b). Date work commenced if a start has been made on the site? ..../.........../.........

4(c). Have there been any incidents on the site which could have given rise to a claim? **YES/NO**
   If "yes" give details at 10 below.

4(d). Target completion date ..../.........../.........
   Standard policy is for 15 months.

THE BUILDING

5(a). Is the building a completely new structure? **YES/NO**
   If "no" refer to DMS Services on 01909 591652 or provide details at 10 below.

5(b). State the value of the new building at builders reinstatement cost. (The minimum premium is for the value up to £80,000)   £

5(c). Will the new dwelling have brick or masonry walls with or without a timber frame under a tile or slate roof? **YES/NO**
   If "no" refer to DMS Services on 01909 591652 or provide details at 10 below.

5(d). Will the building qualify for N.H.B.C., Zurich Custombuild or surveyors or architects progress certificates **YES/NO**
   If "no" refer to DMS Services on 01909 591652 or provide details at 10 below.

THE SITE

6. Is the site and any existing building on it subject to any special hazard such as flooding, subsidence or other ground conditions **YES/NO**
   If "yes" give details at 10 below.

7. Do the Planning Consent or Building Regulation Approvals indicate any special requirements or special precautions to be taken in the construction of the building? *If "yes" give details at 10 below.* **YES/NO**

SECURITY

8. Does the proposer intend to live within 25 metres of the new work during the construction period? **YES/NO**
   If "yes" a discount can be claimed on the proposal form opposite

9. Will security arrangements on site be to good standard practice on building sites in the local area? **YES/NO**
   (A limit of £20,000 will apply to unfixed electrical, plumbing, heating, kitchen and bathroom fitments which must be contained in a locked building, hut or steel container whenever left unattended)

SPECIAL CIRCUMSTANCES

10. State the circumstances of any unusual circumstances or other facts which might influence the decision of the insurer when considering this proposal.
   If insufficient space please continue on a separate sheet.

I/we declare that all the work to which this proposal relates will be carried out in accordance with the Building Regulations, and that arrangements for the approval or certification of the works under the regulations will be made before any works are carried out.

I/we declare that to the best of my/our knowledge and belief all the statements and particulars made with regard to this proposal are true and I/we agree that this proposal shall be the basis of the contract of insurance between me/us and Guardian Insurance Ltd. I/we consent to the seeking of information from other insurers to check the answers I/we have provided, and I/we authorise the giving of information for such purposes.

Signature _____   Date _____

BUILDERS RISKS INSURANCES
FOR THOSE BUILDING ON THEIR OWN LAND

NORWICH UNION

The Norwich Union is able to offer an insurance package for those who are building for their own occupation private dwellings of traditional construction with or without the help of builders or sub-contractors. It does not apply to the extension, alteration, repair or renovation of existing buildings. This affords Contract Works, Public Liability and Employers' Liability cover and automatically includes the interest of any Mortgagee. Cover is provided in one policy document, summarised as follows. This description of insurance must be regarded only as an outline. The policy is a legal document and as such defines the insurance in precise terms. A specimen copy of the policy form is available on request.

CONTRACT WORKS

Cover	"All Risks" of loss or damage to:
	(a) the new building whilst under construction and materials for incorporation therein
	(b) plant, tools, equipment, temporary buildings and caravans.
Sum insured	The full rebuilding cost of the property, excluding the value of the land.
Including	(a) your own and hired plant, tools and equipment used in connection with the work up to a total sum insured of £2000 (can be increased if required).
	(b) Employees personal effects and tools whilst on the site up to a sum insured of £330 any one employee in accordance with standard Building Industry/Union agreements.
	(c) Architects, Surveyors and other fees necessarily incurred in rebuilding following loss or damage.
	(d) the cost of removing debris following any claim.
Excluding	(a) The first £50 of each and every claim for loss or damage to employees personal effects or tools.
	(b) The first £500 of each and every other loss.

EMPLOYERS LIABILITY (compulsory by law)

Cover	Your legal liability for death or bodily injury to employees, including labour only sub-contractors, arising out of the building work.
Limit	£10,000,000 each occurrence.
Including	Legal costs and expenses in defending any claim.
Note	A Certificate of Insurance will be provided, and must by law be displayed on site.

PUBLIC LIABILITY

Cover	Your legal liability to members of the public, (including sub-contractors working on the site not classed as employees) for death, bodily injury or damage to property, arising out of the building work.
Limit	£1,000,000 any one loss. (Can be increased if required)
Including	Legal costs and expenses in defending any claim
Excluding	The first £250 of any claim for damage to property.

PERIOD	From the commencement date you specify (which should be no earlier than the date you complete the proposal form) up to completion of the building work, subject to a maximum of 24 months. Extensions to this period may be available on payment of an additional premium. There is no refund for early completion.
THE POLICY	Will be sent direct to you by DMS Services Ltd. on behalf of the Insurance Company.
THE PREMIUM	£5.95 per 1,000 on the rebuilding cost of the property. (Minimum £80,000). This is a total rate for all the cover set out above, subject to submission of the completed proposal form overleaf, and includes insurance premium tax at 4%. Proposal forms should be accompanied by cheques for the relevant premium made out to DMS Services Ltd. or credit card details should be provided

Rebuilding Cost Up to £	Premium £	Rebuilding Cost Up to £	Premium £	Rebuilding Cost Up to £	Premium £
80,000	476.00	100,000	595.00	140,000	833.00
85,000	505.75	110,000	654.50	150,000	892.50
90,000	535.50	120,000	714.00		
95,000	565.25	130,000	773.50	Over 150,000 @ £5.95 per £1000	

TAX	The scale of premiums shown in this prospectus and proposal are inclusive of Insurance Premium Tax at 4% and are only valid while the rate of tax remains at this level. DMS Services Ltd. will advise on revised premiums should the rate of tax change.

REBATE VOUCHER

If you complete within 6 months without any claims you will be entitled to use the Discount Voucher of £40 towards a Norwich Union Home Plus Policy

IMPORTANT The above terms only apply:
(a) up to 31st December 1998. Amended terms may be necessary for proposal forms completed after that date.
(b) to risks in Mainland Great Britain only. Proposals from N. Ireland are quoted individually and special excesses may apply. Phone 01909 591652 or fax 01909 591031 for a quotation. Proposals cannot be accepted from Eire.
(c) Where there is no abnormal exposure to risk of floods, storm damage or vandalism.

THE AGENCY

The Agency is DMS Services Ltd., a company which provides specialised insurance services to those building on their own. The proposal form overleaf should be completed and sent to the agency with a cheque or Credit Card details for the premium payable to DMS Services Ltd.

D.M.S. Services Ltd., Orchard House, Blyth, Worksop, Notts. S81 8HF.
Phone 01909 591652 Fax 01909 591031

Agency: DMS Services Ltd   Agency Reference: 50GA59   Policy No.

Proposal – BUILDING OWN PRIVATE DWELLING
The Insurer: Norwich Union Insurance Limited

NORWICH UNION

Name of Proposer
MR/MRS/MISS

Phone No.

Full Postal Address
....
.... Postcode ....

Address of property to be erected
....
....

Name and address of any interested party – eg Bank or Building Society
....

Commencing date
of insurance
....

Important – Please give a definite answer to each question (block letters) or tick appropriate boxes

| | Yes | No | If "Yes" please give details |

1. Have you made any other proposal for insurance in respect of the risk proposed?   ☐ ☐

2. Has any company or underwriter declined your proposal?   ☐ ☐

3. Have you ever been convicted of (or charged but not yet tried with) arson or any offence involving dishonesty of any kind (eg fraud, theft, handling stolen goods)?   ☐ ☐

4. Will the property be

   (a) a completely new structure and not an extension, conversion or restoration of an existing building?   ☐ ☐   (If "No" please refer to DMS Services Ltd.) Phone 01909 591652

   (b) of conventional construction, either in loadbearing masonry, or with a timber frame, and built to drawings approved under the requirements of the Building Regulations as meeting the requirements of the regulations in full?   ☐ ☐

   (c) occupied as your permanent residence on completion?   ☐ ☐   (If "No" please refer to DMS Services Ltd.) Phone 01909 591652

5. (a) Will the total value of plant, tools, equipment and temporary buildings, whether hired or owned on site at any one time exceed £2,000. If so see overleaf for the additional premium required (cover for plant on site can be altered at any time while the policy is in force). Phone 01909 591652 if in doubt.   ☐ ☐   Contractors plant hired in with operators, such as excavators, need not be included if proposers are wholly satisfied the hirers insurances cover all risks. However if cover is required on such machines phone DMS Services on 01909 591652

6. Is there any abnormal exposure to risk of flooding, storm damage or vandalism?   ☐ ☐

7. State estimated value of building work on completion at builder price for reinstatement.   £ ____   It is important that this sum is the cost of a professional building firm rebuilding the entire dwelling should it be completely destroyed just prior to completion. This will be the limit of indemnity for item (A) of the Contract Works section, and payments of premium on a lesser figure will result in any contracts works claim being proportionately reduced. Please discuss with DMS Services Ltd if in any doubt

8. Material facts – state any other material facts here. Failure to do so could invalidate the policy. A material fact is one which is likely to influence an insurer in the assessment and acceptance of the proposal. If you are in any doubt as to whether a fact is material it should be disclosed to the insurer.   If work on site has started certify here that there have been no incidents on site which would have given rise to a claim

Note: 1. You should keep a record (including copies of letters) of all information supplied to the insurer for the purpose of entering into the contract.
2. A copy of this proposal form will be supplied by the Insurer on request.
3. Please note that the details you are asked to supply may be used to provide you with information about other products and services which the Norwich Union Group can offer.

Declaration To be completed in all cases
I desire to insure with the Insurer in the terms of the Policy used in this class of Insurance. I declare that the above statements and particulars are true to the best of my knowledge and belief and that I have not withheld any material information. I agree to give immediate notice to the insurer of any alteration to the circumstances described herein and that this proposal shall form the basis of the contract between us.

Proposer's signature

Date

Send completed form to DMS Services Ltd., Orchard House, Blyth, Worksop, Notts. S81 8HF, together with a cheque made payable to DMS Services Ltd. or provide credit card details. Any queries to DMS Services. Phone 01909 591652

Norwich Union Insurance Limited. Registered in England No. 99122. Registered Office: Surrey Street, Norwich NR1 3NS. Member of the Association of British Insurers. Member of the Insurance Ombudsman Bureau.

HOME PLUS COVER
Quotations will be provided for household insurances when the building approaches completion. If this is not required please tick box – ☐